V. E. TARRANT

The U-Boat Offensive 1914–1945

Dedicated to the memory of my grandfather,
Arthur Evan Coles (1894–1977),
a soldier of the Great War
and my stepfather, Reginald Henry Parry (1921–1982)
an airman of the Second War
nulli secundus

Below: *U35* in the Heligoland Bight with a battleship of the *Baden* class in the background.

V. E. TARRANT

The U-Boat Offensive 1914–1945

NAVAL INSTITUTE PRESS

German naval officer ranks and British equivalents

Grossadmiral	Admiral of the Fleet
Generaladmiral	no equivalent
Admiral	Admiral
Vizeadmiral	Vice-Admiral
Konteradmiral	Rear-Admiral
Kommodore	Commodore
Kapitän zur See	Captain
Fregattenkapitän	no equivalent
Korvettenkapitän	Commander
Kapitänleutnant	Lieutenant-Commander
Oberleutnant zur See	Lieutenant
Leutnant zur See	Sub-Lieutenant
Oberfähnrich zur See	no equivalent
Fähnrich zur See	Midshipman

Compiled from the Naval Intelligence Division document (B.R.634G) 'Dictionary of Naval Equivalents' (1943).

Published and distributed in the United States of America by the Naval Institute Press, Annapolis, Maryland 21402

Library of Congress Catalog Card No. 89-60238.

ISBN 0-87021-764-X

Jacket illustrations: Front, 'A German submarine in heavy seas at the blockade zone', painted by Hans Bohrdt in 1917 (courtesy of the Staatsbibliothek, Berlin). Back, top, U9 with a Helgoland Class dreadnought in the background. Smoke from the ventilation pipes of the earliest U-boats was conspicuously visible by day and night. Back, below, the commissioning of U802 (Type IX C/40) alongside the Seebeckwerft, Bremerhaven, on 12 June 1943. The commanding officer, Kapitänleutnant Rolf Steinhaus is in the front row (standing) with the white cap cover.

The illustrations in this book have been collected from many sources, and vary in quality owing to the variety of circumstances under which they were taken and preserved. As a result, certain of the illustrations are not of the standard to be expected from the best of today's equipment, materials and techniques. They are nevertheless included for their inherent information value, to provide an authentic visual coverage of the subject.

Designed and edited by DAG Publications Ltd.
Designed by David Gibbons; edited by Michael Boxall; layout by Anthony A. Evans; typeset by Typesetters (Birmingham) Ltd.; camerawork by M&E Reproductions, North Fambridge, Essex; printed and bound in Great Britain by The Bath Press, Avon.

Contents

Foreword

by Captain Kurt Diggins (FG Navy, ret.), President, Verband Deutscher U-bootfahrer

The development, establishment and operational implementation of Germany's submarine arm forms an important part of those two dramatic events – the World Wars – which changed the world in our century.

The potential of submarines to destroy a nation's merchant shipping and thus dramatically affect the course of the war had been recognised late, or had been underestimated, in Germany as well as in Great Britain. This book, based on comprehensive studies of special sources, provides a summary of strategic and tactical U-boat operations performed in both the First and Second World Wars. At the same time it demonstrates the interdependence of policy, politics and strategy. In both wars the U-boats almost succeeded in cutting off Britain's life-lines, which were the sea lanes across the Atlantic, thereby capturing the upper hand. But for Germany they did become a fatal factor: it was precisely the U-boat offensive that twice caused the United States to enter the war. With that, a decisive turn of the war was brought about.

This chronological description of the U-boat offensive shows that in the First as well as in the Second World War there did exist the possibility that the U-boats could lead towards a favorable outcome of the war for Germany. The opportunities for this, however, were never exploited because the experiences of the First World War were overlooked.

The numerical weakness of the U-boat arm at the beginning of each war and the hesitant stance of the political leadership with regard to their maximum use in the tonnage war gave Great Britain (which in 1939 relied too much on Asdic) enough time to set up a defensive system which to a great extent obtained its technological superiority through the outstanding results of operational research.

The Battle of the Atlantic was decided, in the end, by insufficient German U-boat construction and the enormous naval construction capacity of the United States. On the one hand this led to an unfavorable ratio of successes to losses for the U-boats and on the other to the impossibility of replacing the growing German losses through the construction of new U-boats. In fact, the competition between ships sunk by U-boats and the enormous construction programme of Liberty Ships in the United States could not be won by Germany because the significance of the Battle of the Atlantic was never clearly understood by the continent-oriented German political and military leadership.

Today it is but an academic question whether Great Britain could have resisted the attrition offensive of the U-boats in the long run had the commander of Germany's submarine force, Admiral Dönitz, had the 300 U-boats at his disposal which he considered necessary to defeat Great Britain.

This excellent account, absolutely fair and impartial, provides a summary of two cruel wars at sea. Both sides fought with courage and determination. May their sacrifices provide a reminder and an example to be followed by all of us to maintain peace in freedom and justice.

Preface

The concept of this book was inspired by Eberhard Rössler's *The U-Boat* (published by Arms & Armour Press, 1981) which is the definitive work on the *technical evolution* of Germany's *Unterseeboote*. My aim has been to complement Rössler's work by chronicling the *strategical and tactical evolution* of the U-boats through the two world wars, tracing how vessels originally conceived as coastal defence units evolved into a deadly menace and came close to being the single decisive factor in both wars. I have approached the work in the spirit of – to quote Talleyrand – '*Je ne blâme ni n'approuve: Je raconte*'; in so doing I have tried to be totally objective and non-partisan even though I have relied heavily on German source material. Notable are, for the period 1914–18, Konteradmiral Arno Spindler's German official account of the U-boat offensive against shipping, the five-volume *Der Handelskrieg mit U-Booten*, and, for the second war, the

translated but unpublished three-volume Admiralty monograph *The U-Boat War In The Atlantic* written by Dönitz's one time chief of staff, Fregattenkapitän Günther Hessler. The statistics of merchant shipping losses which I have compiled are based entirely on post-war German research. These figures, the result of many decades of research, are undoubtedly more accurate than the British official assessments and therefore, supersede those in the *Statistical Review of the War Against Shipping* (1918), and the appendices of the official history of *The Second World War At Sea* by Captain Stephen Roskill.

V. E. TARRANT
CARDIFF
SEPTEMBER, 1988

A Weapon of Uncertain Value

August to December 1914

At the outbreak of war, during the first week of August 1914, the Kaiserliche Marine (Imperial German Navy, 1871–1919) had 28 U-boats (*Unterseeboote*) in service. A further two, *U29* and *U30*, were nearing completion and another fourteen, *U31–U41* and *U43–U45* (there was no *U42*) were in advanced stages of construction. Of the 28 boats in service, four, *U1–U4*, were of primitive design and, being small and of very little fighting value, were employed throughout the war as training boats. The remaining 24 operational boats (*Frontboote*) were divided into two flotillas: each flotilla being further sub-divided into half-flotillas:

1st Flotilla (Commanded by Korvettenkapitän Hermann Bauer)
1st half-flotilla: *U5, U6, U7, U8, U9, U10, U11*
2nd half-flotilla: *U12, U13, U14, U15, U16, U17, U18*

2nd Flotilla (Commanded by Korvettenkapitän Otto Feldman)
3rd half-flotilla: *U19, U20, U21, U22, U24*
4th half-flotilla: *U23, U25, U26, U27, U28*

Four of these boats, *U6, U11, U12* and *U26*, were in dockyard hands undergoing refits during August. In accordance with the German mobilization plan, orders were placed during the first month of the war for the building of another eleven boats (*U46–U56*), although the first of these was not completed until December 1915 and the last, *U56*, not until June 1916. As operational units all fourteen U-boats of the 1st Flotilla were handicapped by their unreliable Körting heavy oil engines. The considerable quantity of thick white smoke and showers of sparks these engines produced (which rendered the boats

conspicuously visible by day and night while on surface trim) necessitated the fitting of tall, heavy ventilation pipes which had to be lowered and stowed before the boats could submerge. The larger, more modern boats of the 2nd Flotilla had no need of these cumbersome fitting, being powered by far more reliable diesel engines.

Strategic role of the U-boats

At this time the German Naval Staff (Admiralstab) had little faith in the capabilities of their *Unterseeboote* and small understanding of their formidable latent potentialities. Indeed, the initial strategical role they perceived for their undersea arm was purely defensive. This was a direct result of the Admiralstab's obsession with the idea that, in the event of war, the full might of the British Grand Fleet would drive headlong into the Heligoland Bight, there to engage decisively the battle squadrons of the German High Seas Fleet (*Hochseeflotte*). In accordance with this fixation the two U-boat flotillas were based in the harbour of Heligoland (a small fortified island, 1,800 yards long and 650 yards wide), some 30 miles north of the River Jade where the High Sea Fleet was assembled.

The two flotillas formed an integral part of the defensive arrangements in the Bight, which was designed to give a timely warning of the expected British naval onslaught. By day an outer observation line, comprised of a destroyer flotilla, patrolled on a concentric arc 35 miles NW of Heligoland, while a division of torpedo-boats formed an inner line 23 miles distant from the island. The U-boats (usually a half-flotilla at a time) formed a static line, surfaced and riding at mooring buoys, between these two lines. The plan called for the outer line of destroyers to draw any approaching enemy forces over the line of U-boats, stationed six miles astern, which were to submerge and launch torpedo attacks. Along with massed torpedo attacks launched by destroyers, the Admiralstab hoped that the U-boats would be able to weaken the numerical superiority of the British forces, to a point at which the weaker High Seas Fleet would be offered a more reasonable chance of success when it sallied forth from the Jade.

Although the possibility had been mooted before the war that the British might adopt the *strategical defensive*, by sealing off the North Sea with lines of blockade (across the twenty miles of the Dover Straits and the 200-mile stretch from the Orkneys to the Norwegian coast), the Germans could not bring themselves to believe that historical prestige would permit the Royal Navy to renounce the *strategical offensive*; they would seek battle in the waters close to German bases at the first possible

Below: *U1* the very first of the U-boats that were commissioned into the German Navy and became operational through the two world wars. Of very little military value, *U1* was used as a training boat throughout the First World War. She is now preserved in Munich Museum.

opportunity. When the expected onslaught into the Bight failed to materialize, however, the premise upon which the Germans had based their strategy was overturned. This resulted in the U-boats being assigned a more aggressive strategical task than passively bobbing around at their moorings off Heligoland.

From 6 to 14 August 1914, three separate groups of U-boats were dispatched on their pioneering war patrols. Their objectives were to discover the location of the patrol lines which the British had established to blockade the North Sea, and once discovered to whittle down the superiority of the Grand Fleet to a *Kräfteausgleich* – an approximate equalization of forces – by torpedoing their capital ships. The *raison d'être* of the British blockade lines, it must be mentioned, was, of course, to deny the egress of German surface warships into the Atlantic to attack Britain's vital seaborne trade, and at the same time bring economic pressure to bear on Germany by cutting off her equally vital maritime trade. (Germany was the second largest owner of mercantile tonnage – 11.9 per cent of the world total – next to the British Empire's 47.9 per cent.)

Initial operations
The first of these operations commenced on 6 August. Ten of the older submarines from the 1st Flotilla (chosen because these boats had the more experienced commanders) sailed from Heligoland at 04.20 in thick, rainy weather and poor visibility. Reaching a position east of the south-west patch of the Dogger Bank that same evening, they spread out on a 60-mile front

(seven miles between each boat) and steered north-west to begin a sweep up the central sector of the North Sea which was to extend to the latitudes north of the Orkneys. Running in a line west to east, the disposition of the boats was: *U7, U14, U15, U16, U17, U18, U9, U8, U13* and *U5*. (The latter boat had to return to base when one engine broke down on the morning of the 8th.) The attack on enemy warships, if and when discovered, was to be carried out in accordance with the operational orders issued by Korvettenkapitän Bauer, commanding the 1st Flotilla: 'The main object is to attack the main body of the enemy's fleet (i.e., battleships) . . . (also) attack all battlecruisers, cruisers and light cruisers, which may be encountered, light cruisers only if opportunities for firing are favourable. On the return passage every type of ship is to be attacked and the enemy damaged by every possible means.'[1]

Throughout their 350-mile north-westerly surface sweep, the nine remaining U-boats sighted nothing of the enemy until noon on 8 August. Ten miles south-east of Fair Island (situated roughly midway between the Orkneys and Shetlands) *U15* (Pohle) sighted three dreadnought battleships (*Orion, Monarch* and *Ajax*) carrying out target practice. Submerging and closing for an attack position, Pohle attained the distinction of being the first U-boat commander to launch a torpedo at a British warship. The torpedo he fired at the 25,000-ton *Monarch* missed, and he was denied another chance by the evasive course of the battleships, which quickly disappeared out of periscope view. Late in the evening of that same day, having reached the

Right: *U15*, the first U-boat to be lost to enemy action. She was rammed and sunk by the light cruiser HMS *Birmingham* on 9 August 1914. There were no survivors.

Right: *U13* mysteriously disappeared without trace while returning to the Heligoland Bight from a North Sea operation on 12 August 1914.

Left: *U7* (nearest the camera) with *U8* and *U6* among units of the German High Seas Fleet.

northerly limits of their sweep, the line of boats turned south-east to retrace their course. Reaching a position on the latitude of the southern tip of the Orkneys they hove-to in the early hours of the 9th. Their orders were to remain stopped and surfaced on this line for 39 hours before commencing the homeward run early in the evening of the 10th. The strategic thinking behind this idea was little more than moving the static line which the U-boats occupied in the Bight to more northerly reaches, in the hope that British forces would unwittingly attempt to cross them.

Shortly after U15 reached this position, disaster struck. At 03.40 the light cruiser *Birmingham*, one of a cruiser screen thrown out on a wide arc, 30 miles ahead of the British battle fleet, sighted U15 lying motionless amidst wraiths of mist. According to *Birmingham's* report, sounds of loud hammering inside the U-boat's hull could be heard, indicating that the crew were probably trying to remedy engine trouble. Altering course, *Birmingham* bore down on the unsuspecting U-boat (it seemed that no watch was being kept) and struck her a glancing blow on the stern. While the light cruiser turned a tight circle to deliver another attack, at the same time opening fire with all

guns that could be brought to bear, U15 attempted to get under way. She was beginning to move slowly through the water, prerequisite to diving, when *Birmingham*, foaming along at full speed, rammed her square amidships cutting her clean in half. The two severed parts floated for several minutes (possibly because the sheared plates were folded over, causing partial sealing) before they slipped beneath the waves. There were no survivors.

An hour later U18 (Spindler) sighted another cruiser of the scouting screen, one mile distant. U18 dived to launch an attack, but when Spindler searched for his quarry through the periscope the cruiser had already disappeared in a passing rain squall. It was the last sighting of the enemy by any of the boats throughout the remainder of the sweep, which was completed on the afternoon of 12 August when seven of the original force arrived back in Heligoland. One other boat, U13 (Arthur von Schweinitz), was missing. The last that was heard from U13 was a radio report early on the 12th, announcing her approach to the Bight. Nothing was heard or seen of her again. (Most historians surmise that U13 struck a mine in the defensive fields laid in the Bight; seemingly unaware that no defensive mining was undertaken by the Germans in the area until 9 September, and the first British minefield in the Bight was not laid until January 1915.)

The results of this pioneer operation did very little to vindicate the value of the *Unterseeboote* in the eyes of the Admiralstab. They had failed to damage, let alone sink, a single enemy warship, yet had lost two of their number in the attempt. Neither had they been able to discover the location of the British lines of blockade. In the words of the German official history: 'The observations made left it uncertain whether the British forces sighted belonged to the regular patrol line, whether there was any patrol line in that position, or whether

the presence of a patrol line further north, in the latitude of the Shetlands, might be assumed.'[2]

The results obtained from the other two war cruises, carried out from 8 to 19 August, were equally negative. Four diesel-engined boats from the 3rd half-flotilla, *U19, U21, U22, U24*, were dispatched on 8 August to attack the warships covering the crossing of the British troop transports to France. Two boats, *U19* and *U21*, were forced back by heavy seas. *U22* and *U24* did manage to push on into the Hoofden (Flanders Bight) but they returned to Heligoland on the 11th, having sighted nothing but a few destroyer patrols. Another attempt to discover the northern blockade line by *U20* and *U21*, from 15 to 19 August, also proved totally unproductive; as did a sweep by *U22* which reconnoitred the approaches to the Humber, which was believed (erroneously) to be a base for capital ships.

These operations led the Admiralstab to conclude that: 'The British Main Fleet and probably all war vessels which are worth attacking by U-boats, are so far away from Germany that *it is beyond the technical capacities of our U-boats to find them.* Neither is it possible for U-boats to lie in wait off the bases [of the Grand Fleet] for long periods owing to their distance from Germany. *U-boat operations will therefore be abandoned for the present.*' (author's italics)[3] Having failed to prove their value in offensive and reconnoitering operations, the U-boats were relegated in their entirety to the static lines of defence in the Heligoland Bight. It wasn't until 30 August, when information was received by the

Admiralstab that heavy ships were anchored off Rosyth in the Firth of Forth, that the U-boats were given another chance.

On 2 September, Korvettenkapitän Bauer (who had been designated flag officer of the U-boat flotillas – Führer der U-boote (*F.d.U.*) – at the end of August) dispatched two boats with orders to penetrate the estuary of the Forth and attack any incoming or outgoing warships. At about 15.00 on the stormy afternoon of 5 September, one of these boats, *U21* (Hersing), which was approaching the Forth, sighted the small cruiser *Pathfinder* (2,940 tons) on patrol south-east of May Island. Manoeuvring for an attack position (the range was down to about 1,600 yards by 15.45) Hersing fired one torpedo. Although *U21* was pitching and plunging in the rough seas, a direct hit ignited the cruiser's magazine and *Pathfinder* plunged to the bottom bows first, taking the majority of her crew with her. This was the first of nine British warships that would succumb to U-boat attack during the next four months, although, during this period, the majority of the *Frontboote* were still held back in the Bight. Two weeks after the loss of *Pathfinder*, *U9* (Weddigen) sank the three old armoured cruisers *Aboukir*, *Cressy* and *Hogue* twenty miles NW of the Hook of Holland on 22 September. When *Aboukir* began to sink after being torpedoed, her Captain recklessly ordered the other two cruisers to close and rescue suvivors. Lying stopped, *Cressy* and *Hogue* presented sitting targets for *U9*. Within an hour of the first torpedo striking *Aboukir* (06.30) all three 12,000-ton cruisers were on the bottom: 62 officers and 1,397 men went down with them.

On 15 October, *U9* triumphed again when she sank the 7,350-ton cruiser *Hawke* off Peterhead, causing Fisher, the First Sea Lord, to lament, 'More men lost [in the four cruisers] than by Lord Nelson in all his battles put together.' During the same month *U27* (Wegener) sank the British submarine *E 3* off the Borkum Riff (18 October), blowing her in half with one torpedo, and the 5,600-ton seaplane-carrier *Hermes*, which went down eight miles WNW of Calais (31 October). The only success throughout November and December was the sinking of the 810-ton gunboat *Niger* (11 November) which *U12* (Forstmann) torpedoed while the ship was lying at anchor off Deal pier. The final victim in this phase was the old 15,000-ton predreadnought battleship *Formidable*, which succumbed to one torpedo from *U24* (Schneider) off Portland, at 02.30 on New Year's Day, 1915: 35 officers and 512 men of her complement of 780 were drowned. Very near misses were also achieved in torpedo attacks on three cruisers and two destroyers.

All the ships that had fallen victim to the U-boats were old and subsidiary patrol units; the full might of the British dreadnought battle fleet being unscathed. However, an enterprise carried out by *U18* (Hennig) could well have resulted in losses to the Grand Fleet that would have gone a long way to achieving the equalization of forces that the Admiralstab desperately hoped to attain. On 23 November *U18* succeeded in penetrating the Hoxa entrance to Scapa Flow by following in the wake of a steamer. Unluckily for Hennig his efforts to negotiate the racing

Left: Korvettenkapitän Hermann Bauer, the very first Führer der U-Boote, and the first to advocate the use of U-boats in an offensive against British seaborne trade.

Right: The primitive *U9*, under the command of the intrepid Kapitänleutnant Otto Weddigen, returning to base after sinking the three British armoured cruisers *Aboukir*, *Cressy* and *Hogue* on 22 September 1914.

the most powerful battlefleet in history to abandon its base and retreat to a second base, and then to a third, each being progressively more remote from the main theatre of naval hostilities – the North Sea. Gone was the "containing" position in the Orkneys, and with it the support for the Northern Blockade. In a word, the bottom of the whole strategical situation was knocked out for a time by the German U-boats.'[4] Anti-submarine obstructions were not fitted to the three main entrances into the Flow (Hoxa, Switha and Hoy Sound) until February 1915. By not launching more concerted U-boat attacks on Scapa during the first four months of the war, the Germans lost a golden opportunity, but they were labouring under the misapprehension that Scapa was as heavily defended as their own naval bases (which the loss of U18 seemed to confirm).

The German Naval Command was equally as surprised as their opponents by the capabilities of the U-boats. 'Our U-boat cruises extended further afield,' Admiral Scheer explains.

'On 15 October, U16 returned to Heligoland after a cruise of fifteen days, and on her return reported that she was still perfectly effective. October also witnessed the first cruise to circumnavigate the coast of the British Isles. U20 [Droescher], which had been sent out to attack troop transports in the English Channel, found herself compelled by damaged diving gear, to avoid the Straits of Dover, which were heavily patrolled, and therefore returned via the Irish Sea and around Scotland. The passage took eighteen days in all. The proof of the ability of the U-boats to remain at sea for a long period had been attained . . . so that from being merely a coastal defence machine, as was originally planned, they became a very effective long-range weapon.'[5]

Having proved themselves to be the most formidable offensive weapons in the German naval arsenal, the catalytic agency of necessity would now invent an even more deadly strategic role for the U-boats; the success or failure of which would decide the outcome of the war.

currents of the Pentland Firth were in vain: the anchorage was empty; the battle squadrons of the Grand Fleet were carrying out a sweep in the North Sea. If the full concourse of battleships had been in their usual berths, lined up like ninepins, U18 would have had them at her mercy up to the number of the six torpedoes she carried (roughly the margin of superiority in battleships the British had over the High Seas Fleet). On the way out of Hoxa the periscope of U18 was sighted and she was rammed one mile off the entrance, first by the armed trawler *Dorothy Gray* and later by the destroyer *Garry*. With the hydroplanes damaged U18 rose and sank erratically. Trying desperately to grope her way eastwards away from the patrolling vessels, she was caught in the powerful Pentland tidal streams and carried on to the sharp rocks of the Skerries, where she was scuttled by her crew. During December, two more U-boats were lost. Neither boat left any survivors and the exact cause of their loss is unknown, but it is highly probable that both U11 (Suchodoletz) and U5 (Lemmer) were blown up on British minefields laid north of Zeebrugge.

The demoralizing effect of these U-boat exploits on the Royal Navy was even greater than the material losses. The Admiralty had adjudged Scapa Flow, some 475 miles from the German naval bases, to be beyond the reach of the U-boats; the premise being based on the endurance of British submarines which were incapable of such extended operations. As a consequence Scapa was devoid of any anti-submarine defences (mines, nets or booms). The discovery of U-boats in the vicinity of Scapa came as a shock, haunting Jellicoe (CinC, Grand Fleet) with the prospect of U-boats penetrating the Flow by night and sending his fleet to the bottom. As a result of a U-boat scare (an erroneous report of a periscope sighting inside the anchorage on 1 September) Jellicoe hustled the fleet out to sea and proceeded to Loch Ewe on the north-west coast of Scotland. Although the fleet returned to Scapa on 24 September, Jellicoe withdrew the dreadnoughts to an even more distant base at Lough Swilly on the north coast of Ireland after another false scare on 16 October. They did not return to Scapa until 9 November. The situation is summed up by Gibson and Prendergast: 'A few submarines [the average number at sea on any one day through September to December was 4] had forced

U-boat losses August to December 1914

Date	Boat	Commander	Cause and location
9 Aug	U15	Pohl	Rammed by light cruiser *Birmingham*: North Sea.
12 Aug	U13	Schweinitz	Unknown. Disappeared while approaching Heligoland Bight.
23 Nov	U18	Hennig	Rammed by trawler *Dorothy Gray* and destroyer *Garry*: Pentland Firth.
9 Dec	U11	Suchodoletz	Unknown, presumed mined: off Zeebrugge.
5 Dec	U5	Lemmer	Unknown, presumed mined: off Zeebrugge.

Analysis of causes

Rammed by warships	2
Unknown	3
Total	5

Unsheathing the Sword
November 1914 to February 1915

Strategic reassessment

While the operations against enemy warships were taking place, the spectre of the terror which the U-boats were to launch against the world's mercantile shipping slowly, almost imperceptibly, began to raise its menacing head. The very first victim of the 8,209 Allied merchant vessels totalling 27,200,678 tons that the U-boats were to sink during the two world wars, was the British steamer *Glitra* (866 tons), outward bound from Grangemouth to Stavanger with a mixed cargo of coal, iron plate and oil. On 20 October 1914, she was brought-to fourteen miles off Skudesnaes by *U17* (Feldkirchner), and sunk by a boarding-party which opened her sea-cocks. Acting in strict accordance with international law, Feldkirchner not only gave the crew time to take to the lifeboats before scuttling the *Glitra*, but towed them to within easy rowing distance of the Norwegian coast. Six days later, however, an event occurred, which painfully illustrated the difficulties inherent in a U-boat commander's ability correctly to identify the nature of a vessel through the restricted view of a periscope. On 26 October, *U24* (Schneider) sighted the French steamer *Amiral Ganteaume* (4,590 tons) off Cap Gris-Nez. Through the periscope Schneider took the crowds on deck to be troops (the ship was in fact carrying 2,500 Belgian refugees), and as *U24* had been sent into the Channel for the express purpose of attacking troop transports, Schneider did not hesitate to torpedo the ship without warning. Although the majority of the refugees were taken off by a British steamer, and *Amiral Ganteaume* did not sink but was towed into Boulougne, forty lost their lives in the panic which broke out.

During November, *U21* (Hersing) sank two British steamers off Le Havre: *Malachite* (718 tons) on the 23rd, and *Primo* (1,366 tons) on the 26th. Acting within the confines of international maritime law, Hersing allowed the crews of both ships time to take to the boats (they were in sight of the French coast) before

sinking the steamers with his deck gun. During the remaining weeks of 1914, only one other merchant ship was attacked (the 1,209-ton passenger vessel *Colchester*), 22 miles off the Hook of Holland, but she managed to escape by using her superior speed to outrun the surfaced U-boat. The sinking of three small British steamers with a combined gross tonnage of 2,950 tons was a flea-bite out of the British Empire mercantile marine tonnage of 18,356,000 (world total 34,835,000 tons) and was totally unimpressive in contrast to the promising method of offensive action against Britain's naval supremacy. Yet it was against the commercial objective that the U-boats were to be directed.

With the endurance factor of the U-boats now apparent, Führer der U-boote Bauer was the first to realize the deadly potential of using his boats in an all-out attack on British seaborne trade, with the object of starving the British Isles into submission. Bauer advocated this proposal as early as October, complaining to the CinC, High Seas Fleet, von Ingenohl, of the uselessness of employing the bulk of the U-boats in narrow defensive circles round Heligoland. Von Ingenohl was impressed with the idea and he submitted a report to Admiral von Pohl, the chief of the Admiralstab: 'I beg to point out that a campaign of U-boats against commercial traffic on the British coasts, will strike the enemy on his weakest spot, and will make it evident both to him and his allies, that his power at sea is insufficient to protect his imports.'[1]

Pohl vetoed the suggestion on the grounds that such a radical method of warfare would be a crude violation of international maritime law with regard to the method of destroying enemy merchant ships, to which Article 112 of German Naval Prize Regulations conformed. To act within the spirit of Article 112, a U-boat would have to surface, stop the intended victim, either by signal or a warning shot with its deck gun, send a boarding-party to the vessel to establish whether it

Left: *U17* firing her deck gun while under the command of Kapitänleutnant Feldkirchner. She sank the British 866-ton steamer *Glitra*, the first of the 8,209 Allied merchant vessels grossing 27,200,678 tons that the U-boats sank during the two world wars.

Right: Admiral von Pohl, Chief of the German Naval Staff, who, after initial doubts, became the main advocate of the U-boat offensive against shipping.

belonged to a belligerent or neutral country, and, if it were of the enemy marine, make adequate provisions for the safety of the crew and passengers before sinking the vessel, either by gunfire, torpedo or, as in the case of *Glitra*, scuttling. It being patently impossible for a U-boat, a small, cramped vessel, to take aboard the personnel of a large ship, the best provision that could be made for crew and passengers was a chance to use the lifeboats and brave the perils of the sea. If the vessel were sunk out of sight of land this 'best provision' was clearly inadequate within the definition of maritime law.

Pohl was also apprehensive that the accidental destruction of neutral merchantmen might bring the neutral powers so affected into conflict with Germany. His attitude changed, however, when, on 2 November, Britain violated international law by declaring the whole of the North Sea a War Zone. This declaration was intended to tighten the effect of the blockade on Germany, by seizing all supplies 'ultimately' destined for Germany, even though carried in neutral ships which were bound for ports in neutral countries neighbouring Germany. Britain also infringed international law by instructing British merchantmen to fly neutral flags as a *ruse de guerre*. The effect of the former was (in the words of Admiral Scheer) that '. . . free trading of neutral merchant vessels in the North Sea (with Germany and the neutral states of Holland, Denmark, Norway and Sweden) was made impossible . . . because every ship that

did not follow the instructions of this declaration [i.e., submit to examination: the cargo being either seized or, if that couldn't be justified, purchased] was exposed to the risk of destruction.' This resulted in, 'all important trade with Germany both by land and sea being strangled and, in particular, the importation of food was made impossible. When the starvation of Germany was recognized as the goal the British were striving to reach, we had to realize what means we had at our disposal to defend ourselves against this danger.'[2]

As the German Fleet was considered too weak to destroy the Grand Fleet, which was the backbone of the British blockade, the U-boats, against which the numerical strength of the Royal Navy was powerless, provided the logical and only answer to the German predicament. This was the premise of a memorandum submitted to Pohl by the senior officers of the High Seas Fleet Command (Kommando der Hochseeflotte), which not only endorsed Bauer's original proposal, but enlarged on its radical nature by advocating an *unrestricted* campaign by the U-boats (sinking ships without warning and without regard for the safety of the crew) as opposed to a *restricted* campaign in which crew and passengers would at least be allowed the chance to use the lifeboats.

'As England is trying to destroy our trade it is only fair if we retaliate by carrying on the campaign against her trade by all possible means. Further, as England completely disregards international law in her actions, *there is not the least reason why we should exercise any restraint in our conduct of the war.* We can wound England most seriously by injuring her trade. By means of the U-boat we should be able to inflict the greatest injury. We must therefore make use of this weapon, and do so, moreover, in the way most suited to its peculiarities. The more vigorously the war is prosecuted the sooner will it come to an end . . . *Consequently a U-boat cannot spare the crews of steamers, but must send them to the bottom with their ships.* The shipping world can be warned of these consequences, and it can be pointed out that ships which attempt to make British ports run the risk of being destroyed with their crews. *This warning that the lives of steamers' crews will be endangered will be one good reason why all shipping trade with England should cease within a short space of time.* The whole British coast, or anyway a part of it, must be declared to be blockaded, at the same time the aforesaid warning must be published. The declaration of the blockade is desirable in order to warn neutrals of the consequences. *The gravity of the situation demands that we should free ourselves from all scruples which certainly no longer have any justification.* It is of importance too, with a view to the future, that we should make the enemy realize at once what a powerful weapon we possess in the U-boat, with which to injure their trade, *and that the most unsparing use is to be made of it.*'[3] (author's italics)

Although von Pohl was converted to the idea of a counter-blockade by the U-boats – indeed he became its main advocate – most members of the Admiralstab were unconvinced of the memorandum's wisdom, sharing the views of the German Chancellor, Bethmann-Hollweg and the Foreign Office (Auswärtiges Amt), foremost of which was the Foreign Secretary, von Jagow, that a trade war by the U-boats, although justified in principle, ran the risk of provoking the neutral states, above all America, into joining the enemy. However, after protracted argument, von Pohl succeeded in convincing first the Admiralstab (January 1915) and finally the Chancellor (1 February) to agree to the proposal.

Pohl reasoned that a proclamation, issued before the campaign was inaugurated, would frighten neutral shipping away from British waters (intimidation was to be the essence of the plan), so that diplomatic conflict with the neutrals need not necessarily arise (the loss of neutral ships and their crews was less likely to occur). It was his contention that the combined effects of the destruction of Britain's shipping and the dissuasion of the neutrals to trade with her, could well compel Britain to end her blockade of the North Sea (in return for a reciprocal move by Germany to call off the U-boat blockade) and might even make her willing to consider peace proposals advantageous to German war aims. The volte-face by the Chancellor and the Auswärtiges Amt was brought about in part by Pohl's dialectic, which stressed that the campaign should commence before the deliveries of cereals from South America arrived in Britain, ensuring food for the country for many months, but also by the pressure of public opinion in Germany. Fired by Grossadmiral von Tirpitz's optimistic remarks about the outcome of a U-boat campaign on commerce to an American journalist (published in the Press during December), the German public began to believe that an attack on enemy trade by the U-boats could decide the outcome of the war.

Tirpitz was Secretary of the Naval Cabinet (Staatssekretär des Reichs-Marine-Amt); a position which was roughly equivalent to the British First Lord of the Admiralty. Pohl's position as Chief of the Admiralstab was equatable with the British First Sea Lord. After the Tirpitz interview had echoed through the German Press, the naval command and the political authorities were assailed by a mass of papers written by eminent financiers, shipping and industrial magnates, politicians and scientists, urging them not to be deterred from using a decisive weapon by any false misgivings. The Kaiser's ratification was obtained by Pohl on 4 February (the day on which he relieved Ingenohl as CinC, High Seas Fleet, the post of chief of the Admiralstab going to Admiral Bachmann). On the following day a proclamation signed by Pohl was published in The Imperial Gazette (*Reichsanzeiger*), declaring '*all the waters around Great Britain and Ireland, including the whole of the English Channel a war zone (Kriegsgebiet)*', with a warning that from 18 February all British merchant shipping in these waters '*will be destroyed, nor will it always be possible to obviate the danger with which the crews and passengers are thereby threatened*'. In an attempt to frighten away neutral traders from the prohibited area they were warned that '*neutral ships, too, will run a risk in the war zone, for in view of the misuse of neutral flags ordained by the British Government . . . and owing to the hazards of naval warfare, it may not always be possible to prevent the attacks meant for hostile ships from being directed against neutral ships*'. To allow neutral shipping access to Germany and the neighbouring non-combatant states a safe from attack channel was left open, '*north of the Shetland Islands, in the eastern part of the North Sea and on a strip thirty nautical miles wide along the Dutch coast*'.[4]

Political complications

Although the British blockade was causing the USA substantial economic losses (relationships between the two governments were strained), Germany's declared intention to attack and destroy *any* vessel entering the prescribed area was viewed as a far more serious matter, considered by Washington to be 'an act unprecedented in naval warfare', in that it threatened the *lives* of peaceful traders on the High Seas. The ominous tone of an American diplomatic note, which threatened armed conflict, alarmed the Chancellor and the Auswärtiges Amt to the extent that they replied with an assurance that the U-boat commanders would receive orders not to molest neutral ships, '*if they were recognizable as such*'.[5] The naval command protested vigorously that these limiting precautions would make success impossible. They could no longer hope to terrorize neutral ships (which carried a quarter of British imports) into avoiding the war zone, and how, for instance, could a U-boat commander operating off a busy British port be expected to distinguish between enemy and neutral shipping, particularly at night, and in view of the fact that British ships had been advised to fly false colours? Admiral Bachmann, the new chief of the Admiralstab, remonstrated that if the undertaking was allowed to stand, the campaign would have to be abandoned outright. As this was out of the question, the die having been cast by the publicly announced proclamation of 4 February ('the campaign being most hopefully regarded by the German public'), the impasse was circumvented by the issue of new instructions on 18 February (the commence date was deferred until the 22nd), which was a compromise between the diplomatic objections and the conflicting arguments of the Admirals.

Ships flying neutral colours, unless *definitely* identified as being of enemy nationality (by 'structure, place of registration, course and general behaviour') were immune from attack, along with hospital ships (unless 'they are obviously being used for the transport of troops from England to France') and ships belonging to the Belgian Relief Commission (funded primarily by America to provide food for the impoverished Belgian population under German occupation). On the other side of the coin, the U-boat commanders were urged to prosecute the campaign 'with all possible vigour', along with the assurance that they would not be held responsible '*if in spite of the exercise of great care mistakes should be made*'.[6]

So it was that the two strongest naval powers in the world embarked on maritime campaigns in which each would attempt to starve the other into submission. For Britain with her superior battle fleet and geographical advantage (lying like a great 600-mile long breakwater across the oceanic approach routes to Germany), the total severance of German imports, keeping within the 'accepted' standards of naval warfare with the use of surface craft, was a relatively humane and easy matter. With the weaker fleet and geographical disadvantage, Germany had only one hope of winning the war of strangulation and only one recourse – the U-boat offensive.

Opening Gambit
The first offensive against shipping, February to September 1915

Throughout January and up until 22 February 1915, the U-boat commanders pre-empted the official commencement of the offensive by sinking one French and ten British merchantmen totalling 24,861 tons. Of these, five were torpedoed without warning, resulting in the loss of 27 lives. Seven other vessels were also attacked but managed to escape. One of these, the Norwegian tanker *Belridge* (7,020 tons), was the first neutral to be torpedoed without warning (*U16* on 19 February); the *Belridge* did not sink and she was towed into Folkestone. At a time when the German diplomats were trying to placate American sabre-rattling with assurances of restraint, the aggressive tactics of the U-boat commanders was evidence that the naval command was unleashing a force over which they could not exercise proper control. The situation is summed up by A. C. Bell, the official historian of the Blockade of Germany: 'A handful of naval officers, most of them under thirty years of age, without political training, and isolated from the rest of the world by the nature of their duties, were thus given a vague and indefinite instruction to give a thought to politics before they fired their torpedoes.'[1] Serious infractions of the assurances given to the Americans was the inevitable result.

During January two U-boats had been lost. *U31* (Wachendorff) disappeared without trace; it is surmised that she blew up on a mine off the east coast of England. *U7* (König) was accidentally torpedoed by *U22* (Hoppe) off the Dutch coast. When *U7* failed to reply to Hoppe's recognition signal, Hoppe attacked, believing the U-boat to be a British submarine. There was only one survivor. This brought the total number of boats lost since the outbreak of war to seven. The eighteen remaining boats of the original 24 *Frontboote*, were reinforced by twelve new boats which had been taken into service since August 1914: *U29–U41* (not including the lost *U31*), giving a total of thirty *Frontboote* with which to prosecute the campaign. Another 29 boats were under construction: *U43–U56*; *U57–U62*; *U66–U70* (which were being built for Austria and were requisitioned); and the large ocean-going minelayers (*Hochsee Minenunterseeboote*) *U71–U74*. These only became operational between the end of 1915 and December 1916. In addition to these High Seas Fleet U-boats (*U-boote der Hochseeflotte*) two new types of small boats – the 127-ton coastal UB and the 168-ton minelaying UC boats – were nearing completion. Orders for these boats had been placed after the German Army captured the Belgian coastal ports. As these ports afforded ideal bases from which to harry the east coast and English Channel traffic (a 300-mile passage from the German naval bases) it was decided that small U-boats with a contractual building time of four months should be

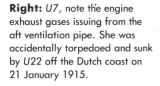

Right: *U7*, note the engine exhaust gases issuing from the aft ventilation pipe. She was accidentally torpedoed and sunk by *U22* off the Dutch coast on 21 January 1915.

constructed (the average building time of conventional boats was eighteen months). In fact the first of the UB series, which were a quarter the size of the High Seas Fleet U-boats, were completed by Germaniawerft (Kiel) in the remarkably short time of 75 days. Most of these small boats were transported to their operational bases by rail, each boat requiring about five long wagons – one for each of the three main hull compartments and others for the conning tower, engines and batteries. After being assembled in Antwerp, which took approximately fourteen days, they were towed through the Scheldt and the Ghent-Bruges Canal to the base of the newly inaugurated (29 March) Flanders Flotilla under the command of Korvettenkapitän Bartenbach.

The Marine Corps in Flanders, based in Bruges, which encompassed warships, bases, coastal defences and naval brigades ashore, including the new flotilla of small coastal U-boats (*Unterseeboote für küstengewässer*) were under the overall command of Admiral Schroder. Egress to the sea from Bruges was facilitated by two canals which linked the base to Zeebrugge (eight miles) and Ostend (eleven miles). Altogether seventeen of the UB and fifteen of the UC classes were completed between the end of January and mid-July 1915, but it wasn't until the latter part of April that six of the UB boats became operational; while the first of the UC boats did not begin to dump her lethal cargo of mines until early in June. Even with these additions, the means available to commence the campaign were ridiculously small given the objective of attempting to blockade the whole of the British Isles (Tirpitz favoured a more modest blockade of the Thames estuary).

Before the war Kapitänleutnant Blum had, in an unofficial paper, deduced, very accurately, as experience was to prove, that an effective blockade of the British Isles would require at least 222 operational boats to maintain permanent patrols in 48 operational areas (or stations).[2] In Bauer's plan only four stations were envisaged: the South Western Approaches and the Irish Sea covering the trade routes to Liverpool and the Bristol Channel ports; the English Channel covering the routes to Southampton and London; and the north-east coast covering the routes used by the Baltic and Scandinavian traders and the colliers from Newcastle. When the commence day dawned (22 February) most of the newer boats, *U35–U41*, were still running their sea trials, and many of the older boats were undergoing lengthy overhauls. After initially underestimating the potential of their *Unterseeboote*, the Admiralstab was now grossly overvaluing the ability of the small numbers they possessed. As A. C. Bell points out: 'The assumption that shipping of all nations would fly in terror from four to six U-boats, posted off a few British harbours was extraordinary.'[3] This paucity of available means inspired Winston Churchill (First Lord of the Admiralty) to reassure the House of Commons on 15 February, that: 'Losses will no doubt be incurred, of that I give full warning, but we believe that no vital injury can be done if our traders put to sea regularly . . . we expect the losses will be confined within manageable limits, even at the outset, when the enemy must be expected to make his greatest effort to produce an impression.'[4]

Churchill's optimism, although not unfounded, proved dangerous in that the Admiralty failed to sense the urgency of developing efficient anti-submarine (A/S) weapons.

British counter-measures

The principal methods and weapons relied on during 1915 all proved to be relatively ineffective in various degrees. In the area of the densest traffic – the Western Approaches to the British Isles – diverse light craft (sloops, armed yachts, trawlers, drifters and some destroyers) of the Western Approaches Command, based on Queenstown, thrashed about in what was optimisti-

cally termed 'offensive patrolling'. Although the number of craft at Queenstown had reached 450 by May 1916, the vast area of water they had to cover, the whole of the Irish Coast (including the Irish Sea), St. George's Channel, Bristol Channel and the entrance to the English Channel (the area of the South-Western Approaches with the principal landfalls of Fastnet and the Scilly Islands alone covered 100,000 square miles of water) made their chances of intercepting a U-boat hardly more than accidental. The small craft of this force, armed yachts, trawlers and drifters, belonged to the Auxiliary Patrol flotillas. In theory a continuous protective belt around the coastal waters of the British Isles was supposedly formed by Auxiliary Patrol flotillas, which were deployed in 23 different patrol areas. But the number of craft available (827 in January 1915, increasing to 2,595 by January 1916 and 3,301 by the beginning of 1918) for such a large expanse of water obviously reduced the theory of a continuous protective belt to little more than wishful thinking. Throughout the entire war they accounted for very few U-boats in return for a vast amount of effort.

To protect the English Channel traffic 7,154 mines in 22 fields were laid to the east of the Dover Straits from 2 October 1914 until 16 February 1915. This mine barrage proved no obstacle to the U-boats because the British mines were defective. Apart from being visible on the surface at low water they commonly failed to explode when struck. Moreover about 4,000 of the total laid either sank uselessly to the bottom or drifted away owing to the 5cwt sinkers being too light. One mine, for example, was found to have dragged eighteen miles in three weeks; eventually many, carried by wind and current, washed up on the Dutch coast.

Behind these minefields were two other lines of defence. The first of these was a line of drifters (of the Dover Auxiliary Patrol flotilla) towing 'indicator nets'. These were made of light steel wire mesh of high tensile strength, 300 feet long and 30 feet deep, and were kept in an extended position by being towed at low speed by the drifters. The nets were attached to bottle-glass buoys ingeniously devised so as to ignite a carbide flare if a section of net was fouled by a U-boat. With the U-boat's presence thus revealed, patrol craft (destroyers or armed trawlers) were to close in to attack by ramming or gunfire should the U-boat surface in an attempt to get clear of the net. If, however, the U-boat remained submerged, the only weapon available to deal with it was the 'explosive sweep'. This, towed by the patrol craft, consisted of a long looped wire, to which were affixed nine 80lb explosive charges. This weapon, which was only effective at slow speed, was to account for only one U-boat (*U8*) up until the time it was superseded by the more effective 'explosive paravane' (or high-speed sweep) in 1916. Thirty drifters were riding their nets across the Straits by February 1915, but bad weather took a heavy toll, 90 nets (i.e., 4½ miles) were swept away in one three-day gale. Bases for net drifters were also established at Cromarty, Peterhead, Firth of Forth, Yarmouth, Harwich, the Nore, Portsmouth, Portland, Poole, Falmouth, Devonport and Larne.

The third measure designed to bar the straits to the passage of U-boats was the intention to stretch a 20-mile long boom of heavy harbour-defence steel nets from Folkestone to Cap Gris-Nez on the French coast. The boom consisted of wooden floats, nine feet by five feet and weighing four tons, moored to buoys, to which were affixed 2in wire nets, 100 feet deep and 200 yards long. 'Strong gales and heavy seas played "Old Harry" with the heavy floats and large hawsers,' according to Admiral Bacon in command of the Dover Patrol. 'Above all, the strain on the chain cables, due to the strong tides pressing against the floats and nets, was enormous, and produced unforeseen erosion in the bolts of the shackles as the sea lifted and lowered the whole structure.'[5] These insurmountable difficulties and the heavy cost of maintenance caused the Admiralty to abandon the only half-constructed boom as impracticable in May 1915, and the sections of the boom were removed. As we shall see, the net drifters and the boom were to have an effect on U-boat strategy out of all proportion to their true potential. An attempt was also made to seal off the entrances to the Irish Sea with drifters towing indicator nets. The St. George's Channel was far too wide to be completely covered, but in the narrow and deep North Channel, an area twelve miles wide and thirty miles long was patrolled and netted (there were seven lines of drifters in all) so as to force the U-boats to make a deep and prolonged dive, which would exhaust their batteries and force them to surface where the patrol craft would be waiting for them. That, at least, was the theory. In practice the strong tides of the North Channel, along with gales, frequently turned the out-stretched nets into hopeless tangles.

Slightly more effective counter-measures were obtained by the defensive arming of merchant ships with light calibre guns (766 had been armed by December 1915) and the employment of decoy ships plying the trade routes in the U-boats' operational areas. These decoys became known as 'Q-ships' after the Admiralty gave them all 'Q' numbers in the latter part of 1916. These were usually small tramp steamers armed with concealed guns. The idea was to entice a U-boat to surface and close in for the kill with gunfire, as the Q-ships were too small to be worth a torpedo, whereupon the Q-ship would open fire at pointblank range. More than 180 ships were so fitted throughout the course of the war and they accounted for eleven U-boats in all, but at the disproportionate cost of 27 of their own number. Through the auspices of Room 40 (in which intercepted German naval wireless signals were decoded) the British were well aware of, not only the operational strength of the U-boat flotillas, but also the areas for which they were bound because the boats made frequent position reports to U-Boat Command on their outward passage. Although the Admiralty sent out general warnings of the dangerous areas four times a day (at 03.00, 09.00, 15.00 and 21.00 hours) in the Merchant Navy code, it had very little effect on the general situation as very few merchant ships were equipped with wireless sets in those days. In all the lack of effective counter-measures tended to compensate the Germans for their lack of *Frontboote*.

The opening of the offensive

On the day 'the great gamble began' there were only three U-boats at sea. Of these *U30* was returning to base north around the Shetlands after operating in the Irish Sea; while *U34*, which was *en route* from Heligoland to her operational area off the north-east coast, had to return to base with engine trouble on 24 February. This left only one boat, *U8* (Stoss) to blood the campaign with the first kills. Having set out from Heligoland on the 21st for the English Channel, *U8* negotiated the British minefields east of the Dover Straits and tore through the net barrage without much difficulty. During the 23rd and 24th *U8* opened the campaign by sinking without warning five British steamers off Beachy Head, grossing 15,049 tons. This brought the grand total of tonnage sunk by U-boats for the whole of February to eight ships of 21,787 tons. To put this figure into perspective it must be set against the fact that some 4,000 merchant vessels either arrived or departed from British ports during the same month. But from this unimpressive start, the campaign gradually gathered momentum as more and more boats became operational.

Because the available *Frontboote* could only work in relays, due to the necessity of maintenance and replenishment after each patrol, the average number of boats at sea daily from March until September 1915 was only 7.3, yet even this meagre number were able to account for 480 merchant vessels and fishing craft grossing 790,016 tons (including vessels that came to grief on the scattered minefields of from six to twelve mines laid by Flanders' UC minelayers – of which see below). These are the German official figures compiled by Konteradmiral (Rear Admiral) Arno Spindler.[6] There is a discrepancy of 153 vessels of 16,470 tons between Spindler's figures and those compiled by the British Admiralty, accountable by the fact that the British figures do not include vessels under 500 gross tons or fishing craft. During the same period the U-boats sank twelve British warships (all theatres): two predreadnought battleships (*Triumph* and *Majestic* torpedoed by *U21* off Gallipoli); four destroyers; two torpedo-boats; two armed merchant cruisers and two submarines.

From March to May 1915, when the average number of U-boats at sea daily was only 5.6 (maximum number at sea on any one day, twelve), they accounted for 115 merchant and fishing vessels grossing 257,900 tons in the North Sea and the waters surrounding the British Isles. The breakdown of figures (with the number of ships and the British figures in parentheses) month by month is as follows:[7]

March	(29)	89,517 tons	(26 ships of 72,441 tons)
April	(33)	41,488 tons	(23 ships of 38,614 tons)
May	(53)	126,895 tons	(35 ships of 106,293 tons)

Of the total, 22 vessels of 31,118 tons were neutrals.

The U-boat attack fell most heavily in the South-Western Approaches (the waters between the southern Irish coast and the north-west coast of France): the area in which the ships following the ocean routes passed through, and which bore most of the essential imports upon which Britain was chiefly dependent. This vital area, along with the Irish Sea, could only be reached by the twenty diesel-engined boats of the High Seas Fleet flotillas (*U20–U41*). The older, heavy-oil engined boats (*U6–U17*) operated in the English Channel (until 10 April), which they reached via the Dover Straits, and in the North Sea including the north-east coast station. The U-boats operated as individual units and their targets, the mass of merchant shipping, also sailed as independents; the concept of merchant vessels sailing in convoy, and concentrated attacks being mounted upon them by groups of U-boats acting in concert (wolf-packs) were measures undreamed of at this stage.

During April the small 127-ton UB coastal boats (they carried only four 19.7in torpedoes and no deck gun) became operational. Until June their activities were confined to the Hoofden, after Bauer ordered all boats not to attempt the passage through the Dover Straits (effective from 10 April). This order had the effect of adding 1,400 miles (an extra seven days) to each cruise of the High Seas Fleet boats, which could, consequently, only reach the South-Western Approaches and Irish Sea, north about Scotland, and closed the English Channel to the small boats of the Flanders Flotilla. The reason for this constricting order is explained by Führer der U-boote Hermann Bauer (who was promoted to Fregettenkapitän on 16 April 1915). In the war diary of the *F.d.U.*, Bauer made the following entry on 10 April:

'The Führer der U-boote has decided to give up operations in the English Channel for a while . . . Necessity for this withdrawal had been confirmed by a report by the Commander of *U33* (Gansser) according to which the approach to the Straits of Dover (from Sandettie Bank to the Goodwin Sands, and Fairy Bank to the Falls) is blocked by three dense minefields and it is also probable that between Gris-Nez and Dover wire nets are spread, which reach to a depth of 25 metres (82 feet). There remains no point, therefore, at which a U-boat can still pass the Straits of Dover without grave danger. However, the British minefields known hitherto still offer comparatively little danger, because at low water the mines lie on the surface, and the barrage can be easily seen and comparatively easily traversed in good weather when the current is favourable. According to recent experience it appears that to proceed under water at a depth of 20 metres (66 feet) is a particularly good way of avoiding the British mines. While proceeding this way (17/18 March), *U35* caught a small steel line round her propeller, which on later examination proved to be the mooring rope of a British mine. Meanwhile there has been frequent confirmation of the report current for some time that there is also a net barrage in the Straits of Dover. Furthermore, *U28* brings news from Ostend that French deep mines have been discovered off Gris-Nez. This means that the U-boats cannot reach their area of operations in the Channel via the Straits without any great anxiety. Moreover *U37* (which left port on 20 March) must be considered as lost, and it will probably be right to put this down to a mine in the Straits of Dover. The route through the Straits must therefore be avoided for the present.'[8]

According to Professor Grant,[9] Bauer was motivated by the interception, on 6 April, of a British wireless message which made mention of numbered buoys in the Straits which were

Right: UB boats of the Flanders Flotilla in Zeebrugge.

Right: A yard model of *UB54*.

attached either to mines or to moored nets. Actually, the message must have referred either to indicator nets or to the incomplete nets between Folkestone and Cap Gris-Nez. Bauer believed, however, that a real net barrage had been laid across the Straits. Spindler is critical of Bauer's over caution: 'A considerable time passed before there was any certainty as to whether the dangers of the Straits, veiled in mystery, really existed and the momentous order to take the wearisome circuitous route was unjustified.'[10] Especially, it must be added, in view of the fact that the UB boats of the Flanders Flotilla began to pass through the Straits into the English Channel without loss during June. And yet Bauer's interdiction on the Straits route for the High Seas Fleet U-boats remained in force until December 1916.

UC minelaying operations

During May the small 168-ton UC minelayers (they carried twelve mines, but no torpedoes or deck gun) began laying small, but deadly minefields, of between six to twelve mines, off the French coast between Calais and Dunkirk, and off the mouths of the commercial harbours on the south-east coast of England. From May to September 1915, they laid a total of 420 mines in 46 fields: the largest percentage being laid in the Thames estuary. The maiden minelaying cruise by a UC boat was carried out by *UC11* (Schmidt) which set out from Zeebrugge on 29 May. Despite becoming temporarily fouled in a net of the indicator-net barrage east of the Straits and unwittingly, but harmlessly, passing through a British minefield west of the Ruytingen Sand, Schmidt laid the first field of twelve mines close to the South Foreland in the Downs. 'The hardihood of the UC voyages is difficult to exaggerate,' wrote the author of a naval staff monograph on the subject. 'To navigate among the shoals and swirls of the east coast of England in a UC boat whose maximum speed was 6¼ knots on the surface and less below it, seems itself sufficiently difficult; but in addition to that, to cross continually waters known to be mined and to penetrate through a patrol (the Auxiliary Patrol) keenly alert and ready with indicator nets and guns, calls for a special degree of courage. Yet, in spite of all the opposition and danger they knew they could expect, the UC boats fouled with their mines all parts of the British coast within their reach.'[11] To counter the UC mine-layers small 'trap' minefields were laid in British coastal waters. Commencing in April 1915, a total of twenty trap fields were laid by the end of the war.

The boats of UCI class had one drawback. Each boat carried twelve mines in tubes which occupied the whole of the fore part, and the mines were immersed in sea water while so stowed. During a cruise the mines were, therefore, inaccessible from the interior of the boat, and the depth setting had to be carried out in harbour before the mines were placed in the tubes and could, consequently, only be laid in the depth of water for which they were set. With the later classes of UCII, UCIII and the large ocean-going UE minelayers, this problem was eradicated by having dry storage tubes within the interior of the boat.

The *Lusitania* incident

Of the 115 merchant vessels sunk from March until May, slightly more than half had been torpedoed without warning, 22 of these being neutrals. As 'one flag is very like another seen against the light through a periscope', conflict with America was bound to occur sooner or later. On 1 May the American tanker *Gulflight* was torpedoed by *U30* off the Scilly Isles. Although *Gulflight* did not sink, the master and two of her crew died (the master suffered a heart attack and the other two drowned after jumping overboard in panic). With emotions already aroused by this incident, a bitter diplomatic feud between Washington and Berlin was sparked off when more American lives were lost in an attack on a British liner on 7 May 1915.

At 14.20 (German time) Kapitänleutnant Walter Schwieger, commander of the *U20*, which was operating in the Western Approaches, sighted a four-funnelled steamer fourteen miles distant. The war pilot of *U20* (a merchant marine officer carried by U-boats to assist in the identification of targets) was certain that the steamer was either the *Lusitania* or *Mauretania*, which were described as Armed Merchant Cruisers in Schwieger's 1914 copies of *Jane's Fighting Ships* and *The Naval Annual*. It was also believed by the Germans that these two great liners were being used as troop transports. With what Schwieger considered to be a legitimate target in his sights, he ran *U20* at high speed in order to get ahead of the oncoming ship, and at 15.10 fired a bowshot at a range of 700 metres. The torpedo detonated behind the bridge on the starboard side of the ship. According to Schwieger's log 'the ship stopped immediately and quickly

heeled over to starboard, immersing simultaneously at the bow'.[12] Twenty minutes later she plunged to the bottom, leaving the water black with hundreds of drowning men, women and children. *U20* had sunk the 30,396-ton Cunard liner *Lusitania* which was not armed and not engaged in trooping. Among the 1,201 passengers who lost their lives were 128 American citizens, 'some of enormous wealth and influence'. This tragedy evoked a series of strongly worded protests from Washington to Berlin.

To begin with, President Wilson virtually demanded the complete cessation of the U-boat campaign against commerce: 'The objection to the present method of attack against trade lies in the practical impossibility of employing U-boats in the destruction of commerce without disregarding those rules of fairness, reason, justice and humanity, which all modern opinion regards as imperative.'[13] But, being persuaded that a decision at sea could not be secured by any other measure than the U-boat campaign, the Admiralstab was determined not to give way to political pressure. Admiral Scheer gave expression to the general conviction: 'In a comparatively short space of time U-boat warfare against commerce has become a form of warfare which is more than retaliation (to the British blockade); for it is adapted to the nature of modern war and must remain a part of it . . . For us Germans, U-boat warfare upon commerce is a deliverance; it has put British predominance at sea in question . . . Being pressed by sheer necessity we must legalize this new weapon, or, to speak more accurately, accustom the world to it.'[14]

After a lengthy exchange of diplomatic notes, the German Chancellor managed to satisfy President Wilson, in a note dated 28 August, with assurances that the U-boat commanders would not hence forward endanger the safety of neutral ships and large passenger liners even if the latter were flying belligerent colours. But the chief of the Admiralstab (Bachmann) stubbornly insisted that the restrictions were untenable and that the campaign must either be abandoned outright or continued without modification. As the Chancellor could not accept the responsibility of calling an end to the campaign in the face of German popular opinion, and could not, as he put it, 'go on sitting on top of a volcano', he overcame the impasse and scored a *fait accompli* by the contrivance of replacing Admiral Bachmann with Admiral von Holtzendorff, a personal friend of the Chancellor's, who not only shared Bethmann-Hollweg's views on political problems, but also believed that the U-boat campaign was greatly overvalued and was, furthermore, determined that it should be properly regulated.

Throughout the summer and autumn months, while the German Chancellor and Auswärtiges Amt were trying to placate American opinion, the U-boat commanders continued to attack without warning whenever they were unable to distinguish the flag of a vessel; each one of these attacks being a potential source of future armed conflict with the USA. The average number of U-boats at sea daily from June to September was 8.6 (maximum number at sea on any one day, eighteen). Although this was only a percentage increase of 3 over the March–May figure, they

were able to more than double the rate of sinkings: 365 ships of 532,116 tons, as the monthly breakdown shows (number of ships sunk and British official figures in parentheses):

June	(114)	115,291 tons	(58 ships of 118,091 tons)
July	(86)	98,005 tons	(55 ships of 105,145 tons)
August	(107)	182,772 tons	(74 ships of 181,691 tons)
September	(58)	136,048 tons	(56 ships of 151,271 tons)

Failure of the first offensive

Despite this achievement, Churchill could still boast that 'the failure of the German submarine campaign was patent to the whole world'.[15] Indeed the Germans were under no illusions that the campaign was failing in its essential aims. Despite heavy losses, the neutral traders had not been intimidated in the way Pohl and the Admiralstab had so confidently expected. Neither had the economic pressure reached anywhere near the scale necessary to coerce Britain into lifting her blockade of the North Sea, let alone sue for peace. Between 1,000 to 1,500 sailings a week in and out of British ports had been maintained, and the monthly imports of foodstuffs and raw materials actually exceeded in volume the imports during the last corresponding months of peace in 1913. Thanks to the great number of German and Austro-Hungarian merchant ships captured, seized or detained in the early months of the war, the total tonnage available to Britain and her allies was greater in the autumn of 1915 than it had been at the outbreak of war. But if the U-boats continued to exert pressure of the scale witnessed during the campaign the situation for Britain would very soon begin to change for the worse. As Fayle, the official historian of *Seaborne Trade* explains: 'New merchant tonnage launched, which amounted to 416,000 tons for the last quarter of 1914, fell in the quarter ending March 1915 to 267,000 and in the June and September quarters it was only 148,000 tons and 146,000 tons respectively [the latter being roughly a third of the tonnage sunk during the corresponding quarter of the campaign].'[16] Not only were the shipbuilders' yards, material and labour being taken up more and more for the construction and repair of warships, but 20 per cent of British ocean-going tonnage had been requisitioned for the transport of troops, munitions, stores and military supplies: a loss for trade carrying purposes far heavier than anything the U-boats had been able to achieve.

The *Arabic* incident and the suspension of the campaign

Before the effects of the campaign began to reach fruition, a sudden check occurred after the sinking, without warning, of two British passenger liners. The 15,801-ton White Star liner *Arabic* was sunk twenty miles from the Smalls by *U24* (Schneider) on 19 August (three Americans were among the 44 casualties); and the 10,920-ton liner *Hesperian* went down 80 miles south-west from Fastnet with the loss of 32 lives on 6 September, after being torpedoed by *U20* (Schwieger – who had sunk the *Lusitania*). No Americans were lost on the *Hesperian*, but as the sinking of these two liners was contrary to the assurances made to President Wilson and to the instructions to the commanders in force at the time (and as relations between Germany and the United States had reached a precarious low), Holtzendorff issued an order on 18 September, withdrawing all the U-boats from the English Channel and South-Western Approaches where the densest concentration of US shipping occurred. He also decreed that operations in the North Sea could henceforth only be carried out in strict accord with Prize Regulations. These orders virtually suspended the campaign in the war zone for the rest of the year, for rather than conform to Holtzendorff's instructions, von Pohl, as CinC, High Seas Fleet, withdrew his boats from the North Sea. As a soporific to German public opinion both Holtzendorff and Pohl agreed an alternative arrangement whereby the campaign was to be prosecuted on a smaller scale in the Mediterranean theatre where very few US merchantmen were to be found. As it was, the campaign in home waters was beginning to peter out anyway because of the lack of *Frontboote*.

Since the start-date the original thirty *Frontboote* had been reinforced by the addition of two U-boats (*U43* and *U44*), seventeen UB boats and fifteen UC minelayers. During the same period twelve U-boats, two UB boats and one UC minelayer had been lost. In addition *U25* had been withdrawn from active service due to mechanical problems (she was used as a training boat for the rest of the war), and *U30* had accidentally foundered in Borkum Roads: she was salvaged three months later and after a lengthy overhaul re-entered service. This brought the total number of *Frontboote* available at the end of September (in all theatres) to fifty (including fourteen UC minelayers). This figure, however, is deceptive because, of the High Seas Fleet boats in home waters only five were not in need of lengthy docking for repairs, so that the addition of the six boats (*U45*, *U66–U70*) running their sea trials during September, would do very little materially to affect the situation.

During December a raid by one of the High Seas Fleet boats took place. *U24* (Schneider) left the Bight on 16 December with orders to attack the troop transports which were regularly entering the French port of Le Havre. Taking the northerly route around the Shetlands *U24* sank five merchant ships grossing 22,767 tons in the South-Western Approaches *en route* to the English Channel. However, heavy weather damaged the U-boat and injured two of her crew, whereupon Schneider abandoned the proposed attack on the transports and turned for home, arriving in the Bight on 4 January.

The most important lesson of the campaign was the obvious one: that a much larger fleet of *Frontboote* was necessary to impose an effective U-boat blockade of the British Isles. It was also apparent that imposing politically motivated restraints on the tactical use of the boats blunted their potential. Of the 274 attacks on British merchantmen, 69 were submerged torpedo attacks made without warning of which 40 vessels were sunk and 29 (or 42 per cent) escaped through the torpedoes missing the mark. In comparison, of the 205 attacks by surfaced U-boats – acting in accordance with Prize Regulations – 163 vessels were sunk and 111 (or 54 per cent) escaped, usually by superior speed and/or counter-attack by those that had been defensively armed with guns. Moreover, surfacing to act in accordance with Prize Regulations not only gave the intended victims a 12 per cent better chance of escape, but also placed the U-boats in greater danger from counter-attack. Seven of the fifteen boats lost from February to September were sunk as a direct result of this prescription which deprived them of their submerged defensive secrecy. Three boats, *U36*, *U27* and *U41*, were sunk by the concealed guns of Q-ships; *U14* and *UB4* were destroyed in a like manner by trawlers armed with light-calibre guns; while *U23* and *U40* were torpedoed by British submarines acting in concert with trawlers.

Below: *U23*, which was torpedoed and sunk, on 20 July 1915, by the British submarine *C27* which was being towed submerged by the decoy trawler *Princess Louise*.

The latter method was quite ingenious. A trawler towed a submerged submarine. When a U-boat surfaced with the intention of sinking the trawler either with gunfire or explosive charges, the trawler would telephone down to the submarine below, by way of the umbilical link, which would then slip the tow and attack the U-boat with torpedoes. 'Secrecy', Professor Grant explains, 'was obviously the essence of this method. Unfortunately the secret got back to Germany when survivors from U23 passed information on to German civilian prisoners in England who were about to be repatriated.'[17] As a result no further U-boats fell for this ruse.

The other boats were lost by a variety of means: U12 and U29 were rammed by warships (the latter by the battleship *Dreadnought* while U29 (Weddigen) was attempting to torpedo the battleship *Neptune*); U6 was torpedoed by a British submarine; UC2 blew up on her own mines and U8 was blown up by the explosive sweep of a destroyer. The fate of the other three boats is uncertain. It is surmised that U37 and U26 were sunk by mines, but nothing is known of the fate of UB3 which disappeared mysteriously in the Aegean Sea during May.

Mediterranean waters

The latter boat was one of the thirteen sent out to form a half-flotilla of five U-boats (all of the '30s' class) based on the Austro-Hungarian Adriatic ports of Pola and Cattaro (*Deutsche U-halbflotille Pola*) for operations in the Mediterranean; and a flotilla comprised of one U-boat, four UB boats and three UC minelayers based on the Turkish capital of Constantinople, for operations in the Black Sea and Aegean (*U-boote der Mittelmeer-division in Konstantinopel*). The boats in these two groups began the campaign against commerce in the latter part of September 1915. Although the Austro-Hungarian Navy had seven U-boats in commission, they did not enter the war against commerce

until 1917. The Adriatic-based boats quickly made their presence felt in the Mediterranean. The combination of the most experienced commanders and the powerful new boats of the '30s' class, in conjunction with the vastly better weather and visibility conditions than prevailed in the North Sea, produced optimum results. Acting by and large in conformity with Prize

---

Flotilla dispositions of *Frontboote*, February to September 1915

War losses are marked with an asterisk; dates boats joined flotillas are in parentheses

High Seas Fleet Flotillas (*U-boote der Hochseeflotte*)
Führer der U-boote (F.d.U.): Korvettenkapitän Bauer (promoted to Fregattenkapitän 16 April 1915).

I. U-Halbflotille (half-flotilla)
Chef: Kapitänleutnant Mühlau (succeeded by Kapitänleutnant Pasquay 29 June 1915)
U6*, U8*, U9, U10, U12*, U14*, U16, U17. U9 and U10 were transferred to the Baltic, 7 July 1915.

II. U-Halbflotille
Chef: Korvettenkapitän Spindler
U34, U35, U36*, U37*, U38, U39, U40*, U41*. U34, U35 and U39 were transferred to the Adriatic, Aug 1915.

III. U-Halbflotille
Chef: Kapitänleutnant Gayer
U19, U20, U21, U22, U23*, U24. U21 was transferred to Constantinople, June 1915.

IV. U-Halbflotille
Chef: Kapitänleutnant Prause
U27*, U28, U29*, U30, U32, U33.
U30 accidentally foundered in Borkum Roads, 22 June 1915, but was later salved and repaired; U33 was transferred to the Adriatic, Aug 1915.

Flanders Flotilla
U-boote des Marinekorps U-Flotille Flandern (from March to Sept 1915)
Chef: Kapitänleutnant Bartenbach (promoted to Korvettenkapitän 18 Sept 1915)
UB2, UB4*, UB5, UB6, UB10, UB12, UB13, UB16, UB17, UC1, UC2*, UC3, UC5, UC6, UC7, UC9, UC11.

Adriatic
Deutsche U-Halbflotille Pola
Chef: Kapitänleutnant Adam
Although the headquarters of the flotilla was Pola, the operational base was Cattaro. The U-boats only used Pola for major overhauls and repairs. Dates the boats joined the flotilla are in parentheses.
U33 (16 Sept 1915), U34 (23 Aug 1915), U35 (23 Aug 1915), U39 (15 Sept 1915), UC12 (27 June 1915).

Black Sea
U-boote der Mittelmeer division in Konstantinopel
Dates the boats joined the division are in parentheses.
U21 (5 June 1915), UB3* (23 May 1915), UB7 (13 June 1915), UB8 (4 June 1915), UB14 (24 July 1915), UC13 (26 Aug 1915), UC14 (18 July 1915), UC15 (20 July 1915).

Below: *U35 (nearest the camera) with other units of the Deutsche U-Flotilla Pola in Cattaro.*

Regulations, this small force of five boats sank 99 merchant ships of 346,786 tons from September to December 1915. In comparison the boats based on Constantinople sank only one small vessel of 200 tons. As was the case in the war zone there was very little in the way of A/S measures to hinder the carnage the Cattaro boats wreaked on the lanes of seaborne commerce in the Mediterranean. Lacking sufficient patrol craft, the Allies attempted to bar the passage of the U-boats from the Adriatic into the Mediterranean by sealing off the Straits of Otranto with a mobile indicator net barrage.

By December 1915 a total of 92 drifters sent out from Britain, and based on the Italian port of Brindisi, were stretching their towed nets across the straits. It was a hopeless task. The width (45 miles) and depth (300–500 fathoms) of the Otranto Straits gave the U-boats ample room for manoeuvre. They either slipped through on the surface at night, or found a way through the gaps in the nets and on occasions dived deep to pass beneath them (the maximum diving depth of the early U-boats was 160 feet). The nets of the mobile barrage accounted for only one boat during the entire war: the Austro-Hungarian *UVI* (von Falkenhausen) which surfaced after fouling a net on 13 May 1916, and was destroyed by the gunfire of a drifter. Despite the achievements of the Cattaro Flotilla, strategically the campaign in the Mediterranean theatre was merely an auxiliary campaign from which no decisive result could be expected. However, powerful centrifugal forces at work in Germany were soon to revive the campaign in home waters.

U-boat losses January to September 1915

Date	Boat	Commander	Cause and location
15 Jan	U31	Wachendorff	Unknown.
21 Jan	U7	König	Accident: torpedoed by U22 off Dutch coast.
4 March	U8	Stoss	Explosive sweep of destroyer: English Channel.
10 March	U12	Kratzsch	Rammed by destroyer *Ariel*: North Sea.
18 March	U29	Weddigen	Rammed by battleship *Dreadnought*: North Sea.
1 April	U37	Wilcke	Unknown.
? May	UB3	Schmidt, S.	Unknown: Aegean Sea.
5 June	U14	Hammerle	Gunfire of trawlers: off Peterhead.
23 June	U40	Fürbringer, G.	Torpedoed by submarine C24 acting in concert with trawler *Taranaki*: off Aberdeen.
2 July	UC2	Mey	Accident, own mines: off Yarmouth.
20 July	U23	Schulthess	Torpedoed by submarine C27 acting in concert with trawler *Princess Louise*: North Sea.
24 July	U36	Graeff	Gunfire of Q-ship *Prince Charles*.
16 Aug	UB4	Gross	Gunfire of trawler: off Yarmouth.
19 Aug	U27	Wegener	Gunfire of Q-ship *Baralong*: off Scillies.
30 Aug	U26	V. Berckheim	Unknown: Baltic.
15 Sept	U6	Lepsius	Torpedoed by submarine E16: off Stavanger, Norway.
24 Sept	U41	Hansen	Gunfire of Q-ship *Baralong*: off Scillies.

Analysis of causes
Cumulative total in parentheses

Rammed by warships	2	(4)
Unknown	4	(7)
Accidental causes	2	(2)
Explosive sweep	1	(1)
Q-ship gunfire	3	(3)
Torpedoed by submarine	3	(3)
Gunfire of small craft[1]	2	(2)
Total	17	(22)

[1] Trawlers, drifters, armed yachts, motor launches, P-boats, sloops, etc.

Left: The minelayer *UC37* in the Adriatic base of Cattaro.

The Blunt Edge of the Sword

The second offensive against shipping, February to April 1916

The effects of the British blockade

By the end of 1915 Germany was beginning to feel the pinch of the British blockade, and the first signs of hardship and war-weariness had begun to manifest themselves. During the first campaign 743 neutral ships carrying supplies to Germany had been waylaid by British patrols and their cargoes either seized or purchased; this number was more than three times the losses suffered by the British from U-boat attack during the same period. By imposing a rationing system on Holland, Denmark, Norway and Sweden, whereby they were only allowed to import sufficient supplies for home consumption, Germany was also deprived of her usual imports of surplus foodstuffs and raw materials from her neutral neighbours. 'The food supply was giving cause for anxiety,' Fayle explains.

> 'While there was as yet no appreciable general shortage, there were many local and temporary shortages of particular kinds of food, especially in the large towns ... it was, however, the future rather than the present which was the real cause of anxiety. Germany's dependence was not so much on imported foods as on imported fodder and fertilizers, and it was in respect of these that the blockade assumed its most threatening aspect. Without a free use of fertilizers the poor and sandy soil of Germany would not yield anything approaching the normal harvests ... This shortage of fertilizers had a very serious effect on the production of cereals both for direct human consumption and for use as fodder. If the war were prolonged, it was apparent that the impoverishment of the soil by deprivation of its accustomed nourishment must inevitably be cumulative in its effects.[1]

In short, Germany was facing the possibility of being starved into suing for peace in the foreseeable future even though her armies remained undefeated in the field.

The decision to launch the second offensive

On 30 December, two solutions to the German predicament were presented by General von Falkenhayn, the chief of the German General Staff, at a conference attended by the generals and naval leaders. Falkenhayn had decided to launch a major offensive in the new year against the French fortified town of Verdun; a point of attack for which the French Command would have to fight to the last man to hold: Verdun being the gateway to Paris. The essence of Falkenhayn's plan was to turn the approaches to Verdun into an abattoir into which the French forces would be drawn and bled to death: the actual capture of the town was secondary and of no real importance. By this method of attrition Falkenhayn was confident that France would be knocked out of the war by the end of 1916. Falkenhayn's second proposal was to revive the U-boat campaign in home waters with the object of discouraging Britain so that she would, with her main ally beaten, be inclined to make peace. Despite Holtzendorff's initial doubts with regard to the value of the U-boat offensive, his opinion had undergone a radical transformation for he now believed that if the campaign were restarted soon and executed ruthlessly, it would have the effect on Britain Falkenhayn predicted.

Holtzendorff's conclusion was largely based on a report submitted by a number of German shipping experts on the state of the British carrying trade. The Germans were well informed about the large proportion of the carrying tonnage (20 per cent) which had been put to military use. They also knew that because the shipbuilding yards had been so depleted of men (who had been called to the colours) and of material (diverted to the construction of warships) only some 650,000 tons of new shipping could be delivered for the whole of 1916. Working on the simple mathematical formula that if the monthly average of British shipping destroyed throughout the campaign had been 80,000 tons, and this had been achieved by a fleet of 35 U-boats, it followed that with 70 boats in service the average monthly loss of British shipping might easily be doubled to 160,000 tons. For the whole of the year this would accumulate to close on 2,000,000 tons, depleting the British carrying trade by 1,270,000 tons with the construction figure of 650,000 tons taken into account. Such a depletion, Holtzendorff reasoned (erroneously as it turned out), would be insupportable. With France and Britain brought to their knees the fear of America's entry into the war could be disregarded, as it was not conceivable that she would be able to give any material assistance to the Western Allies before they succumbed to the double blow delivered on land and sea. Holtzendorff therefore submitted a resolution to the German Chancellor that U-boat warfare should be restarted in the War Zone, especially in the South-Western Approaches and the Irish Sea, and that all enemy merchant ships, with the exemption of passenger liners, should be destroyed without warning.

When this resolution was laid before Bethmann-Hollweg, however, another bout of protracted wrangling between the Admiralstab and the Chancellor, supported by the Auswärtiges Amt, broke out afresh. The Chancellor argued that it would be foolish to disregard conflict with the United States, which would surely happen if Holtzendorff's call for an unrestricted campaign were inaugurated, since increasing the number of Germany's enemies still further would invite sheer ruin – *finis Germaniae!* As for the prediction of the consequences of an unrestricted campaign, the Chancellor argued that it could not be calculated by simple arithmetic with regard to tonnage, as the success or failure of the campaign would be decided by Britain's endurance: a factor not calculable by figures. The Kaiser agreed with Bethmann-Hollweg to the extent that he could not, as head of state, sanction a totally unrestricted campaign which would provoke the United States into declaring war. On the other hand he accepted Holtzendorff's calculations, and made a median decision whereby the U-boat campaign in home waters was ordered to re-commence on 29 February, but with the following limitations:

1. Enemy vessels in the War Zone are to be destroyed outright (i.e., without warning).
2. Enemy vessels outside the War Zone are only to be attacked without warning if they are armed.
3. Enemy passenger steamers are not to be attacked either inside or outside the War Zone by submerged U-boats, no matter whether they are armed or not.[2]

Tirpitz, who supported the immediate commencement of a campaign devoid of all limitations, resigned his post over the issue (12 March), his place as Naval Secretary being taken by Admiral von Capelle who held more moderate views.

U-boat strength

Although the operations of the High Seas Fleet U-boats had been quiescent since September 1915, the UB and particularly the UC minelayers of the Flanders Flotilla had remained active. From October 1915 until February 1916, the UB boats sank seventeen vessels grossing 5,034 tons in the Hoofden; while the small minefields laid by the UC boats accounted for 78 vessels grossing 44,843 tons. In all the UC boats had laid 842 mines in 87 fields off the south-east coast ports and on the French coast between Cap Gris-Nez and Boulogne. By March 1916 Germany had a total of 52 *Frontboote* with which to prosecute the second offensive against shipping. Of these sixteen were formed into the reconstituted 3rd and 4th Half-Flotillas. Decimation from losses and transfers to the Mediterranean theatre meant that the 1st and 2nd Half-Flotillas had to be temporarily disbanded.

3rd Half-Flotilla (commanded by Korvettenkapitän Gayer)
  U19, U20, U22, U24, U43, U44, U45, U46, U47
4th Half-Flotilla (commanded by Kapitänleutnant Prause)
  U28, U32, U66, U67, U68, U69, U70
The Flanders Flotilla had twelve UB boats and eight UC minelayers:
  UB2 (which was transferred to the Baltic on 15 March), *UB5, UB6, UB10, UB12, UB13, UB16, UB17, UB18, UB19, UB26, UB29, UC3, UC4, UC5, UC6, UC7, UC10, UC11, UC12*

The new UBII and UCII Classes, which were only just coming into service, were much more powerful than their predecessors. Both the new UB and UC boats now carried light-calibre deck guns and the UC minelayers also carried torpedoes (seven 19.7in), making them more suitable for commerce warfare. In the Baltic there were four boats: *U9, U10, UB5* and *UB20*, which formed the newly inaugurated 5th Half-Flotilla (which was retitled the *Kurland* Flotilla on 1 November 1916).

Left: The German Kaiser with Admiral Scheer on his immediate left.

At Cattaro in the Adriatic were seven boats: *U21, U34, U35, U38, U39, UB42* and *UC14*; and with the *Mittelmeerdivision* in Constantinople five boats: *U33, UB7, UB8, UB14* and *UC15*.

From October 1915 until the beginning of March 1916, one boat (*U17*), had been withdrawn from service and relegated to training; two boats had been lost. *UC9* had blown up on her own mines near the Long Sands light vessel (October); and *UC13* had run aground in the Black Sea and had to be abandoned (29 November); while *UC8* had run aground off Terschelling on the night of 4 November, and was interned by the Dutch.

During the five-month period April–August 1916, a further 38 boats (including ten of the UEI class ocean-going minelayers – nicknamed the 'Children of Sorrow') would become operational which would bring the total of *Frontboote* to 88, not taking into consideration probable losses.

The development of British counter-measures

The British had developed two new major A/S weapons with which to counter the new offensive. In January 1916 the Type D depth-charge (300lb explosives) for fast ships, and the Type D* depth-charge (120lb explosives) for slow ships, not fast enough to be clear of the heavier jolt of the Type D when it exploded, came into service. These charges were fired by a hydrostatic pistol with 40 and 80 feet predetermined settings. Limited supply, however, restricted the allowance to the totally inadequate number of two charges per A/S vessel: a state of affairs that did not improve until June 1917. The effectiveness of these prototypes was also limited by the fact that they did very little material damage to the submerged U-boats unless they exploded within a short distance of the target: within about 14 feet to sink them and about 28 feet to disable and force them to the surface. As the depth-charges were simply dropped over the stern of the A/S vessel from chutes – either by hydraulic gear operated from the bridge or by an ordinary slip operated by hand – the degree of accuracy needed was difficult to achieve, especially in view of the fact that methods of underwater detection were still in their infancy. The first success came on 22 March 1916, when the Q-ship *Farnborough* sank *U68* (Güntzel) off the coast of Kerry, Ireland. Throughout the remainder of 1916, only two other boats (*UC19* and *UB29*) were lost as a direct result of depth-charge attack. According to Spindler the Germans first became aware of the new weapon after unsuccessful attacks on *U67* and *U69* (15 and 20 April respectively).

Superseding the ineffective 'explosive sweep' was the 'explosive paravane' with a 400lb charge. Originally fitted to destroyers, it was eventually extended to smaller craft of high speed. Its advantage over the 'explosive sweep', in addition to higher speed, was that, with a paravane well out and deep down on each quarter, it swept through a greater amount of water both in area and in depth (200 feet). The functions of the depth-charge and the 'explosive paravane' were complementary. The former was for use against a U-boat whose position was

comparatively accurately known, while the latter dealt with a submerged U-boat whose position was in doubt.

In another unsuccessful attempt at barring the passage of the Flanders U-boats through the Dover Straits, 2,070 mines in six new fields were laid to the east of the Straits. Another measure designed to counter the Flanders boats was a Zareba of moored mine nets eighteen miles long (light steel net supported by mooring buoys and studded with mines) along with double lines of deep and shallow minefields (4,862 mines in sixteen fields) which were laid from April to July at a distance of twelve miles off, and running parallel to, the Belgian coast between Nieuport and the Scheldt. Apart from restricting the egress and ingress of the Flanders boats from and to their bases at Zeebrugge and Ostend to one small channel off West Capelle on the Dutch coast, it is also presumed that *UB13* (Metz) struck a mine in the Zareba on 24 April. The unremedied defective qualities of the mines undoubtedly robbed the British of much greater success. For instance *UB10* became entangled in the mine nets during April, and although it took her eight hours to get clear she escaped unscathed. Gibson and Prendergast are of the opinion that 'had the type of British mine then in use been more efficient it is probable that several U-boats would have been destroyed immediately after the laying of the barrage'.[3]

New strategic counter-measures in the Mediterranean also proved ineffective. At an Allied naval conference which was held in Paris at the beginning of December, it was decided to divide the Mediterranean into eighteen zones which were to be covered by roving patrols of A/S vessels. Four zones were assigned to the British (Straits of Gibraltar; Malta and the south coast of Sicily; the Dardanelles and Aegean; and the coastline of Egypt): four to the Italian Fleet and ten to the French. That these roving patrols proved ineffective is not surprising considering that to patrol the vast areas of the British zones all the Admiralty could provide was a total of eleven yachts (only nine of them armed), thirty sloops, four destroyers and 96 armed trawlers: these were based as far apart as Gibraltar, Malta and Egypt. During the first five months of 1916 only one German U-boat was lost in the Mediterranean and she (*UC12*) blew up on her own mines while laying a field off Taranto harbour (16 March).

The course of the second offensive

As was the case during the opening of the first campaign a year previously, the new offensive was inaugurated by a solitary U-boat. Two boats had in fact put to sea at the end of February, but of these *U22* (Hoppe) had to return to base, without any kills to her credit, because of mechanical defects to her port dynamo and forward diving rudder. This left *U32* (Spiegel) to blood the offensive on 4 March by sinking the British *Teutonion* (4,824 tons) bound for Avonmouth with 6,000 tons of oil, 36 miles south-west of Fastnet in the South-Western Approaches: the area in which the heaviest blow of the campaign was once more to be delivered. Spiegel gave the crew time to abandon ship before sinking the tanker with gunfire and one torpedo. As in the first campaign, the High Seas Fleet boats were dispatched to the South-Western Approaches as independent units via the northern route around Scotland.

Altogether eight boats put to sea to operate in that vital zone from 26 February until 29 March, followed by five boats which left their bases in northern Germany from 4 to 24 April. Two of the new UBII class, *UB27* (Dickmann) and *UB21* (Putzier), which joined the 1st Half-Flotilla during the middle of April, put to sea at the end of the month to operate off the Firth of Forth.

Although the total number of *Frontboote* (50 in all theatres) was 21 in excess of the number available in February 1915, the actual number of the larger, High Seas Fleet boats which were capable of reaching the South-Western Approaches via the northerly route was only sixteen, five less than in the previous February. However, according to Spindler, these boats (including *UB27* and *UB21*) accounted for 57 vessels grossing 157,009 tons during March and April, to which must be added the loss of the British steamer *Sabbia* of 2,802 tons, which blew up off the Firth of Forth on a minefield of 34 mines laid by *U74* (Weisbach), the first of the UE ocean-going minelayers to become operational at the end of March.

Spindler's figure of the total tonnage sunk by all forms of U-boat action throughout March and April is 152 vessels of 347,843 tons when the achievements of the boats in the Mediterranean (27 ships of 76,483 tons), Black Sea (one ship of 5,350 tons) and the Flanders Flotilla operating in the Hoofden and the eastern waters of the English Channel (66 ships of 106,199 tons) are added. However, Holtzendorff's equation for success was based solely on the depletion of British carrying trade alone at the rate of 160,000 tons a month. This had not been achieved. The Admiralty figures for British losses during March and April 1916 show that only 69 vessels of 240,282 tons (an average of 120,141 tons per month) were sunk. But with 38 new *Frontboote* due to be commissioned during the next five months, a 160,000-ton monthly loss of British shipping could be confidently expected if not exceeded. During March and April the UC boats had laid a total of 710 mines in 73 fields in home waters, off the south-east coast, in the Channel off both the English and French coasts, and off the Belgian port of Nieuport. Spindler gives the number of vessels lost on these fields as thirty totalling 46,383 tons, plus a further five vessels grossing 5,252 tons which were lost on minefields laid in the Mediterranean, adding up to a grand total of 35 vessels of 51,635 tons. It was during early April that the second UE minelayer, *U73* (Siehs), became operational. She was sent out to the German Mediterranean Flotilla based in Cattaro, where she arrived on 30 April. On her outward passage she laid a field of twelve mines off Lisbon in the estuary of the River Tagus (17 April), and another of 22 mines off Malta (27 April). In the Lisbon field a Norwegian steamer of 3,580 tons foundered, while the field off Malta accounted for the 14,200-ton predread-nought battleship *Russell*, the sloop *Nasturtium*, the armed yacht *Aegusa* and the armed trawler *Crownsin*.

During March and April the Germans lost four boats in home waters. The first U-boat lost due to enemy action, *U68* (Güntzel), during the second campaign, was as a direct result of the Prize Law prescription. Surfacing to bring-to what appeared to be an innocent looking collier, Güntzel, who was on his first war cruise and had not had the advantage of a trial cruise with a more experienced commander, found himself under gunfire from what turned out to be the Q-ship *Farnborough*. Hit several times, *U68* dived to escape, only to become the first U-boat to be destroyed by depth-charges which *Farnborough* dropped over the position where *U68* had submerged. The bows of the stricken U-boat rose out of the water; five more rounds were fired into her and she vanished for the last time. Spindler comments that Güntzel 'had recapitulated everything which during the summer of 1915 had led to many such defeats of U-boats by British Q-ships'.[4] In April *UB26* (Smiths), which was operating off Le Havre, fouled the indicator net of *Endurance*, one of the six British drifters that were based in the port. When the U-boat's overworked batteries caught fire, filling the boat with chlorine gas, she was forced to surface and scuttle herself. The French later raised the wreck and after repairs she was commissioned into the French Navy as the *Roland Morillot*. *UB13* (Metz) was also lost in April, probably to a mine in the Zareba north of Zeebrugge; while *UC5* (Mohrbutter) ran aground on the Shipwash Shoal on the 27th and was captured intact by two British destroyers which towed her into Harwich.

The *Sussex* incident

Before the validity of Holtzendorff's calculations could be put to the test an incident occurred that sparked off yet another diplomatic crisis with the United States. It was not the general orders relating to the conduct in which the second campaign was to be prosecuted that occasioned the new crisis, but a subsidiary order that had been in force for four months. On 12 November 1915, the Admiralstab ordered the UB boats of the Flanders Flotilla to operate against troop transports entering or leaving the French and English channel ports. This order was a dead letter for three months, for it was not until the beginning of March 1916 that the Flanders Flotilla was reinforced by boats of the UBII class which alone were sufficiently powerful to operate effectively in the central parts of the English Channel. During March these new boats put to sea to execute a 3-month-old order which had not been revised or reconsidered in the interval. Moreover the order had been drafted in such a way as to intimate, quite erroneously as it turned out, that passenger ships were only plying on the Folkestone–Boulogne route, and that vessels on all other cross-Channel routes could be sunk without warning, and without fear of disregarding the pledges made to the United States that passenger ships of every nationality were to be spared molestation.

So it came about that during the afternoon of 24 March, *Oberleutnant* Pustkuchen, in command of the new *UB29*, sighted through his periscope a steamer about to enter Dieppe whose upper foredeck was crowded with what Pustkuchen, through the

restricted view of the periscope, took to be troops. Believing her to be a transport, and in accordance with the orders issued four months previously, Pustkuchen torpedoed the ship without warning. The ship was not a troop transport but the French cross-Channel vessel *Sussex* carrying 325 passengers on her usual trip from Folkestone to Dieppe. Among them were 25 US citizens, some of whom were included among the 50 casualties caused when the torpedo exploded against the hull of the ship. Two other victims were the outstanding Spanish composer and pianist, Enrique Granados, returning to Spain after a recital tour in the USA, and his wife. 'For the third time running the one principle on which the Washington authorities stood firm was breached by a young fellow, less than thirty years old, with

nothing to guide him but his periscope, and his desire for professional distinction.'[5] US reaction was stern. The US Press declared that the sinking of the *Sussex* was an outright challenge to the United States, made without even 'the decencies and punctilio of a challenge'. President Wilson, like the newspaper editors, considered that the United States was being defied and contemptuously treated. The German Government was presented with the sharpest indictment, threatening war:

'If it is still the purpose of the Imperial Government to prosecute relentless and indiscriminate warfare against vessels of commerce by the use of U-boats without regard to what the Government of the United States must consider the sacred and indisputable rules of international law and universally recognized dictates of humanity,

Below: The coastal minelayer *UC5* which was captured by British destroyers after running aground on the Shipwash Shoal on 27 April 1916. This photograph was taken at Sheerness in 1918.

the Government of the United States *is at last forced to the conclusion that there is but one course it can pursue.* Unless the Imperial Government should now immediately declare and effect an abandonment of its present methods of U-boat warfare against passenger and freight-carrying vessels, the Government of the United States can have no other choice but to sever diplomatic relations with the German Reich altogether. This action the Government of the United States contemplates with the greatest reluctance but feels constrained to take in behalf of humanity and the rights of neutral nations.'[6]

Bending before this threat, the German Government renewed its pledges and instructed Holtzendorff to issue orders (24 April) to the High Seas Fleet and Flanders Flotillas that, 'Until further orders, U-boats may only act against commerce in accordance with Prize Regulations.' That is, the U-boats were not to destroy ships, even if they were of belligerent nations, without first examining the papers and taking proper steps for the safety of their crews, 'unless the ships attempt to escape or offer resistance'.

The abandonment of the offensive

Although Admirals Capelle and Holtzendorff were of the conviction that sinkings of 160,000 tons a month could still be achieved despite the tactical restraints, Admiral Reinhard Scheer, the new CinC, High Seas Fleet (he relieved Pohl who was dying of cancer in January 1916), arrogantly refused to comply, and on 25 April he recalled all the U-boats to base by wireless, announcing to the Admiralstab that the campaign against commerce had ceased, much as he regretted, 'the cessation of the most effective form of attack on England's economic position, the effect of which might under certain circumstances, have become decisive in regard to the final issue of the war'.[7] Bartenbach, Chef der U-Flotille Flandern, took similar action, recalling the UB boats. This meant the virtual abandonment of the second campaign in the War Zone: only the Flanders UC minelayers and the boats in the Mediterranean were not affected.

When the recall signal was made there were three High Seas Fleet boats at sea: *U19* (Weisbach) was already returning to base; *U45* (Sittenfeldt), outward bound for the South-Western Approaches, was nearing the Irish coast; while *U20* (Schwieger), also bound for the South-Western Approaches, was one day out from Germany. None of these boats took in the recall signal with the result that from 27 April to 8 May, *U45* and *U20*, unaware that the campaign had been called off, sank eight vessels between them grossing 26,751 tons. The last vessel sunk (8 May) was the 13,370-ton liner *Cymric*, outward bound for the United States, which was torpedoed without warning by Schwieger (who had sunk the *Lusitania*) in *U20*, 140 miles WNW from Fastnet with the loss of five lives. *Cymric* was the 37th unarmed liner to be sunk by U-boats since the loss of *Lusitania*, and the fourth passenger liner to be sunk (one of which was a Dutch neutral) during the second offensive, despite the orders of limitation.

Scheer maintained that his reason for suspending the campaign was quite simply that 'war waged according to prize law by U-boats in the waters around England could not possibly have any success, but on the contrary, must expose the boats to the greatest danger [from attack by Q-ships, patrol craft and the defensive armament of merchantmen]'. His decision was no doubt influenced by Bauer – F.d.U – who had made a voyage in *U67* (Nieland) during the campaign to study conditions for himself; an experience which convinced him beyond doubt that it was too dangerous for the U-boats to act in accordance with prize laws. Scheer was also motivated in the belief that the political consequences of his action would force Bethmann-Hollweg, the main opponent of an unrestricted campaign, to resign his office in the face of indignation in the Reichstag when it learned that the U-boat campaign had been called off. But the popular uproar which Scheer hoped to provoke was weaker than he expected and the Chancellor 'boldly faced his critics in Reichstag'. His gambit failed, Scheer downgraded the strategic role of the U-boats to attacks on enemy warships, in the hope that the stranglehold of the British blockade could be broken by a fleet action, after the ever-growing numerical superiority of the Grand Fleet had been whittled down to an equalization of forces. Germany's hopes of victory still rested with her *Unterseeboote*.

U-boat losses October 1915 to April 1916

Date	Boat	Commander	Cause and location
20 Oct	UC9	Schürmann	Accident, own mines: off Longsands light vessel.
29 Nov	UC13	Kirchner	Accident: ran aground in Black Sea and abandoned.
16 March	UC12	Fröhner	Accident, own mines: Taranto (Italy).
22 March	U68	Güntzel	Depth-charges of Q-ship *Farnborough*: South-Western Approaches.
15 April	UB26	Smiths	Indicator nets of drifter *Endurance*: off Le Havre.
25 April	UB13	Metz	Unknown. Presumed mined in zareba: off Zeebrugge.
27 April	UC5	Mohrbutter	Accident: ran aground on Shipwash Shoal and captured by British destroyers.

Analysis of causes
Cumulative total in parentheses

Rammed by warships	0	(4)
Unknown	1	(8)
Accidental causes	4	(6)
Explosive sweep	0	(1)
Q-ship gunfire	0	(3)
Q-ship depth-charges	1	(1)
Torpedoed by submarine	0	(3)
Gunfire of small craft	0	(2)
Indicator nets	1	(1)
Total	7	(29)

The Horns of Dilemma
May to August 1916

With a fleet of U-boats three times as large as they had possessed in the latter months of 1914, and with vastly more powerful and efficient units than those which had scored notable successes against the enemy fleet in the first five months of the war, it was not unrealistic for the German naval high command to feel confident that the U-boats could tip the balance of power at sea in their favour by successful attacks on the British dreadnought battle fleet, which would bring about a *Kräfteausgleich* (equalization of forces). In an attempt to break the stranglehold of the British blockade by a fleet action a *Kräfteausgleich* was the necessary preliminary. Scheer was well aware that before this condition was attained, seeking a battle *à outrance* with the markedly numerically superior Grand Fleet would be courting suicide. By May 1916 British superiority had grown to the ratio of 37:21 in dreadnoughts and battlecruisers and 105:76 in light forces.

Scheer's plan to redress the balance centered on luring the Grand Fleet into an ambush of U-boats lying off the main British bases. To entice the British to sea Scheer planned a High Seas

Fleet sortie in the form of a raid on Sunderland where establishments of military importance would be shelled. With the operation set to commence on 23 May, the U-boats began putting to sea on the 17th. Nine boats carried out a thorough reconnaissance of the central sector of the North Sea which lasted until 22 May, and on 23 May took up their positions off the enemy bases to form the proposed ambush. Two boats, *U43* (Jürst) and *U44* (Wagenführ), lay in wait off the Pentland Firth to attack the British battle fleet as it emerged from Scapa Flow. Seven boats, *U66* (Bothmer), *U63* (Schultze), *U51* (Rumpel), *U32* (Peckelsheim), *U70* (Wünsche), *U24* (Schneider), and *U52* (Walther), took up position off the Firth of Forth to intercept the British battlecruiser fleet which was based on Rosyth. Each of the latter boats were assigned adjoining sectors, the lines of which were drawn from a central point lying off the estuary of the River Forth. Their orders were to remain on station until the evening of 1 June and to avoid being discovered prematurely at their waiting positions. Wireless reports were therefore only to be made on the sighting of the enemy's main forces putting

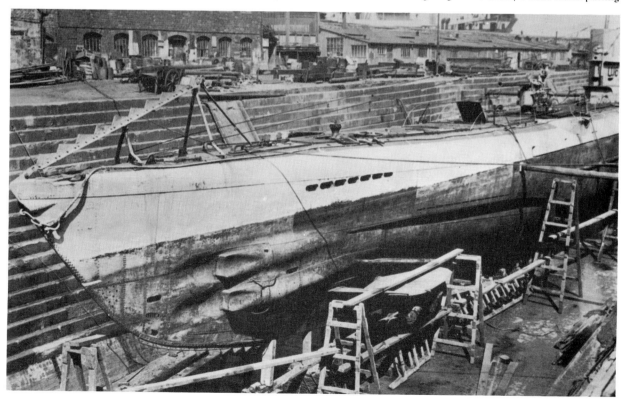

Right: The business end of *U62*. Note the forward torpedo tubes.

to sea, and then only after an attack had been made on them or all possibilities of attack had been exhausted. In order that the U-boats at sea might be informed, without arousing suspicion, that the main operation was about to commence, it was proposed to notify them of the actual time of sailing of the High Seas Fleet by means of the following phrase: 'Take into account that enemy's forces may be putting to sea.'

In addition to this main force, eight other boats were assigned to subsidiary roles. U47 (Metzer) reconnoitred the area off Sunderland, the proposed point of attack, during the night of 21/22 May, to establish that there were no enemy minefields in the area, and then proceeded north to take up a waiting position (24 May) off Peterhead; presumably to intercept enemy forces moving directly southward from the Moray Firth (eight dreadnoughts, four armoured cruisers, and ten destroyers were based on Cromarty). To guard the southern flank of the fleet as it advanced on Sunderland, U46 (Hillebrand) and U67 (Nieland) took up position to the north-westward of Terschelling. Two boats of the 1st Flotilla (Hochseeflotte), UB21 (Hashagen) and UB22 (Putzier), sailed on 21 May to keep the Humber under observation (it had been reported erroneously that numerous warships were assembled there), while UB27 (Dickmann), also from the 1st Flotilla, was sent out on 20 May with orders to force her way into the Firth of Forth with the object of attacking any warships entering or leaving. Although UB27 actually penetrated the Forth as far as Inchkeith, she became entangled in an anti-submarine net. With the port propeller fouled, Dickmann was obliged to abandon any intention of attack and had to limp back to Germany on one engine. Finally three of the new UE minelayers were dispatched to lay minefields off the enemy bases. If, as intended, the sortie of the High Seas Fleet immediately succeeded the laying of these mines, there was a chance that the enemy would not have time to locate them with the result that some of their forces might run into the fields as they put to sea. U72 (Kraft) was unable to complete her mission of laying mines off the Forth due to a leaky outer oil bunker which left a broad trail of oil in the boat's

wake. She turned for home on the 26th. U74 (Weisbach) was caught on the surface by four armed trawlers of the auxiliary patrol, 25 miles south-east of Peterhead, and sunk by gunfire (27 May) before she could lay her mines. Only U75 (Beitzen) successfully completed her mission, laying a field of 22 mines west of the Orkneys. (It was on this field that the cruiser Hampshire, with Kitchener aboard, foundered on 5 June.)

Pre- and post-Jutland operations

Due to a postponement of the High Seas Fleet sortie, which did not commence until the night of 30/31 May (an alternative plan for an advance on the Skagerrak had been adopted), the U-boats were subjected to a long and fruitless wait of eight days, during which they were constantly harassed by patrol vessels. When the code phrase, warning them to expect the egress of the British forces from their bases, was finally broadcast on 30 May, only four boats, UB22, U32, U67 and U70 actually received it with the result that the ambush, of which Scheer had expected so much, proved to be a complete and disappointing failure. Only two (U32 and U66) of the boats setting the ambush off the northern bases actually sighted units of the Grand Fleet, and only U32 managed to launch a torpedo attack (two fired at the light cruiser Galatea, at 03.55 on 31 May, both of which missed). At midnight on the 30th, six UB boats of the Flanders Flotilla, UB17 (Wenniger), UB29 (Pustkuchen), UB19 (Becker), UB12 (Kiel), UB10 (Saltzwedel) and UB6 (Neumann), also put to sea to form a line eighteen miles long to the east of Lowestoft, with the object of attacking the light forces (five light cruisers and nineteen destroyers) based on Harwich, should they put to sea. Two other Flanders boats, UB18 (Steinbrinck) and UB23 (Voigt), scouted along the Dutch coast as far as Terschelling. Their efforts were no more successful than the northern boats. Only one, UB10, sighted destroyers of the Harwich Force, and they were too far distant for an attack to be launched.

The failure of the U-boat ambush resulted in the High Seas Fleet becoming engaged, unwittingly, with the full and un-diminished might of the Grand Fleet in what became known as

Below: U75, one of the UE-I class of ocean-going minelayers which were nicknamed 'The Children of Sorrow'. Note the minelaying tube in the stern.

the Battle of Jutland (Skagerrak to the Germans). It was only because of Scheer's bold and great tactical skill, aided by poor visibility, the onset of night and Admiral Jellicoe's excessive tactical caution, that the Germans were able to escape a disastrous battle à outrance and beat a hasty retreat to the safety of their harbours. Only two boats sighted units of the returning Grand Fleet and although they launched attacks (U51 on the battleship Warspite and U46 – which had been ordered north from her position off Terschelling – on the battleship Marlborough) they scored no hits with their torpedoes and the Grand Fleet sailed back through the areas of the carefully laid ambush without further molestation.

The second attempt at ambush

Disappointed by the U-boat's failure to bring about a Kräfteausgleich, Scheer, none the less, laid plans early in August for another attempt at ambushing the Grand Fleet with a U-boat trap. It was considered that faulty dispositions had been the root cause of the negative results obtained prior to Jutland. The system of posting the U-boats in radiating sectors extending from central points off the enemy bases, had resulted in the boats bunching and getting in one another's way when they hugged the entrances and, alternatively, becoming needlessly dispersed when they stood out to sea, which left broad, unwatched avenues through which the majority of the British forces had passed. In the new plan, which was essentially the original Sunderland plan (the Fleet was to venture across the North Sea during the night of 18 August and bombard Sunderland on the following morning), the U-boats were to be disposed in lines (Standlinie) in the path of the enemy's probable line of advance down the English coast. The problem of divining the possible movements of the Grand Fleet was made relatively simple by the existence of three large minefields, which the Germans had laid earlier in the war off the Tyne, Humber and western part of the Dogger Bank, which restricted the most direct approach to the Sunderland area to a broad channel between the coast and the inner edge of these fields. The U-boats were thus stationed accordingly.

In all, 24 boats were disposed in five Standline. Sailing on the 18th, nineteen of the boats were to be in position by 08.00 on 19 August. Standlinie I, II and III were composed of High Seas Fleet boats. Twenty miles off Blyth, U44, U67, U65, U52 and U53 formed line I, covering a front 35 miles long. Standlinie II, twelve miles off Flamborough Head, also covering a 35-mile front, was formed by U63, U49, U45, U66 and U64. To cover the retirement of the Fleet and guard the approach to the Bight, U48, U69, UB35, U55 and U56 formed a rear (rückwärtige) line (III) off the Dogger Bank, about 120 miles north-west from Heligoland. These five boats took up their position on the morning of 20 August. To attack the light forces based on Harwich and to guard the southern flank of the fleet's advance, nine boats of the Flanders Flotilla formed two lines in the Hoofden. Line I, lying level with the Humber off the Swarte Bank, was composed of UB39, UB23, UB18 and UB29; while

UB37, UB19, UB16, UB6 and UB12 formed Line II, twelve miles off Texel.

Warned of the German intentions by intercepted signals, the Grand Fleet put to sea at 16.00 on the 18th, five hours before the Germans actually sailed. Scheer, as events turned out, was dissuaded from bombarding Sunderland by a false report made by a scouting Zeppelin, which mistook the light craft of the Harwich Force for a detached squadron of enemy battleships (Scheer's dream of destroying a detached squadron of the Grand Fleet, seemed on the point of realization). Turning south-east away from Sunderland to chase the phantom battleships, Scheer held on until 14.35 when, with his southerly advance barred by the Humber minefield, and made aware by a report from U53 of the Grand Fleet closing on him from the northward 65 miles distant, he turned the High Seas Fleet ESE and headed for home. Having missed the Germans by a small margin, Jellicoe began his retirement at 15.53. On this occasion the U-boat trap proved slightly more successful. At 05.57 on the 19th, U52 (Hans), which was approaching her position on Standlinie I (off Blythe), ran in with the advanced light cruiser screen of the British Battlecruiser Fleet making its way south. Manoeuvring for an attack position, U52 fired two torpedoes at the light cruiser Nottingham, both of which struck home on the port side. Although the cruiser remained on an even keel, she lost all power of manoeuvre, and at 06.25 U52 hit Nottingham with one more torpedo, which finally sank her. U66 (Bothmer) managed to hit the light cruiser Falmouth (04.45) with two torpedoes on the starboard side, fired at a range of 1,000 yards. Although flooded forward and aft, Falmouth's midship section remained watertight, and with her engines intact she began to crawl towards the Humber, 65 miles distant. Although she was screened by three destroyers and an armed trawler, U66 continued to dog the crippled Falmouth with the intention of finishing her off. Despite being repeatedly attacked by the escorting destroyers – a depth-charge attack blew out all the lights, and the clips of two ports were blown off resulting in a large amount of water flooding in before they could be closed – Bothmer fired several torpedoes at Falmouth, which missed their target by a narrow margin, before he finally sheered off more than two hours after making the first attack. Falmouth toiled along under tow at 2 knots until noon the following day, when, passing over Standlinie II on her direct route to the Humber, she was finally sunk by two torpedoes fired by U63 (Schulze).

The decision to launch the third offensive

The sinking of two light cruisers hardly credited the operation as successful. In short the events of 19 August convinced the Admiralstab that 'while such bold sorties might damage the British Fleet, they would not produce an important, let alone a decisive, result'. The stranglehold of the British blockade had not even been dented let alone broken, and the failure to bring about the desire results impressed upon the Germans that their only hope of winning the war of economic strangulation rested with an all-out unrestricted U-boat campaign against commerce. Indeed, on 4 July, Scheer in his confidential report to the Kaiser on Jutland (*Immediatbericht*), concluded:

'There can be no doubt that even the most successful outcome of a Fleet action in this war will not *force* England to make peace. The disadvantages of our military – geographical position in relation to that of the British Isles, and the enemy's great material superiority, cannot be compensated by our Fleet to the extent where we shall be able to overcome the blockade or the British Isles themselves – not even if the U-boats are made fully available for purely naval

operations. A victorious end to the war within a reasonable time can only be achieved through the defeat of British economic life – that is, by using the U-boats against British trade. In this connection, I feel it my duty to again strongly advise Your Majesty against the adoption of any half-measures, not only because these would contradict the nature of the weapon and would produce commensurate results, but also because in British waters, where American interests are strong, it is impossible to avoid incidents, however conscientious our commanding officers may be; unless we can act with full determination, such incidents involve us in the humiliation of having to give way.'[1]

Above: *U55* of the 715-ton series *U51–U56*.

Flotilla dispositions of *Frontboote*, October 1915 to January 1917

War losses are marked with an asterisk; dates boats joined flotillas are in parentheses

High Seas Fleet Flotillas (*U-boote der Hochseeflotte*)
Führer der U-boote: Fregettenkapitän Bauer. On 1 Oct 1916, the four 'half-flotillas' were redesignated 'flotillas'.

I. U-Halbflotille
Chef: Kapitänleutnant Pasquay
U71 (7 April 1916), *U72* (11 April 1916), *U74** (18 March 1916), *U75* (29 June 1916), *U76** (29 June 1916), *U77** (29 June 1916), *U78* (9 July 1916), *U79* (30 July 1916), *U80* (27 Aug 1916), *U51*, *U52*, *UB21* (14 April 1916), *UB22* (14 April 1916), *UB27* (14 April 1916), *UB34* (27 July 1916), *UB35* (18 Aug 1916), *UC24* (18 Nov 1916), *UC29* (19 Oct 1916), *UC30* (16 Nov 1916), *UC31* (10 Dec 1916), *UC32* (27 Nov 1916), *UC33* (16 Dec 1916), *UC40* (15 Dec 1916), *UC41* (18 Dec 1916), *UC43* (25 Dec 1916). *U72* was transferred to the Adriatic, Aug 1916; *U51* and *U52* were transferred to the II U-Halbflotille, 25 May 1916.

II. U-Halbflotille
Chef: Kapitänleutnant von Rosenberg-Gruszczynski
*U51** (25 May 1916), *U52* (25 May 1916), *U53* (31 May 1916), *U54* (2 July 1916), *U55* (29 July 1916), *U56** (18 June 1916), *U57* (7 July 1916), *U58* (16 Oct 1916), *U59* (20 Nov 1916), *U60* (13 Jan 1917), *UB41* (2 Nov 1916). *U52* was transferred to the Adriatic, Nov 1916.

III. U-Halbflotille
Chef: Kapitänleutnant Gayer (promoted to *Korvettenkapitän*, 24 April 1916)
U19, *U20** , *U22*, *U24*, *U43*, *U44*, *U45* (11 Nov 1916), *U46* (29 March 1916), *U47* (8 May 1916), *U48* (8 June 1916), *U49* (7 Aug 1916), *U50* (30 Aug 1916). *U19* and *U22* were transferred to the V U-Halbflotille (Baltic), 18 Aug 1916; *U47* was transferred to the Adriatic, 8 Aug 1916.

IV. U-Halbflotille
Chef: Kapitänleutnant Prause
U28, *U30* (15 Oct 1916), *U32*, *U63* (2 May 1916), *U64* (31 May 1916), *U65* (2 July 1916), *U67* (22 Oct 1915), *U68** (28 Nov 1915), *U69* (4 March 1916), *U70* (9 Feb 1916), *U81* (18 Oct 1916), *U82* (21 Nov 1916), *U83* (31 Oct 1916), *U84* (3 Dec 1916), *U85* (15 Jan 1917). *U30* accidentally foundered in Borkum Roads on 22 June 1915, was later salved and underwent repairs from 17 Sept 1915 to 16 April 1916. *U32*, *U63*, *U64* and *U65* were transferred to the Adriatic on 16 Oct 1916, 2 May 1916, 31 May 1916 and 2 July 1916 respectively.

Flanders Flotilla
U-boote des Marinekorps U-Flotille Flandern
Chef: Korvettenkapitän Bartenbach
UB2, *UB5*, *UB6*, *UB10*, *UB12*, *UB13** , *UB16*, *UB17*, *UB18* (16 Feb 1916), *UB19** (1 March 1916), *UB23* (19 May 1916), *UB26** (21 March 1916), *UB29** (8 March 1916), *UB37** (5 May 1916), *UB38* (10 Oct 1916), *UB39* (21 June 1916), *UB40* (3 Oct 1916), *UC1*, *UC3** , *UC5** , *UC6*, *UC7** , *UC8** , *UC9** , *UC10** , *UC11*, *UC16* (11 Sept 1916), *UC17* (2 Oct 1916), *UC18* (19 Oct 1916), *UC19** (9 Nov 1916), *UC21* (14 Nov 1916), *UC26* (12 Sept 1916), *UC46* (29 Nov 1916), *UC47* (23 Jan 1917). *UB2* and *UB5* were transferred to the Baltic, 15 March 1916 and 6 Oct 1915 respectively. From 17 Oct 1915 to 11 Aug 1916 *UC11* was used as a training boat at Kiel before being transferred back to the Flanders Flotilla.

Baltic Flotilla
U-boote der Ostseestreittkräfte V. U-Halbflotille, später U-Flotille Kurland (based on Kiel, Danzig and Libau)
Chef: Kapitänleutnant Schött
UA, *U9*, *U10** , *U17*, *U19* (19 Sept 1916), *U22* (23 Aug 1916), *U47* (9 Aug 1916), *U66* (17 Oct 1915), *UB2* (19 March 1916), *UB5* (9 Oct 1915), *UB20* (12 March 1916), *UB30* (8 May 1916), *UB32* (25 May 1916), *UB33* (10 June 1916), *UB36* (27 June 1916), *UC4*, *UC25* (12 Sept 1916), *UC27* (15 Sept 1916). *UA* (21 May 1916), *U9* (20 April 1916), *U17* (10 Jan 1916), *UB2* (19 March 1916) and *UB5* (21 Sept 1916) all became training boats at Kiel on the dates indicated, and remained as such until the end of the war. *U66* was transferred to IV Halbflotille, 15 Jan 1916.

Adriatic
Deutsche U-Flotille Pola (HQ Pola-flotilla based in Cattaro)
Chef: Kapitänleutnant Adam
Flotillenchef: Korvettenkapitän Kophamel
U21, *U32* (8 Nov 1916), *U33*, *U34*, *U35*, *U38* (11 Nov 1915), *U39*, *U47* (27 Dec 1916), *U52* (24 Dec 1916), *U63* (6 Nov 1916), *U64* (19 Nov 1916), *U65* (18 Nov 1916), *UB42* (23 March 1916), *UB43* (24 April 1916), *UB44** (11 May 1916), *UB45* (26 May 1916), *UB46* (12 June 1916), *UB47* (4 July 1916), *U72* (17 Sept 1916), *U73* (30 April 1916), *UC12** , *UC14*, *UC20* (11 Dec 1916), *UC22* (12 Oct 1916), *UC23* (13 Oct 1916), *UC34* (8 Jan 1917), *UC35* (25 Dec 1916), *UC37* (12 Jan 1917), *UC38* (23 Jan 1917). *U33* (2 March 1916), *U38* (12 May 1916), *UB45* (3 Aug 1916), *UB46* (23 Sept 1916) and *UC23* (20 Nov 1916) were transferred to the *Mittelmeerdivision* on the dates indicated.

Black Sea
U-boote der Mittelmeerdivision in Konstantinopel
U33 (11 March 1916), *U38* (22 May 1916), *UB7** , *UB8*, *UB14*, *UB45** (12 Aug 1916), *UB46* (7 Oct 1916), *UC13** , *UC15** , *UC23* (6 Dec 1916). *U33* and *UB8* were transferred to the Adriatic on 27 Nov 1916 and 7 Sept 1916 respectively.

Scheer's *Immediatbericht* marked the beginning of yet another bout of wrangling between the admirals and the political authorities over the U-boat question, motivated by the dilemma in which Germany found herself by the August of 1916. Falkenhayn's plan to knock out France by bleeding her armies to death in the abattoir of the Verdun battle had failed. Although they had inflicted 377,231 casualties on the French, the German armies had bled themselves to the tune of 337,000 casualties in the attempt. The Battle of the Somme, launched by the British in July, was still raging (this ghastly battle of attrition would cost the Germans a further 400,000 casualties), the Austro-Hungarian armies were in full retreat before the Russian 'Brusilov' offensive and Roumania had entered the war (27 August) on the Allied side. In a conference summoned on 31 August at the general headquarters at Pless, Holtzendorff (Chef des Admiralstab) supported by Admiral von Capelle and the new chief of the general staff, Field Marshal von Hindenburg (who had replaced the discredited Falkenhayn on the day before) along with his quartermaster-general, General Ludendorff, set about trying to convince the German Chancellor and Jagow, the Foreign Minister, that, 'A country in danger must make every exertion possible, and that unrestricted U-boat warfare was on that account inevitable and had better commence at once. *Finis Germaniae*', he argued, 'consists not in the use, but in the withholding of a weapon which cripples England's ability to support her allies and continue the war.'[2]

Although Jagow remained as strongly opposed as ever to such a measure, arguing that if the United States entered the war (which Holtzendorff's proposal would surely invoke) the effect on the other neutrals would be incalculable – 'Germany will be treated like a mad dog against which everybody will combine' – Bethman-Hollweg, for the first time, was far less decisive in his opposition and admitted, in the light of Germany's predicament, that he no longer doubted that an unrestricted U-boat campaign was the only answer remaining, but that the moment was not right for the unleashing of such an extreme measure. He warned that the declaration of an

unrestricted campaign might cause a breach between the northern neutrals and Germany; a warning that weighed heavily with Hindenburg and Ludendorff. As the last reserves of the German Army from both the Eastern and Western Fronts had to be sent to help the Austro-Hungarians stem the Brusilov and Roumanian offensives, Ludendorff explained that there would be nothing left to oppose Holland and Denmark if they declared war. Hindenburg agreed, in view of the Chancellor's appreciation, that the risks of armed conflict with Holland and Denmark could not be run until the military position against Russia and Roumania had been stabilized. He therefore pronounced autocratically that 'a decision [with regard to a declaration of an unrestricted campaign] is not possible at present. *I shall make the time for it known*'.[3] In short, agreement had at last been reached by all parties that the question was no longer whether the campaign should, or should not, be pursued without restraint; only the appropriate moment to throw this 'measure of desperation' into the struggle remained to be decided. In the meantime, as an interim measure, it was decided that a campaign, conducted according to Prize Regulations, was to be recommenced in home waters. Confident that an unrestricted campaign would soon follow, Scheer raised no objection, and the scene was set for the third offensive against Allied maritime trade to begin.

U-boat losses May to September 1916

Date	Boat	Commander	Cause and location
27 May	U74	Weisbach, E.	Gunfire of several trawlers: off Peterhead.
27 May	UC3	Kreysern	Mine in zareba: off Zeebrugge.
? May	U10	Stuhr	Unknown. Presumed Russian mine in Gulf of Finland.
5 July	UC7	Haag	Mine in zareba: off Zeebrugge.
? July	U77	Güntzel	Unknown: North Sea.
14 July	U51	Rumpel	Torpedoed by submarine H5: Ems estuary.
? Aug	UB44	Wäger	Unknown. Agean Sea?
21 Aug	UC10	Albrecht, W.	Torpedoed by submarine E54: Schouwen Bank.
? Sept	UB7	Lütjohann	Unknown: Black Sea.

Analysis of causes
Cumulative total in parentheses

Rammed by warships	0	(4)
Unknown	4	(12)
Accidental causes	0	(6)
Explosive sweep	0	(1)
Q-ship gunfire	0	(3)
Q-ship depth-charges	0	(1)
Torpedoed by submarine	2	(5)
Gunfire of small craft	1	(3)
Mines	2	(2)
Indicator nets	0	(1)
Total	9	(38)

The Growing Menace
The third offensive against shipping, October 1916 to January 1917

Although U-boat operations against trade had been quiescent in home waters since May, there had never been a complete suspension. While traversing the North Sea to and from the operational areas for attacks on the enemy fleet, the High Seas Fleet boats had accounted for 78 vessels (including a large number of fishing boats) grossing 29,311 tons (21 of them neutrals). Another three vessels of 1,838 tons had blown up on minefields laid by the large ocean-going UE minelayers of the High Seas Fleet flotillas (from 29 May until 12 September they laid eleven fields, usually of 34 mines, around the coast of Britain). The UC minelayers of the Flanders Flotilla had also continued dumping their deadly cargoes between the Thames estuary and Flamborough Head (664 mines in 75 fields) and off Boulogne and between Calais and Nieuport (102 mines in fourteen fields). In all, 25 vessels (including one fishing boat) totalling 30,529 tons sank on these small and scattered fields from June until August; while another eighteen ships of 6,747 tons were accounted for in the central part of the English Channel by the Flanders UB boats (all during August).

Mediterranean waters
During the same period the U-boats of the Cattaro Flotilla, with the number of boats at sea at any one time varying from only three to five, had wreaked a veritable slaughter on the Mediterranean sea lanes, sinking 153 vessels of 282,925 tons. Most of the losses occurred in the western basin of the Mediterranean – the Gulfs of Lyons and Genoa, along the eastern seaboard of the Spanish coast, off the Algerian coast and in the narrows between Tunisia and Sicily. All three areas were within the French patrol zone, in which no U-boats were accounted for. As Newbolt explains, 'The French could only do as the British were doing in the approach routes to the British Isles: vary the tracks that shipping followed, and patrol the terminal points. They were short of patrol craft, and the defence never kept the attack in check; also the line of British drifters (towing indicator nets) across the Otranto Straits did nothing to impede the in- or out-going passages of the Cattaro Flotilla.'[1] It was during the period 26 July–30 August 1916, that the commander of U35, Kapitänleutnant Lothar von Arnauld de la Periere, who was destined to become Germany's supreme U-boat ace (his achievements were unequalled during the two world wars), carried out his most destructive cruise. Operating between the north-eastern coast of Spain and the Gulf of Genoa, this intrepid ace sank 54 steamers of 91,000 tons in three weeks. Carrying a picked gun-layer from the High Seas Fleet, Arnauld wreaked this enormous amount of destruction with his single

4.1in deck gun (expending 900 rounds of ammunition as against only four torpedoes). When he returned to Germany in March 1918, to take command of U139, he had accounted for the incredible total of two warships, one auxiliary cruiser, five troop-ships, 125 steamers and 62 sailing vessels, grossing 453,716 tons.

U-boat strength
From the end of May until September the Germans lost eight boats. UC3 (Kreysern) and UC7 (Haag) struck mines in the Zareba off the Belgian coast; U51 (Rumpel) and UC10 (Albrecht) were torpedoed by British submarines (in the Ems estuary and off the Schowen Bank in the Hoofden); and four boats disappeared, causes unknown: U10 (Stuhr) in the Baltic, U77 (Güntzel) in the North Sea, UB44 (Wäger) in the Aegean Sea, and while on passage from Cattaro to Constantinople, UB7 (Lütjohann), in the Black Sea. This left the Germans with 96 Frontbotte (all theatres) with which to prosecute the new offensive, which were disposed as follows: 36 with the High Seas Fleet flotillas; 22 in the Flanders Flotilla; fourteen in the Kurland (Baltic) Flotilla; eighteen at Pola (Adriatic), and six with the Mittelmeerdivision (Constantinople).

British counter-measures
Only one new device had been developed as an A/S measure by the British with which to counter the new offensive. This

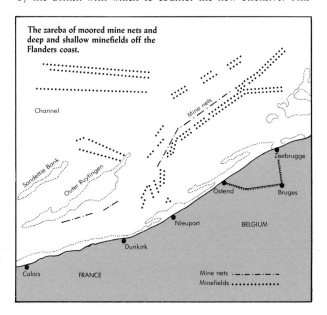

The zareba of moored mine nets and deep and shallow minefields off the Flanders coast.

was an attempt to detect U-boats by acoustic means in the form of the hydrophone: a submerged microphone capable of detecting the beat of a U-boat's propellers from between one to two miles. There were two main types: one for harbour defence, which was fixed on the sea bottom and connected to a shore station. The other was for use with patrol vessels, the hydrophone being suspended over the side of the ship. The latter suffered from the disadvantage that it was not possible to use it while the patrol vessel was moving, as the noise of the ship's engine and of the sea washing along the hull prevented the beat of the U-boat's propellers being detected; alternatively if the patrol vessel stopped to listen, she then became a sitting target for a torpedo attack. To make matters worse the early hydrophones proved ineffective in that, even when they did detect a U-boat, they possessed no accurate directional qualities and could only indicate the presence of a U-boat 'somewhere' in the vicinity. In short the new device was next to useless, leaving it still necessary actually to sight a U-boat or its periscope, or follow up a torpedo track, before an attack by gunfire, depth-charge or explosive paravane could be mounted. But the chances of a sighting were slim, as evinced by the fact that during one week early in September 1916, three UB boats of the Flanders Flotilla, while operating in the English Channel between Beachy Head and the Eddystone light, sank more than thirty British and neutral ships without once running into a patrol vessel. This despite the fact that the patrol forces in the Channel totalled 570 A/S vessels of all types.

Yet it was on the 'offensive' patrolling of the approach routes to the British Isles by small craft, particularly in the South-Western Approaches, that the British principally relied. By November 1916 there were 2,994 patrol craft of all kinds involved in countering the U-boats, yet their success rate was abysmal. From the outbreak of war until January 1917 offensive

patrolling by these A/S forces, including the action of Q-ships, had accounted for only fourteen U-boats (a monthly average of only 0.46). The problem was that the vast amount of water the patrol vessels had to cover made their task too much like hunting for a needle in a haystack. A more promising counter-measure was the defensive arming of merchant ships. Although not responsible for the loss of a single U-boat, this did mitigate to some extent against the loss of merchantmen as an analysis of U-boat attacks against British shipping in the last quarter of 1916 shows. Of the total of 206 attacked, 98 were sunk and 108 escaped. Of the total that escaped 80, or 74 per cent, were armed in comparison to 28, or 26 per cent, of those that were unarmed. By September 1916, 1,749 British merchantmen had been fitted with guns. By February 1917 this number had risen to 2,899. But of course this antidote only worked against surfaced U-boats, and would be nullified to a large extent by the unleashing of an unrestricted campaign whereby the U-boats would by and large torpedo without warning and maintain their defensive secrecy by remaining submerged.

Another attempt was made to construct a fixed barrage across the Dover Straits to bar the passage of the U-boats into the Channel. The idea was inspired by the apparent success of the Zareba of moored mine nets which had been laid parallel to the Belgian coast earlier in the year. Commencing on 2 September 1916, a line of indicator nets (each net studded with two electric-contact mines) suspended from 2in head wires secured to buoys moored 500 yards apart, was stretched from the southern end of the Goodwin Sands across the straits to the Ruytingen Bank (reached in October) and extended to the Snouw Bank (off Dunkirk). This was completed in February 1917. The pressure of the strong tides on the barrage was so great that nets of only 30 to 84 feet in depth, held down by 3-cwt anchors and 500 yards of heavy chain attached to the footing of each net, were practicable. To compensate the shallow depth of the nets, under which the U-boats could dive, three rows of deep minefields were laid half-a-mile to the westward of the barrage. The cross-Channel barrage, illuminated by light buoys at 3-mile intervals with the object of exposing U-boats trying to cross the barrage on the surface at night, was patrolled by a totally inadequate small force of drifters (mostly unarmed), supported by armed yachts and trawlers. 'There can be no doubt', laments the author of the naval staff monograph on the Dover Command, 'that the barrage never fulfilled its object of stopping the passage of the U-boats.'[2] Bad weather made it extremely difficult to maintain the efficiency of the indicator nets, as evinced by a statement made by the officer in charge of the barrage maintenance, Captain Bird, who reported that during the winter months subsequent to its construction only 25 per cent of the entire line of nets could be regarded as efficient.[3] Part of the problem lay with the deep minefields, the mines of which constantly dragged their moorings and fouled the nets, becoming by May 1917 a menace to the vessels maintaining or patrolling the barrage (four were damaged by mine explosions in May alone).

Below: *UB41 of the 274-ton series UB30–UB41*. Note the net cutter fitted to the bow.

A captured German report relating to the passage of the barrage, which was salved from a sunken U-boat in 1917, illustrates its ineffectiveness by giving particulars of 190 passages made from 23 December 1916 to 6 June 1917. These were chiefly made at night, and during these six months there were only eight reports of boats touching a net and eight reports of boats being forced to dive to avoid the patrols. In short, the Dover Straits remained a sieve, not only to the Flanders boats but, from December 1916, the High Seas Fleet boats, after Bauer lifted the interdiction on the route which he had imposed in April 1915, making it an optional route thus shortening their passage to and from the South-Western Approaches by 1,400 miles. 'The ineffectiveness of the barrage', concludes the naval staff monograph, 'must be attributed to the lack of efficient deep minefields to catch the U-boats if they dived, and of an intensive system of patrol to deal with them if they tried to pass on the surface'.[4] From May to July 1917, the western section of the barrage, from the South Goodwins to the Outer Ruytingen, was lifted and the mines swept up. The nets were then relaid, with strengthened moorings, to the south-west of their old position to clear any remaining mines; despite these improvements the barrage still presented little more than an inconvenience to the U-boats.

The course of the third offensive

The resurgence of the campaign in home waters was inaugurated during September by the UB boats of the Flanders Flotilla. With the new and powerful UBII class of boats in commission their area of operations, which had previously been confined to the Hoofden and the western side of the Dover Straits, extended to the western entrance to the English Channel where they sank a mass of shipping between the Scilly Isles and the French port of Brest (78 vessels of 82,068 tons – 22 of them neutrals). From October 1916 to January 1917 their depredations spread even farther afield into the South-Western Approaches and along the coastal waters of the entire French western seaboard as far south as the Gironde. During these four months they accounted for a total of 289 merchantmen grossing 289,558 tons (104 ships being neutrals). The heavy rate of sinkings accomplished by the UB boats in the English Channel, brought about a critical situation in the vital Anglo-French coal trade. French factories began closing down for the want of coal which the British colliers, either being sunk or bottled up in port by the U-boat threat, could not deliver in sufficient quantities. The operational areas of the Flanders UC minelayers also began to spread, thanks to the larger UCII class of boats, into waters hitherto undefiled by their lethal cargoes. In the 4-month period October 1916–January 1917, apart from continuing to lay fields on the east coast, between the Thames estuary and Flamborough Head, and off the Downs and the French coast between Boulogne and Nieuport (734 mines in 83 fields), they began laying their small minefields (usually of twelve mines) off the Channel ports – Portsmouth, Plymouth, Portland, Falmouth, Cherbourg, Le Havre and Dieppe – in the Bristol Channel (Swansea Bay) and

off the French Atlantic ports of Brest, St-Nazaire and in the mouth of the Gironde (a total of 219 mines in 45 fields). In all, sixty vessels of 82,379 tons (thirteen of them neutrals) foundered on these fields.

The progressive expansion of the U-boat danger zones, which the British Admiralty viewed 'with the anxiety of a physician who studies the steady, unrelenting spread of a harmful sympton', as they extended beyond the range of the A/S patrols, became more pronounced when the ocean-going boats of the High Seas Fleet flotillas joined in the affray. It was on 6 October that Scheer received orders from the Admiralstab for his boats to resume operations, under Prize Regulations. Although the weight of their attack fell once more upon the vital South-Western Approaches, they began to range into the Bay of Biscay, down the Atlantic coastline of Spain and Portugal and, more alarmingly, as far afield as the east coast of the USA, although only one U-boat carried matters that far. This singular raid (17 September–28 October) was carried out by U53 (Rose) which, after a 24-hour stay in the American port of Newport to refuel, sank five steamers (three British, one Norwegian and one Dutch) grossing 20,388 tons off the Nantucket light vessel to the east of Long Island. 'When U53 actually carried submarine war to the American coast,' wrote Newbolt, 'strong feelings were aroused among the American public, at the sinking of vessels with the assistance of American navigational marks and under the eyes of American light-keepers. The proceeding was defended on the plea that the sinkings had been made outside territorial waters and according to the rules of cruiser warfare; but popular indignation is not easily subdued by quotations from books of maritime law. The agitation took a threatening shape. The President himself took note of it and warned the German Ambassador that the incident must not be repeated.'[5]

The field of operations also spread northward into the Arctic. For two years an unceasing flow of munitions and supplies had been passing to the port of Archangel from Britain, the USA and other neutral states, furnishing Russia with essentials that she lacked and urgently required for the

Above: This photograph was taken from the conning tower of *U35*; the torpedoed steamer was one of the 194 victims accounted for by Arnauld de la Periere, Germany's supreme Ace U-boat commander.

maintenance of her war fronts. During the summer of 1916 alone, more than 600 steamers – roughly four a day – had delivered a million tons of coal and a million and a half tons of munitions, food and raw materials. To interfere with this traffic, two of the large UE minelayers (*U75* and *U76*) laid 72 mines in three minefields off the Kola Peninsula, which accounted for four vessels of 13,974 tons. And from the end of September until early November 1916, five of the High Seas Fleet boats, *U43* (Jürst), *U46* (Hillebrand), *U48* (Buch), *U54* (Freiherr von Bothmer) and *U56* (Lorenz), raided the shipping routes off the North Cape and along the Murmansk coast, sinking 22 vessels of 48,111 tons (thirteen of them neutral Norwegian).

In all zones (including the Arctic and the singular raid on the US coast) the High Seas Fleet boats sank a total of 253 vessels of 446,306 tons (including fifteen vessels of 34,786 which foundered on the UE-laid minefields around the British coast). When the depredations of the Cattaro Flotilla on the Mediterranean shipping lanes (153 vessels of 506,540 tons) and the one vessel of 116 tons accounted for in the Black Sea (*Mittelmeerdivision*) plus twelve vessels of 2,319 tons sunk in the Baltic, are added to the achievements of the Flanders and High Seas boats, the grand total of British, Allied and neutral ships sunk from September 1916 until January 1917 comes to 768 ships grossing 1,535,863 tons. Of these, 500 vessels were neutrals. This brought the average monthly losses of merchant ships during the five months of the third offensive to 307,172 tons which was more than double the monthly average achieved during the seven months of the first offensive (114,580 tons), and an increase of 56.6 per cent over the monthly average of the March and April losses of the second offensive (173,921 tons). The obvious common denominator in the progressive upward trend of the losses through the three offensives, in the absence of any significant change in tactics, was quite simply the increase in the number of *Frontboote* available at the commencement of each offensive: 30 in February 1915; 52 in March 1916; and 96 in October 1916.

From being an inconvenience the U-boats had suddenly become a very serious menace to Britain. In addition to the 1,535,863 tons of lost shipping, a further 178 vessels grossing 788,595 tons had been damaged by U-boat action, the majority of which would be in need of lengthy repairs. U-boat warnings had also caused delays in sailings which further decreased the carrying power of the merchant marine by an estimated 30 per cent. In addition, the intimidation factor with regard to neutral traders also began to take effect. During the first quarter of 1916, 3,442,000 tons of neutral shipping had entered and been cleared in British ports. During the last quarter of the year this had slumped to 959,000 tons. But for the enterprise and courage displayed by the Norwegian shipowners and seamen the comparison would have been far more unfavourable; indeed it was only under the Norwegian flag that any considerable volume of trade continued to be carried. (Norwegian shipping entered and cleared during the last quarter of 1916 amounted to 723,000 tons.) Jellicoe summed up the seriousness of the

situation in a memorandum to the First Lord of the Admiralty (Arthur Balfour):

'There appears to be a serious danger that our losses in merchant ships, combined with the losses in neutral merchant ships, may by the early summer of 1917 have such a serious effect upon the import of food and other necessaries into the Allied countries as to force us into accepting peace terms, which the military position on the Continent would not justify and which would fall far short of our desires. The methods which have been used in the past for attacking submarines are not meeting with success ... The reasons for our present want of success ... are, firstly, the increased size and radius of action of enemy submarines, which enables them to work in waters so far afield as to make it increasingly difficult to trap them; secondly, the fact that they are attacking more frequently with the torpedo, and that this prevents the use of methods which were applicable to submarines which came to the surface [i.e., the defensive arming of merchantmen and the employment of Q-ships]; thirdly, the very powerful gun armament now carried by submarines, which makes them more than a match for our smaller patrol craft, who are therefore unable to work far afield and are forced to some sort of concentration, thus reducing their sphere of action; fourthly, the fact that the enemy having become aware of the methods hitherto in use, are therefore more or less able to avoid destruction by these means.'[6]

In short, the rub of the matter was that Britain would be defeated by the U-boats unless 'new methods of attack (could) be devised and put into execution at the earliest possible moment'.[7] From October 1916 until January 1917 the Germans lost ten boats, which brought the total losses from August 1914 until January 1917 to 48, or an average loss of only 1.6 per month. When boats lost from accidental and unknown causes are deducted, the total losses directly attributable to Allied action is only 22, or a mere 0.73 per month. During the same period the Germans had completed an average of 2.56 boats per month or 77 in total.

Jellicoe believed that 'to destroy (enemy) submarines at a greater rate than the output of the German shipyards ... was the surest way of counteracting their activities'. With this object in mind he formed the Anti-Submarine Division (ASD) of the Naval Staff on taking up the post of First Sea Lord on 4 December 1916.

'Prior to Jellicoe's coming to the Admiralty,' Professor Marder explains, 'no one division [of the Naval Staff] dealt with the submarine menace as a single problem. the Trade, Operations, and Intelligence Divisions and the Submarine Committee all had a hand in it. These branches of the Admiralty War Staff were now co-ordinated by the ASD, which also absorbed the duties and personnel of the old Submarine Committee; it had been concerned with technical measures against the U-boat. The overall charge of the ASD was to co-ordinate existing, and to devise new, measures and devices in the A/S campaign.'[8] Jellicoe saw only three ways of dealing with the U-boats. 'The first, naturally, was to prevent the vessels from putting to sea; the second was to sink them after they were at sea; and the third was to protect the merchant ships from their attack.'

As regards the first method, Admiral Beatty (who had relieved Jellicoe as CinC, Grand Fleet) suggested (January 1917) a very extensive semi-circular mine barrage (shallow and deep mines forming a vertical barrier) across the entrance to the

Heligoland Bight from the Rote Kliff Bank to Ameland which, he believed, would largely hinder the submarines (of the High Seas Fleet Flotilla) coming or returning in safety. Jellicoe vetoed the idea replying to Beatty that he had an 'exaggerated view of the value of mines against submarines'. This he pointed out was 'proved by the ease with which submarines pass the Dover barrage'.[9] It was in any case impracticable as there were only 1,100 mines in stock (Beatty had envisaged the laying of 80,000). Not only was the amount available grossly inadequate, but the Admiralty had done nothing after thirty months of war to remedy the shortcomings of British mines (more often than not failing to explode when struck and failing to keep their intended depth).

It was not until the spring of 1917 that production commenced on a reliable type of mine (Mark H-2), which was arrived at by the simple expedient of copying a captured German contact mine. Orders for 100,000 were immediately placed, but by September only 1,500 were ready for laying, and not until December 1917 had any significant number (12,450) been produced. Sporadic mining of the Heligoland Bight had been going on since January 1915, but the objective had been German surface warships rather than as an A/S measure. In any case, as Newbolt points out, 'These fields [6,320 mines in 26 fields had been laid during 1915 and 1916] accounted only for some half-dozen enemy trawlers; they did not cause the loss of a single outgoing or incoming submarine, and were always discovered after fairly short intervals.'[10]

Jellicoe also vetoed the third method (protecting merchant ships from attack) of which the convoying of merchantmen was the only application. 'Such knowledge as was then at my disposal', wrote Jellicoe after the war, 'led me to think that the objections to a general convoy system . . . would be insurmountable. I knew that we were very short of cruisers and destroyers for escort work and was doubtful about merchant ships in convoy being kept in sufficiently accurate station to ensure safety by a comparatively small number of escorting destroyers.'[11] The Operations Division of the Admiralty War Staff were of the same opinion. 'Wherever possible, vessels should sail singly . . . The system of several ships sailing in company, as a convoy, is not recommended in any area where submarine attack is a possibility. It is evident that the larger the number of ships forming the convoy, the greater the chance of a submarine being enabled to attack successfully, and the greater the difficulty of the escort in preventing such an attack.'[12] Rear-Admiral Duff, Director of the ASD, also objected to convoy on the grounds of the variation in speed of merchant ships, their inability to zigzag, and their tendency to straggle made convoy impracticable.

It was in the second method (sinking the U-boats at sea), which was of course the existing A/S strategy, that Jellicoe believed the answer to the problem lay, and that, accordingly, there was a pressing need for a great increase in A/S craft, weapons and devices; which gave birth to what one officer termed the 'thousands scheme' – thousands of patrol craft,

thousands of mines, thousands of nets, etc. To begin with, the production rate of depth-charges was speeded up. The average monthly production during 1916 was 264. This had risen to an average of 1,678 during 1917, and to 4,647 a month throughout 1918. Up until June 1917 the low output restricted the supply to two depth-charges per A/S vessel; this had increased to four by July and six by August, and 30 to 40 by early 1918. By the end of 1917 great improvements had also been made to the hydrostatic pistol of the charges, which made them a more effective weapon. Whereas the early depth-charges could only be set to explode at predetermined depths of either 40 or 80 feet, the improved pistols increased the range to predetermined depths of 50, 100, 150 or 200 feet. The result was that all vessels, whether fast or slow, could safely use the Type D (300lb charge) and the Type D* (120lb charge) was therefore withdrawn. A further improvement in the effectiveness of this weapon was the introduction of the depth-charge thrower (August 1917), which could project the charges up to a distance of forty yards on the beam of the attacking vessel. The 'throwers' were usually fitted one on each quarter so that the charges could be thrown out on the quarter while others were dropped over the stern, thus greatly increasing the chances of damaging or sinking the U-boat under attack. During 1917 between 100 and 300 depth-charges a month were expended in attacks upon the U-boats; during the last six months of the war, this had increased to an average of 1,745 a month.

Closely allied to the depth-charge was the innovation of the howitzer (rifled gun) or bomb-thrower (smooth-bore gun) which fired bombs with explosive charges ranging from 11lb up to 113lb, set to explode some 40 to 60 feet under water at ranges from between 650 to 2,600 yards (eight types were developed in all, the most extensively used being the 7.5in howitzer). These weapons first came into service in July 1917. By the end of the war a total of 1,277 had been mounted in ships, 735 of these in defensively armed merchantmen. As Professor Marder points out, these 'were in a way the ancestors of the 'Hedgehog' and 'Squid' of the Second World War, although these were *ahead*-throwing weapons.'[13] Of course, depth-charges, howitzers and bomb-throwers were only effective when the position of the U-boat was reasonably well determined. As we have seen the early hydrophones were as good as useless in detecting the position of a submerged U-boat due to the fact that they had no directional qualities and could only be operated from a stationary vessel. By October 1917, after much research and experiment, these shortcomings had been remedied and the 'Nash Fish' (named after its inventor) type of hydrophone came into service, which not only had directional qualities (albeit limited) but was effective while being towed by a slow-moving ship. After the introduction of the 'Nash Fish' hydrophones, U-boat-hunting flotillas were established composed of trawlers, drifters and motor launches equipped with the new acoustic device and depth-charges. The inherent shortcomings of the 'Nash Fish', which could not accurately compute the position of a submerged U-boat with anything like the proficiency of the ASDIC sets of the Second World War, together with the low speed of the trawlers and drifters and the effects of bad weather on the much faster but flimsy motor launches mitigated against the success of these hunting flotillas to the extent that they only accounted for one U-boat during the entire war.

Commander M. G. Saunders, the one time German Navy expert of the Admiralty, discounts the value of the hydrophones entirely. 'To avoid detection by hydrophones', he explains, 'the U-boat would proceed at 'silent running speed', i.e., on electric motors at about one to two knots, at depths ranging from periscope depth to 100 or 120 feet, depending on the situation, and heading away from the enemy on varying courses. Our hydrophone equipment in World War I was rather primitive, and until relatively late in the war the U-boat captains did not have to worry too much about being chased ... The fact is that the U-boats used their own hydrophones to much greater effect on their targets than British A/S craft could.'[14]

As a part of the 'thousands scheme', 1,108 new A/S craft were ordered (May 1917) made up of 97 destroyers, ten 'P' boats (small motor boats), 34 sloops, 114 minesweepers, 486 trawlers, 215 drifters, 36 Q-ships, 56 motor launches and 60 submarines. A new A/S innovation was the formation of 'hunting forces', composed of destroyers and 'P' boats to operate in U-boat transit areas and on information provided by D/F bearings. These 'hunting forces', which were to operate outside the areas in which shipping was concentrated, were formed in order to leave the remaining 'patrol forces' to work on their fixed beats where shipping was concentrated, i.e., the approach routes to British ports. Previously destroyers and 'P' boats had been detached from their fixed beats to hunt for U-boats known to be operating within striking distance. The inclusion of a large number of submarines in the 'thousands scheme' was a result of the Admiralty's belief that they could be advantageously employed in purely offensive operational roles against the U-boats. Beatty, for one, was convinced that the 'only real reply to the U-boat menace is that wherever a German U-boat is,

there must be also a British submarine'. The foundation of this belief was elucidated by Duff (Director ASD):

'The enemy submarine [will never] be sure that he is not being stalked, and consequently he must either: (a) keep diving, or (b) keep continually under way at a moderate speed (eight to ten knots) and zigzag. If (a) is chosen our object is attained. If (b): (i) his personnel is under continual tension. (ii) His engines are continually being used, which means in effect a longer time laid up between cruises. (iii) The time he can remain out is limited by his increased consumption of fuel. (iv) He is much more likely to be sighted than if at rest on the surface, and so avoided. Whenever he makes an attack, whether successful or not, he will always have the feeling that unseen submarines may be closing him, and this will act as a strong inducement to remain submerged and safe.'[15]

Despite the paucity of successful results obtained from the sporadic use of submarines against U-boats up until the spring of 1917 (out of 56 contacts only six occasions arose in which a submarine managed to attack a U-boat which resulted in the sinking of five, – two of these through decoy trawlers towing a submarine), Beatty and Duff's optimistic expectations led to the establishment of submarine patrols in the areas in which the U-boats were known to pass *en route* and in which they operated against shipping. Early in 1917 diving patrols (in the hope of catching the U-boats on the surface) were established in the Channel and were gradually extended to the west coast of Ireland (Atlantic Patrol), the east coast (North Sea Patrol), off the Shetland Islands, the North Channel between Ireland and Scotland, in the Hoofden and the Dover Straits. 'The submarines in the latter', Jellicoe explains, 'were fitted with occulting lights on top of the conning tower [for recognition purposes] and were moored at night to buoys in the Dover Net Barrage, in places where U-boats were likely to pass in order that they might have a chance of torpedoing them.' Submarine watching patrols in the Heligoland Bight (off the German bases) and off the Horns Reef, which had been instituted at the outbreak of war, were also maintained. Results did not vindicate Beatty and Duff's optimism, due in the main to a shift in U-

Below: *U89* of the 757-ton series *U87–U92*.

boat tactics during 1917 whereby the commanders gave preference to night attacks and were thus very rarely found on the surface in daylight. During the last quarter of 1917, 54.2 per cent of attacks on British shipping in home waters occurred at night. Further, the low underwater speed of British submarines mitigated against success on the rare occasions when contact was actually made, due to the difficulty of obtaining a position to launch torpedoes. In any case a U-boat did not make an easy target given the small area of the boat showing above the water in anything but very smooth seas when surfaced, and the difficulty in estimating the course and speed of such a small target.

The extent of the difficulties is illustrated by the fact that of contacts made by British submarines in the U-boats' operational areas the ratio of destructive hits to contact was 1:222; while contacts made with U-boats on passage faired better with a ratio of 1:39. Throughout 1917 and 1918 twelve U-boats were accounted for by British submarines, giving a wartime total of seventeen out of the total German losses of 178 (a French submarine accounted for one other in 1917). A more efficient torpedo would undoubtedly have given them a higher score. As it was British torpedoes were as bad as their mines, frequently running straight to the bottom after launch and producing little effect when detonating against the target (on seven occasions hits were scored on U-boats but the torpedo failed to detonate). Parenthetically: throughout 1917–1918, British submarines made contact with U-boats on 564 separate occasions, and in attacks they scored nineteen hits with torpedoes which gives the ratio of hits to contacts as 1:29.7. To obviate the low underwater speed of British submarines as the principal hindrance to the achievement of better results, designs were prepared (autumn 1917) for a special class of 'hunter-killer' submarine. The resulting 'R' class were small boats (163 feet long, 420 tons surface displacement, armed with six 18in bow torpedo tubes), but with a phenomenally high submerged speed, for those days, of sixteen knots (7½ knots surfaced). Twelve of this class were laid down in December 1917, but only five had come into service before the war ended. Only one contact was made with a U-boat (R-7, on 13 October, in the Irish Sea), but she dived before an attack could be made. All twelve of the 'R' class were sold for scrap immediately after the war.

The use of aircraft and airships in A/S work was dismally unproductive as Professor Marder explains:

'Despite the extensive network of coastal air patrols established in 1916, the results had been disappointing. No U-boats were destroyed as a result of surface and air hunts, and U-boat attacks on shipping in coastal waters, although only a percentage were made without warning, were not curtailed. The creation of the ASD led to a great increase in the activities of all types of A/S aircraft – aeroplanes, seaplanes, and airships. Their operations were reorganized, systematized, and co-ordinated with other U-boat counter-measures ... Prior to the introduction of convoys in 1917, A/S aircraft were employed exclusively on patrol work. Until 1917 the emphasis was on lighter-than-air-craft, in the form of non-rigid airships. They were capable of more extensive operations under

Above: UB67 in heavy seas in the Bight. The island of Heligoland is visible in the background.

favourable weather conditions than were aeroplanes and seaplanes, whose low performance and limited endurance relegated them to inshore work. By the end of 1916, fifty S.S. (submarine scout) airships were in operation and 27 improved 'C' (coastal) types had been commissioned. Hitherto heavier-than-air A/S operations had been concentrated off the east coast and in the mid and eastern stretches of the Channel. West of Portland there were only airship stations. It was now appreciated that the decisive theatre of U-boat operations was in the Western Approaches to the English Channel, where the oceanic shipping converged on the British Isles and where defence by dispersion was proving impracticable. It was therefore decided to supplement the existing patrols with seaplanes, and by February 1917, seaplane stations had been established at Plymouth, Newlyn (Cornwall), in the Scillies and at Fishguard ... In April [1917], to meet the demand for more air patrols, as no seaplanes were available, aeroplanes were brought into use, airfields being opened in the vicinity of the seaplane stations. Systems of routine patrols by airships, seaplanes, and aeroplanes were established by which the main areas in the St. George's Channel, Bristol Channel and Western Approaches, and in the Channel itself, were covered. Off the east coast seaplanes and airships operated similar patrols, and later in the year aeroplanes were also brought into use here. By September 1917 there were 21 aeroplane or seaplane stations, with 190 planes, on the east coast and in the English Channel, and 10 airship stations, with 50 airships, on the east coast and in the English and Irish Channels. These air patrols supplemented the numerous surface patrols operating in the coastal areas and in the Western Approaches.'[16]

During the whole of 1917, aeroplanes, seaplanes and airships flew a total of 1,526,746 hours, sighted 169 U-boats (average 14.08 per month) and attacked 106 (average 8.8 per month). Throughout the ten wartime months of 1918, these craft flew a total of 4,801,152 hours, sighted 192 U-boats (average 19.2 per month) and attacked 131 (average 13.1 per month). Yet this enormous effort was singularly unproductive. During 1917–1918 (indeed during the entire war) only one U-boat (UB32) was sunk by air attack (bomb dropped by a seaplane). Professor Marder:

'These results are not difficult to explain. Airships proved too sluggish as attackers of U-boats sighted, and the vast majority of the aeroplanes and seaplanes used in A/S work were old trainers with an unreliable engine, very limited endurance, and capable of carrying in addition to the pilot only an observer *or* a bomb load. Forward view was very limited from these aircraft, there was no sighting for bomb-dropping on U-boats, and the 100lb A/S bomb was often defective, and in any case proved to be too light to cause lethal damage. Moreover, its fuze setting (2½-second delay action) was found to be too deep for shallow-dived U-boats and too shallow for deep-dived ones.'[17]

As the 2½-second delay caused the bombs to detonate at about 80 feet under water, the U-boat commanders quickly learnt to counter aerial bomb attacks by diving either to periscope depth or deep (180 feet was sufficient), with the result that in either case the bomb would detonate too far away to do any harm. It was only in fairly shallow water or in the case of a U-boat being caught passing the 80-feet mark during its descent that damage could be done. As a result of the greater air activity in 1917 the U-boat commanders became very wary of aircraft, and by 1918 altiscopes (a periscope with a top prism that could be elevated) with which to search the skies before surfacing were fitted to most U-boats. The work of aircraft, seaplanes and airships was 'but a small contribution to the problem of defeating the stranglehold of the submarine,' writes H. A. Jones, the official historian of 'The War in The Air':

'It was an essential and valuable contribution. The air patrols imposed caution on the submarine commanders and considerably hampered their freedom of action. In the more important shipping lanes they made it hazardous for a submarine to break surface by day. By keeping them submerged, too, the patrols restricted their effective radius of action. Much of the work of the air patrols may appear negative in value, but their mere presence averted many attacks on merchant vessels. When all is said, however, the whole wide network of the A/S organization, absorbing an enormous amount of material and energy, could do little more than blunt the edge of the submarine weapon.'[18]

In summation all of these A/S craft, methods, weapons and devices, new and old, singly or in combination, proved to be no panacea to the U-boat menace. Jellicoe's contention that the key to the problem lay in sinking the U-boats once at sea, had its roots firmly implanted in the collective emotional, rather than rational, preference of the Royal Navy for the offensive, which in this instance entailed thousands of A/S craft of both sea and air fruitlessly hunting over vast expanses of water in an endeavour to harry an elusive and largely invisible foe. The fallacy of this method was soon to be ignominiously driven home when the Germans finally unleashed the full fury of the storm that had been gathering in intensity since August 1914.

U-boat losses October 1916 to January 1917

Date	Boat	Commander	Cause and location
3 Nov	U56	Lorenz	Unknown.
4 Nov	U20	Schwieger	Accident: ran aground on west coast of Jutland and abandoned.
6 Nov	UB45	Palis	Mines: off Varna, Black Sea.
? Nov	UC15	Heller	Unknown: Black Sea.
30 Nov	UB19	Noodt	Gunfire of Q-ship *Penshurst*.
6 Dec	UC19	Nitzsche	High-speed paravane (modified explosive sweep) of destroyer *Ariel*: South-Western Approaches.
7 Dec	UB46	Bauer, C.	Mines: Bosporus.
13 Dec	UB29	Platsch	Depth-charges of destroyer *Landrail*: South-Western Approaches.
14 Jan	UB37	Günther	Gunfire of Q-ship *Penshurst*: English Channel.
22 Jan	U76	Bender	Rammed by Russian armed trawler and storm damage: North Cape.

Analysis of causes
Cumulative total in parentheses

Rammed by warships	1	(5)
Unknown	2	(14)
Accidental causes	1	(7)
Explosive sweep	0	(1)
High-speed paravane	1	(1)
Q-ship gunfire	2	(5)
Q-ship depth-charges	0	(1)
Torpedoed by submarine	0	(5)
Gunfire of small craft	0	(3)
Mines	2	(4)
Destroyer depth-charges	1	(1)
Indicator nets	0	(1)
Total	10	(48)

Shipping losses in the Western Approaches, Channel and East Coast

1. Five months of the restricted third offensive, September 1916 to January 1917

The Sharp Edge of the Sword

Unleashing the unrestricted campaign
February to April 1917

Holtzendorff's equation for victory

During August 1916, Hindenburg and Ludendorff had been dissuaded from pressing for an unrestricted U-boat campaign, because of the lack of reserves available should Holland and Denmark be provoked into declaring war on Germany. By the first week of December, with Roumania crushed and the British 'Somme' and Russian 'Brusilov' offensives successfully checked (thus releasing the necessary German reserves), the Chief of the General Staff and the Quartermaster-General renewed their demand. Once more, however, they agreed to a postponement pending the result of a peace overture made to the Allies by the German Chancellor on 12 December. When a negative reply was received at the end of December ... 'the overture made by the Central Powers is but an attempt calculated to work upon the evolution of war and of finally imposing a German peace ...'[1] Hindenburg insisted that the 'diplomatic and military preparations for the unrestricted U-boat war should be begun, so that it may for certain commence at the end of January'.[2]

Buoyed by the success of the autumn campaign in which the U-boats had sunk an average monthly total of 307,000 tons of Allied shipping, Holtzendorff (Chef des Admiralstab) added weight to the General Staff's demand in a memorandum, dated 22 December, which argued for an early opening of the unrestricted campaign. 'A decision must be reached before the autumn of 1917, if the war is not to end in the exhaustion of all parties, and consequently disastrously for us. Of our enemies, Italy and France are economically so hard hit that they are only upheld by England's energy and activity. If we can break England's back the war will at once be decided in our favour. England's mainstay is her shipping, which brings to the British Isles the necessary supplies of food and materials for war industries, and ensures their solvency abroad.'[3] Holtzendorff reckoned that Britain was fed and supplied by $10\frac{3}{4}$ million tons of shipping ($6\frac{3}{4}$ million British, 900,000 captured enemy shipping, and 3 million neutral). Judging from the previous experience of U-boats operating under the restraint of Prize Regulations, he argued that acting without restraint the U-boats should be able to account for 600,000 tons of British shipping each month; and at least 1,200,000 tons of neutral shipping would be frightened away (which the reaction of the neutrals in the autumn campaign seemed to confirm). After five months, he computed, shipping to and from Great Britain would be reduced by some 39 per cent.

'England would not be able to stand that ... I do not hesitate to assert that, as matters now stand, we can force England to make peace in five months by means of an unrestricted U-boat campaign.

Left: Admiral von Holtzendorff, Chief of the German Naval Staff, who calculated that the U-boats would have to sink 600,000 tons of shipping a month to achieve a decisive result.

But this holds good only for a really unrestricted campaign ... I arrive, therefore, at the conclusion that an unrestricted U-boar war, started at the proper time, will bring about peace before the harvesting period of the 1917 summer, that is, before August 1st; the break with America must be accepted; we have no choice but to do so. In spite of the danger of a breach with America, unrestricted U-boat war, started soon, is the proper, and indeed the only way to end the war with victory.'[4]

Holtzendorff's new figure of 600,000 tons of British shipping a month, was a far more realistic equation for success in comparison to his earlier calculation of 160,000 tons a month on which the second offensive was launched.

A final 'Crown Council' on the matter took place at General Headquarters (Grosses Hauptquartier) in Pless on 9 January 1917. The conference was attended by the Kaiser, Bethmann-Hollweg (Chancellor), Holtzendorff, Hindenburg, Ludendorff and the chiefs of the Military and Naval cabinets. Faced with a definite, uncompromising demand by Hindenburg and Ludendorff, who had arrogantly constituted themselves as the deciding authority on the question with no regard to the Chancellor, and the weight of Holtzendorff's impressive reasoning, the Kaiser concurred that 'U-boat warfare should begin *with the utmost severity* on 1 February'. Bethmann-Hollweg also capitulated with the comment: 'The prospects for unrestricted U-boat warfare are, doubtless very favourable . . . but it must be admitted that they cannot be demonstrated by proof . . . *U-boat warfare is the last card.* We are making a very serious decision, but if the military authorities consider it essential, I am not in a position to contradict them.'[5]

As for the American reaction, so long feared by the Chancellor and Auswärtiges Amt, both Hindenburg and Ludendorff were contemptuously dismissive. As well they could be, as things stood. Despite two years of sabre-rattling, the US Government had done nothing to prepare their armed forces for the eventuality of war. During the spring of 1917 the USA had only 55 military aircraft in any fit state to fly and most of these were old and outdated, while her army numbered 200,000 officers and men, of which 67,000 were national guardsmen. As it would take some considerable time before the United States could mobilize and train her vast manpower resources, the General Staff were confident that the U-boats could starve Britain into submission before US troops could arrive in France, in any appreciable numbers, to stave off an Allied defeat (in fact only 100,000 half-trained American troops had arrived in France by January 1918). Besides, the United States would be faced with the problem of transporting the army across the North Atlantic, a move which could, it was believed, be easily countered by the U-boats which would find rich pickings among the transports.

The demands of the military and naval leaders, the Kaiser's acquiescence and the Chancellor's abdication of authority had a common denominator – realistically there was no alternative but to make the ultimate decision with regard to the strategic use of the U-boats, because Germany's situation was desperate.

Below: Hindenburg and Luedendorff (nearest) with Admiral Tirpitz directly behind. All three pressed for the unleashing of an unrestricted U-boat campaign.

On all war fronts the manpower situation was loaded against the Central Powers, which could only dispose a total of 304 divisions against an Allied total of 405: on the Western Front alone 2,500,000 German troops were facing 3,900,000 French, British and Belgian troops. With no prospect of bringing the war to a successful conclusion on land, this was reason enough for the decision taken at Pless. But it was the internal problems in Germany, brought about as a direct result of the stranglehold of the British naval blockade, that provided the decisive factor in the decision making. Although the German armies continued to be reasonably well fed and equipped, the German Government had protected their armed forces by exposing the civil population to the full shock of economic warfare. The sufferings of the 'turnip winter' of 1916–17 (so called because turnips provided the staple diet during the period) were telling heavily upon both the physical and moral powers of the German people. A. C. Bell explains:

'The rations allowed were not always obtainable. Many thousands of individuals could only be sure of five slices of bread, half a small cutlet, half a tumbler of milk, two thimblefuls of fat, a few potatoes and an egg-cup of sugar in the course of a day. To this the more fortunate could add a precarious, irregular supply of jams, green vegetables and nuts. These supplies were, however, only obtainable by waiting for long hours in food queues, exposed to the rain, snow and slush of the bitter German winter; after obtaining them, the women as often as not returned in their soaking clothes to houses that were not heated or even warmed . . . they were reduced to a condition that no community will endure indefinitely. The majority of the urban population were either cold, or wet, or hungry for the greater part of the day.'[6]

'The poor, the weak and the elderly were very badly hit,' writes Professor Berghahn, 'whereas the better-off who had savings were able to obtain supplies on the black market at exorbitant prices. Infant mortality rose dramatically, and according to some estimates more than 700,000 people died of starvation or hypothermia.' In short, the unrestricted U-boat campaign was Germany's only remaining hope, for, as Admiral Scheer explains, 'If we did not succeed in overcoming England's will to destroy us then the war of exhaustion must end in Germany's certain defeat. There was no prospect of avoiding such a conclusion by the war on land . . . In such a situation it was not permissible to sit with folded hands and leave the fate of the German Empire to be decided by chance circumstances.'

With the die cast the Kaiser sent Scheer a telegram, via Holtzendorff, commanding that the unrestricted U-boat campaign begin on 1 February 'with the utmost energy'. All Allied and neutral shipping was to be sunk on sight, without warning, in prohibited zones (*Sperrgebiet*) which covered the English Channel, the western half of the North Sea, the western coasts of Scotland, Ireland, England and France, extending about 400 miles west into the Atlantic bounded by the meridians 62° North and 20° West (extended to 30° West on 22 November 1917). The Mediterranean was forbidden to shipping, except for narrow passages south and east of Spain, around the Balearics, and a narrow corridor to Greece (the latter being incorporated into the *Sperrgebiet* on 22 November).

The neutral governments were not notified until the day before the start of the campaign, as it was considered 'that the proclamation and the actual commencement of unrestricted U-boat warfare should occur more or less simultaneously. Only in that way would it be possible to achieve the psychological effect on the population of Britain and the deterrent effect on the neutral powers which was an essential factor in the whole plan.'[7] The orders issued by Bauer (*F.d.U.*) to the U-boat commanders (dated 27 January) demanded a supreme effort in the prosecution of the campaign: '. . . unrestricted U-boat warfare is to force England to make peace and thereby decide the whole war. *Energetic* action is required, and above all *rapidity* of action. The campaign is therefore to be prosecuted with the utmost vigour. No vessel must remain afloat, the sinking of which is authorized [hospital ships were exempt, except those encountered in the English Channel, which the Germans believed were being used as transports: neutral steamers, Belgian relief ships and *unarmed* passenger steamers were to be dealt with in accordance with Prize Regulations up until midnight of 6/7 February, after which they too were to be sunk without warning].

'Orders must be carried out with exactitude . . . Leave [for U-boat crews] is only possible hitherto when repairs to the boat are not affected by it. For this reason, food allowances of U-boats are increased. The sole aim is, that each boat shall fire her entire supply of ammunition as often as possible. The standard of achievement is not to be judged by each separate enterprise, but on the total result over any given period. Therefore short cruises, with short visits to the dockyard, result in a considerable curtailment of effort and are to be avoided. The best form of practice is for the U-boat to remain at sea for 14 days in each month with the object of firing her full supply of torpedoes and gun ammunition. During periods of overhaul, only what is absolutely necessary is to be done. The crew and reserve personnel are to be made the utmost use of. Venereal diseases represent an avoidable loss from a military standpoint – often a very serious loss – which must be eliminated in the future . . . special orders regarding the suppression of venereal diseases are being issued. Our object is to cut England off from traffic by sea, and not to achieve occasional results at far-distant points. As far as possible, therefore, stations must be taken up near the English coast, where routes converge and where divergence becomes impossible. When the weather is so bad that weapons cannot be used, better weather conditions and chance successes are not to be sought at far-distant points at sea, but the boat is to remain on her station, if necessary submerging to avoid damage. An improvement in the weather will then be perceived immediately and can at once be utilized without any delay in reaching the spot. The principal advantageous methods of prosecuting ruthless U-boat warfare are: (1) Attack submerged all ships which are armed or suspect, whenever the U-boat is in a position for attacking submerged, or is able by means of her speed to reach such a position. (2) Utilize all chances of attack by night. (3) Open immediate effective firing when a ship is stopped by gunfire, without wasting time on warning shots. (4) No boat to ship communication (i.e., sending a boarding-party to examine the ship's papers and cargo); consequently, when holding up a ship, the position of the U-boat and her distance from the enemy ship can be determined from the military standpoint . . . Way

should always be kept on the U-boat to render a counter-attack more difficult, particularly that of an enemy submarine, and in order that the boat herself may remain completely under control, so as to avoid a torpedo, if necessary. When a ship, abandoned by her crew, is to be sunk by gunfire, she should be approached from aft; she is then not in a position either to ram or to open fire, as the U-boat traps (a reference to Q-ships) with hidden armament, reported to date, in every case had their guns on the broadside. A trap will endeavour without exciting notice to keep her beam on to the U-boat and will turn accordingly. Beware of this! When approaching keep one bow torpedo ready for firing, with the tube flooded, and keep the enemy under fire; have the boat ready for diving and no men on deck except those actually required. As a rule, expend only one torpedo on each ship stopped . . . she should be finished off with gunfire, if possible. A sharp lookout must be kept for the approach of any further vessels, particularly any which lie hidden under the lee of the ship attacked. An approach from astern permits observation on both sides.'[8]

To obtain the maximum effort from the High Seas Fleet's U-boats, the previously optional choice of using the Dover Straits route was now made compulsory, for reasons set out by Bauer in his orders:

'(1) To shorten the cruise, so that each boat may make as many cruises as possible in a given period of time. (2) To shorten the period spent in the dockyard corresponding with the shortening of the cruise, particularly as the heavy strain on the boat in the northern part of the North Sea and in the Atlantic is avoided. (3) In cases where bad weather is met with in the area of operations, to allow the boats time to await an improvement, instead of their being obliged after a short while to start on the long homeward voyage round the Shetlands – without having attained any result, as has frequently happened.'[9]

U-boat strength
Germany began her unrestricted campaign with 105 *Frontboote* (Spindler's figures)[10] which were distributed as follows: 46 with the High Seas Fleet flotillas (based on the German North Sea ports), 23 in the Flanders Flotilla (based on Zeebrugge and Ostend), 23 in the Adriatic (based on Pola and Cattaro), ten in the Baltic and three in Constantinople. During March the number of *Frontboote* grew to 117 increasing to 120 in April. Orders were also placed in February for 51 further boats (six large U-boats and 45 UBIII coastals) along with the conversion of seven *Deutschland* class 'merchant cruisers' (originally built with the idea of circumventing the British economic blockade with large, cargo-carrying submarines) to U-cruisers armed with two 19.7in torpedo tubes and a heavy deck armament of two 5.9in guns. Admiral von Capelle, Secretary of the Navy, was averse to embarking on a larger programme, as it was believed that German industry would be unable to cope with a heavier burden. Anyway, it was reasoned, if the campaign was designed to achieve its goal within six months, what was the point in building cohorts of U-boats which would not be completed until the spring of 1918 at the earliest. In a word, the U-boats at hand and in immediate prospect would have to carry out the great 'drive' against sea-borne commerce. 'Put in a nutshell,' as Gibson and Prendergast neatly sum up the situation, 'the whole effort

Right: The Mercantile U-boat *Deutschland* returning to Heligoland after her maiden voyage to America. She was converted to a UA Cruiser in 1916.

Below: Crew members of *U35* unloading spent shell cases in Cattaro, April 1917. *U35* was the most successful U-boat of the First World War, being credited with 224 ships grossing 535,900 tons.

was to be a gigantic "smash and grab" raid: the brittle glass of the world's shipping was to be shattered, so that the U-boats could grab the gems of victory and decamp before Policeman America could lay a hand upon them.'

Unleashing of the unrestricted campaign

During the first three months of the unrestricted campaign it seemed that Holtzendorff's prediction would be realized. Although the average number of *Frontboote* actually at sea in February (all theatres) was only 36 (maximum in any one day 44), rising to 40 in March (maximum 57) and 47 (maximum 58) in the climacteric month of April (during which the sinkings would never be surpassed again in any month during the two world wars), they accounted for a total of 1,945,243 tons of shipping or a monthly average of 648,414 tons. The monthly breakdown of the figures, with the British figures in parentheses are as follows:

February	520,412 tons	(254 ships of 500,573 tons)
March	564,497 tons	(310 ships of 556,775 tons)
April	860,334 tons	(413 ships of 873,754 tons)
Total	1,945,243 tons	(977 ships of 1,931,102 tons)

More than half the losses (1,045,367 tons) were accounted for by the boats of the High Seas Fleet flotillas; the main weight of their attack falling on the vital South-Western Approaches. The Flanders Flotilla, operating in the Hoofden, the English Channel and along the French Atlantic coast as far south as the Gironde accounted for 349,000 tons, with a further 127,300 tons falling prey to the small minefields sown by the UC minelayers. Although only 23 boats were operating in the Mediterranean, of which only one-third were at sea at any one time, they accounted for 422,498 tons, while a mere 251 tons of shipping went down in the Black Sea and 787 tons in the Baltic. In addition, a further 321,000 tons of British and foreign shipping had also been damaged by U-boat action during this quarter (113,000 tons in April alone). More than 270,000 tons of this total were British, and with the shipyards already choked with repair work, the carrying power of the vessels seriously damaged would obviously be lost for a considerable period of time. The German intimidatory intentions with regard to neutral shipping also bit as the neutrals practically abandoned attempts to trade with Britain; Norwegian, Danish, Dutch and Swedish ships suspended their voyages, and neutral ships already in British harbours refused to sail. During February alone more than 600 neutral vessels refused to clear. Shipping entering British ports during February and March 1917 was only about a quarter of what it had been a year earlier. The seriousness of the situation for Britain is summed up by Fayle:

'The full menace of the unrestricted U-boat campaign could now be seen. It had raged for three months, and during those three months the world's tonnage had been reduced by over 2 million tons [*sic*], of which nearly a million and a quarter were British ... compared with such losses, the acquisitions of shipping by new construction or transfer from foreign flags sank into insignificance. New ships of 1,600 tons gross or over, brought into service under the British flag, amounted for the three months to under 200,000 tons. About 60,000 tons had been obtained from other sources, but the net reduction in ocean-going tonnage, after allowing on the one hand for all gains and on the other for war and marine losses, was some 940,000 tons or about 5.66 per cent of the total tonnage available on February 1st. In other words the wastage of ocean-going tonnage was at the rate of nearly 23 per cent per annum. It was, however, the acceleration in the rate of loss during the second half of April which was the most alarming feature in the situation. While the ratio of war losses for the three months (without regard to replacements) was about 7 per cent, or 23 per cent per annum, the losses suffered during the fortnight April 17th to 30th inclusive were at the appalling rate of over 50 per cent per annum on the available tonnage. On the basis of the same period, it was estimated that the risk to an individual steamer homeward bound from a port more distant than Gibraltar was about 2 in 11; to an outward-bound steamer, which could be more easily stayed or diverted, about 1 in 14. Her chances of leaving the United Kingdom on such a voyage and returning safely were only about 1 in 4 ... it was evident that the continuance of losses, even at the average for the three months which had elapsed since the opening of the unrestricted campaign, would soon bring the Germans within measurable distance of the decision on which they had staked so much.'[11]

The enormous acceleration in the rate of tonnage sunk by the U-boats (343,265 tons in excess of the 305,149 tons monthly average achieved during the third offensive) was a direct result of the removal of the tactical restraints inherent in the Prize Regulations that had previously handicapped the commanders. Of the 781 merchant ships attacked from 1 February until the end of April, 516 had been attacked with torpedoes and without

warning, of which 374 (72.5 per cent) had been sunk and 31 (6.0 per cent) had been damaged while 111 (21.5 per cent) had managed to escape. By comparison, 105 (39.6 per cent) of the 265 ships attacked by gunfire had effected escape (154 or 58.1 per cent had been sunk, and six or 2.3 per cent had been damaged). The attacks by gunfire had, of course, not been made for any humanitarian reasons, but purely to save on torpedoes and thus obtain the optimum results from each cruise.

The cost to the Germans in this supreme effort had been ten boats; two of which had blown up on their own mines (*UC32* and *UC68*) and one (*UB6*) had run aground off Hellevoetsluis and was interned by the Dutch authorities, which meant that only seven (or a monthly average of 2.3) had been accounted for by British A/S measures. Three of these losses could have been avoided if the commanders had paid heed to the warnings with regard to Q-ships explicit in Bauer's orders. On 17 February, *U83* (Hoppe) torpedoed without warning a steamer in the South-Western Approaches. Although the steamer was slowly sinking by the stern, and there was no reason to surface, Hoppe did so, only 300 yards from the stricken ship, presumably to deliver the *coup de grâce* with gunfire. It proved fatal. *U83* had in fact torpedoed the Q-ship *Farnborough* which turned the tables on Hoppe by uncovering her concealed guns and sinking *U83* withe 25 rounds of well-aimed gunfire. *Farnborough* was later beached after being taken in tow by sloops which answered her distress call. In similar circumstances *UC18* (Kiel) was sunk by the Q-ship *Lady Olive* in the Channel on 19 February, while *U85* (Petz) went down under the gunfire of the Q-ship *Privet* off Start Point on 12 March. Two other boats, *U84* (Röhr) and *U93* (Peckelsheim), were both badly damaged in encounters with Q-ships in the South-Western Approaches, but managed to struggle back to Germany on surface trim. As a result of the institution of submarine diving patrols, during early 1917, in the areas through which U-boats were accustomed to pass ('the tracks which the larger U-boats followed were known with tolerable accuracy'), the British submarine *G13*, patrolling the waters off the Shetlands sighted and sank by torpedo *UC43* (Sebelin) on the afternoon of 10 March. The other three losses, all UC minelayers, were accounted for by destroyer patrols (*UC46* and *UC39*) and British mines (*UC30*). To balance these losses the Germans commissioned thirteen new boats during the same period.

There was one consequence of the campaign, which although it had no immediately perceptible influence, did in fact have a profound immediacy which was to have far-reaching and decisive results. This was the declaration of war on Germany (6 April 1917) by the United States, brought about in the main by U-boat attacks on US shipping and partially by the interception and decoding of the 'Zimmermann telegram' (a German proposal that Mexico should be instigated into inviting Japan to join in an attack on the United States, should President Wilson declare war on Germany). The immediacy of this event was that American intervention, which provided badly needed naval reinforcements (especially in destroyers and other small craft), was the deciding factor in convincing the Admiralty of the practicality of introducing Mercantile Convoy, which, in the words of Admiral Karl Doenitz, was destined to rob the U-boat arm of its opportunity to become a decisive factor'.

Left: A U-boat's 5.9in deck gun crew in action.

Left: The UA cruiser *U139* (1,930 tons) armed with two 5.9in guns.

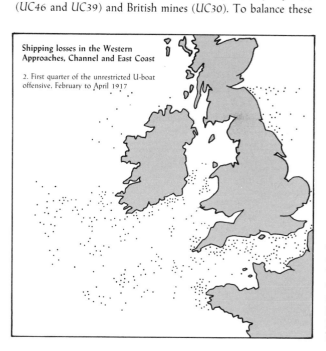

Shipping losses in the Western Approaches, Channel and East Coast

2. First quarter of the unrestricted U-boat offensive, February to April 1917

U-boat losses February to April 1917

Date	Boat	Commander	Cause and location
8 Feb	UC46	Moecke	Rammed by destroyer *Liberty*: south-east of Goodwin Sands.
8 Feb	UC39	Ehrentraut	Depth-charges of destroyer *Thrasher*: off Flamborough Head.
17 Feb	U83	Hoppe	Gunfire of Q-ship *Farnborough*: South-Western Approaches.
19 Feb	UC18	Kiel	Gunfire of Q-ship *Lady Olive*: English Channel.
23 Feb	UC32	Breyer	Accident; own mines: off Sunderland.
10 March	UC43	Sebelin	Torpedoed by submarine *G13*: off Muckle Flugga.
12 March	U85	Petz	Gunfire of Q-ship *Privet*: off Start Point.
13 March	UC68	Degetau	Accident; own mines: off Start Point.
21 April	UC30	Stenzler	British minefield: off Horns Reef.

Analysis of causes
Cumulative total in parentheses

Rammed by warships	1	(6)
Unknown	0	(14)
Accidental causes	2	(9)
Explosive sweep	0	(1)
High-speed paravane	0	(1)
Q-ship gunfire	3	(8)
Q-ship depth-charges	0	(1)
Torpedoed by submarine	1	(6)
Gunfire of small craft	0	(3)
Mines	1	(5)
Destroyer depth-charges	1	(2)
Indicator nets	0	(1)
Total	9	*(57)*

Victory on the Horizon
May to July 1917

The holocaust being wreaked among the world's shipping by the U-boats cast a dark shadow of pessimism over the Admiralty. An analysis of the situation conducted by Sir Leo Chiozza Money came to the conclusion that, after taking in allowances for replacements by building, repairing and buying from abroad, the merchant vessels in the service of Britain would be reduced from 8,394,000 tons (the April 1917 figure) to 4,812,000 tons by the end of 1917, and this would barely suffice for the importation of adequate food stocks. In short, defeat was staring the country in the face. When Admiral Sims of the United States Navy met Jellicoe at the Admiralty on 10 April, he was handed a memorandum on the British and neutral shipping losses of the last few months. 'I was fairly astounded', wrote Sims after the war, 'for I had never imagined anything so terrible. I expressed my consternation to Admiral Jellicoe.'

'Yes,' he said, as quietly as though he were discussing the weather and not the future of the British Empire. 'It is impossible for us to go on with the war if losses like this continue.'

'What are you doing about it?' I asked.

'Everything that we can. We are increasing our anti-submarine forces in every possible way. We are using every possible craft we can find with which to fight submarines. We are building destroyers, trawlers, and other like craft as fast as we can. But the situation is very serious and we shall need all the assistance we can get.'

'It looks as though the Germans are winning the war,' I remarked.

'They will win, unless we can stop these losses – and stop them soon,' the Admiral replied.

'Is there no solution for the problem?' I asked.

'Absolutely none that we can see now,' Jellicoe announced.

'He described the work of destroyers and other anti-submarine craft, but he showed no confidence that they would be able to control the depredations of the U-boats ... the disconcerting facts which faced the Allies were that the supplies and communications of the forces on all fronts were threatened; that German U-boats were constantly extending their operations farther and farther out into the Atlantic; that 3 years' constant operations had seriously threatened the strength of the British Navy, and that Great Britain's control of the sea was actually at stake. Nor did Admiral Jellicoe indulge in any false expectations concerning the future. Bad as the situation then was, he had every expectation that it would grow worse. The season which was now approaching would make easier the German operations, for the U-boats would soon have the long daylight of summer and the more favourable weather. The new few months, indeed, both in the estimation of the Germans and British, would witness the great crisis of the war ...'[1]

British counter-measures

In desperation the Admiralty adopted three new measures with which to counter the fury of the storm which was threatening to engulf the country. These measures consisted of: (1) An attempt to build merchant ships faster than the enemy was sinking them (this became the responsibility of the Scottish shipowner Sir Joseph Maclay, who was appointed to head the newly created Ministry of Shipping Control); (2) To carry out an extensive mining policy in the Heligoland Bight and (3) To introduce experimental mercantile convoys.

For the first measure, Maclay set up a programme in which 1,200,000 tons of new merchant shipping was to be constructed during 1917. This figure was the largest output that Maclay could venture to hope for. To achieve this it was necessary to find a further 35,000 skilled workers for the shipyards (who had to be recalled from military service), and to increase the weekly steel supply allotted to merchant shipbuilding from 13,000 to 22,000 tons (achieved by the Admiralty having to cancel the construction of five light cruisers and the three sister ships of the battlecruiser *Hood* which were in the process of building). The standardization of merchant ship design with respect to both engines and hull was also necessary. The types approved are described by Fayle:

'... 2 principal types, known as 'A' and 'B' were both 400-foot freighters of 5,030 tons gross; but whereas 'A' was a single-decked steamer of 8,175 tons dead weight capacity, 'B' had 2 decks with a consequent reduction in capacity of 100 tons. The third type, 'C', was a smaller vessel with a length of 331 feet, a gross tonnage of 3,000, and a dead weight capacity of 5,050 tons. A still smaller ship, type 'D' of 285 feet length, 2,300 tons gross, and 2,980 dead weight was produced, mainly in response to Admiralty demands for vessels of this size for naval employment. In all four types the simplification of design was carried to such a length that the number of steel sections required in construction was reduced to 8 or 10 as compared with 30 to 40 normally used in ships of the same size. Further, only 2 types of engine were required for the 4 designs. All were single-screw ships with a speed of 11½ knots.'[2]

In all, sixteen 'A', 45 'B', 24 'C' and 21 'D' type were completed during the war (the average number of days under construction being 314). Despite the fact that a frenzied programme of purchase from neutrals was also put in hand ('The world's ports were ransacked for tonnage ... decrepit steamers fetched fabulous prices, and even old sailing vessels, derelict or used as harbour hulks, were reconditioned and set out to sea again.')[3] for the whole of 1917 only 1,163,000 tons of new shipping was brought on to the register, which was roughly a quarter of the British Empire losses of 4,010,000 tons (from all forms of enemy

action plus marine loss, i.e., collisions, storm or running aground).

Equally dismal were the results of the second measure: the mining of the Heligoland Bight. Although Jellicoe had vetoed Beatty's suggestion, of January 1917, to form a vertical barrier across the Bight from the Rote Kliff Bank off the Schleswig coast to the island of Ameland off the Dutch north coast, a policy of laying small independent minefields on a much wider semi-circle than originally suggested (from the island of Texel to the north of the Horns Reef) was carried out. During 1917 a total of 15,686 mines were laid in 76 fields. During 1918 until October, this was increased to 21,105 mines in 129 fields, for a wartime total of 43,111 mines in 231 fields. All this effort had very little effect. As Newbolt explains:

'They [the minefields] were always discovered before they caused serious loss, and as soon as they were known to exist the necessary measures were taken to clear them, or to discover their exact position and to mark them suitably . . . if German mining had never seriously interrupted the commercial traffic round the British Isles, it needed some faith to believe that the German U-boats would ever be pinned to their bases by British mines, or even that they would suffer any serious losses when entering or leaving harbour, seeing that they could always choose their time of sailing or return, and need never move until all the necessary precautions had been taken.'[4]

Throughout the whole of the war the extensive minefields in the Bight accounted for only five U-boats.

The introduction of the mercantile convoy
As for the third measure, despite Rear-Admiral Duff's earlier objections to the idea of convoy, the variation in speed of merchant ships, their inability to zigzag and tendency to straggle making it impracticable (none of these objections proved to be valid), he had changed his opinions by the end of April to the extent that he minuted the First Sea Lord (Jellicoe) on the advisability of introducing 'a comprehensive scheme of convoy'. Practical experience had been the catalyst in changing Duff's views. The heavy sinkings by the boats of the Flanders Flotilla in the English Channel during the last quarter of 1916, caused a 39 per cent reduction in the deliveries of coal to France. As the French needed to import a minimum of 1½ million tons of coal a month to keep her vital armament factories in full production, it was decided, after representations made by the French naval authorities, to introduce a system of 'controlled sailings' to ensure the safe and speedy passage of the 800 colliers that crossed the Channel every month.

The system that evolved was in fact convoys of up to 45 colliers escorted by three or four armed trawlers of the Auxiliary Patrol. The first convoy of colliers sailed on 10 January 1917. By the end of April 2,600 colliers had been convoyed, and although they traversed one of the most consistently lucrative areas of U-boat operations only five were sunk by U-boat action: a loss rate of a mere 0.19 per cent. The 'unexpected immunity from successful U-boat attack on the French coal trade' (together with the success of similar experiments carried out with ships employed in the Dutch trade between the Downs and the Hook of Holland, and trade between Scandinavia and the North Sea ports) afforded Duff 'sufficient reason for believing that we can accept the many disadvantages of large convoys with the certainty of a great reduction in our present losses'.[5] His minute to Jellicoe went on to postulate that, 'It would appear that the larger the convoy passing through any given danger zone, provided it is moderately protected, the less the loss to the Merchant Service.'[6]

Duff submitted his minute on 27 April, together with detailed proposals for a trial Ocean Convoy from Gibraltar. Jellicoe approved, prepared to see a fair trial made, although his heart was not in it. Duly, on 10 May 1917, a convoy of sixteen merchant ships, organized in three columns (speed 6½ knots), sailed from Gibraltar escorted by three armed yachts and two Q-ships as escorts. Eight days later the convoy was met on the edge of the danger zone (the U-boats' operational area) some 200 miles from the English Channel by eight destroyers from Devonport. The convoy reached port on 20 May unscathed. Not a ship had been lost, no U-boats had been encountered and station-keeping by the merchant ships had proved on the whole quite satisfactory. This success led to an experimental North Atlantic homeward-bound convoy of twelve ships (speed 9 knots) which sailed from Hampton Roads, Virginia on 24 May. Ocean escort was provided by the cruiser *Roxburgh*, and, on arrival in the danger zone on 6 June, by eight destroyers. Although two slow steamers straggled and had to drop out (one of them being torpedoed by a U-boat and sunk), the ships in convoy arrived safely at their destinations. Despite fog and heavy weather, station-keeping had been excellent.

These trial runs having invalidated the main objections, a general scheme of convoy was slowly introduced (the immense organizational problems mitigated against a speedy adoption on a large scale and several months elapsed before it became fully operational). During June a further four Atlantic convoys were run from Hampton Roads; a total of sixty laden ships being convoyed homewards without loss. In July the system was extended to include homeward-bound convoys from Gibraltar, New York and the Canadian port of Sydney (Cape Breton). By the end of July a total of 21 Atlantic convoys had been run, and of the 354 ships convoyed only two had been sunk by U-boats: a loss rate of a mere 0.56 per cent. The success rate is even more pronounced when the figures for the total number of ships convoyed in the period, May to July, including the Scandinavian, Dutch, French coal trade and Atlantic convoys, are considered. Of 8,894 ships convoyed, only 27 were sunk by U-

boat attack; a loss rate of only 0.30 per cent. In comparison 356 ships sailing as independents during the same period were sunk by U-boats; giving a ratio between the independent loss rate and convoy loss rate of 18:1.

These meagre losses invalidated yet another objection to convoy that had been voiced at the Admiralty: namely that convoys would offer fat, inviting targets, and that a U-boat set loose in the middle of such a concourse of ships would be able to wreak tremendous carnage and havoc. In practice the U-boats found that they were forced to keep their distance by the escorts which, together with the zigzag course of the convoy, increased the difficulties in taking up a favourable position for a torpedo attack. More often than not the U-boat commander found that he had only the chance of a 'browning shot' (a random shot in the hope of hitting one ship in the convoy), which might or might not hit. Vice-Admiral Hezlet explains the problem:

'When all shipping sailed independently, U-boats were presented with a long succession of targets at which to fire, and they had time to take deliberate aim and then reload before the next victim appeared. With convoy there would be only one chance to fire as the enemy swept by *en masse*. While the selected ship was being attacked, the rest of the convoy would slip by unscathed and a second shot was seldom possible even if the escorts permitted it.'[7]

However, the limited number of ships convoyed on the Atlantic routes (all of which passed through the Western Approaches) up until the end of July (354 out of a total of about 3,000 ocean-going ships) did little to limit the amount of destruction that the U-boats continued to inflict on world shipping (Hezlet calculates that about 35 of the total number convoyed would have been sunk if they had all sailed as independents).

U-boat strength

By May the number of available *Frontboote* had grown to 126. Of these the average number at sea daily in May was 47, growing to 55 in June, falling to 41 in July. The shipping these boats accounted for rose (reaching the second climactic month of the

Below: The UA Cruiser *U155* (1,512 tons) armed with two 5.9in guns.

war in June) and fell almost in direct proportion to the average number of *Frontboote* at sea:

May	616,316 tons	(285 ships of 589,603 tons)
June	696,725 tons	(286 ships of 674,458 tons)
July	555,514 tons	(224 ships of 545,021 tons)

Once again the lion's share of this slaughter was accounted for by the U-boats of the High Seas Fleet flotilla (averaging 58 boats for the period): almost half (910,133 tons) of the total losses sustained in the entire three months (1,868,555 tons). And once again their attack struck at the heart of the ocean carrying trade in the South-Western Approaches. During June the boundary of the U-boats' operational area was pushed out into the Atlantic as far as the Azores, when the first of the large U-cruisers (*U155*) undertook her maiden war cruise. On her 104-day patrol (24 May–4 September), which extended as far south as the Azores, *U155* (Meusel) sank a total bag of ten steamers and seven sailing vessels grossing 52,000 tons mainly by gunfire and explosive charges. It was the longest passage (10,220 miles, of which only 620 were run submerged) made by a U-boat to date. Although the boats of this class were clumsy to handle and endowed with bad diving qualities, their phenomenal endurance and heavy armament (two 5.9in guns and eighteen 19.7in torpedoes) made them formidable adversaries, carrying the U-boat campaign far out of reach of the British A/S patrols. From May to July the Germans lost fifteen boats (seven in May, two in June and six in July); three of these were lost through unknown causes and two by accidents. Although this number represented the highest number lost in any previous quarter during the war, the exchange rate, i.e., number of ships sunk in ratio to each U-boat lost, was still highly favourable: 53 ships (or 124,570 tons) per U-boat sunk. This was not as favourable as the exchange rate of the previous quarter – 86.3 ships (or 194,524 tons) per U-boat lost – but was far more favourable than in the quarter of the second offensive (February–April 1916): 39.2 ships (or 88,586 tons) per U-boat lost. Moreover the fifteen boats lost were more than replaced by the 24 new boats commissioned by the Germans during the same period (May, five; June, eight; July, eleven); and, as Spindler points out, a proportionate rise in losses must inevitably accompany the higher the number of *Frontboote* at sea. On this basis he argues that the losses during the whole of 1917 *calculated as a percentage of Frontboote* were in fact no higher than in previous years: 1914 – 4.0; 1915 – 4.6; 1916 – 2.7; 1917 – 4.3.[8] The low percentage for 1916 is accountable by the fact that during a considerable part of the year the U-boats were not used in trade warfare in the waters around Britain.

In short, the losses suffered by the U-boats during the summer of 1917, were not as a result of any greater efficiency on the part of the British A/S patrol and hunting forces, as a major operation mounted in June graphically illustrates. From 15 to 24 June a special hunting operation ('the most elaborate operation that had as yet been undertaken against the German U-boats') was mounted. Thirty-five destroyers and fifteen submarines were concentrated in zones around the north of

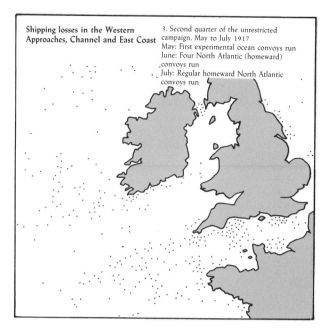

Shipping losses in the Western Approaches, Channel and East Coast

3. Second quarter of the unrestricted campaign, May to July 1917
May: First experimental ocean convoys run
June: Four North Atlantic (homeward) convoys run
July: Regular homeward North Atlantic convoys run

Scotland, which were distributed over the known outward and homeward-bound routes used by the U-boats. 'The results achieved', says Newbolt, 'only gave additional proof of the extraordinary difficulty of intercepting U-boats, even when their routes were known. The outcome was that U-boats were sighted 61 times by our forces on patrol, and attacked on twelve occasions. None of the attacks caused loss or damage, or affected U-boat activities in the approach routes farther south.'[9]

The course of the unrestricted campaign

The situation for Britain was growing ever more serious. Statistics prepared by Maclay, the shipping controller, in June showed plainly that by 1 December 1917, assuming a monthly rate of loss of about 300,000 tons of *British shipping* (from February until the end of June the average monthly loss of British shipping had in fact been 379,924 tons), there would not be enough tonnage left to import necessities into the country. For direct war requirement, Maclay computed, about 1,300 British ships were available for overseas imports. With a loss rate of twenty ships a week, 1,040 would be lost in one year; at 25 a week: 1,300; at 30: 1,560. As an average of 31.15 British merchant ships had been lost each week from February until the end of June, and only 300 ships could be constructed in the next twelve months, it was vital 'that by some means equilibrium *must* be brought about between losses and gains with the least possible delay'.[10] With the rate of merchant ship construction far below the loss rate, only decreased loss by means of more effective protection, i.e., the rapid extension of the general scheme of convoy could save the situation.

Ironically enough while Maclay, full of gloom and foreboding, was expounding the statistics of impending defeat, the German leaders were beginning to appreciate that their belief, which they had proclaimed to the whole nation, that the unrestricted campaign would bring Great Britain to final ruin within six months, was not going to be realized. As Admiral Hezlet explains:

'The whole of Holtzendorff's plan depended on terrorizing the neutrals and depriving the Allies of the carrying power of their ships and of their building capacity. The Germans did succeed at the beginning of the campaign in scaring away a very great proportion of neutral shipping from British trade. Diplomatic skill, hard bargaining and pressure exerted in various other ways managed, however, to get a great deal of this back before the end of the period and by July the entrances of foreign ships were only 20 per cent less than the normal. A consequence of this was that the U-boats had to expend a great deal of their effort in sinking neutral ships and only 400,000 tons a month, out of the average sinkings of 600,000 tons, was British. As a result the British merchant fleet lost a total of 2¼ million tons instead of von Holtzendorff's estimate of over 3½ million tons ... In spite of the fact that the U-boats sank what they said they would ... the tonnage available to the Allies was not reduced by anything like what they had hoped.'[11]

This, however, did not imply that the Germans had lost faith that the campaign would ultimately bring them victory; they were of the opinion that they had merely been too optimistic in setting a date for the inevitable outcome. Their redirected optimism was well founded (as Maclay's statistical appraisal bore out). The rate at which the *Frontboote* were being destroyed was below the new commissioning rate, while, conversely, the losses they were inflicting on mercantile trade was well above the world's capacity for replacement. The essential now was to redouble the U-boats' efforts in an all-out attempt to win the war before the American armies could be deployed in France in any strength. As it was deemed impossible for the rate at which each *Frontboote* could sink more ships in each patrol to be improved (for the quarter February–April, seven ships or 15,814 tons had been accounted for by each boat, falling to 5.5 or 13,066 tons per boat in the subsequent quarter), the only apparent solution was to get greater numbers of *Frontboote* to sea. To achieve this, the decision of February 1917, not to embark on a larger programme of new construction over and above the 51 U-boats ordered at that time was overturned. It was now (June 1917) 'adjudged essential for the prosecution of the war that everything that could be built in any possible way by 1st January 1919 be put in hand immediately, as the general outlook of the war gave no justification for any reduction in the most-committed work on improvements to, and increase in number of U-boats.'[12] Consequently, at the end of June 1917, a total of 95 new U-boats were ordered, for completion between the summer of 1918 and early 1919; an indication that the Germans were no longer under any illusion that the campaign could force a speedy decision.

German hopes now rested on a substantial increase in the reduction of world shipping, which, they believed, could be obtained by throwing a larger number of *Frontboote* into the fray. Britain's only hope rested on the attempt to thwart the German design by what appeared to be the only effective counter-measure – the extension of the general scheme of ocean convoy.

U-boat losses May to July 1917

Date	Boat	Commander	Cause and location
1 May	U81	Weisbach	Torpedoed by submarine *E54*: off west coast of Ireland.
8 May	UC26	V. Schmettow	Rammed by destroyer *Milne*: Thames estuary.
14 May	U59	V. Firks	Accident; ran on to German minefield: near Horns Reef.
? May	UB39	Küstner	Mine: east of Dover Straits.
19 May	UC36	Buch	Unknown. Presumed blew up on own mines: off the Needles.
21 May	UB36	Keyserlingk	Rammed by steamer: off Ushant.
24 May	UC24	Willich	Torpedoed by French submarine *Circe*: off Cattaro (Adriatic)
7 June	UC29	Rosenow	Gunfire of Q-ship *Pargust*: South-Western Approaches.
12 June	UC66	Pustkuchen	Depth-charges of trawler *Sea King* (of a hydrophone patrol).
7 July	U99	Eltester	Torpedoed by submarine *J2*: North Sea.
12 July	U69	Wilhelms	Depth-charges of destroyer *Patriot*: east of Shetlands.
19 July	UC1	Mildenstein	Unknown; presumed sank on minefield: off Nieuport.
26 July	UC61	Gerth	Accident, ran aground between Gris-Nez and Boulogne and blown up to avoid capture.
28 July	UB20	Glimpf	Unknown, presumed struck mine off Zeebrugge while undergoing diving trials.
29 July	UB27	V. Stein	Rammed by gunboat *Halcyon*: off Smith's Knoll (Harwich).

Analysis of causes

Cumulative total in parentheses

Rammed by warships	2	(8)
Rammed by merchant ship	1	(1)
Unknown	3	(17)
Accidental causes	2	(11)
Explosive sweep	0	(1)
High-speed paravane	0	(1)
Q-ship gunfire	1	(9)
Q-ship depth-charges	0	(1)
Torpedoed by submarine	3	(9)
Gunfire of small craft	0	(3)
Depth-charges of small craft	1	(1)
Mines	1	(6)
Destroyer depth-charges	1	(3)
Indicator nets	0	(1)
Total	15	(72)

The Struggle for Mastery
August to December 1917

The expansion of the convoy system

With an ever-increasing number of homeward-bound merchant ships being organized in convoys, the U-boats shifted their attack, during the latter part of July, to the unescorted outward-bound traffic from the British Isles; all of which still sailed independently. Previous to this tactical shift, 'the danger to homeward-bound vessels had been considerably greater than to those outward-bound', Newbolt explains, 'because they converged and were more easily found, because they were not in possession of the latest U-boat information and because they were loaded and therefore more valuable than outward vessels which were often in ballast. In April, for example, the risk attaching to the homeward-bound vessel was more than twice as heavy as that of the outward-bound one, but by August the proportion had been reversed.'[1]

With the U-boats sinking almost exclusively outward-bound shipping, and with convoy a proven success, the logical step of expanding the scheme of convoy to embrace outward shipping was adopted during the second week of August. The shortage of escorts was overcome by dispersing the ships of the outward-bound convoy when clear of the danger zone and the escort meeting up simultaneously with a homeward convoy to escort it through the dangerous waters of the *Sperrgebiet*

(prohibited zone). During August, eighteen outward convoys were run (from Milford, Falmouth, Queenstown, Buncrana and Devonport) and of the 219 ships convoyed only two were sunk by U-boat attack. A further expansion – South Atlantic convoys running from Sierra Leone (started 11 August) and Dakar (22 September) – resulted from the cruise of the U-cruiser *U155* in the region of the Azores. Finally, on 3 October, local convoys were commenced in the Mediterranean, followed by *through* Mediterranean convoys at the end of the month (i.e., sailing from the UK to pass through the Mediterranean bound for the Suez Canal and beyond and vice versa). By the end of November, 90 per cent of *British* ocean-going shipping was sailing in convoy. This brought about yet another shift in U-boat tactics.

The shift of the attack to inshore waters

Beginning in early October they had, by November, virtually abandoned operations in the Western Approaches to seek targets in inshore waters – the Irish Sea, English Channel, Bristol Channel and the coastal waters around the British Isles under ten miles from land where shipping continued to sail independently, either to the convoy assembly ports for outward-bound convoys or after dispersal from a homeward convoy. The latter

Right: The hulk of *UB77* moored in Portsmouth harbour. Nelson's flagship *Victory* is in the background.

dispersed off the North Channel, if 'north-about' Ireland; if 'south-about' they dispersed off the Smalls (for the Irish Sea and Bristol Channel ports) and off St. Catherine's Point (for the Channel and east coast ports).

During the pre-convoy period the U-boats had worked far out to sea, especially in the South-Western approaches. For example, during the period February–July 1917, 55 per cent of shipping sunk by the U-boats had gone down more than fifty miles from land, 25 per cent from ten to fifty miles and only 20 per cent under ten miles from land. In comparison, from August to December the situation had been entirely reversed with only 8 per cent being sunk more than fifty miles out to sea and 58 per cent under ten miles from the coast (34 per cent had gone down ten–fifty miles out – mainly accountable to the operations of the Flanders Flotilla in the confines of the English Channel). With convoy a proven antidote to the U-boats, it is incomprehensible why the Admiralty did not immediately institute interlocking coastal convoys. Of the British merchantmen employed in overseas trade, 33 per cent of those sunk by U-boats from October to December had occurred among those sailing independently in coastal waters from the embarkation ports to the outward convoy assembly ports, and more than 40 per cent among those that had dispersed from homeward convoys to make their way to the various ports of disembarkation.

In their lecture on convoy in maritime strategy, prepared for the Historical Section of the Admiralty, Lieutenant-Commander Waters and Commander Barley point out that 'Had coastal convoy been developed around the east, south and west coasts of England and the west coast of France ... the large number of independent losses would not have occurred. As it was, many ships were still being sailed independently in coastal waters although the loss rate of independent ships on all routes was ten times as high as that of ships sailed in convoy. Moreover, the inclusion of more ships in convoy would not have resulted in a significant increase in the number of convoyed ships sunk.'[2]

The statistical evidence in support of this statement admits of no doubt on this point. For the quarter August–October 1917, a total of 12,098 ships had been convoyed, of which only 49 had succumbed to U-boat attack; a loss rate of a mere 0.41 per cent. During the same period the U-boats accounted for 221 British independents, giving a ratio in favour of convoy of 15:1. However, the constant shifts in tactics, in which the U-boats kept probing for and attacking the weakest links in the shipping defences, i.e., ships out of convoy, resulted in the sinking of 2,009,881 tons of shipping in the 5-month period August–December, or a monthly average of 401,976 tons. The monthly breakdown with the British figures in parentheses are:

August	472,372 tons	(186 ships of 509,142 tons)
September	353,602 tons	(158 ships of 338,242 tons)
October	466,542 tons	(159 ships of 448,923 tons)
November	302,599 tons	(126 ships of 289,095 tons)
December	414,766 tons	(160 ships of 382,060 tons)

Flotilla dispositions of *Frontboote*, February to December 1917

War losses are marked with an asterisk; dates boats joined flotillas are in parentheses

High Seas Fleet Flotillas (*U-boote der Hochseeflotte*)
Führer der U-boote: Fregattenkapitän und Kommodore Bauer. On 5 June 1917, Bauer was replaced by Befehlshaber (Commander-in-Chief) der U-boote (B.d.U.): Kapitän zur See und Kommodore Andreas Michelsen

I. U-Flotille
Chef: Kapitänleutnant Pasquay
U71, U75*, U78, U79, U80, UC29*, UC30*, UC31, UC32*, UC33*, UC40, UC41*, UC42* (1 Jan 1917), UC43*, UC44*, UC45 (10 Feb 1917), UC49 (1 March 1917), UC50 (18 Feb 1917), UC51 (8 April 1917), UC55* (15 Feb 1917), UC75 (10 Feb 1917), UC76 (13 Feb 1917), UC77 (5 March 1917). UC45 sank in a diving accident off Heligoland on 17 Sept 1917, but was raised in 1918 and after refitting was recommissioned into the I Flotilla. UC50 (6 Nov 1917), UC51 (4 Aug 1917), UC75 (22 July 1917), UC77 (4 July 1917), were transferred to the Flanders Flotilla on the dates indicated. UC76, damaged by a mine explosion in the Bight on 10 May 1917, was recommissioned in 1918.

II. U-Flotille
Chef: Kapitänleutnant Von Rosenberg-Gruszczynski
U52 (27 April 1917), U53, U54, U55, U57, U58*, U59*, U60, U61 (15 Feb 1917), U62 (15 Feb 1917), U99* (7 June 1917), U100 (31 May 1917), U101 (10 July 1917), U102 (5 Aug 1917), U103 (26 Aug 1917), U104 (1 Oct 1917), UB21, UB22, UB27 (21 April 1917), UB34, UB35 (20 April 1917), UB41, UB61 (6 Aug 1917), UB62 (24 Aug 1917), UB63 (4 Sept 1917). UB21 (10 Sept 1917), UB22 (22 Sept 1917), UB34 (10 Sept 1917), UB41 (13 Sept 1917), UB61 (10 Sept 1917), UB62 (1 Oct 1917) and UB63 (30 Sept 1917) were transferred to V Flotilla on the dates indicated. UB27 (21 April 1917) and UB35 (20 April 1917) were transferred to the Baltic on the dates indicated.

III. U-Flotille
Chef: Korvettenkapitän Gayer
U19 (1 May 1917), U21 (4 March 1917), U22 (16 March 1917), U24, U43, U44*, U45*, U46, U48*, U49*, U50*, U87* (24 April 1917), U88* (18 May 1917), U89 (6 Sept 1917), U90 (10 Sept 1917), U91 (13 Dec 1917), U92 (27 Dec 1917). U24 was transferred to the Kiel U-boat training school, 11 Aug 1917.

IV. U-Flotille
Chef: Kapitänleutnant Prause
U28 (10 May 1917), U30, U66*, U67, U69*, U70, U81*, U82, U83*, U84, U85*, U86 (21 Feb 1917), U93 (5 April 1917), U94 (20 April 1917), U95 (24 May 1917), U96 (24 May 1917), U97 (27 Aug 1917), U98 (19 Sept 1917), U105 (3 Sept 1917), U106* (2 Sept 1917), U107 (21 Sept 1917), U110 (22 Nov 1917). U28 transferred to IV Flotilla from the Kiel U-boat training school. U30 became a training boat at Kiel, 19 Nov 1917.

V. U-Flotille (inaugurated on 10 Sept 1917)
Chef: Korvettenkapitän Jürst
UB21, UB22, UB34, UB41*, UB61*, UB62 (1 Oct 1917), UB63 (30 Sept 1917), UB64 (10 Sept 1917), UB65 (30 Sept 1917), UB67 (24 Oct 1917), UB72 (26 Oct 1917), UB73 (30 Nov 1917), UB75* (24 Oct 1917), UB77 (30 Nov 1917), UB82 (30 Dec 1917), UB83 (24 Dec 1917).

Above: The crew of *U35* bathing under a rigged-up shower on the upper deck on an October morning off Madeira in 1917.

On 1 Oct 1917 the Flanders boats were split into two flotillas:

U-Flotille Flandern I
Chef: Kapitänleutnant Hans Walther
UC4, UC11, UC14, UC16, UC17, UC21, UC50, UC51, UC56, UC77, UC78, UC79, UB54, UB55, UB56, UB57, UB58, UB59, UB80, UB81

U-Flotille Flandern II
Chef: Kapitänleutnant Rohrbed
UB10, UB12, UB16, UB17, UB18, UB30, UB31, UB32, UB33, UB35, UB38, UB40, UC21, UC47, UC48, UC62, UC63, UC64, UC65, UC69, UC70, UC71, UC75

Adriatic
Deutsche U-Flotille Pola
Chef: Korvettenkapitän Kophamel, succeeded by Kapitän zur See und Kommodore Püllen, 9 June 1917, under the new title of Führer der U-boote im Mittelmeer and Chef der Deutsche U-Flotille Pola (the old Mittelmeerdivision in Konstantinopel being incorporated into the Adriatic Command Structure).
U21, U32, U33, U34, U35, U38, U39, U47, U52, U63, U64, U65, U72, U73, UB43, UB47, UB48 (2 Sept 1917), UB49 (15 Oct 1917), UB50 (30 Sept 1917), UB51 (19 Oct 1917), UB52 (13 Oct 1917), UB53 (1 Nov 1917), UB68 (15 Dec 1917), UB69 (26 Dec 1917), UC20, UC22, UC24* (21 Feb 1917), UC25 (15 April 1917), UC27 (30 April 1917), UC34, UC35, UC37, UC38*, UC52 (23 May 1917), UC53 (27 May 1917), UC54 (29 June 1917), UC67 (29 March 1917), UC73 (6 June 1917), UC74 (17 March 1917). U21 transferred to III Flotilla, 4 March 1917. U52 transferred to II Flotilla, 27 April 1917. UB43 and UB47 transferred to the Austro-Hungarian Navy in July 1917.

U-Cruisers
U-Kreuzer Flotille (inaugurated on 27 March 1917)
Chef: Korvettenkapitän Koch (promoted to Fregattenkapitän on 26 April 1917)
U151 (21 July 1917), U152 (20 Oct 1917), U155 (19 Feb 1917), U156 (28 Aug 1917), U157 (22 Sept 1917).

Baltic
U-boote der Ostseestreitträfte U-Flotille Kurland (disbanded, 10 Oct 1917)
Chef: Kapitänleutnant Schött
U19, U22, UB20, UB27 (21 April 1917), UB30*, UB31, UB32, UB33, UB35 (20 April 1917), UB36, UC25, UC27, UC56 (14 Sept 1917), UC57* (6 May 1917), UC58 (9 May 1917), UC59 (21 July 1917), UC60 (1 Sept 1917), UC78 (21 March 1917), UC79 (7 Aug 1917). U19 (1 May 1917) and U22 (16 March 1917) were transferred to III Flotilla on the dates indicated. UB20 (26 March 1917), UB27 (19 July 1917), UB30 (16 Feb 1917), UB31 (23 Feb 1917), UB32 (24 Feb 1917), UB33 (24 Oct 1917), UB35 (19 July 1917), UB36 (23 Feb 1917), UC56 (11 Dec 1917), UC78 (21 March 1917) and UC79 (7 Aug 1917) were all transferred to the Flanders Flotilla on the dates indicated. UC25 (20 March 1917) and UC27 (1 April 1917) were transferred to the Adriatic on the dates indicated. UC58 (11 Dec 1917) and UC59 (21 July 1917) were transferred to I Flotilla on the dates indicated. UC60 (25 Nov 1917) became a training boat on 25 Nov 1917.

Constantinople
U-Halbflotille Konstantinopel
UB14, UB42, UB66, UC23. UB66 was commissioned into service on 15 Nov 1917, the day on which she sailed from Kiel for Cattaro, which she reached on 29 Dec 1917. On 10 Jan 1918 she sailed from Cattaro bound for Constantinople.

Flanders
U-boote des Marinekorps U-Flotille Flandern
Chef: Korvettenkapitän Bartenbach
UB6*, UB10, UB12, UB16, UB17, UB18*, UB20* (26 March 1917), UB23*, UB27* (19 July 1917), UB30 (8 Aug 1917), UB31 (23 Feb 1917), UB32* (24 Feb 1917), UB33 (24 Oct 1917), UB35 (19 July 1917), UB36* (23 Feb 1917), UB38, UB39*, UB40, UB54 (8 Aug 1917), UB55, UB56* (10 Sept 1917), UB57 (20 Sept 1917), UB58 (10 Oct 1917), UB59 (4 Nov 1917), UB80 (6 Nov 1917), UB81* (11 Nov 1917), UC1*, UC4, UC6*, UC11, UC14*, UC16*, UC17, UC18*, UC21*, UC26*, UC36* (3 Feb 1917), UC39*, UC46*, UC47*, UC48 (3 Feb 1917), UC50 (5 July 1917), UC51* (4 Aug 1917), UC56 (11 Dec 1917), UC61* (27 Feb 1917), UC62* (25 March 1917), UC63* (27 April 1917), UC64 (13 May 1917), UC65* (3 Feb 1917), UC66* (3 Feb 1917), UC68* (16 Feb 1917), UC69* (6 March 1917), UC70 (22 Feb 1917), UC71 (4 March 1917), UC72* (17 Feb 1917), UC75 (22 July 1917), UC77 (4 July 1917), UC78 (11 Dec 1917), UC79 (7 Aug 1917).

Although the situation remained serious for Britain and losses were still in excess of new construction, the worst was clearly over. Of the total tonnage lost, only 1,223,310 tons was British: a monthly average of 244,662 tons, which was 59 per cent short of Holtzendorff's 600,000 ton equation for victory. The shift of the attack to coastal waters resulted in another unfavourable factor for the Germans. Among the mercantile losses were an ever-growing number of smaller vessels used in the coasting trade, and consequently a decreasing number of losses among the larger, more vital ocean-going steamers which had previously been the U-boats' principal targets. For instance, the average size of the merchant ships sunk in the four months preceding the adoption of ocean convoy (March to June) was 5,084 tons gross. During the four months July–October this had fallen to 4,342 tons; as the process was continuous the average size continued to fall so that by September 1918 it was only 2,827 tons.

U-boat strength and tactical considerations

With the tide clearly turning against them, the Germans, rather than develop tactics to counter the convoy system, clung blindly to the conviction that they could redress the situation by getting ever greater numbers of *Frontboote* to sea. This belief is evinced in Scheer's report to Admiral Capelle, dated 8 November 1917: 'The U-boat enters a critical stage; the enemy is growing in strength and the convoy system limits out opportunities for attack to ever-decreasing locations and fewer sea routes … Experienced commanders are being lost, and new ones cannot initially replace them adequately … *The reduction in overall effectiveness can only be arrested by increasing the number of U-boats available for the U-boat campaign.*'[3]

This led to orders being placed for 108 new boats to be completed by 1919. Yet the statistical evidence contradicted the basis of this conviction – that a large number of U-boats at sea must inevitably account for a correspondingly larger number of enemy ships. For instance, the average number of *Frontboote* at sea daily during the last five months of 1917 was 48.8; they had accounted for a total of 2,009,881 tons of shipping during that period. In comparison, the average number of *Frontboote* at sea for the 5-month period March–July had been 46, yet they had accounted for 3,293,386 tons of enemy shipping: or a favour-ability factor over the success rate of the boats operating during the subsequent 5-month period of 27,902 tons per boat. The following table illustrates the point:

Month	Average number of *Frontboote* at sea daily	Total tonnage accounted for	Average per boat
March	40	564,497	14,112 tons
April	47	860,334	18,304 tons
May	47	616,316	13,113 tons
June	55	696,725	12,667 tons
July	41	555,514	13,549 tons
August	46	472,372	10,268 tons
September	55	353,602	6,429 tons
October	56	466,542	8,331 tons
November	39	302,599	7,758 tons
December	48	414,766	8,640 tons

Although a large fleet of U-boats was obviously a primary requisite for a successful blockade of Britain, this factor only held good if the tactical use of the boats was effective. It follows, therefore, that unless the Germans evolved a tactical counter to the convoy system, their U-boat fleet, however large, would be incapable of sinking enemy tonnage to the extent required to force Britain into submission. With the benefit of hindsight it is obvious that the only effective tactical riposte to convoy – which in its essential was simply a *concentration* of both merchant ships and their defending A/S forces – was a corresponding *concentration* by the attacking force (i.e., the pack – *Rudel* – tactics which was introduced in the early part of the Second World War). Hermann Bauer (*F.d.U.* until June 1917, when he was superseded by Kapitän zur See und Kommodore Andreas Michelsen with the title of Befehlshaber der Unterseeboote – Commander-in-Chief, U-boats) maintains in his autobiography *Als Führer der U-boote im Weltkriege*, written after the war, that he had in fact submitted a proposal in *April 1917* that foreshadowed the wolf-pack tactics in the Second World War.

'The first consideration was to counter convoys with the attackers similarly organized. The U-boats were, for this purpose, to be stationed either singly or in groups in such a way that a maximum number could mass for attack on any convoy reported. Consequently it was essential to make contact as early as possible with an approaching convoy. The manner in which the contact and concentration by U-boats would actually work out, and how it would subsequently develop, were questions to be solved by practical experience. A Headquarters on the west coast was required to try out this principle and thereafter probably for the duration of the conduct of U-boat warfare; such a base must be equipped with wireless personnel and instruments of the type for which the ordinary U-boat could neither find stowage space, nor which she could manipulate. The solution presenting itself seemed to be to use the *Deutschland* cargo-carriers which had been converted into U-cruisers (*U151–U157* class). These were vessels of over 1,500 tons displacement, having plenty of available space, very seaworthy, in short just as if specially built for the intended operation. One of these boats was to be stationed on the west coast, fitted with extensive wireless equipment and manned by picked, trained W/T personnel who had also been taught deciphering of foreign signals; she would be far out to sea and beyond the patrols, where she would have her W/T equipment in complete readiness by day and night … with her large carrying capacity, [she] could also be used as a depot-ship carrying oil fuel and provisions for the U-boats operating

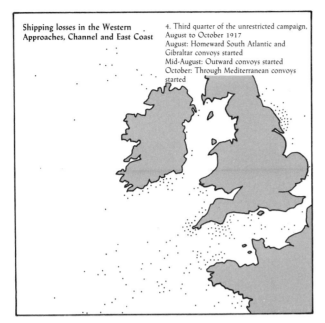

Shipping losses in the Western Approaches, Channel and East Coast

4. Third quarter of the unrestricted campaign, August to October 1917
August: Homeward South Atlantic and Gibraltar convoys started
Mid-August: Outward convoys started
October: Through Mediterranean convoys started

Shipping losses in the Western Approaches, Channel and East Coast

5. Fourth quarter of the unrestricted campaign, November 1917 to January 1918
Ocean convoy system fully developed

in the Atlantic. Her main task as an HQ boat was primarily planned so that the main line of advance of convoys would be reported by intercepting the wireless traffic between the Admiralty and the convoy Commodores. Then these courses had to be reported at definite and constantly changing times of transmission and in concise signals, on receipt of which each U-boat commander who considered he had an opportunity to attack the convoy could do so ... If such a procedure turned out successfully and kept pace with the expected defensive measures of the British, the military advantages of the convoy system would in this way be rendered nugatory; there was even a possibility that such a concentration of maritime traffic would expose the convoys to attack by U-boats to a greater extent.'[4]

Bauer's imaginative and perfectly sound idea was the obvious tactical answer to convoy – in short, meeting defensive concentration with a concentration of the attacking force – but, fortunately for the Allies, the Admiralstab rejected the proposal, preferring to cling blindly to the conviction that a larger number of *Frontboote* would save the situation. One curious point in Bauer's account is that he maintains he submitted his proposal in *April 1917*. This makes no sense, because the first trial convoy did not sail until 10 May, and it was August before convoys were sailing in any significant numbers. However, the Germans' intention to increase the number of *Frontboote* at sea was already being compromised by a dramatic rise in the number of U-boats being lost in action. During the last five months of 1917 a total of 37 boats had been sunk: an average of 7.4 a month, which was only 1.4 below the commissioning rate of 8.8 a month for new boats during the same period. The main reason for the sudden upsurge in losses was due, in the main, to the new H2 horned mine which the British had begun to lay in significant numbers during September. This new and vastly more deadly mine had definitely accounted for nine U-boats, and possibly sixteen (seven of the boats lost through unknown causes are all pesumed to have been mined). As the commissioning rate during 1918 would actually fall slightly to an average of 8.6 a month, any increase in the rate at which U-boats were being lost, over and above the 7.4 a month average for the latter months of 1917, or even if the latter figure could be maintained, would deprive the Germans of the one card on which they were betting so heavily. In comparison with the two previous quarters, the heavy U-boat losses during the last five months drastically reduced the exchange rate of merchant ships sunk in ratio to each U-boat lost. Compared to the exchange rate of the quarter February–April – 86.3 ships (or 194,524 tons) per U-boat lost – the ratio for the period August–December had fallen by 75 per cent to 21 ships (or 54,321 tons) per U-boat lost.

But despite the gloomy statistics filling the German side of the balance sheet, the British account was still tottering on bankruptcy. In May Sir Leo Chiozza Money had calculated that 4,812,000 tons of British shipping was the irreducible minimum necessary for the importation of food. The total available at the beginning of April 1917 had been 8,394,000 tons. During the subsequent nine months, 2,909,155 tons had been sent to the bottom (through all forms of enemy action), while only 917,000 tons of new shipping had been brought on to the register during the same period. The balance, therefore, of British shipping available for the importation of necessities at the end of December 1917 was 6,401,845 tons. But included in this figure was 925,000 tons of shipping that had been damaged, most of which would be out of service from between four to six months. This left only 5,476,845 tons immediately available: a margin of a mere 664,845 tons above the irreducible minimum. It is clear, therefore, that although the British had weathered the worst of the storm, the situation remained precarious, and the U-boats, despite the setbacks, still had it in their power to achieve victory in 1918.

U-boat losses August to December 1917

Date	Boat	Commander	Cause and location
4 Aug	UC44	Tebenjohanns	Accident, ran on to minefield laid by UC42: off Waterford, southern Ireland.
12 Aug	U44	Wagenführ	Rammed by destroyer Oracle: off southern Norwegian coast.
20 Aug	UC72	Voigt	Gunfire of Q-ship Acton: Bay of Biscay.
21 Aug	UC41	Foerste	Accident, own mines: Tay estuary.
31 Aug	U50	Berger	Unknown, presumed British mines: off Terschelling (Bight minefields).
2 Sept	U28	Schmidt, G.	Accident, explosion of munitions ship which U28 had torpedoed: off North Cape.
3 Sept	U66	Muhle	Unknown, presumed mined: Dogger Bank.
5 Sept	U88	Schwieger	British mines: off Terschelling (Bight minefields).
10 Sept	UC42	Müller, H. A.	Accident, own mines: off Cork.
11 Sept	U49	Hartmann	Rammed by steamer: west of Bay of Biscay.
12 Sept	U45	Sittenfeld	Torpedoed by submarine D7: west of Shetlands.
22 Sept	UB32	V. Ditfurth	Bombed by seaplane: English Channel.
26 Sept	UC33	Arnold	Rammed by PC61: St. George's Channel.
27 Sept	UC6	Reichenbach	Mine nets: off the North Foreland.
29 Sept	UC55	V. Lilienstern	Scuttled to avoid capture after accidental flooding: off Lerwick.
? Sept	UC21	V. Zerboni di Sposetti	Unknown, presumed British mines: off Zeebrugge.
3 Oct	UC14	Feddersen	British mines: off Zeebrugge.
5 Oct	UB41	Ploen	Mines (presumed German?): off Scarborough
7 Oct	U106	Hufnagel	Unknown, presumed mines: off Terschelling (Bight minefields).
14 Oct	UC62	Schmitz, M.	Unknown, presumed British mines: off Portland.
14 Oct	UC16	Reimarus	Unknown, presumed mines: off Belgian coast.
1 Nov	UC63	Heydebreck	Torpedoed by submarine E52: south of Goodwins.
3 Nov	UC65	Lafrenz	Torpedoed by submarine C15: off Dartmouth.
17 Nov	UC51	Galster	British mines: off Start Point.
17 Nov	U58	Amberger, G.	Depth-charges of American destroyer Fanning (convoy escort): off Milford Haven.
18 Nov	UC47	Wigankow	Rammed by P57: off Flamborough Head.
18 Nov	UC57	Wissmann	Russian mine: Gulf of Finland.
24 Nov	U48	Edeling	Accident, ran aground on south-west Goodwins and blown up to avoid capture.
29 Nov	UB61	Schultz, T.	British mines: north of Vlieland (Friesian Islands).
2 Dec	UB81	Saltzwedel	British mines: off Isle of Wight.
6 Dec	UC69	Thielmann	Accident, rammed by U96: off Cap Barfleur (Channel).
9 Dec	UB18	Neimeyer	Rammed by trawler Ben Lawer (convoy escort): English Channel.
10 Dec	UB75	Walther, F.	Unknown, presumed British mines: off Flamborough Head.
13 Dec	U75	Schmolling	British mines: off Terschelling (Bight minefields).
14 Dec	UC38	Wendlandt	Depth-charges of French destroyers Lansquenet and Mameluk (convoy escorts): Agean Sea.
19 Dec	UB56	Valentiner, H.	Mine: Dover Barrage.
25 Dec	U87	V. Speth-Schülzburg	Rammed by sloop Buttercup and PC56 (convoy escorts): Irish Sea.

Analysis of causes

Cumulative total in parentheses

Rammed by warships	5	(13)
Rammed by merchant ship	1	(2)
Unknown	7	(24)
Accidental causes	7	(18)
Explosive sweep	0	(1)
High-speed paravane	0	(1)
Q-ship gunfire	1	(10)
Q-ship depth-charges	0	(1)
Torpedoed by submarine	3	(12)
Gunfire of small craft	0	(3)
Depth-charges of small craft	0	(1)
Mines	9	(15)
Destroyer depth-charges	2	(5)
Bombed by seaplane	1	(1)
Indicator nets	0	(1)
Mine nets	1	(1)
Total	37	(109)

Finis Germaniae!
January to November 1918

The Dover mine barrage and the Northern barrage

Despite the proven success of the convoy system, it was still looked upon at the Admiralty as a purely *defensive* measure. In the Admiralty's opinion only *offensive* methods could ultimately defeat the U-boats. As mining was considered to be an *offensive* measure, the year 1918 opened with the Admiralty bent on a grandiose scheme to seal off the North Sea completely with two huge mine barriers: one across the Dover Straits and the other – a truly mammoth endeavour – stretching 250 miles across the northerly latitudes of the North Sea from the Orkneys to the approaches of Norway's Hardanger Fiord.

The first of these schemes to be undertaken was the laying of a deep mine barrage in the Dover Straits. The old mine-net barrage laid in the winter of 1916–17, stretching from the South Goodwins to the Snouw Bank (off Dunkirk), had proved to be utterly ineffective in denying the passage of the Straits to the U-boats. For instance, from 1 February to the end of May 1917 the large UBII and UCII types of the Flanders Flotilla passed safely through the straits on 122 separate occasions. Taking the year 1917 as a whole, British Naval Intelligence estimated that at least thirty U-boats (*of all types*) were passing through the Straits every month. Early in 1918 the mine-net barrage was abandoned; the buoys and nets were simply not replaced when they broke adrift. To end the porousness of the Straits it was decided to lay a vertical deep mine barrage of parallel fields, laid at differing depths of between 30 and 100 feet below low water, across the entire width of the Straits from Folkestone to Cap Gris-Nez. To make it impossible for U-boats to pass through the Straits on the surface at night, the whole area above the minefields was to be brilliantly illuminated with flares burned by trawlers and searchlights worked by old 25-knot destroyers, P-boats and paddle-minesweepers. The illumination in conjunction with a large concentration of patrol craft (80 to 100 vessels patrolled the Straits day and night) would, it was hoped, force the U-boats to dive into the deep minefields. Work began on 21 November and was completed by February 1918. It was constantly strengthened until the end of the war by which time 9,573 mines had been laid. In its final form (October 1918) the barrage consisted of twenty main parallel lines of mines, covering an area about six miles wide stretching across the entire width of the Straits, broken only by traffic 'gates' off the English and French coasts, and by the mid-Channel sandbars (the Varne and le Colbart). Results were immediate: 'marked, if not sensational,' is Professor Marder's assessment.

Shortly before midnight on the night of 19/20 December, the outward-bound *UB56* (Valentiner), attempting to slip

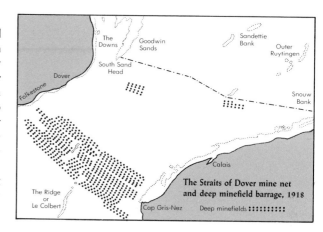

The Straits of Dover mine net and deep minefield barrage, 1918

Deep minefields ::::::::::

through the Straits on the surface, was forced to dive by the brilliant illuminations and blew up in the deep fields laid between le Colbart and Gris-Nez. Another two boats (*U109* and *UB38*) were lost in exactly the same manner (26 January and 8 February respectively) before the barrage was completed. During the remainder of 1918 another nine boats perished in the deep minefields of the barrage for a wartime total of twelve with one other, *UC50* (Seuffer), as a possible (her fate has never been definitely ascertained).

The strategic effect of the Straits barrage was far greater than the material. In his orders dated 27 January 1917, Bauer made the Straits passage compulsory for the High Seas Fleet U-boats. However, during February, numerous complaints were made by U-boat commanders of difficulties experienced while passing through the Straits. Instances are *U54* which became entangled in the old mine-net barrage and only escaped by dropping to the bottom; and *U85* which, diving to avoid patrols, snagged a mine cable and when she eventually surfaced found that she was towing a mine. Deciding that it was inexpedient to enforce an order which the High Seas Fleet U-boat commanders regarded as impracticable, Bauer once more made the Straits passage optional, despite all the attendant disadvantages of using the northerly route around Scotland. Michelsen (Befehlshaber der U-boote) overturned this decision on 1 November 1917, ordering the use of the Straits route once more, but with the proviso that the northerly route could be used when such conditions as fog, full moon, etc., made the Straits an unacceptable risk. But when the Germans became aware of the extent of the new deep mine barrage in the Straits, the commanders of the High Seas Fleet boats became so reluctant to use this route that only five actually attempted it during the whole of January.

Unexplained losses among boats using the Straits route, notably the failure of *U109* to return to base (destroyed in the barrage on 26 January 1918), caused Michelsen at the beginning of February to yet again leave the choice of route to the commanders of the High Seas Fleet boats proceeding to or from their operational areas. In practice the Straits route was now abandoned; the last High Seas Fleet boat to pass through the Straits being *U55* outward bound from Heligoland on 18 February. All of the Flanders boats, however, continued to use the route (26 transits in January and 29 in February) until March, when the majority began to switch their attack from the Channel and French coastal waters in the Bay of Biscay to the independent shipping north of the Humber off the east coast of Britain. Only five of the Flanders boats passed through the Straits in June followed by nine in July. But, by the beginning of September, Bartenbach, Chef der U-Flotille Flandern, finally had to acknowledge defeat (a total of eleven Flanders boats had come to grief in the barrage to date) and the Dover Straits route was finally given up altogether. The last Flanders boat to pass through the Straits was *UB103* (Hundius) on 14 August, outward bound for the Bay of Biscay. This same boat was also the last one to attempt the return passage (16 September), but this time she came to grief, being depth-charged by several drifters of the barrage patrol after betraying her presence with a track of oil from a leaking bunker, evidently caused by mine damage. To add to the dangers and difficulties to which the Flanders boats were subject, sporadic minelaying to the east of the Dover Straits and off the Flanders coast, continued right up to the end of the war, by which time a total of 24,739 mines had been laid. These fields accounted for a wartime total of four definite kills (*UC3*, *UC7*, *UB39*, *UC14*) and eight possibles.

Parenthetically, it must be mentioned that the much acclaimed Zeebrugge raid, carried out on 23 April, with the object of bottling-up the Flanders boats by sinking old cruisers as blockships in the harbour entrances of Zeebrugge and Ostend, although a partial success (only the narrow harbour entrance at Zeebrugge was blocked) did not affect the strategic situation one iota. On the day following the raid the small *UB16* left and re-entered the harbour by negotiating a gap to the east of the blockships. It was only the larger U-boats which had to be diverted for a short period to Ostend for entering or leaving. The trifling effect of the raid is summed up in the German Official History: 'the conduct of the war from Zeebrugge suffered only minor and temporary restrictions'.[1]

The second great mine barrage to be laid, designed to seal off completely the U-boats' egress from the North Sea was, in the strategic sense, an absolute failure. In comparison with the Dover Straits (about twenty sea miles wide and comparatively shallow) the area in which the Northern barrage was laid (from the Orkneys to Norway) was not only 254 miles in length, but the depth of water ranged from 400 to 900 feet. 'This went counter to the fundamental principle of mine-warfare', wrote

Korvettenkapitän Hagen in a post-war German naval monograph *Mine und Seestrategie*, 'in that it was taken through the deepest area to be found in the North Sea . . . which is not only irrational but completely impracticable.'[2]

This enormous undertaking, which it was estimated would require 200,000 mines, was divided into three areas. The westernmost section, Area B, designed to block the Fair Isle Channel, extended from the Orkneys fifty miles to the eastward. The central section, Area A, stretched from the edge of Area B to a point 134 miles to the ENE; while Area C, the easternmost section, covered the remaining seventy miles up to Norwegian territorial waters off Hardanger Fiord (south of Bergen). The laying of the barrage was a joint venture of the British and American Navies. Area B (deep minefields only – to allow room for manoeuvre for the battlefleet) consisted *mostly* of American and *partly* British mines. Area A (mined to the surface) consisted *entirely* of American mines; while Area C (both shallow and deep minefields) consisted of *partly* American and *partly* British mines.

The American magnetic mine (Mark VI) was a new and unproved type. 'This type of mine', Admiral Sims explains, 'could be located at any depth and from it a long antenna (a thin copper cable) reached up to within a few feet of the surface, where it was supported in that position by a small metal buoy. Any metallic substance, such as the hull of a U-boat, simply by striking this antenna at any point, would cause the mine to explode.'[3] The advantage of this kind of mine was that it covered, because of the antenna, a greater area on the vertical plane than the orthodox contact mine, rendering dangerous an area from a depth of 200 feet up to the surface. Unfortunately

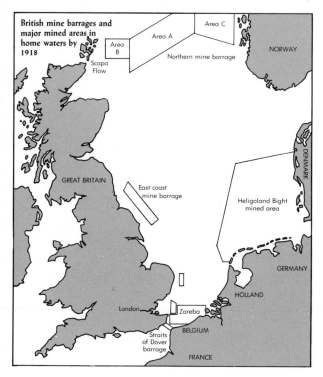

Above: *UB155, the last and largest of the UB coastal classes completed during the First World War. In this photograph, taken after the armistice, she is flying the French Tricolour and has been renamed* Jedon Corre *(1920).*

they proved to be far too sensitive and many exploded for no apparent reason, causing a series of spectacular counter-mining 'ripples' as whole lines of mines went up, one mine setting off a kind of exploding domino effect. Many U-boats passing through the barrage reported distant explosions of this kind.

Laying operations in Area B began on 3 March 1918; Areas A and C were not begun until 8 June. Although a great technical achievement (71,126 mines had been laid by the war's end), the results achieved were meagre in comparison to the enormous expenditure of time, effort and material. Although the U-boats passed through the barrage at the rate of 35 a month, only four U-boats are known to have been definitely destroyed (*UB127, UB104, U156* and *UB123*), with another two possibles (*U92* and *U102*); all these losses occurred during September. In addition, three boats were damaged by mine explosions in the barrage (*U86, U113* and *UB62*). The last boat to make the northward transit through the barrage was *UB86*, outward-bound for the Irish Sea, on 15 October. Returning boats crossed the barrage (Area C) throughout October without loss. The main reason for the Northern barrage's ineffectiveness is summarized by Michelsen:

> 'for some unknown reason many of the mines detonated spontaneously. This tendency was well known to our U-boats . . . Considering the number of mines lost in this way, one will readily appreciate that this barrage was far from being a complete seal to the North Sea's northern exit, and could have no more than a limited effectiveness . . . In fact, it might be said that the barrage was more of a danger to the minelayers than to the U-boats.'[4]

It must be added however that the barrage did have an effect on the morale of the U-boat crews as Gayer admits: 'It is not to be denied . . . that the threat this barrage posed was extremely unpleasant.'[5]

Another large mining scheme was carried out on the east coast. In November 1917, a deep minefield of 960 mines had been laid off Flamborough Head. This area was a favourite hunting ground for the Flanders U-boats; there being a

considerable volume of independent shipping having dispersed from the Scandinavian convoys rounding the coast on their way to the Humber and Thames. In June 1918, increased U-boat activity in the area, consequent on the effective blocking of the Dover Straits, caused the laying of an extensive East Coast Mine Barrage (9,049 mines), incorporating the existing field off Flamborough Head, running from this point NWN as far as the Tyne from fifteen to thirty miles off the coast. There is no evidence to suggest that any U-boats were either sunk or damaged in this barrage, and the U-boats continued to operate in the Yorkshire coastal waters with relative impunity.

The Otranto Straits barrage

One other barrage laid in 1918 also proved to be totally ineffective. To reinforce the mobile indicator-net barrage which the British had maintained in the Straits of Otranto since 1915 (it had accounted for only one Austrian U-boat), it was decided to establish a fixed barrage of mine-nets across the Straits, despite the proved ineffectiveness and abandonment of the mine-net barrage in the Dover Straits. The object was to deny the passage of the thirty U-boats, based on Cattaro, out of the Adriatic into the Mediterranean. Work commenced in April 1918, although the barrage was not completed until the end of September (some five weeks before the war ended). In its final form the barrage, which consisted of mine-studded wire nets reaching to a depth of 150 feet, stretched from the edge of a deep minefield laid seven miles off Otranto (on the Italian coast) across the 45-mile wide Strait (mostly 300 or 500 fathoms deep) to Fano Island (WNW of Corfu). Despite the fact that the waters above the barrage (the top of which lay submerged 33 feet below the surface) were heavily patrolled by destroyers and small craft, and American sub-chasers (purpose-built craft of only sixty tons displacement) patrolled the area to the south of the barrage where U-boats were expected to surface after the deep and prolonged dive to clear the Straits, the barrage was not surprisingly an out-and-out failure. From April to August the

Cattaro U-boats made 121 passages through the Straits, and, although the patrol forces made 58 depth-charge attacks, only one U-boat was lost. This was *UB53* (Sprenger) which, on 3 August, fouled the mine-nets and was badly damaged by two exploding mines. After surfacing Sprenger scuttled the boat to avoid capture.

The main reason for the failure of the mine-net barrage is simple to determine. Because the depth of the water in the Straits was too great (1,800 to 3,000 feet) for deep minefields to be laid (the main destructive agency in the much shallower Dover Straits), the U-boats were able to pass under the nets by diving to the limits of what their pressure hulls could stand (250 feet maximum). Apart from failing in its primary object of stopping the U-boats from getting to sea, the barrage had the adverse effect of increasing the U-boats' offensive potential once they were out into the Mediterranean. This was due to the fact that the strength of the convoy escorts were denuded in order to increase the strength of the barrage patrol. In November 1917 vessels employed as escorts for the Mediterranean convoys totalled 118 (sixteen destroyers, 33 sloops and 69 armed trawlers). When a large proportion of this already small number were withdrawn in April 1918, for duty on the barrage, it left a totally inadequate scale of escorts, with the result that *only* 35 per cent of all Mediterranean shipping could be convoyed, and these convoys could only be escorted by, at most, one sloop and two armed trawlers, more often than not only by the latter. This state of affairs in turn resulted in the overall loss rate in Mediterranean convoys being twice as high as those in Atlantic convoys; while the percentage of ships forced to sail as independents (650 in the month of March alone) gave the U-boats a rich harvest of easy targets. The man responsible for this misappropriation of available A/S forces was Admiral Gough-Calthorpe (CinC, Mediterranean) who, according to Commander Waters, was 'personally antipathetic to the convoy system, regarding it not as a scientific system of A/S warfare, for fighting the enemy in the most effective way, but as a purely

defensive palliative involving the mis-employment of naval forces'.[6]

Notwithstanding these disabilities, however, it was the convoy escorts (which to Gough-Calthorpe's way of thinking were being employed in a purely *defensive* role) that were responsible for the destruction of five of the nine U-boats sunk in the Mediterranean from November 1917 up to the end of the war. As we have seen, the 300 A/S vessels of the barrage patrol which, by the Admiral's definition, were acting in an *offensive* role, only accounted indirectly for one U-boat. Finally, the statistics of the Mediterranean convoy loss rate, although not as favourable as the Atlantic convoys, make a mockery of Gough-Calthorpe's contention that convoy was 'at best a deterrent, and not a reliable safeguard ... and that the true solution is to be found in an increased and unceasing offensive which should, in time, enable us to dispense altogether, with the need for these methods of defence'.[7] Of 11,509 ships convoyed in 1,657 Mediterranean convoys during the last year of the war, only 136 ships grossing some 250,000 tons were lost, while, in comparison, nearly 800,000 tons of shipping that sailed as

Top: *U135* of the 1,175-ton series U135–U138.

Above: *U105* leaving Heligoland harbour.

Right: *UB131* which ran ashore near Hastings on 9 January 1921, while under tow from Britain to France.

Right: *U117*, a UEII class ocean minelayer.

Right: The UA-cruiser *U157* holding up the Spanish liner *Infanta Isabel de Bourbon* on 28 March 1918.

independents in Mediterranean waters were sunk in the same period.

The efficacy of the convoy system

Gough-Calthorpe, however, was not alone in regarding convoy as a purely defensive measure; indeed it had become a platitude in naval thinking, that to provide warship escorts for merchant ships was to act essentially *defensively* which was *ipso facto* bad. What they failed to understand was that convoy contains the essential elements of not only the *defensive* but also the *offensive*, in that convoys gave A/S vessels increased opportunities to attack U-boats: the escorts being in very close proximity to the U-boats' principal targets. Indeed the convoy escorts had a large degree of predictability and probability in their chances of making contact with U-boats, compared with the purely accidental chances of contact inherent in the nature of the hunting and patrol forces, which were attempting to locate a largely invisible enemy intent on evasion in the vast expanses of the sea. Although convoy escorts only accounted for twelve U-boats from August 1917 to October 1918 (*UC38*, *UB58*, *UB18*, *U87*, *UB69*, *U32*, *UC35*, *U64*, *U89*, *UC75*, *UB110* and *UB30*), their score would undoubtedly have been much higher if more suitable craft had been employed. As it was, a very high proportion were either armed trawlers or slow over-aged destroyers. The craft most suitable, including fast modern destroyers, were chiefly employed in the A/S patrol and hunting forces.

Another factor detrimental to the 'kill' score of the convoy escorts was the fact that (and there is evidence to suggest this) a number of the commanding officers of the escorts were defensively-minded: content merely to drive away the attacking U-boat from the convoy rather than doggedly persist in counter-attack until a 'kill' had been made. Of course, it must be added, that without an effective under-water detection device they were seriously disadvantaged. The existing hydrophones were rendered useless by the cacophony of engine and propeller noise made by the ships in the convoy. But the valid point remains that convoy escorts could have accounted for more U-boats destroyed if their commanding officers had realized that their role was also essentially offensive as well as defensive.

The overall scale of escorts afforded to convoys was also insufficient (although home waters and Atlantic convoys were better protected than those in the Mediterranean). For example, of the 5,018 British warships in commission in October 1918, only 257, or 5.1 per cent, were employed as convoy escorts. In March 1918 the ASD expressed doubts about the efficacy of convoy, going so far as to suggest that the number of vessels employed as convoy escorts should be reduced by 30 per cent to strengthen the A/S patrol and hunting forces. These doubts would have been quickly dispelled if the ASD had plotted the number of merchant ships sunk each quarter against the number of ships sailed in all convoys. They would then have realized that as the statistical curve of *ships sailed in convoy* ascended, so the statistical curve of *ships sunk* descended, and that the

Below: *U126* after surrender and flying the white ensign.

Shipping losses in the Western
Approaches, Channel and East Coast

6. Fifth quarter of the unrestricted campaign,
February to April 1918

gradient of the latter was determined by that of the former. No such analysis was undertaken with the result that the ASD's attitude to convoy remained ambivalent to the very end of the war. Although admitting that convoy was a great success in that it afforded a great measure of safety to the mercantile marine, they clung to the dogma that *attack is the best defence* and that only purely *offensive* action by hunting and patrol forces could master the U-boat menace.

Any question as to the efficacy of convoy is dispelled in the final analysis. Of the 16,070 ships sailed in ocean convoys (including 'through' Mediterranean), U-boats sank 96, or 0.60 per cent. Of the 67,888 ships sailed in home waters convoys (coastal, Dutch, French coal trade, Scandinavian), U-boats sank 161, or 0.24 per cent. When Mediterranean local convoys are added, the grand total of ships convoyed is nearly 95,000, with losses of 393, or a loss rate of 0.41 per cent. 'Equally revealing', Professor Marder points out, 'is a comparison between the number of ships convoyed in the Atlantic and home waters in the February 1917–October 1918 period (83,958, of which 16,070 were in ocean convoys) and the number of independent sailings (48,861 for November 1917–October 1918: figures are not available for February–October 1917), on the one hand, and the losses inflicted on both types of shipping (260 and 1,497 respectively), on the other hand. Total losses were, then, 1,757, *with independent losses accounting for 85 per cent.*'[8] In short it was convoy, or more precisely the Germans' inability to develop tactics of concentration in attack to counter the convoy system, that robbed the U-boats of ultimate victory.

While continuing to operate as independent units, the U-boats found themselves faced with numerous tactical disadvantages after the introduction of convoy. Vice-Admiral Hezlet explains:

'The first effect of the convoy system was that the ocean suddenly seemed to the U-boats to be devoid of shipping. This was because, strange as it may seem, a convoy of ships was not much more likely to be sighted than a single vessel. A single ship will probably be seen by a U-boat lurking within ten miles of its track. A convoy of twenty ships is only two miles wide and so would be seen by a U-boat lying within eleven miles of the centre of the track of the convoy. Five convoys of twenty ships each were not, therefore, very much more likely to be seen than five single ships and were obviously much harder to find than a hundred independents. The result was that the vast majority of ships when in convoy were never seen, and the greatest advantage of the system was the difficulty the U-boats had in finding the convoys at all.'[9]

When a U-boat commander did sight a convoy, he then had to overcome the difficulty of obtaining a favourable position for attack without exposing his presence to the escorts and inviting an inevitable counter-attack. If he were not well before the convoy's beam on first sighting, the U-boat's low submerged speed made it unlikely that the commander would be able to obtain a favourable position without surfacing to make use of higher speed, with which to manoeuvre ahead of the convoy, and run the risk of being sighted. If such a position were successfully obtained (attacks were made from about 700 yards) further difficulties presented themselves, as Commander Waters explains:

'... attacking a ship in convoy is one of the most difficult and most dangerous operations of war ... This is because a U-boat can sink a ship only by attacking her within a peripheral attack area whose radii are determined largely by the U-boat's weapon performance and relative speed of attack. If a surface A/S escort is disposed around a convoy at the probable U-boat attack range and an air escort is present, in order to sink a ship the U-boat commander must penetrate the defence perimeter; concentrate on attacking the ship and not on evading the escorts and aircraft; must remain in the attack area long enough to identify, aim and fire at a target successfully; yet, when attacking must avoid betraying his presence to the surface and air escorts although they are trained and disposed to anticipate attack; must betray his presence by a successful attack, and will probably betray it by an abortive one; yet, if not sunk before, must withdraw from the scene of the attack in the presence of alerted surface and air escorts operating within the probable range of detection and of counter-attack. Attacking unescorted ships [independents] ... is a much less hazardous operation, the U-boat commander has fewer diverse problems to attempt to solve concurrently and fewer distractions.'[10]

These difficulties are illustrated by the fact that during the 18-month period June 1917–November 1918, of the hundreds of convoys that were run, the U-boats only achieved 84 successful attacks on convoys, and in 69 of these instances only one ship was sunk. Each war cruise by individual boats was also rendered less productive because the convoy escorts gave them far fewer opportunities to attack with gunfire. For obvious reasons the U-boat commanders were forced to resort to submerged torpedo attacks. This restricted the number of attacks to the limited number of torpedoes carried (twelve in the *Mittel-U* classes). Faced with these unresolved and debilitative problems, the majority of U-boat commanders continued to concentrate their attack in British coastal waters; particularly in the Irish Sea, Bristol Channel and off the south and east coasts of England. In these waters a rich harvest was still to be reaped among large ocean-going independents, sailing to the convoy assembly ports or after dispersal from homeward convoys, along with a host of smaller vessels engaged in coastal trade. The absence of any interlocking coastal convoys resulted directly in the loss of 375 ships grossing 779,216 tons, which was 59.9 per cent of the grand total of 622 ships of 1,299,647 tons sunk by U-boats from January to April 1918 in all theatres (a monthly average of 324,911 tons):

January	(160)	295,630 tons	(123 ships of 302,088 tons)
February	(138)	335,202 tons	(115 ships of 318,174 tons)
March	(190)	368,746 tons	(169 ships of 244,814 tons)
April	(134)	300,069 tons	(112 ships of 273,355 tons)

These figures represent a slight decrease of 59,466 tons on the monthly average sunk in the previous 4-month period (September–December 1917). More importantly, of the grand total only 817,569 tons was British shipping, or a monthly average of 204,392 tons (approximately one-third of Holtzendorff's equation for victory). When the 320,000 gross tons of new British shipping, brought on to the register for the quarter January–March 1918, is deducted, the effective monthly average is reduced to a mere 124,392 tons, or less than a quarter of Holtzendorff's demand.

Part of the reason for the overall decline in the rate of sinkings was the substantial reduction of losses (117,125 tons in 1918) incurred by the minefields laid by the UC and UE minelayers which had peaked in 1917 (532,272 tons). The reason for this reduction is explained by Professor Marder: 'Convoy was in itself almost a complete antidote to the German mining operations ... for the simple reason that ships were under continuous operational control of naval vessels with the latest information as to where mines had been discovered or were suspected. As a consequence, ships in convoy could be diverted around or stopped from entering minefields.'[11] Throughout the war the Germans had laid 11,000 mines in 1,360 groups in British home waters, and these had accounted for a total of 1,224,225 tons of British, Allied and neutral shipping.

Hopes of the *Unterseeboote* forcing a decision at sea were obviously rapidly slipping away. A fact made all the more obvious when the losses suffered by the U-boats – 24 from January to April – are compared with the commissioning rate of 27 new boats during the same period. This dealt a severe blow to the Germans' efforts to get a higher monthly average of *Frontboote* to sea; their conviction remaining unshaken that this factor alone would stem the tide that was clearly flowing against them with ever-gathering strength. High losses and an average commissioning rate of only 6.4 boats during the first four months of 1918, resulted in the daily number of *Frontboote* at sea actually falling from 49.5 (September–December) to an average of 45. One of the reasons for the high losses of U-boats during this period was, that by operating in the constricted area

Left: Minelayer *UC 56* (UCII class) in the Spanish port of Santander on 24 May 1918. She was interned there after suffering damage and taking refuge.

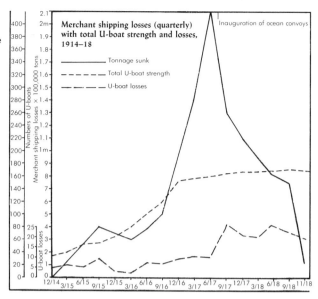

Merchant shipping losses (quarterly) with total U-boat strength and losses, 1914–18

— Tonnage sunk
--- Total U-boat strength
-·- U-boat losses

Inauguration of ocean convoys

Left: *UC100*, a UCIII class of coastal minelayer.

Left: *UC172* of the UCIII 427-ton series *UC65–UC73*.

of British coastal waters, they sacrificed a very great deal of their evasive capabilities which operations in the vast expanses of deeper waters afforded. This factor gave much greater potency to the otherwise relatively impotent patrol forces, which accounted for six U-boats in the North Channel and the St. Georges Channel entrances to the Irish Sea. A further six boat (*U109*, *UB38*, *UB58*, *UB54*, *UB33* and *UB55*) were lost in the deep minefields of the Dover Barrage.

The institution of coastal convoys

All hopes of the U-boats forcing a decision finally evaporated when coastal convoys were instituted in the areas where losses among independents was highest. From June onwards the proportion of ships sailed in coastal convoys increased until practically the whole of the trade on the east coast and Irish Sea was included. Once again as the statistical curve of *ships in coastal convoy* ascended so the curve of *losses* decreased, while losses among the few ships that proceeded out of convoy remained high. Of the 16,102 ships that sailed in east coast convoys during 1918, a mere 35 (or 0.2 per cent) were lost to U-boat attack. The relative immunity of the coastal convoys was due in part to the emphasis in the A/S air effort being shifted from 'area patrol' to 'close convoy escort' which became effective in July 1918. Of a total of 564 aeroplanes, seaplanes and airships employed on A/S operations in home waters, an average of 310 were engaged daily to provide A/S convoy escort cover. During the last five months of the war this force flew a total of 83,807 hours, sighted 167 U-boats and attacked in 115 instances; and, although they did not sink any U-boats, their attacks did manage to frustrate all but six of the daylight attacks made by U-boats against the coastal convoys, only two of which were successful.

The combination of coastal convoy and effective air cover had a profound influence on both U-boat strategy and tactics.

The strategic effect was that the U-boats abandoned in large measure, although not entirely, the concentration of their forces in British coastal waters, and reverted to their old deep water hunting ground in the Western Approaches, which was beyond the range of existing maritime aircraft. ('The difficulties of interception in these wider waters being preferred to the danger of air attack inshore.') Tactically, to avert air attack the U-boats resorted increasingly to night attacks. Indeed it became the predominant form of attack in the closing months of the war, by which time the percentage had reached almost two-thirds. Night attacks had other advantages as Rear-Admiral Bellairs explains:

'Night attacks were the initial, and perhaps logical, reaction to the introduction and expansion of air escort ... for convoys in 1918. Night surface attacks, while usually freeing the U-boats from the attentions of air escorts, also enabled them to exploit their relatively high surface speed, and to make the most of the difficulty the surface escorts always experienced in sighting the low silhouette of a U-boat in the darkness near a convoy. Moreover the U-boats' own powers for observation in a night attack were increased by using the surface tactics.'[12]

With the last weak link in the British defences tightened, the rate of world shipping losses from U-boat attack began to decline steeply:

May	(139)	296,558 tons	(112 ships of 294,019 tons)
June	(110)	268,505 tons	(101 ships of 252,637 tons)
July	(113)	280,820 tons	(95 ships of 259,901 tons)
August	(154)	310,180 tons	(104 ships of 278,876 tons)
September	(91)	171,972 tons	(79 ships of 186,600 tons)
October	(73)	116,237 tons	(52 ships of 112,427 tons)
November	(3)	10,233 tons	(15 ships of 26,857 tons)

This steep decline sounded the death-knell of the U-boat campaign, for as the downward curve of sinkings fell it crossed the upward curve of British mercantile construction: new shipping brought on to the register for the period April to October exceeded the tonnage sunk by 202,933 tons.

The failure of the offensive

Although heavy losses – 45 U-boats were sunk in the last seven months of the war – and the consequent loss in experienced commanders and crews played a part, it was, unquestionably, the Germans' inability to develop viable tactics with which to defeat the convoy system that resulted in the failure of the U-boat campaign to starve Britain into submission.

Although the Germans had perceived that the convoy system had proved to be the decisive manoeuvre in the struggle at sea, they made only one feeble attempt to disrupt it. From 10 to 25 May, six boats (*U103*, *U70*, *U55*, *U94*, *U43* and *UB72*) gathered off the approaches to the English Channel with the object of attacking the convoys that passed through the area. This 'concentration' should not be confused with pack tactics, as the boats, although in wireless contact with one another and under the direction of Kapitänleutnant Rücker in *U103*, were widely separated over a large area. Only two of the six boats made contact with the convoys. Of these *U103* was rammed by the troop transport *Olympic* and sunk before she could launch an attack (12 May), and *U70* failed to sink a single vessel. The latter boat ran in with convoy HS38, comprised of 35 merchant ships formed up in nine parallel columns and escorted by eight destroyers and three sloops. 'It would have been imagined that the U-boat commander had an exceptional opportunity,' writes Newbolt. 'It was a fine summer morning, the sea was smooth, and what wind there was blew from the west. The convoy covered a wide front and should have been a good target; yet all the German could do was to fire two torpedoes, which both missed, at the rear ship of the starboard wing column, and then get out of the way.'[13] One other boat in this group, *UB72* (Träger), was also sunk. She was caught on the surface at dawn on 12 May by the British submarine *D-4* which sent her to the bottom with two torpedoes fired at a range of 600 yards. That this kind of experiment was not repeated is comprehensible in light of the result. Nineteen homeward and eleven outward convoys passed through the group's operational area from 10 to 25 May without loss, while a third of the attacking force had been destroyed.

Having failed in their primary aim the U-boats also failed in another respect and, in so doing, sealed the fate of the German Empire. After provoking the United States into declaring war by unleashing the unrestricted campaign, the military and naval authorities promised the German people that the U-boats would prevent the transportation of US troops across the North Atlantic to the Western Front. However, this boast was made before the introduction of the convoy system, and as the US troops crossed the Atlantic in transports organized in heavily escorted convoys the U-boats did not have the tactical expertise to stop them. Moreover the tactical problems were purely academic, simply because the Germans did not possess enough *Frontboote* to maintain their attack on merchant-men in British coastal waters and the Western Approaches, and simultaneously launch a separate campaign directed solely at the troop transports which slipped past the U-boats' operational areas by disembarking in the French Biscay ports. From march 1918 until the end of the war, 2,000,000 US troops were transported to France, for the loss of only 56 lives when the 9,500-ton transport *Moldavia* was torpedoed on 23 May. Only two other transports were sunk – the 18,168-ton *President Lincoln* by *U90* (Jetz) on 31 May, and the 16,339-ton *Covington* by *U86* (Patzig) on 1 July – but these were both empty, west-bound ships making the return trip to the USA.

As the campaign to starve Britain into submission was clearly failing, it is arguable that the Germans would have been better served by switching the U-boat attack and directing it entirely against the US troop transports. The reason they did not is explained by Ludendorff:

'From our previous experience of the U-boat campaign I expected strong forces of Americans to come, but the rapidity with which they actually did arrive proved surprising. General von Cramon, the German military representative at the Austro-Hungarian Head-quarters, often called me up and asked me to insist on the sinking of American troopships; public opinion in Austria–Hungary demanded it. Admiral von Holtzendorff could only reply that everything was being done to reduce enemy tonnage and to sink troopships. It was not possible to direct the U-boats against troopships exclusively. They could approach the coasts of Europe anywhere between the north of England and Gibraltar, a front of some fourteen hundred nautical miles. It was impossible effectively to close this area by means of U-boats. One could have concentrated them only on certain routes; but whether the troopships would choose the same routes at the same time was the question. As soon as the enemy heard of U-boats anywhere he could always send the ships new orders by wireless and unload at another port. It was, therefore, not certain that by this method we should meet with a sufficient number of troopships.'[14]

The campaign in American waters

The only attempt to interfere directly with US shipping and indirectly with the troop convoys, was a minor campaign (more in the nature of a defiant gesture than anything else) carried out on the eastern seaboard of North America from May to

October 1918. Five of the large U-cruisers fitted to carry mines (*U151*, *U152*, *U155*, *U156*, *U140*) and one UC ocean-going minelayer (*U117*) operated in an area stretching from Cape Hatteras (North Carolina) as far north as Newfoundland. Apart from preying on unescorted shipping (mainly with gunfire), these six U-boats also laid mines at different points off the convoy assembly ports on what the Germans believed to be the convoy traffic routes. In all they accounted for a trifling 110,000 tons of shipping which for the most part consisted of small coasters and sailing vessels, the only notable exception being the armoured cruiser USS *San Diego* which sank after striking a mine off Fire Island (New York) on 19 July. They did nothing to impede the passage of the 2,000,000 US troops to the Western Front, whose arrival rendered the German military situation untenable. The final and desperate attempt to break through on the Western Front – the *Kaiserschlacht* (Emperor's battle) launched on 21 March – only served to consume the last of Germany's manpower reserves. Beginning on 8 August (the black day of the German army) when the Allied armies, reinforced by the great influx of US troops, began their counter-offensive, the Germans started a general retreat that marked the end of their resistance.

Conditions inside Germany

The German people on the home front were also at the end of their tether. The comparative effects of the British blockade of Germany and the counter-blockade by the U-boats are spelled out by Professor Marder:

'Whereas at no time in the war was there any widespread privation in Britain, though there were shortages and queues in 1917–18, it was quite different in Germany. There the growing demoralization of the home front in 1918 caused by the blockade, and which culminated in a revolutionary outbreak, had given the *coup de grâce* to the German military effort. The cumulative effects of food and clothing shortages, and the absence of any hope of real improvement proved too much for the German people.'[15]

The condition to which the German people had been reduced by the British blockade is illustrated by Fayle:

Below: The 512-ton *UB122* (UBIII class) was commissioned in March 1918 and accounted for only one ship, of 3,150 tons, in her short career.

'Apart from the restricted quantity of the food, its monotonous, unpalatable, and indigestible character, and in particular the terrible shortage of fats, deprived it of much of its nutritive value. The effects of a semi-starvation diet were aggravated by the shortage of beer, coffee and tobacco, and above all by the want of adequate clothing. The various substitute fabrics woven out of nettles or paper had proved exceedingly unsatisfactory, and a large proportion of the population were miserably ill-equipped to withstand the cold of the approaching winter ... These conditions, it must be remembered, had now been going on for a long time, and their effects were cumulative. To a population whose powers of resistance had been undermined by two years of persistent underfeeding, each reduction in the rations, temporary or permanent, was a heavier blow both morally and physically than when, in 1916, they had been nerved to endurance by the hope of speedy victory.'[16]

Defeat

Driven by their suffering the German people hoisted the red flag of revolt. To avert a revolution similar to that which had overwhelmed the Russian royal dynasty, the Kaiser appointed a new Chancellor, Prince Max of Baden, with authority to seek an armistice. Subsequently, on 5 October, the Chancellor asked President Wilson for the immediate conclusion of an armistice, to which Wilson replied that negotiations were out of the question while the U-boats continued to sink passenger ships. Despite Admiral Scheer's protests (he had relieved Holtzendorff as chief of the Admiralstab on 11 August) 'that to comply with this condition would be tantamount to a complete cessation of U-boat warfare', and that, 'in so doing we should lay aside our chief weapon, while the enemy could continue hostilities and drag out the negotiations as long as he pleased',[17] the Chancellor, to speed up negotiations, accepted Wilson's demand. Accordingly Scheer abandoned the campaign against shipping entirely and, on 20 October, ordered the recall of all U-boats at sea.

Earlier in October the Flanders Flotilla had been broken up when the bases on the Belgian coast has to be evacuated as the Allied armies advanced upon them. Ostend was evacuated on the 17th and Zeebrugge and Bruges on 19 October. Ten boats (three UC minelayers and seven UB boats) made their way to German ports, while four unseaworthy, obsolete or damaged boats were blown up to prevent capture. Later in October, when the collapse of the Austro-Hungarian Empire became imminent, the Germans were also forced to abandon their bases at Pola

and Cattaro in the Adriatic. Of the 26 boats in the *Deutsche U-Flotilla Pola*, ten boats that were undergoing repairs and could not be made ready for the long, perilous passage back to Germany were blown up. Of the sixteen that navigated their way safely past the Otranto barrage for the very last time at the end of October, thirteen made it back to Germany (arriving after the armistice). Of the other three, *U34* (Klasing) was sunk on the night of 8/9 November, depth-charged by patrols while trying to get through the Straits of Gibraltar; and *U35* and *UC74* sought refuge in Barcelona. As a parting blow on behalf of the *Deutsche U-Flotilla Pola*, which had sunk a total of 3,671,471 tons of shipping in the Mediterranean, *UB50* (Kukat) sank the 16,350-ton predreadnought battleship *Britannia* off Cape Trafalgar on 9 November. When Turkey surrendered unconditionally on 30 October, the four boats at Constantinople (*UB14*, *UB42*, *UC23* and *UC37*) fled to Sevastopol where they eventually surrendered on 26 November.

With the German Empire in its death throes, the Admiralstab decided to embark on one last desperate gamble in which the U-boats were to play out their last operational role. The plan was a bold variation on the unsuccessful attempts made in 1916 to lure the Grand Fleet over a U-boat ambush. The major difference in the 1918 variant was that this time the Germans were intent on a final battle *à outrance* even if the U-boats failed to reduce the Grand Fleet's numerical superiority. To provoke and draw the Grand Fleet south over the U-boat positions and finally into battle, the entire High Seas Fleet under the command of Vizeadmiral Hipper was to advance into the Hoofden and demonstrate its presence by attacking warships and shipping off the Flanders coast and the Thames estuary. Although Scheer expressed a vague hope that 'a tactical success would bring about a reversal of the military position and avert surrender',[18] the operation was in essence to be a 'death ride' of the High Seas Fleet. Hipper believed that 'an honourable battle by the fleet – even if it should be a fight to the death', was necessary because it would 'sow the seed of a new German fleet of the future', as there could 'be no future for a fleet fettered by a dishonourable peace'.[19] In all, 22 U-boats put to sea and took up positions off the east coast on the Grand Fleet's probable line of advance. The operation was set to commence on 30 October, but when the battle squadrons of the High Seas Fleet began to assemble in the Schillig Roads, outside Wilhelms-

Left: While in command of *U86* Oberleutnant Helmut Patzig sank the hospital ship *Llandovery Castle* on 27 June 1918. He then committed an act of inhumanity unparalleled by any other U-boat Commander in the entire war by firing on the survivors.

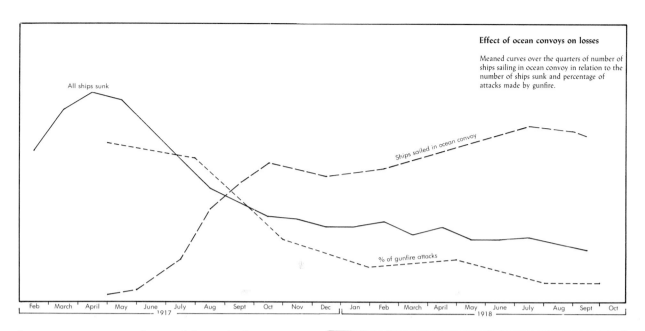

Effect of ocean convoys on losses

Meaned curves over the quarters of number of ships sailing in ocean convoy in relation to the number of ships sunk and percentage of attacks made by gunfire.

All ships sunk

Ships sailed in ocean convoy

% of gunfire attacks

Feb | March | April | May | June | July | Aug | Sept | Oct | Nov | Dec | Jan | Feb | March | April | May | June | July | Aug | Sept | Oct
— 1917 — — 1918 —

haven, mutiny in various forms and degrees broke out in many of the large ships, by crews who had no intention of being needlessly sacrificed for honour's sake. Hipper had no choice but to abandon the operation and disperse the squadrons to different ports in an attempt to quell the mutiny. Although the red flag of revolution was flying at all the main German naval bases by 4 November, it says a lot for the morale of the U-boat crews that they remained loyal and unaffected by the mutiny without exception.

Finally, at 05.00 on 11 November, the 1,586th day of the war, the Germans accepted the Allies' armistice terms and hostilities ceased at 11.00 that day. It was all over. 'The U-boat weapon had broken in the hand of Germany,' is Gibson and Prendergast's succinct conclusion. 'It had brought ruin and disaster instead of swift and decisive victory. It had made America enter the raging conflict on the side of Germany's enemies, whereas, by adroit handling, Berlin had at certain periods a chance of winning the great Republic of the West to her side . . . The U-boat was the weapon which indirectly caused her doom. It ranged the whole of the civilized world against her; the victory promised to the German nation by its agency had

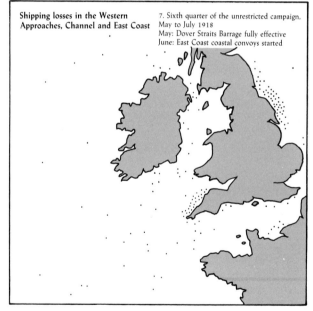

Shipping losses in the Western Approaches, Channel and East Coast

7. Sixth quarter of the unrestricted campaign, May to July 1918
May: Dover Straits Barrage fully effective
June: East Coast coastal convoys started

Right: The 821-ton *U161* armed with a 5.9in gun, the heaviest calibre of naval ordnance carried by German submarines during the First World War.

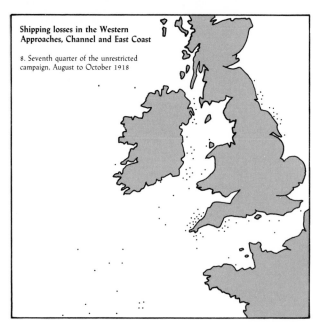

Shipping losses in the Western
Approaches, Channel and East Coast

8. Seventh quarter of the unrestricted
campaign, August to October 1918

Germans were still in possession of 171 U-boats at the time of the armistice, with a further 149 in various stages of construction. With such a fleet, Germany was obviously still capable of prosecuting the U-boat campaign with great vigour, and it is difficult to see how Professor Grant arrived at the conclusion, in his book *U-Boats Destroyed*, that 'anti-submarine warfare decisively defeated the U-boats during the last year of the war'.[21] That they were *thwarted* from achieving their objective by the convoy system is obvious, but to suggest that they were *decisively defeated* by A/S warfare is clearly overstating the case. As we shall see, the Admiralty's mistaken belief that the combination of their A/S measures *had* decisively defeated the U-boats during the Great War was to cost them dearly in the future.

Flotilla dispositions of *Frontboote*, 1918

War losses are marked with an asterisk; dates on which boats were transferred between flotillas are unavailable.

Befehlshaber der U-boote Kapitän zur See und Kommodore Andreas Michelsen

High Seas Fleet Flotillas *(U-boote der Hochseeflotte)*

I. U-Flotille
Chef: Korvettenkapitän Pasquay
U71, U78*, U79, U80, U117, U118, U119, U122, UC17, UC31, UC40, UC45, UC49, UC58, UC59, UC71, UC76, UB21, UB34, UB67, UB73, UB77, UB98, UB99, UB127*, UB130, UB132.

II. U-Flotille
Chef: Kapitänleutnant von Rosenberg-Gruszczynski
U52, U53, U54, U55, U57, U60, U61*, U62, U100, U102*, U103*, U104*, UB62, UB64, UB65, UB72*, UB80, UB88, UB89, UB90*, UB91, UB92, UB93, UB94, UB95, UB96, UB97, UB111, UB117.

III. U-Flotille
Chef: Kapitänleutnant Forstmann
U19, U21, U22, U43, U46, U89*, U90, U91, U92*, U135, U136, UB83*, UB86, UB87, UB112, UB116*, UB118, UB119*, UB120, UB121, UB122, UB123*, UB124*, UB125, UB126.

IV. U-Flotille
Chef: Korvettenkapitän Prause
U67, U70, U82, U84*, U86, U93*, U94, U95*, U96, U97, U98, U105, U107, U108, U109*, U110*, U111, U113, U114, U160, U161, U162, U163, U164, U165.

V. U-Flotille
Chef: Korvettenkapitän Jürst
UB21, UB22*, UB34, UB62, UB63*, UB64, UB65*, UB67, UB72, UB73, UB74, UB77, UB78, UB82*, UB83, UB85*, UB86, UB87.

Flanders Flottillas
U-Boote des Marinekorps
Führer der Unterseeboote in Flandern: Korvettenkapitän Bartenbach

I. U-Flotille Flandern
Chef: Kapitänleutnant Walther
UB21, UB54*, UB55*, UB57*, UB58*, UB59, UB74*, UB78*, UB80,

not been gained.'[20] Essentially true, but this assessment must be balanced by the fact that strategically Germany had no choice but to use the U-boats to the utmost of their potential if she were to have any chance of winning the war.

When the advance of the German Army through Belgium and northern France bogged down into a muddy stalemate, Germany was forced thereafter to fight, with the exception of Verdun and the spring offensive of 1918, a defensive war of attrition against the Western Allies. With a battle fleet too weak to challenge the Grand Fleet, which was the backbone of the British blockade, the U-boat was the only weapon left in the German strategic arsenal capable of undertaking an unremitting offensive and winning the war by means of a counter-blockade. That the unleashing of the *unrestricted* campaign in February 1917, was strategically sound, despite the attendant risk of provoking the United States into war, is beyond question. The results achievable by a *restricted* campaign could never have been consummate with victory. If the peak of sinkings which had been achieved in the spring of 1917 could have been maintained, Britain would undoubtedly have been forced into submission by the end of 1917 or the spring of 1918 at the latest. In any event, American intervention would have been too late to save the collapse of the Western Front which France could not have held alone.

That the German strategy ultimately failed is attributable simply to their inability to evolve suitable tactics with which to negate the success of the convoy system. For without convoy the combination of all the other A/S measures developed by the Allies during the war could not have prevented the U-boats maintaining, *ad infinitum*, the success rate achieved in the spring of 1917. Although a total of 178 U-boats were destroyed during the war (of which nineteen were lost by accidental causes) the

UB88, UB103*, UB108*, UB109*, UB115*, UB116, UB117, UC4, UC11*, UC17, UC40, UC50*, UC56, UC77*, UC78*, UC79*.

II. U-Flotille Flandern
Chef: Kapitänleutnant Rohrbeck
UB10, UB12*, UB16*, UB17*, UB30*, UB31*, UB33*, UB34, UB35*, UB38*, UB40, UB104*, UB107*, UB110*, UB111, UB112, UB113*, UC31, UC48, UC49*, UC64*, UC70*, UC71, UC75*.

Mediterranean Flotillas
Führer der Unterseeboote im Mittelmeer: Kapitän zur See Gratzhoff

I. U-Flotille Mittelmeer
Chef: Korvettenkapitän Otto Schultze
U32*, U33, U34*, U35, U38, U39, U47, U63, U64*, U65, UB52*, UB53*, UB68*, UB69*, UB70*, UB71*, UB105, UB128, UB129, UC20, UC73.

II. U-Flotille Mittelmeer
Chef: Korvettenkapitän Ackermann
U72, U73, UB48, UB49, UB50, UB51, UC22, UC25, UC27, UC34, UC35*, UC37, UC52, UC53, UC54, UC67, UC74.

Constantinople
U-Halbflotille Konstantinopel
Chef: Kapitänleutnant Krueger (until April 1918); Kapitänleutnant Adam (from April 1918)
UB14, UB42, UB66*, UC23, UC37.

U-Cruisers
U-Kreuzer-Flotille
Chef: Fregattenkapitän Koch (until end of Sept 1918); Korvettenkapitän Iyszka (from 1 Oct 1918)
U35, U38, U62, U91, U117, U139, U140, U141, U151, U152, U153, U154*, U155, U156*, U157.

U-boat losses January to November 1918

Date	Boat	Commander	Cause and location
7 Jan	U95	Prinz	Rammed by steamer: English Channel.
8 Jan	UC50	Seuffer	Unknown, presumed mine: Dover Barrage.
9 Jan	UB69	Klatt	High-speed paravane of sloop Cyclamen (convoy escort): off Bizerta.
19 Jan	UB22	Wacker	Mine: Heligoland Bight.
26 Jan	U109	Ney	Mine: Dover Barrage.
26 Jan	U84	Röhr	Rammed by PC62: St. George's Channel.
26 Jan	UB35	Stöter	Depth-charges of destroyer Leven: north of Calais.
? Jan	UB66	Wernicker	Unknown.
? Jan	U93	Gerlach	Unknown.
? Jan	UB63	Gebeschus	Unknown.
8 Feb	UB38	Bachmann	Mine: Dover Barrage.
12 Feb	U89	Bauck	Rammed by cruiser Roxburgh (convoy escort): off Malin Head.
10 March	UB58	Löwe	Mine: Dover Barrage.

Date	Boat	Commander	Cause and location
15 March	UB17	Branscheid	Unknown.
15 March	U110	Kroll	Depth-charges of destroyer Michael: off Northern Ireland.
19 March	UB54	Hecht	Mine: Dover Barrage.
26 March	U61	Dieckmann	Depth-charges of P51: St. George's Channel.
? March	UC79	Krameyer	Unknown.
11 April	UB33	Gregor	Mine: Dover Barrage.
17 April	UB82	Becker	Depth-charges of several drifters: North Channel.
21 April	UB71	Schapler	Depth-charges of motor-launch (ML413): Straits of Gibraltar.
22 April	UB55	Wenninger	Mine: Dover Barrage.
25 April	U104	Bernis	Depth-charges of sloop Jessamine: St. George's Channel.
30 April	UB85	Krech	Gunfire of drifter Coreopsis: North Channel.
2 May	UB31	Braun	Mine: Dover Barrage.
5 May	UB70	Remy	Unknown.
8 May	U32	Albrecht	Depth-charges of sloop Wallflower (convoy escort): between Sicily and Malta.
8 May	UC78	Kukat	Mine: Dover Barrage.
9 May	UB78	Stosberg	Rammed by troop transport Queen Alexandra: north of Cherbourg.
10 May	UB16	Lühe	Torpedoed by submarine E34: off east coast.
11 May	U154	Gercke	Torpedoed by submarine E35: off Cape St. Vincent.
12 May	U103	Rücker	Rammed by steamer: English Channel.
12 May	UB72	Träger	Torpedoed by submarine D4: English Channel.
17 May	UC35	Korsch	Gunfire of French patrol vessel Ailly (convoy escort): off Sardinia.
19 May	UB119	Kolbe	Depth-charges of American destroyers Patterson and Allen: west of Cardigan Bay.
23 May	UB52	Launburg	Torpedoed by submarine H4: west of Durrazo, Adriatic.
26 May	UB74	Steindorff	Depth-charges of patrol yacht Lorna: Lyme Bay.
31 May	UC75	Schmitz	Rammed by destroyer Fairy (convoy escort): off Flamborough Head.
17 June	U64	Moraht	Gunfire of sloop Lychnis (convoy escort): between Sardinia and Sicily.
20 June	UC64	Schwartz	Mine: Dover Barrage.
26 June	UC11	Utke	Mine: off sunk light vessel.

Date	Boat	Commander	Cause and location
4 July	UB108	Amberger	Mine: Dover Barrage.
10 July	UB65	Schelle	Accident: explosion, cause unknown.
12 July	UC77	Ries	Unknown.
19 July	UB110	Fürbringer	Depth-charges of several vessels (convoy escorts): off Yorkshire coast.
20 July	UB124	Wutsdorff	Depth-charges of several destroyers: North Channel.
27 July	UB107	Prittwitz	Depth-charges of destroyers and trawlers: off Scarborough.
3 Aug	UB53	Sprenger	Mine: Otranto Barrage.
8 Aug	UC49	Kükenthal	Depth-charges of destroyer *Opossum* and motor-launches: off Start Point.
13 Aug	UB30	Stier	Depth-charges of armed trawlers (convoy escorts): off Whitby.
14 Aug	UB57	Losz	Unknown, presumed mine: off Zeebrugge.
19 Aug	UB12	Schoeller	Unknown.
28 Aug	UC70	Dobberstein	Depth-charges of destroyer *Ouse*: off Yorkshire coast.
29 Aug	UB109	Ramien	Mine: Dover Barrage.
? Sept	U92	Ehrlich	Unknown, presumed mined: Northern Barrage.
9 Sept	UB127	Scheffler	Mine: Northern Barrage.
10 Sept	UB83	Buntebardt	Depth-charges of destroyer *Ophelia*: Pentland Firth.
16 Sept	UB103	Hundius	Depth-charges of several drifters: off Cap Gris-Nez.
25 Sept	U156	Feldt	Mine: Northern Barrage.
29 Sept	UB115	Thomsen	Depth-charges of several destroyers and trawlers: off Sunderland.
? Sept	U102	Beitzen	Unknown, presumed mined: Northern Barrage.
? Sept	UB104	Bieber	Mine: Northern Barrage.
? Sept	UB113	Pilzecker	Unknown.
4 Oct	UB68	Dönitz	Gunfire of steamer *Queensland*: off Malta.
16 Oct	UB90	Mayer	Torpedoed by submarine *L12*: in Skagerrak.
18 Oct	UB123	Ramm	Mine: Northern Barrage.
28 Oct	U78	Vollbrecht	Torpedoed by submarine *G2*: North Sea.
28 Oct	UB116	Emsmann	Mine: Hoxa entrance to Scapa Flow.
9 Nov	U34	Klasing	Depth-charges of (ex-Q-ship) *Privet* and motor-launches: Straits of Gibraltar.

Analysis of causes

Cumulative total in parentheses

Rammed by warships	3	(16)	Q-ship depth-charges	0	(1)
Rammed by merchant ship	3	(5)	Torpedoed by submarine	6	(18)
Gunfire of merchant ships	1	(1)	Gunfire of small craft	3	(6)
Unknown	13	(37)	Depth-charges of small craft	10	(11)
Accidental causes	1	(19)	Mines	19	(34)
Explosive sweep	0	(1)	Destroyer depth-charges	9	(14)
High-speed paravane	1	(2)	Bombed by seaplane	0	(1)
Q-ship gunfire	0	(10)	Indicator nets	0	(1)
			Mine nets	0	(1)
			Total	69	(178)

Tod und Auferstehung
(Death and Resurrection), 1918 to 1939

Surrender

Having been brought within measurable distance of defeat by the U-boats, and to ensure that this future source of danger should be nullified, the Allies demanded, in Article XXII of the naval terms of the armistice, that the Germans

'... surrender at the ports specified by the Allies and the United States all submarines at present in existence (including all submarine-cruisers and minelayers), with armament and equipment complete. Those that cannot put to sea shall be deprived of armament and equipment and shall remain under the supervision of the Allies and the United States. Submarines ready to put to sea shall be prepared to leave German ports immediately on receipt of wireless orders to sail to the port of surrender, the remainder to follow as soon as possible. The conditions of this Article shall be completed within fourteen days of the signing of the Armistice.'[1]

Harwich was chosen as the port of surrender and duly on the morning of 20 November 1918, 'The long, low-lying, sinister forms of twenty German submarines were seen being shepherded into captivity by the RN destroyers of the Harwich force.'[2] Anxious that there be no demonstration suggesting any crowing over a beaten enemy, Commodore Tyrwhitt, in command of the Harwich Force, honorably ordered the men under his command to maintain a strict silence when passing or being passed by German U-boats. 'Twenty miles from port, British crews boarded the U-boats and took them over from the Germans; and, as they passed the gates, the White Ensign was hoisted above the German flag.'[3] This humiliating almost funeral-like proceeding was repeated over the next eleven days by which time (1 December) a total of 114 U-boats had been surrendered.

This left the Germans with 62 seaworthy U-boats and construction continuing on another 149. However, when this retention of a considerable potential for U-boat warfare was discovered by the Allied Naval Commission, which visited Germany in December, the Germans were ordered to surrender immediately all the remaining boats which could put to sea or be towed, destroy those under construction and cease all further U-boat building forthwith. Eventually, the Germans surrendered a total of 176 U-boats. A further seven foundered *en route* to Harwich (U97, UC91, UC71, UC40, U16, U21, UB89) while the 149 boats under construction and ten old, unseaworthy boats were broken up in Germany. The surrendered boats were divided among the Allies: Britain 105; France 46; Italy ten; Japan seven; United States six and Belgium two. Of these France retained ten for incorporation into her fleet (serving until the

early 1930s) while all the rest were sold for scrap. To avoid this humiliation the Germans had originally planned to scuttle all their U-boats, but this was vetoed when the Allies warned that if Germany failed to surrender her U-boats intact the Allies would permanently occupy the island base of Heligoland. Such was the ignominious end of an élite which had almost wrested Britain's century-old undisputed command of the sea from her. During 51 months of war, the U-boats had sunk by torpedo, gunfire, mine and explosive charge a total of 5,282 British, Allied and neutral merchant ships and fishing craft grossing 12,284,757 tons, at the relatively small cost of 178 U-boats and 511 officers and 4,576 men. An exchange rate of almost thirty ships of 69,000 tons per U-boat lost.

Having suffered most and borne the brunt of the U-boat offensive, Britain pressed for the entire abolishment of submarines of all nations by international decree. But faced with strong French and Italian opposition (the ban was impracticable anyway because in time of war one or more combatant states could quickly rearm with submarines), Britain had to be content with Article 191 of the Treaty of Versailles (signed by Germany on 28 June 1919) which forbade '... the construction and acquisition of any kind of submarine, even for trade purposes ... by Germany.'[4] With the signing of the Peace Treaty it seemed that Germany's once deadly and menacing U-boat arm had passed safely into history and would never rise again. But within less than three years the Germans began sowing the seeds which would eventually bear the fruit of a far greater fleet of U-boats than they had possessed in the world conflict.

Resurrection

In April 1922 German (shipbuilding) yards, with the approval of Admiral Behnke, CinC, Navy, founded in the Hague a German Submarine Construction Office under cover of a Dutch firm NV Ingenieurskaantor voor Scheepsbouw (IvS). This office, directed by a former Chief Constructor at the Germaniawerft, Kiel (Hans Techel), with a German naval representative (Korvettenkapitän Ulrich Blum), was to provide an efficient U-boat construction staff to keep abreast of all technical developments by means of practical work for foreign navies. 'Mentor Bilanz', a dummy Berlin company (directed by the former Korvettenkapitän and commander of U64, Robert Moraht), provided the link between IvS and the German Admiralty. In 1927 a technical department was set up in Mentor Bilanz, staffed by personnel from the Admiralty Construction Office. This became the Admiralty's secret U-boat technical section. Mentor Bilanz, was liquidated in 1928 for internal political reasons and a new dummy company 'Igewit' (*Ingenieur-büro für Wirtschaft und Tecknik*), was formed to make preparations for a speedy and effective rebuilding of the German U-boat arm – in such a way that the Navy and Government would not be compromised. U-boat constructional drawings were prepared there in accordance with German Navy specifications. Data in respect of submarine developments outside Germany were supplied by IvS, and German naval advisers abroad.

In October 1924, Admiral Zenker replaced Admiral Behnke as CinC, Navy. He in turn was succeeded by Admiral Raeder in October 1928. On 15 November 1932 – before the National Socialists came into power – Reichswehrminister von Schleicher had approved a plan for rebuilding the German Navy. This included sixteen U-boats to be built in three stages up to and after 1938. Von Schleicher stipulated, however, that no U-boats were to be purchased or commenced until he considered the political situation favourable. The National Socialists came into power on 30 January 1933. General Blomberg subsequently replaced von Schleicher as *Reichswehrminister*. On 13 October 1933 the German Admiralty discussed a programme, known as 'New Construction Plan A', for the rebuilding of the German Navy, and it was decided that the U-boats already planned should be built. In addition, large U-boats were to be built as far as the available dockyard capacity allowed. A target of six small U-boats a month was to be reached as soon as the necessary facilities could be provided. Germany had already built and tested the prototypes of the U-boats now scheduled to be constructed. In 1927 an agreement had been concluded with the King of Spain for the technical section of Mentor Bilanz to build a 750-ton U-boat in Cadiz. After thorough trials this boat was sold to Turkey at the end of 1931. Under 'Plan A' two U-boats of this type were to be built.

A small 250-ton U-boat built in Finland in 1930 with the permission of the Finnish Government was the prototype for the first 25 German coastal U-boats to be constructed (Types IIA and IIB). This prototype was also used in 1933–34 to give practical experience to a number of German naval officers. On 16 march 1935, Hitler repudiated the Treaty of Versailles, announcing his intention of building up the German Air Force. Three months later, on 18 June, Germany voluntarily entered into a Naval Agreement with Britain, undertaking to restrict her naval tonnage in the ratio of 35 to 100 to the aggregate naval tonnage of the British Commonwealth. This was to apply to all categories of ships with the exception of submarines, in which Germany was given the right to possess a tonnage equal to that of Britain. She agreed, however, not to build beyond 45 per cent of British submarine tonnage unless special circumstances arose. (The increased tonnage allowed in the category 'submarines' was to be compensated by a corresponding reduction in tonnage of other categories of vessels, so that the overall ratio of German tonnage to British remained at 35 to 100.) Preliminary work on U-boat construction was so far advanced that eleven days after the Agreement had been signed, that is on 29 June, Germany commissioned her first U-boat since 1918. By the end of 1935 fourteen U-boats had been commissioned. On 22 July 1935, the German Admiralty laid before von Blomberg a proposal for a U-boat building programme of 48 U-boats to be completed by October 1939. During November 1935, budget difficulties necessitated deferment of eight boats of the 1935 programme, but in the 1936 and 1937 programmes this reduction was eliminated and one boat was added to the 1937 programme – so that the total number of boats intended to be in commission by October 1939, was raised to 49.

Germany entered into a second Naval Agreement with Great Britain on 17 July 1937, which stipulated, *inter alia*, that no submarine built was to exceed 2,000 tons in standard displacement or carry a gun in excess of 5.1in in calibre. The Signatory Powers also undertook to exchange information regarding their annual building programmes, and affirmed that all matters relating to submarines were governed exclusively by the agreement of 18 June 1935. But in the German Navy Estimates for the year 1938 allowance was made for the fact that

Left: *U1*, Type IIA coastal, the first of the second generation of German U-boats. Commissioned on 29 June 1935, *U1* was torpedoed and sunk by the British submarine *Porpoise* SW of Stavanger on 16 April 1940.

the U-boat fleet might have to be increased to parity with the British. This would require the raising of the U-boat tonnage from 22,000 tons to 70,000 tons. By May 1938, Hitler had decided that France and Britain must be regarded as potential opponents of Germany. He therefore instructed Raeder on 27 May to take all measures for bringing the German U-boat fleet up to parity with that of Britain. Raeder informed him that preliminary orders to achieve this had already been placed. A review of U-boat construction issued on 19 September 1938, gave the position as follows: 39 U-boats had been completed and 33 were building. The total of these (72 boats) represented 45 per cent of the British submarine tonnage. In addition, from May to August 1938, contracts had been placed for a further 25 boats, drawings and preparations completed for 26 boats and six had been projected. The overall figure of 129 U-boats thus built, building or planned corresponded to 100 per cent of the British tonnage.

Although these detailed plans had been made by September 1938, it was not until 7 November that Raeder informed Keitel (Chief of Staff, Supreme Command) of them, requesting him to arrange to notify the British Government accordingly. On 12 December 1938, the German Government notified the British Government of its intention to exercise its treaty rights and increase its U-boat tonnage to 100 per cent of that of Britain. A British Mission, led by Vice-Admiral A. B. Cunningham, left London for Berlin on 28 December to discuss matters arising from the above notification. The discussions were very friendly, but from the German point of view a mere formality, as the decision to achieve parity had already been taken and Germany had no intention either of withdrawing or excusing it. British public opinion, while deploring the German decision, recognized that it was nevertheless permissible by the terms of the Anglo-German Naval Agreement of 18 June 1935.

In view of the international situation in the latter part of 1938 (Czechoslovak Crisis, Munich Agreement, 29 September 1938, etc.) the German Admiralty had on 24 November reviewed the possibility of expanding their entire building programme. As a result of these deliberations a plan, known as the 'Z' plan, was drawn up on 16 December, provisionally approved by Raeder on 31 December as the basis for all further expansion of the Navy, and circulated in the German Admiralty on 6 January 1939. In this plan it was proposed that by 1943 the German U-boat fleet should number 162 boats; by 1945 – 230 boats, and by 1948 – 247 boats. By 10 March 1939, 72 U-boats had been built or were building; of these, 48 were in commission. One of the 175 further U-boats required to complete the 'Z' plan, contracts had been placed for 46.

On 28 April 1939, Hitler denounced the Anglo-German Naval Agreements in the *Reichstag*. He stated that he had been prompted to enter into and observe the agreements by a feeling of friendliness towards England, but he now maintained that Britain's attitude to Germany – both in the Press and officially – was one of active hostility. Alleging that the basis of mutual confidence upon which the agreements were built had been undermined by England, he now resolved to terminate the agreements. A note to this effect was sent to the British Government on 29 April 1939.'[5]

Britain's sleepy complacency in allowing Germany to re-acquire U-boats (which must be set against the backdrop of political appeasement of the era) was a direct result of the Admiralty's belief, persisting since 1918, that the U-boat danger had been mastered, and that U-boats would never again be able to present Britain with the problem she had faced in 1917. The foundation of this optimism was the Admiralty's erring belief that the A/S measures of 1918 in conjunction with convoy, had in the past and would in the future, provide an effective panacea (a case – to paraphrase A. J. P. Taylor – of men seeing the past when they peer into the future). This confidence was reinforced when Germany denounced unrestricted U-boat warfare in accordance with the London Protocol which Germany and the other Powers signed in November 1936 (that the Admiralty should pay any heed to this German avowal was in Churchill's

Right: *U9* Type IIB Coastal boat caught by Russian aircraft in Constanza on 20 August 1944 and sunk.

words 'the acme of gullibility').[6] Finally the Admiralty took comfort in the value of the new ASDIC submarine detecting device which had been under development since 1918. The ASDIC device, named after the *Allied Submarine Detection Investigation Committee* which had initiated the project, was capable of accurately locating the position of a submerged submarine by means of high-frequency sound waves passed through the water and which echoed back as a 'ping' from any metal structure they met. As the speed of sound waves in water is accurately known (4,820 feet per second) the direction and distance of a submerged submarine could be determined. The effective range of ASDIC was 1,500 yards on either beam, with an extreme, but unreliable range of 2,500 yards. Although this device was a great improvement over the next to useless hydrophones of the First World War, the early sets had the disadvantage of being unable to determine the depth of a submarine, and it wasn't until the summer of 1944 that a depth-finding set was introduced. In 1943 the term ASDIC was replaced by the newer, US-originated Sonar, which derives from Sound Navigating and Ranging.

The result of the Admiralty's backward-looking complacency of the 1930s resulted in the U-boats being able to bring Britain, once more, to the very brink of defeat. Convoy would no longer provide the degree of immunity from attack that it had afforded in the first war, because, since 1936, the new *FdU*, Kapitän zur See und Kommodore, Karl Dönitz, developing Bauer's suggestion of 1917, had been secretly experimenting with the concept of concentration in attack, which eventually evolved into *Die Rudeltaktik* or, as they are better known, wolf-pack tactics. In this respect Dönitz, had by the summer of 1938, arrived at the tactical postulate that '. . . The plain basic thinking of the battle against the convoy by U-boats is: essential effect against a *gathering* of steamers in convoy can only be realized when a *great number* of U-boats can be successfully set on the convoy . . . This is conditional on the U-boat in touch with the convoy *calling up* others. Then gradually ever more U-boats could come on to the convoy, its position would become ever more difficult, and also the strength relationship, the cover afforded by its *escort*, would become ever less, so that great losses from the convoy could be expected.'[7]

As for the Admiralty's confidence in ASDIC, they apparently overlooked the fact that in the latter months of 1918 two-thirds of U-boat attacks had been carried out on the surface at night, in which they exploited not only their high surface speed but more importantly their low silhouette in the darkness. Against such attacks ASDIC, which could only operate efficiently against submerged U-boats, would be useless. The Germans had not forgotten the value of this form of attack. According to Lieutenant-Commander Waters and Commander Barley, 'It was, indeed, before the war *publicly stated* to be the intention [of the Germans] to operate the U-boats in surfaced night attacks.'[8]

The vanquished had obviously learnt the lessons of the first war far better than the complacent victors, for the tactical combination of wolf-packs, night surface attacks and an aggressive unrestricted strategy would wreak havoc with the British defences. Shortly after the outbreak of the Second World War, during the first week of September 1939, Hitler is quoted as saying that behind him lay only an armistice, whereas before him was 'the victory we threw away in 1918'.[9] And once again it was the U-boats that were to come very close to obtaining that victory for Germany.

Left: *U11* (nearest quay), *U8* and *U9*. All Type IIB 278-ton coastal U-boats. The circular device affixed to the conning towers are radio direction-finders.

Action Replay
The first phase, September 1939 to May 1940

U-boat strength and strategy

At the outbreak of the Second World War, on 3 September 1939, the German Navy (*Kriegsmarine*, 1935–45) had 57 U-boats in commission. Of these 39 were *Frontboote* (fully operational), the remaining eighteen either being used for training purposes or running sea trials. Another six were in advanced stages of construction and would be commissioned into service from October to December. Despite the small number of *Frontboote* available the *FdU* planned to launch an immediate offensive against Britain's merchant shipping. The reason behind this decision was spelled out by Hitler from a draft composed by the Supreme Naval Command (*Oberkommando der Marine* = OKM):

'Our mortal enemy is England. Her goal is the destruction of the German *Reich* and the German people. Her method is not open war, but the mean and brutal starving out . . . of the weak and defenceless not only in Germany, but in the whole of Europe. [This, of course, was a reference to the institution of a British naval blockade of Germany identical with the strategy she had employed so successfully in the previous conflict.] The head of the British Government remained true to this historic attitude when on September 26th, before the Lower House, he declared that the present siege of Germany by England by means of a naval blockade was no different from a siege by land, and it had never been the custom to permit the besieged free rations. We Germans will neither allow ourselves to starve, nor will we capitulate.'

And in declaring a counter-blockade by U-boats, Hitler threatened: 'Every ship without respect of flag in the war zone around England and France exposes itself from now on to the full dangers of war.'[1] So it was that Great Britain and Germany for the second time in a quarter of a century embarked on maritime campaigns in which each would attempt to starve the other into submission.

With the lessons of the first war in mind, and well aware that the small number of *Frontboote* were inadequate to the task, Dönitz urged Generaladmiral Raeder (CinC, Navy) to begin a large-scale programme of U-boat construction without delay, that would equip Germany with at least 300 U-boats of the Atlantic type. When Raeder put the proposal to Hitler, he approved and plans were made for the construction of U-boats at the rate of $29\frac{1}{2}$ boats a month up to 316 above the existing strength of 57. Hitler refused to sanction absolute priority, however, because he was, at the time, more concerned with ensuring that all Army requirements were met. This resulted in a totally inadequate allocation of metals for U-boat construction and only thirteen boats were commissioned up to April 1940, by which time, due to war losses, the total strength had fallen

to 47. The lack of *Frontboote* in any appreciable numbers and Hitler's insistence that they operate strictly within the prescription of Prize Law (he was hoping that Britain and France would come to terms after the fall of Poland and did not wish to antagonize them with an unrestricted campaign: neither did he wish to antagonize the neutrals, particularly the USA) impaired the U-boats' potential and greatly softened the initial blow.

In an attempt to sink as many merchant ships as possible before the British had time to organize a convoy system, eighteen *Frontboote* (five Type IIC coastals and thirteen ocean-going Types VIIA and VIIB) sailed from Germany at the end of August to take up predetermined positions, covering a wide

Right: Raeder and Dönitz.

front across the North Atlantic trade routes, stretching from the North-Western Approaches southward as far as the parallels of the Azores and Gibraltar. Ironically it was one of these boats, *U30* (Julius Lemp) which torpedoed and sank without warning, on the evening of the first day of the war, the 13,581-ton Donaldson passenger liner *Athenia*, some 250 miles NW of Ireland. Through the dusky light and the restricted view of the periscope Lemp believed he was attacking an armed merchant cruiser. This caused the British to believe that Germany was embarking on an immediate policy of unrestricted U-boat warfare, and resulted in their expediting the institution of convoy (ocean and coastal) much sooner than they had originally intended (the first outward-bound convoy sailed on 7 September). As in the first war, outward-bound convoys were given an A/S escort of sloops and destroyers in the South-Western Approaches as far as 15°West. Here the escorts left the ships. These dispersed and proceeded independently to their destinations, while the escorts joined an incoming convoy. Before the convoy system could become fully operational, however, a very large number of ships continued to sail as

Flotilla dispositions at the outbreak of war, September 1939

The flotillas were named after famous U-boat commanders who were killed in action during the First World War.

Führer der U-boote Kapitän zur See und Kommodore Karl Dönitz (promoted to *Konteradmiral*, 1 Oct 1939 and advanced to *Befehlshaber der U-boote*)

I. U-Flotille (Flotille Weddigen)
Chef: Kapitänleutnant Hans-Günther Looff
U9, U13, U15, U17, U19, U21, U23 (all Type IIB coastal boats).

II. U-Flotille (Flotille Salzwedel)
Chef: Korvettenkapitän Schomburg
U26, U27, U28, U29, U30, U31, U32, U33, U34, U35 (all Type VII Atlantic boats apart from *U26* – Type IA Atlantic boat).

III. U-Flotille (Flotille Lohs)
Chef: Kapitänleutnant Eckermann
U12, U14, U16, U18, U20, U22, U24 (all Type IIB coastal boats).

IV. U-Flotille
In process of formation.

V. U-Flotille (Flotille Emsmann)
Chef: Kapitänleutnant Rösing
U56, U57, U58, U59, U60, U61 (all Type IIC coastal boats).

VI. U-Flotille (Flotille Hundius)
Chef: Korvettenkapitän Werner Hartmann
U37, U38, U39, U40, U41, U42, U43 (all Type IIC coastal boats).

VII. U-Flotille (Flotille Wegener)
Chef: Kapitänleutnant Sobe
U45, U46, U47, U48, U49, U51, U52, U53 (all Type VIIB Atlantic boats).

The following boats were either being used for training at the U-boat school based at the Baltic port of Neustadt, or were running trials: *U1, U2, U3, U4, U5, U6, U7, U8, U10, U11, U25, U36*.

independents, and during September a total of 48 merchant ships grossing 178,621 tons succumbed to U-boat attack. Of this total 43 ships (96.63 per cent) were independents, the majority of which were sunk in accordance with Prize Regulations. Only one ship (0.67 per cent) was sunk in convoy, while four ships (3.37 per cent) were sunk by mines laid by U-boats.

First attempt at wolf-pack tactics

On 7 September ten of the most modern ocean-going boats, which were disposed across the trade routes, were recalled; their places being partially filled by three relieving boats of Type VIIA (*U31*, *U32* and *U35*). The recall was made so that the ten boats might, after a short refit, resume operations in the Atlantic at the beginning of October. 'This decision', writes Günther Hessler, the German authority of the U-boat war in the Atlantic, 'was influenced by radio intercepts and agents' reports, pointing to the probable reduction of British traffic, followed by a large increase in October, with the formation of convoys.'[2] Dönitz's intention was to throw as many boats as possible against this traffic and employ, for the first time, the tactical theory of controlled pack operations against mercantile convoys. To this end it was hoped to have nine boats ready to sail by 15 October. The area designated for the attack was operational area *Rot*, west of the Iberian peninsula, where Dönitz (who had been promoted to Konteradmiral and *Befehlshaber der U-boote* on 1 October) hoped that the pack would fall in with one of the Gibraltar-UK convoys. It was planned that the pack, the boats of which would be proceeding at different times, should gather in the South-Western Approaches. However, the success of the operation was compromised before the boats even sailed from their bases, by a reduction in the size of the pack on account of *U34* and *U25* having to remain in dockyard hands much longer than expected because of mechanical problems, and *U47* (Prien) being detached for a daring attack on the British Fleet in Scapa Flow (which resulted in the sinking of the battleship *Royal Oak*). To make matters worse three boats, *U40*, *U42* and *U45*, were sunk before they could form up with the pack. The remaining three boats, *U46* (Sohler), *U48* (Schultze) and *U37* (Schuch) – the latter carrying Korvettenkapitän Hartmann, Chief of the 6th Flotilla, the tactical commander of the pack – were only capable, because of the pack's diminutive size, in scoring a limited success.

On 17 October, *U46* siighted a northbound convoy (HG.3) and called up the other two boats. From 16.30 to 20.35, in a position 300 miles west of Corunna, in individual attacks, the three boats managed to sink one boat each, grossing a total of 24,468 tons, before being driven off by aircraft. A second attempt at pack tactics, planned on the same lines of the first, also failed owing to the small number of boats available. 'This further comparative failure', writes the German authority, 'caused the U-boat Command to defer their attempts at planned concentration and instead to dispatch each boat to the Atlantic whenever it became ready for operations. Not until June 1940, were pack operations resumed.'[3]

Right: *U60*, Type IIC 250-ton coastal boat.

Right: *U42*, Type IXA, was sunk in a depth-charge attack by the destroyers *Ilex* and *Imogen* in the South-Western Approaches in October 1939.

Right: The victorious *U47*, under Günther Prien, returning to a hero's welcome after sinking the battleship *Royal Oak* in Scapa Flow.

Minelaying and torpedo failures

With the exception of these two operations, U-boat strategy and tactics during the first six months of the war differed little from those during the restricted campaigns of the first war: boats acting individually sought out independent shipping (mainly in the South-Western Approaches) or fired random shots at passing convoys. At the same time as the ocean-going U-boats sailed to take up their Atlantic dispositions, fifteen of the 250-ton IIB and IIC coastal U-boats from the 3rd and 5th Flotillas, took up positions in the North Sea and Hoofden to attack naval and merchant shipping and to carry out minelaying operations in the traffic lanes and harbour mouths off the east coast of Britain. During the autumn and winter 33 mining operations were carried out in which a total of 330 mines of the new magnetic type were laid. These fields would account for 37 merchant ships of 129,419 tons during the First Phase. Hampered by lack of numbers (the daily average of *Frontboote* at sea for the first six months was only 6.3) and the use of restrictive and discredited tactics of another age, the U-boats could hardly pose a serious threat to Britain's survival. To make matters worse the newly developed magnetic detonating pistol and the depth-keeping mechanisms of the torpedoes were defective.

'Many torpedoes were reported to have exploded prematurely at the margin of the safety limit (820 feet from the U-boat), these prematures being due to magnetic pistol failures. Besides rendering an attack abortive, a premature explosion betrayed the U-boat's position. In some cases these near explosions caused slight damage to the firing boat. As a readjustment of the magnetic fields of the pistol failed to remedy the defects, impact pistols were used from 2nd October onwards, and the more powerful effect of magnetic firing was lost. Trials ... also revealed that the depth-keeping mechanism was not functioning properly and that torpedoes were running anything up to 5¾ feet too deep. This defect had apparently been ignored before the war on the grounds that a small increase of depth was not important when using a magnetic pistol. But a depth correction of minus 6½ feet had now to be applied to torpedoes when using impact pistols. As a setting of less than 13 feet was impracticable in high seas, targets drawing less than 13 feet, such as destroyers, would escape being hit. From 10th November magnetic pistols were again used. Though Dönitz doubted the efficiency of the improved pistols, there was not much choice, since impact-firing was also unreliable. But even these modified pistols produced prematures and explosions at the end of the run.'[4]

Dönitz explained that these failures also affected the personnel. 'The inefficiency of the torpedo has had a serious effect on the morale of the U-boat service. At least 25 per cent of the torpedoes fired were failures. Statistics up to 6th January, show that 40.9 per cent of misses were due to this cause ... Confidence in the torpedo has been badly shaken ... The object always is to fire torpedoes from the most advantageous position, but owing to misses and torpedo failures, these bold attacks have often involved risk of losing the boat. It is estimated that these failures have lost us at least 300,000 tons of shipping ... It is bitterly disappointing for all concerned that, despite thorough peace-time training, the U-boats have not achieved the sucess they deserved, simply because of torpedo failures.'[5]

Disappointing results

As a result of all these problems the U-boats were only able to account for 250 merchant ships grossing 854,719 tons during the whole of the 6-month period September–February 1940 (a monthly average of 142,453 tons). The monthly breakdown of the figures have been derived from Dr Jürgen Rowher's *Axis Submarine Success 1939–1945*.

Even this score would undoubtedly have been much lower (despite Dönitz's belief that the torpedo failures had robbed the U-boat's of another 300,000 tons) if a greater proportion of Allied shipping had been in convoy. As it was '... the Allied policy of sailing ships of less than 9 knots and of 13 knots or more as independents, coupled with the policy of some neutrals of not sailing in convoy, accounts for the large number of independent ships available for sinking at this time.'[6] Indeed 72 per cent of the total losses were independents and stragglers from convoy. Mines laid by U-boats in British coastal waters at the focal points of trade accounted for 14.8 per cent, while only 13.2 per cent were sunk as a result of U-boats launching individual attacks on convoys. As the plentiful numbers of easy targets in the form of independents would obviously decline sharply as the convoy system expanded, it was imperative, if the U-boats were to realize their full potential and become, as they had been in 1917, a deadly menace rather than a mere nuisance, that Dönitz's conception of pack tactics be realized and perfected as quickly as possible. But this development was dependant on two factors: a substantial increase in the number of available *Frontboote* and the total abandonment of the tactical restrictions of the Prize Regulations (for obvious reasons a pack attack on a convoy could only be carried out in an unrestricted mode). As the slow commissioning rate during the First Phase barely kept up with the loss rate, any immediate increase in the number of *Frontboote* would not be realized: in fact it was not until the spring of 1941 that Germany's total strength in U-boats would exceed 100. Not until July 1940 did Hitler give the U-boat construction programme the necessary priority in materials, and so enable the Navy to place orders for a com-missioning rate of 25 boats a month during 1941; and it wasn't until August that U-boat construction really got into its stride. 'The slowness with which the Germans expanded their U-boat construction had the most fortunate consequences for Britain.'[7]

Unrestricted warfare

Desperate attempts to get more *Frontboote* to sea, and protracted wrangling between the naval and political authorities over the issue of the politically motivated strategic and tactical restraints on the mode of U-boat warfare, were clear echoes from the first war. However, during the first war it had taken the Admiralstab nearly two-and-a-half years to persuade the German Chancellor of the necessity of an unrestricted campaign. In comparison it took Raeder (with Dönitz's prompting) only two-and-a-half months to convince Hitler of the wisdom of an unrestricted strategy. This process is outlined by the official historian of the War at Sea:

Monthly breakdown of losses

Month	Independent Sailings	Ships in Convoy	By mines laid by U-boats	Total
September	(43) 154,529	(1) 4,060	(4) 20,032	(48) 178,621
October	(16) 41,627	(12) 93,834	(5) 20,695	(33) 156,156
November	(16) 35,492	(6) 22,150	(5) 15,079	(27) 72,721
December	(25) 62,688	(3) 22,860	(11) 16,275	(39) 101,823
January	(42) 106,503	(3) 12,586	(8) 43,940	(53) 163,029
February	(38) 117,513	(8) 51,458	(4) 13,398	(50) 182,369
Totals	(180) 518,352	(33) 206,948	(37) 129,419	(250) 854,719

'Hitler's original orders to the German Navy, including the U-boats, to wage war only in accordance with the Prize Regulations, were not issued in any altruistic spirit but in the hope that, after Poland had been crushed, Britain and France – and especially the latter – would make peace. As soon as it was realized that this hope was vain, removal of the restrictions ... started. On the 23rd September, Hitler, on the recommendation of Admiral Raeder, approved that *"all* merchant ships making use of their wireless on being stopped by U-boats should be sunk ..."* As the immediate dispatch of a wireless signal in such circumstances was included in the Admiralty's instructions to merchant ships and was essential – if for no other reason – to the rescue of their crews, this German order marked a considerable step towards unrestricted warfare. Next day, again as a result of representations by Raeder, the order forbidding attacks on French warships was cancelled. On the 30th September observance of the Prize Regulations in the North Sea was withdrawn; and on the 2nd of October complete freedom was given to attack darkened ships encountered off the British and French coasts. Two days later the Prize Regulations were cancelled in waters extending as far as 15° West, and on the 17th of October the German Naval staff gave U-boats permission "to attack without warning all ships identified as hostile". The zone where darkened ships could be attacked with complete freedom was extended to 20° West on the 19th October. Practically the only restriction now placed on the U-boats concerned attacks on liners and, on 17th of November, they too were allowed to be attacked without warning if "clearly identifiable as hostile". Although the enemy this time carefully avoided the expression "unrestricted U-boat warfare", it can therefore be said that, against British and French shipping, it was, in fact, adopted by the middle of November 1939. Neutral shipping was also warned by the Germans against entering the zone

Above: *U38*, 1,030-ton Type IXA Atlantic boat. Note the net cutter above the bow. These were a hangover from the First World War and were removed after the capture of the Biscay bases made the possibility of having to cut through nets (such as had been suspended across the Dover straits in the first war) improbable.

Right: *U35* Type VIIA Atlantic boat was depth-charged and sunk by RN destroyers *Icarus*, *Kashmir* and *Kingston* east of the Shetlands, November 1939.

which, by American neutrality legislation, was forbidden to American shipping, and against steaming without lights, zig-zagging or taking any defensive precautions; it was not until the following year that more drastic action was threatened.'[8]

Apart from the two unsuccessful attempts at employing wolf-pack tactics against convoys it is clear that the Germans opened the offensive against enemy shipping by and large with the strategic and tactical mentality of 1917–18: even the declared prohibited zone (*Sperrgebiet*) around the British Isles, embracing the English Channel, western sector of the North Sea and extending 20° West into the Atlantic was practically identical with the *Sperrgebiet* declared on 1 February 1917.

British counter-measures

British strategic mentality, in terms of development, ran parallel with the Germans', in that their initial A/S measures were a faithful copy of those they had employed in 1918. During the first two months of the war a replica of the Dover mine barrage of 1918 was laid (10,000 mines in deep and shallow fields with surface patrols). This barrage, like its predecessor, quickly proved effective. After three coastal U-boats fell prey to the mine barrage during October (*U12*, *U40*, *U16*) the Germans abandoned the straits route as being too hazardous. 'Even after the Germans occupied France and the Flanders ports they continued to send their U-boats into the Atlantic north about Scotland. The loss of these three U-boats occurring at this early stage of the war was of great importance. It represented about 8 per cent

of the existing operational U-boat fleet. It also led to the decision to abandon the short route to the South-Western Approaches and confined the small U-boats to the North Sea.'[9]

A replica of the east coast mine barrage of 1918, to protect the convoy lane running the length of the coast between the Tyne and the Thames, was also laid. This barrage ultimately absorbed 35,000 mines, but, like its 1918 predecessor, failed to account for a single U-boat. It was also the Admiralty's intention to attempt sealing the North Sea to the egress of U-boats with a copy of the Northern Barrage of 1918. However, the project was rendered obsolete before it was begun, when the Germans overran Norway in April 1940. But, as the great number of mines ordered for the 250-mile long barrage were being produced in large numbers, it was decided (May 1940) to lay an alternative barrage of even vaster proportions stretching north from the Orkneys to the Faeroes, then north-west to Iceland (a total of 500 miles). Although 81,000 mines (in deep and shallow fields) were absorbed by this enormous endeavour, only one U-boat (*U703* on 30 September 1944) came to grief while crossing it. Minelaying in the Heligoland Bight (which was abandoned after the Germans established U-boat bases in Norway and on the French Biscay coast) also only accounted for one boat (*U25* north of Terschelling on 3 August 1940). Equally unsuccessful were a shallow mine barrage of 10,000 mines stretching from the Cornish coast across the St. George's Channel to the Irish Coast, and deep minefields *under* the shipping routes converging on the North Channel: no U-boats were lost in either of these barrages during the entire war. The relative success of the mine barrages in 1918 had, of course, been dependent on geographical factors – to get to their main operational areas both the High Seas Fleet and Flanders boats had to run the risk of either the Straits or Northern barrages. When the Germans overran both Norway and France the geographical factor and consequently the mine barrages no longer counted.

Despite the lessons of the first war, the old clichés of *defensive* and *offensive* methods continued to dog the Admiralty, with the result that the slender resources in craft suitable as convoy escorts were dispersed to form hunting groups which wasted a lot of time and effort scouring the vast ocean expanses for U-boats. To begin with, Fleet Aircraft Carriers were included as integral parts of these groups. But after a near miss attack by *U39* on *Ark Royal* (14 September) and the torpedoing and sinking of *Courageous* by *U29* (Schuhart) at dusk on 17 September, the carriers were rapidly withdrawn. Because of this misdirected dispersal, the number of escorts that could be afforded to the convoy system was totally inadequate. Apart from an average of only two escorts being available per convoy, the insufficiency also restricted the expansion of the convoy system which accounted for the large number of merchant ships having to sail as independents, and so providing the U-boats with numerous vulnerable targets. Clearly the Admiralty still did not appreciate that '. . . convoy provided the means not only of protecting shipping but of locating and destroying U-boats. The enemy, no matter how elusive, if he was to have any chance to be effective, had to be at this vital point where he could be found and destroyed by the escorts in close action.'[10]

If further evidence were required, the 'kill' rate of escorts versus hunting/patrol craft during the First Phase was conclusive. Convoy escorts sank nine U-boats while the hunting and patrol groups only accounted for three (two of these in coastal waters: the position of one, *U27*, being fairly well determined on account of reports of activities off the Butt of Lewis). Moreover, the number of 'kills' by convoy escorts would undoubtedly have been higher if the inadequate scale of escorts afforded to each convoy had been strengthened by the craft unprofitably employed in the hunting and patrol groups. That this axiom was not apparent to the Admiralty at the time was quite simply because during the inter-war period 'the Trade and Anti-Submarine Divisions' were done away with and not recreated until 1939 . . . this put an end for many years to almost all research on the problems associated with the defence of shipping. Consequently much of the knowledge, as well as of the experience, of the First World War was lost and the Second World War broke out before it had been possible to re-assimilate it.'[11]

Another consequence of this was that aircraft (as well as ships) suitable for convoy escort were neither built nor designed. The value of aircraft in keeping U-boats submerged and denying them surface mobility had not been forgotten. Ocean convoys were given close air escorts (by Ansons) to the convoy dispersal point at 15° West (about 200 miles west of Ireland): coastal and

Scandinavia convoys were also given air cover. But so acute was the shortage of aircraft that only one could be allocated to each convoy, and even unarmed aircraft from local flying cubs (mostly Tiger Moths) had to be commandeered to fly A/S patrols on the convoy routes. To make matters worse the A/S bombs in use were found to be defective. During an attack on *U30* on 14 September, by three Skuas from *Ark Royal*, the A/S bombs exploded prematurely in the air, leaving *U30* unscathed but destroying two of the attacking aircraft. Following the failure of the A/S bomb, the Mark VII depth-charge (which differed little from the charge in use during 1918) was adapted for aerial use by the addition of fins and a fairing to stabilize it during flight. However, these did not come into service until the summer of 1940, and had the disadvantage of being set to explode no shallower than fifty feet. As aircraft were only able to detect surfaced U-boats their attacks were consequently launched mainly against U-boats in the process of diving to escape, and the 50-foot setting was too deep to cause damage. Calculating that the setting most likely to achieve a kill on a submerging U-boat ws 25 feet, a new 250lb aerial depth-charge entered service during the winter of 1942. This, the Mk VIII, had a 25-foot depth fuze, and a concave nose and tail fairing designed to snap off when the charge hit the water, which caused it to roll over on its side and thus reduce its velocity to ensure a 25-foot detonation.

'Kills by aircraft were exceptional and they were to remain so until aircraft were equipped with the aerial depth-charges of 1942. Nevertheless the enemy was extremely chary of exposing himself to

Shipping losses in the Atlantic, September 1939 to May 1940

the possibility of attack and always dived on sighting aircraft. The two U-boats destroyed by aircraft during the first phase received direct hits while surprised on the surface. One [*U31*] was under training in the Schillig Roads; the other, the first ever sunk by naval aircraft [*U64*], was carrying out repairs in a Norwegian fiord.'[12]

The Norwegian campaign

On 4 March the U-boat campaign against merchant shipping was suspended in preparation for the German invasion of Norway and Denmark. The size of the operational area and the peculiar formation of the Norwegian coast required the participation of every available U-boat. All sailings were stopped, and boats already at sea were recalled. U-boat training in the Baltic ceased, and the training boats were quickly brought to operational readiness. During the campaign the majority of the U-boats (28 by 10 April) were stationed off the entrances to the fiords to prevent enemy penetration, while the remainder patrolled off the enemy bases and to the north-east of the Shetlands to intercept British naval forces bound for the Norwegian coast. During the course of the campaign the difficulties the U-boats were experiencing with torpedo failures became critical and robbed them of major successes. Unique opportunities of attacking important targets had been offered, and had been fully exploited. An idea of the results can be gained from Kapitänleutnant Günther Prien's report (he commanded *U47*) on his attack in Vaggsfiord and later on the battleship *Warspite*:

'*15th April.* In the afternoon, area patrolled and searched by enemy destroyers. From the odd courses of the destroyers, presume mines to be laid in several places. In the evening three very large transports (each 30,000 tons) and three smaller transports with two cruisers at anchor in the southern part of Bygden. Disembarkation of troops in fishing smacks in the direction of Lavangen – Gratangen. Transports and cruisers in the narrows of Bygden, some moored so close that they are only just clear of one another and present a continuous target.
2200 – Boat prepares for first submerged attack. Intend to fire one torpedo at each of two cruisers and two large transports (one is a *Suffren* class cruiser), then to reload and attack again.
2242 – Fired four torpedoes. Minimum range 750 metres, maximum 1,500 metres. Depth setting of torpedoes four and five metres. A wall of ships ahead. No hits. Enemy not even startled. Reloaded. After midnight ran in again on the surface. Very precise control data. Thorough check of all settings by Chief Officer and First Lieutenant. Fired four torpedoes, depth setting as in first attack. No hits. One gyro failure, torpedo exploded on a rock. Boat ran aground while disengaging. Got clear only to find ourselves near a patrol vessel. Detected. Depth charge attack. Commenced return passage because of damage to engines.
19th April. Sighted *Warspite* and two destroyers. Fired two torpedoes at the battleship from 900 metres. No hits. A torpedo exploding at the end of its run resulted in attacks on me by destroyers from all directions.'[13]

By analysing each unsuccessful attack with the aid of the commanders' reports and firing records it was estimated that during the Norwegian campaign, if it had not been for the faulty torpedoes, hits would have been certain:

   in one of four attacks on a battleship;
   in seven of twelve attacks on cruisers;
   in seven of ten attacks on destroyers; and
   in five out of five attacks on transports.

The situation was so critical that on 20 April, Raeder appointed a special committee of investigation which led to the court-martialling of several officers of the Torpedo Experimental Command who had been in charge of torpedo development from 1936 to 1939. 'The investigations have revealed insufficient preparation before issue of the torpedoes,' Raeder summed-up the investigations findings. 'The depth-keeping qualities of the G7a and G7e are inadequate for an operational weapon. The magnetic firing mechanism of the pistol is technically inefficient, and the impact firing mechanism does not function satisfactorily.'[14] The result of the investigations shocked U-Boat Command. Dönitz wrote on 15 May:

'The findings are more serious than I had expected. An official of the Torpedo Inspectorate informs me that the mechanism had been accepted in peace time, after only two test runs, the results of which were not entirely satisfactory. Such procedure can only be described as criminal . . . It had been expected that twenty years of experiment would produce a torpedo superior to that of the First World War. A trackless torpedo with splashless discharge has been devised, but everything else is wrong. In all the history of war I doubt whether men have ever had to rely on such a useless weapon.'[15]

Left: Type VIIA Atlantic boat *U30*, which had a lucky escape in September 1939 when attacked by Fleet Air Arm Skuas.

Left: *U52* Type VIIB; she survived the war and was scuttled in Kiel, May 1945.

U-boat losses September 1939 to May 1940

Date	Boat	Cause and location
14 Sept	U39	Depth-charged by RN destroyers *Faulknor, Foxhound, Firedrake*: NW of Ireland.
20 Sept	U27	Depth-charged by RN destroyers *Forester, Fortune*: 60 miles W of Hebrides.
8 Oct	U12	Mine: Straits of Dover.
13 Oct	U40	Mine: Straits of Dover.
13 Oct	U42	Depth-charged by RN destroyers *Ilex, Imogen*: SW of Ireland.
16 Oct	U45	Depth-charged by French destroyer *Cyclone*: Bay of Biscay.
24 Oct	U16	Mine: Straits of Dover.
29 Nov	U35	Depth-charged by RN destroyers *Icarus, Kashmir, Kingston*: E of Shetlands.
4 Dec	U36	Torpedoed by RN submarine *Salmon*: SW of Stavanger.
30 Jan	U55	Depth-charged by RN destroyer *Whitshed*, sloop *Fowey* and RAF aircraft (228 Sqn): 100 miles W of Ushant.
1 Feb	U15	Accident. Rammed by German torpedo-boat *Iltis*: Baltic.
5 Feb	U41	Depth-charged by RN destroyer *Antelope*: S of Ireland.
12 Feb	U33	Depth-charged by RN minesweeper *Gleaner*: Firth of Clyde.
21 Feb	U53	Depth-charged by French destroyer *Fantasque*: North Atlantic.
25 Feb	U63	Depth-charged by RN destroyers *Escort, Imogen, Inglefield*: SE of Shetlands.
11 March	U31	Bombed by RAF aircraft: Schillig Roads: later salved and recommissioned.
20 March	U44	Depth-charged by RN destroyer *Fortune*: SW of Narvik.
12 April	U54	Torpedoed by RN submarine *Salmon*: North Sea.
13 April	U64	Bombed by RN aircraft of battleship *Warspite*: Rombaksfiord.
15 April	U49	Depth-charged by RN destroyer *Fearless*: Vaagsofiord.
16 April	U1	Torpedoed by RN submarine *Porpoise*: SW of Stavanger.
25 April	U22	Mined: Skagerrak.
29 April	U50	Depth-charged by RN destroyers *Amazon, Witherington*: N of Shetlands.
31 May	U13	Depth-charged by RN sloop *Weston*: North Sea.

Analysis of causes

Surface vessels	13
Shared by surface vessels and naval aircraft	—
Shared by surface vessels and shore-based aircraft	1
Naval aircraft	1
Shore-based aircraft	1
Shared by naval and shore-based aircraft	—
Torpedoed by submarine	3
Mines	4
Accidental causes	1
Unknown causes	—
Total	24

Despite technical improvements to the impact system, and to compensate for the uncertain depth-keeping qualities the torpedoes were set to run fairly shallow (which reduced the effect of the detonation), premature detonations and detonation failures continued to dog the U-boats' potential. It wasn't until the beginning of November 1942, when a new magnetic proximity fuze and the TIII electrically propelled torpedo became operational, that these problems were largely overcome.

Results of the first phase

By judging the success of the U-boat campaign against shipping during the first six months of the war (March to May 1940 are not considered because of the suspension of the campaign) the overall performance of 16.6 ships (or 56,981 tons) per U-boat lost was only slightly more favourable (0.93 per cent) than the last six months of 1918 (15.45 ships or 32,824 tons per U-boat lost) when any chance of achieving a decisive victory had collapsed. As virtually all the losses suffered by the British (by all causes) during this period had been made good — for the greater part by new building, and partly by captures from the enemy, the opening attack by the U-boats had been little more than a nuisance. But it was realized that, as the German U-boat construction programme gathered way, the campaign was bound to be intensified, and that the First Phase had been little more than a preliminary skirmish.

Churchill, having been appointed First Lord of the Admiralty on the very day that Britain declared war on Germany, the post he had held at the outbreak of the first war, wrote:

'... that the menace was in thorough and hardening control. It was obvious that the Germans would build submarines by the hundred, and no doubt numerous boats were upon the slips in various stages of completion. In twelve months, certainly in eighteen, we must expect the main U-boat war to begin. But by that time we hoped that our mass of new flottillas and anti-U-boat craft, which was our First Priority, would be ready to meet it with a proportionate and effective predominance.'[16]

Right: *U25*, Type IA Atlantic boat was mined north of Terschelling on 3 August 1940.

U-boat strength during the First Phase: September 1939 to May 1940

and success rate expressed as tonnage sunk per U-boat per day at sea. (Source: German Base Records)

Month	Total no. U-boats	No. of *Frontboote*	Training and trials boats	Monthly average of daily number of boats at sea	Average tonnage sunk per U-boat per day at sea
1939					
Sept	57	39	18	23	258
Oct	51	39	12	10	503
Nov	52	33	19	16	151
Dec	54	34	20	8	410
1940					
Jan	54	33	21	11	478
Feb	50	35	15	15	419
March	50	34	16	13	173
April	47	34	13	24	42
May	49	31	18	8	248

The 'Happy Time'
The second phase, June 1940 to March 1941

Resumption of the attack on shipping

Due to the tardiness with which the U-boat replacement and expansion building programme was put in hand, the commissioning rate of new U-boats failed to keep up with the loss rate, so that when the Second Phase opened the total strength was only 51 (six less than in September 1939). To make matters worse, so many *Frontboote* were in need of extensive repair and overhaul after the Norwegian campaign that the congested German dockyards were unable to get any appreciable number fully operational until the beginning of June. By 9 June, however, a total of sixteen *Frontboote* had, after an absence of three months from the Atlantic, gathered in the Western Approaches and resumed the war on shipping. 'At last', writes Hessler, 'technical improvements in the torpedo began to show results ... torpedo failures decreased and thanks to the favourable traffic situation, the boats achieved an unexpectedly high rate of sinkings ...'[1]

Monthly breakdown of losses

Month	Independent sailings	Ships in convoy	Stragglers*	After dispersal*	Total	
June	(52) 281,259	(9) 62,351	(2) 13,327	–	(63)	356,937
July	(33) 167,687	(4) 25,941	(2) 4,250	–	(39)	197,878
August	(26) 137,226	(23) 113,186	(5) 28,318	(1) 8,406	(55)	287,136
September	(23) 82,202	(25) 154,219	(3) 5,014	(8) 43,142	(59)	284,577
October	(13) 64,258	(41) 207,246	(11) 86,577	(1) 5,186	(66)	363,267
	(147) 732,632	(102) 562,943	(23) 137,486	(10) 56,734	(282)	1,489,795

(*Stragglers from convoy and ships sunk after dispersal from convoy)

The *BdU* also determined that conditions were favourable for another attempt at pack operations. With the intention of launching simultaneous attacks on two separate convoys, one group of six boats under the tactical command of Günther Prien in *U47* (Prien Group) was drawn up in a patrol line 420 miles west of Lorient across the estimated line of approach of convoy HX48 (homeward bound from Halifax); while five boats under the tactical command of Kapitänleutnant Hans Rösing in *U48* (Rösing Group) were disposed to the westward of Cape Finisterre to intercept the north-bound troop convoy WS3 (consisting of *Queen Mary* and two other large liners carrying 26,000 Australian and New Zealand troops escorted by the battlecruiser *Hood*, an aircraft carrier and several cruisers). Information on the movements of these two convoys, which was not precise, had been obtained by the German naval *B-Dienst* (*Funkbeobachtungsdienst*) – literally radio observation service, which apart from the monitoring and interception of enemy naval radio traffic was also a cryptanalytic agency). Having broken the Royal Naval Administrative code at the beginning of the war, *B-Dienst* was able, through extensive reading of the decoded traffic, to obtain valuable operational intelligence with regard to sailings of enemy convoys. They continued to do this until 20 August 1940, when the Royal Navy substituted the more secure Naval Code No. 1.

To the bitter disappointment of the *BdU* (WS3 in particular was a valuable prize) neither of these two convoys was sighted by the waiting packs, for the simple reason that the convoys' rendezvous points with the A/S escorts was much further to the south-west than anticipated. Following this disappointment both the Prien and Rösing groups were disbanded and the boats were directed as individual units to attack shipping at the entrances to the English and St. George's Channels. During June 1940 sinkings by U-boat suddenly shot up to 63 ships of 356,937 tons, which was more than double the 142,453-ton monthly average sunk during the first six months of the war. Of this total 82.54 per cent were independents. This sudden upsurge heralded the onset of what the U-boat men called the 'Happy Time' because of the consistently high level of sinkings and negligible losses in U-boats from June to October. During this 5-month period the U-boats accounted for 282 ships, grossing 1,489,795 tons.

Although the monthly average of 297,959 tons was only 46.42 per cent of the monthly average sunk during the critical months of 1917 (February–June), it must be set against the fact that during the first five months of the Second Phase the daily average number of *Frontboote* at sea was only fourteen compared to an average of 45 during the 5-month period considered in 1917. When this factor is taken into consideration the individual performance of the *Frontboote* during the Happy Time was phenomenal, each boat averaging 106,413 tons in comparison with the average of 71,317 tons per boat during the five opening months of the unrestricted campaign of 1917. The statistics in terms of the exchange rate are equally phenomenal. With only seven U-boats lost (one by accidental cause and two by unknown causes), the ratio of tonnage sunk to each U-boat lost is 212,827 tons, which is 8.6 per cent more favourable than the most favourable ratio factor of 1917 (194,524 tons per boat lost for the quarter February–April). Also marked is the sudden high rise in the percentage of ships sunk while sailing in convoy (36.17 per cent). This was not due to any tactical refinement on the part of the Germans.

'. . . the fall of France (a Franco-German armistice came into effect on 25 June) deprived us of the assistance of the French Navy and involved the retention of anti-invasion forces in the narrow seas, whilst the evacuation of the British Expeditionary Force from the Continent had not only caused convoy escorts to be withdrawn to assist in the operation but had resulted in loss and damage to many of them. Most of those surviving were now retained against invasion. Although the first corvettes were coming into service their numbers were as yet small. Ocean convoys in June and July, even when numbering 30 ships, *rarely had more than one escort*. Air escorts, too, and air patrols were rare. Coastal Command had few suitable aircraft . . . whilst the available aircraft were primarily employed on anti-invasion patrols in the North Sea, and naval reconnaissance in northern waters.'[2]

In short, the withdrawal in large part of the convoy surface and air escorts along with the patrol and hunting groups had denuded merchant shipping of any effective scale of defence and given the U-boats almost a free hand.

Acquisition of the Biscay bases
This was only part of the story because of even greater and more far-reaching consequences was the German acquisition of the French Biscay ports as U-boat bases. On the day of the armistice with France, weapons, fuel, provisions, repair facilities and personnel were sent by road from Wilhelmshaven to the proposed bases at Brest, Lorient, St-Nazaire, La Rochelle and Bordeaux. The first base to be made ready was at Lorient, and on 7 July *U30* (Lemp) entered to embark torpedoes. The strategic advantages of these bases was profound, as Hessler explains:

'The use of these new bases, where repair facilities were quickly made available, relieved the situation in the German dockyards. The periods under repair were shortened, and thus there were more boats at sea. The average number of operational boats available from September 1939 to July 1940 was about 33; the average number at sea was about 14, or approximately 42 per cent of the available boats. From August 1940 to July 1941, the average number available was about 30, of which about 16 or approximately 53 per cent were at sea. Thus in the latter period the proportion of boats at sea was approximately 11 per cent higher. The fact that our bases were nearer to the enemy meant a considerable reduction in the outward and homeward passages, hence a greater percentage of boats in the operational area. The actual gain cannot be accurately stated. The passage from Lorient to the North Channel is some 450 miles shorter than from Wilhelmshaven or Kiel. However, the saving of time was much greater than the saving of mileage, since in the North Sea, Skagerrak and Kattegat there were large areas which, because of the danger of submarines and mines, could only be crossed at night, with escort. Obviously this had often contributed to the lengthening of the passage. At least a week was saved on each sortie, and the number of boats in the operational area was thus raised by 25 per cent and more per month. The further bases established on the Atlantic coast during 1940 and the favourable conditions in the operational area led to a considerable increase in U-boat successes, despite the drop in the number of boats available.'[3]

To avoid the danger of air attack from the airfields the Germans had gained in north-west France, and to distance shipping from the U-boat base at Lorient, the British abandoned the shipping routes in the South-Western Approaches and the English Channel, and from mid-July routed all shipping through the North-Western Approaches either by the North Channel or north about Scotland. This also advantaged the Germans in that it enabled the small 250-ton Types IIB and IIC coastal boats (which had hitherto been confined to North Sea operations) to be brought into action against ocean shipping. Operating from Bergen and Stavanger in Norway they were able to work in the coastal waters of the North-Western Approaches with great effect. According to Hessler:

'There were at times surprisingly high sinking figures in successive short operations near the North Channel. The U-boats pursued homeward-bound ships close in to the coast and attacked convoys whose escorts could not cope even with single U-boat attacks. Particularly successful were the operations of Type IIC boats – the improved 250 ton coastal boats. Equipped with six torpedoes, they were stationed on the main traffic routes in the North Channel, at the north entrance to the Minch and just west of the Pentland Firth. Their diving ability, manoeuvrability and splendid resistance to depth charges and bombs encouraged the commanders to persistent bold operations in the vicinity of the coast.'[4]

The main concentration area of the U-boats was to the east of 15° West, covering the west coast of Ireland extending north to the latitudes of the Orkneys – in effect covering the whole of the North-Western Approaches. However, a number of the large ocean-going boats carried the attack westwards into the Atlantic as far as 25° West, far beyond the 15° West limit where the escorts left the convoys. This expansion of the operational area forced the Admiralty to extend the limit to which convoys were escorted to 17° West (300 miles west of Ireland) in July and to 19° West in October. These extensions further diminished the effectiveness of the inadequate number of existing escort craft, in that their limited radius of action was stretched to the point that convoys had to follow more direct routes and refrain from zigzagging. Neither could the escorts, because of their limited endurance, engage in numerous bursts of high speed, with the result that attacking U-boats could only be kept down long enough to prevent them from catching the convoys on the surface, and could not be hunted to destruction.

Right: The long, sleek shape of the 1,050-ton Type IXB Atlantic boat *U108*. Heavily damaged in an Allied bombing raid on Hamburg, 11 April 1944, she was paid off, and to avoid capture was scuttled in May 1945.

Second attempt at wolf-pack tactics

Such was the state of the defences when the *BdU* decided once more to attempt wolf-pack operations, and the U-boat commanders were issued a standing order to report all convoys against which other boats might be able to concentrate. But, 'with so few boats, it was seldom possible to concentrate them as a result of sighting reports, unless the convoys were outward bound. With inward-bound convoys before the nearest U-boats arrived, most of the targets had disappeared into the North Channel, which was heavily patrolled. There was no purpose in going out to the open Atlantic to operate on homeward-bound convoys, since prospects of finding them were slight. But when data were provided for finding a convoy further west, use was made of them. Such occasions were naturally few.'[5]

B-Dienst's reading of decoded messages helped, but it was seldom that they could deduce the exact position of a convoy. High seas and poor visibility prevented the first attempt by three boats to make contact with an HX convoy on 15/16 August. Bad weather also spoiled the attack by four boats on convoy SC2 during early September. 'In a wind up to Force 8, the four boats approaching one after the other managed to sink only five ships [four totalling 18,509 tons by Prien in *U47* and one of 2,434 tons by Kuhnke in *U28*]. Despite the storm, aircraft appeared, unpleasantly complicating the situation for the U-boats.'[6] However three further *Rudeltaktik* operations carried out during the period 20 September–20 October were so successful that Dönitz wrote in his War Diary that they served to '... justify the principles on which U-boat tactics and training have been developed since 1935, i.e., that U-boats *in packs* should attack the convoys.'[7]

The first of these operations was an attack on the weakly escorted Convoy HX72 (night of 21/22 September) about 350 miles out in the Atlantic by four of the five boats that had been directed by the *BdU* to close on the convoy (it had been sighted by *U47* on the 20th and the route instructions had been intercepted by *B-Dienst*). *U99* (Kretschmer – who became Germany's supreme ace of the Second World War) accounted for three ships of 17,978 tons; *U48* (Bleichrodt) sank one ship of 4,409 tons and damaged another, while *U100* (Schepke) after launching persistent attacks between 23.10 on the 21st and 02.14 on the next day sank seven ships grossing 50,340 tons for a grand total of eleven ships of 72,727 tons sunk and two ships of 13,022 tons damaged (*U32* had torpedoed and damaged SS *Collegian* at 06.46 on the 22nd). Two further wolf-pack attacks which took place in mid-October vindicated beyond doubt the value of Dönitz's tactical theory. Seven boats concentrated on Convoy SC7 (34 slow merchant ships in eight columns escorted by three sloops and two corvettes) and sank twenty ships grossing 79,646 tons, during a battle off the Rockall Bank which lasted over two successive nights (16/17 and 18/19 October). Kretschmer in *U99* accounted for six ships of 27,396 tons during this operation. The four boats which attacked HX79 during the night of 19/20 October sank twelve ships of 75,069 tons, bringing the grand total of merchant ships sunk in these three operations to 43, grossing 227,442 tons. No U-boats were sunk or even damaged.

An account of the part played by *U99* in the attack on Convoy SC7, recorded by Korvettenkapitän Otto Kretschmer in the War Diary of *U99*, gives a graphic description of night-surface attacks by wolf-packs:

'18th October:
1745 Wind: southeast, Force 3; sea 3; moderate cloud. *U101*, which is two or three miles north, signals by searchlight: "Enemy sighted to port."
1749 A warship is sighted, bearing 030°, steering east. Soon afterwards, smoke to left of her. Finally the convoy. While hauling ahead to attack, we sight a steamship in the southeast, apparently on a westerly course.
1928 Submerge for attack.
1950 Surface, as the ship is making off slowly to the east. Haul further ahead: at 2000 pass within a few hundred metres of a U-boat on the surface, apparently *U101* again.
2024 Another U-boat has torpedoed the ship. Shortly afterwards, exchange recognition signals with *U123*. Convoy again in sight. I am ahead of it, so allow my boat to drop back, avoiding the leading destroyer. The destroyers are constantly firing starshells. From outside, I attack the right flank of the first formation.
2202 Weather: visibility moderate, bright moonlight. Fire bow torpedo by director. Miss.
2206 Fire stern torpedo by director. At 700 metres, hit forward of amidships. Vessel of some 6,500 tons sinks within 20 seconds. I now proceed head on into the convoy. All ships are zigzagging independently.
2230 Fire bow toepedo by director. Miss because of error in calculation of gyro-angle. I therefore decide to fire the rest of the torpedoes without the director, especially as the installation has still not been accepted and adjusted by the Torpedo Testing Department. Boat is soon sighted by a ship which fires a white starshell and turns towards us at full speed, continuing even after we alter course. I have to make off with engines all out. Eventually the ship turns off, fires one of her guns and again takes her place in the convoy. I now attack the right flank of the last formation but one.
2330 Fire bow torpedo at a large freighter. As the ship turns towards us, the torpedo passes ahead of her and hits an even larger ship after a run of 1,740 metres. This ship of some 7,000 tons is hit abreast the foremast, and the bow quickly sinks below the surface, as two holds are apparently flooded.
2355 Fire a bow torpedo at a large freighter of some 6,000 tons, at a range of 750 metres. Hit abreast foremast. Immediately after the torpedo explosion, there is another explosion with a high column of flame from the bow to the bridge. The smoke rises some 200 metres. Bow apparently shattered. Ship continues to burn with a green flame.
19th October:
0015 Three destroyers approach the ship and search the area in line abreast. I make off at full speed to the southwest and again make contact with the convoy. Torpedoes from the other boats are constantly heard exploding. The destroyers do not know how to help and occupy themselves by constantly firing starshells, which are of little effect in the bright moonlight. I now start to attack the convoy from astern.
0138 Fire bow torpedoes at large heavily-laden freighter of about 6,000 tons, range 945 metres. Hit abreast foremast. The explosion sinks the ship.
0155 Fire bow torpedo at the next large vessel of some 7,000 tons.

Range 975 metres. Hit abreast foremast. Ship sinks within 40 seconds.
0240 Miss through aiming error, with torpedo fired at one of the largest vessels of the convoy, a ship of the *Glenapp* class 9,500 tons.
0255 Again miss the same target from a range of about 800 metres. No explanation, as the fire control data were absolutely correct. Presume it to be a gyro failure, as we hear an explosion on the other side of the convoy some seven minutes later.
0302 Third attempt at the same target from a range of 720 metres. Hit forward of the bridge. Bow sinks rapidly level with the water.
0356 Fire at and miss a rather small, unladen ship, which had lost contact with the convoy. We had fired just as the steamer turned towards us.
0358 Turn off and fire a stern torpedo from a range of 690 metres. Hit aft of amidships. Ship drops astern, somewhat lower in the water. As torpedoes have been expended, I wait to see if she will sink further before I settle her by gunfire.
0504 Ship is sunk by another vessel by gunfire. I suppose it to be a British destroyer, but it later transpires that it was *U123*. Some of her shells land very close, so that I have to leave the area quickly. The ship was *Clintonia*, 3,106 tons.
0530 I commence return passage to Lorient . . .'[8]

British counter-measures

The most noticeable aspect of Kretschmer's account is the impotence of the five escort vessels in preventing or even impeding the slaughter. Indeed the attacks on Convoys HX72,

Right: *U72*, Type VIIC, in dry dock. She was destroyed in a bombing raid by USAAF aircraft on Bremen, 30 March 1945.

SC7 and HX79 epitomized the strategical bankruptcy of the Admiralty's pre-war faith in the combination of convoy and ASDIC as the means of mastering the U-boat menace. Surface night attacks in packs (or indeed as individual units) by the U-boats rendered ASDIC useless. The only means left of detecting a surfaced U-boat was visual, but attacks by night robbed the A/S craft of even this because, given so few escorts, the chances of sighting the low, long, lean silhouette of a U-boat among the loom of the ships in convoy were slight to say the least. Moreover, not only were escorts virtually powerless to ward off attacks, they were for the most part incapable of pursuing an attacker even when it was sighted, for their speed was less than that of a surfaced U-boat which could use its main engines to effect a rapid withdrawal. In short, the enemy had adopted the one form of attack against which the Admiralty had developed neither tactical nor technical antidotes, and the one form of withdrawal after an attack which the escorts, for the most part, were incapable of preventing because existing A/S craft, and the bulk of the new ones coming into service, had been designed to chase and attack relatively slow-moving *submerged* U-boats.

In an attempt to put matters right, the Admiralty quickly instituted tactical and technical improvements. The tactical response was to co-ordinate the counter-attacks by the escort vessels rather than have them thrashing about in an unco-ordinated mêlée, one vessel not knowing what the others were doing or intended. In effect the intention was to meet the concentration in attack of U-boats by a concentration in counter-attack by the escorts. This was brought about by forming the escorts into groups, each group of vessels under its own group leader, sharing a common training and working as a team. This necessitated rapid communication between vessels, which was in turn facilitated by the technical innovation of high-frequency TBS (talk between ships) radio telephone. TBS also had the advantage of being able to co-ordinate messages between the surface craft and escort aircraft. Previously simple requests had sometimes taken hours to pass.

To overcome the blindness of the escorts during a night attack, and to aid escort and patrol aircraft by day in bad visibility, heavy cloud or fog, a small and primitive radar set (Type ASVII for aircraft and the 286M naval variant) was developed. Although 4,000 sets of the ASVII were ordered, only 45 sets had been fitted to coastal command aircraft by October 1940, and it wasn't until the autumn of 1941 that nearly all coastal command aircraft were fitted. The naval 286M set had the disadvantage of having to have its aerial fixed immovably at the top of the ship's foremast, which restricted the radar beam's arc of detection to 120° ahead of the ship and only approximate bearings could be obtained. It is not surprising, therefore, that the 286M did not prove of great value in detecting surfaced U-boats.

By far the most important counter-measure to the threat of an almost total breakdown in the flow of imports into Britain, was the decision, born of dire necessity, to redeploy the large number of suitable escort craft tied up as anti-invasion forces to their proper function of defending Britain's vital seaborne trade. This redeployment, together with the return of the large number of escorts that had been damaged in the previous summer's fighting, whose numbers were swelled by the new corvettes and A/S-fitted trawlers entering service, and the fifty destroyers acquired from the United States, put a sting back into the tail of convoy: of the eight U-boats lost from November 1940 until March 1941, seven were accounted for by convoy escorts (the eighth boat lost, *U560*, was accidentally rammed in the Baltic). However, the percentage of losses among convoyed ships during the period November–March, actually rose above the 36.17 per cent of the previous five months to 43.00 per cent, while the average monthly loss of mercantile tonnage accounted for by U-boat action (211,676 tons) only declined by a marginal .55 per cent below the previous five months' score:

Strategic and tactical problems

This consistent level of sinkings was achieved by a very small number of boats operating under a number of adverse conditions during the winter of 1940–41. Although the total strength of the U-boat fleet had reached 74 by November 1940, and climbed steadily to 109 by March 1941, the number of *Frontboote* during this period only averaged 24.2 and did not exceed 27. The reason for this was that apart from those running trials a large number were required for training new commanders and crews for the rapidly expanding fleet. This small number of available *Frontboote* resulted in an average of only four to six boats being in the operational area at any one time: 'less', Hessler points out, 'than in any other period of the war'.[9]

The major debilitating factor for this small force was that the concentration of the reinforced enemy surface and air A/S forces in the main operational area restricted the U-boats' freedom of manoeuvre and forced them ever farther westward into the open Atlantic, far beyond 15° West and consequently farther apart, which made their chances of intercepting convoys far more difficult. Indeed, during the winter months of 1940 only one wolf-pack attack was successfully mounted. This was against Convoy HX90 on the night of 1/2 December, when six boats (*U101, U47, U52, U95, U94, U99*) sank ten ships grossing 69,219 tons and damaged three ships of 17,196 tons. Interception of convoys was made all the more difficult without the help of *B-Dienst*, which had been unable to 'read' the British ciphers since August, when the enemy lost their misplaced confidence in the security of the 'Administrative Code' and replaced it with the more secure 'Naval Code No 1'. To compound the problems of U-boat operations they were further prejudiced by the weather. Hessler explains:

'If contact was made in bad weather, the heavy seas caused many misses and torpedo failures due to bad depth-keeping. At times torpedoes could not be fired. Even experienced crews found it

Monthly breakdown of losses

Month	Independent sailings		Ships in convoy		Stragglers		After dispersal		Total	
November	(14)	86,345	(19)	76,632	(1)	5,612	(2)	58,863	(36)	181,695
December	(20)	104,369	(19)	118, 61	(4)	21,618	(3)	11,705	(46)	256,310
January	(14)	84,442	(3)	16,085	(5)	24,155	(1)	5,029	(23)	129,711
February	(11)	49,877	(14)	83,149	(16)	94,173	(6)	26,919	(47)	254,118
March	(11)	54,768	(28)	173,918	(1)	5,759	(1)	2,104	(41)	236,549
	(70)	379,801	(83)	468,402	(27)	151,317	(13)	58,863	(193)	1,058,383

impossible by day to keep their boats at periscope depth. At night the commanders sometimes saw their targets pass close by, while their boats plunged in the heavy seas without being able to aim with any prospect of success ... A typical day was 24th November, when no less than four convoys were sighted by U-boats, but the weather prevented a concentration of boats for attack.'[10]

During November welcome reinforcements materialized when the Italians sent 26 of their U-boats to the base prepared for them at Bordeaux. Early in November six of the Italian boats began operating to the west of the North Channel between 15° and 20° West, beyond the reach of enemy air patrols and coastal A/S forces. Although Dönitz did not expect many sinkings, he hoped that the Italian U-boats would serve to extend his reconnaissance. Apart from attacking convoys, they were to shadow them for the German boats. They did not give the expected support. Although they sighted many convoys, it was never possible to bring up the German boats, because the sighting reports either came in too late or were corrupt, or again, contact was lost at once. Dönitz's opinion of the Italians can be judged from the following extract in his War Diary of 4 December:

'I did not expect the Italians immediately to sink many ships in a strange area, with sea and weather conditions outside their experience – they are not sufficiently well trained. But I did at least hope that they would contribute to better reconnaissance of the operational area. During the whole period I have not received a single useful sighting report from them. Several belated, almost incomprehensible messages or inaccurate reports are all I have received. They failed to shadow even for short periods ... The main reasons for their failure are: (a) They cannot attack unobtrusively or remain undetected. (b) They do not understand the technique of hauling ahead of a slow target. (c) They have no idea of surface attacks by night. (d) They do not understand how to shadow and report ... Actually their support is quite useless and I am compelled to dispose the German U-boats for operations without considering the Italians.'[11]

The Italian boats' operational record bears out Dönitz's assessment. During the five months November 1940–March 1941 only fourteen of the 26 Italian *Frontboote* based on Bordeaux scored any kills – their total score being 21 merchant ships of 86,079 tons: the average sinking rate per boat per month being a mere 0.80.

In an attempt to overcome the problems of intercepting convoys, the Germans attempted to use shore-based aircraft on reconnaissance for the U-boats. During the summer and autumn of 1940 Dönitz had been able to obtain spasmodic assistance from the Luftwaffe, but on 7 January 1941, the thirty bombers of *I/KG.40* (1st *Gruppe* of the 40th Bomber *Geschwader*) was allocated and subordinated to the *BdU*. This group was composed of Focke-Wulf Condor 200 bombers which were capable of long-range reconnaissance as far as 20° West. The results were disappointing as Hessler explains:

'The aircraft available from *I/KG.40* were too few to allow the U-boats to abandon their own reconnaissance. Usually only two aircraft operated each day. Whenever a special area was to be reconnoitred by four or five aircraft, ot when a special bomber

operation was planned, this necessarily depleted the air reconnaissance both before and after the air operations. Thus air reconnaissance was still only an occasional aid, and the BdU still had to place his boats "where he thought best". This "hit or miss" policy was even less satisfactory than before, for in January 1941, the British began to spread the convoy routes over a wider area, and to send the convoys further north ... Until 10th February the U-boats operated west of the North Channel as far as 20° West, when they began to follow up the convoy diversions to the north. The battle area stretched in stages as far as the coast of Ireland. The longest north-south extension occurred on the 27th February and again on 2nd March, when seven boats were stretched between Iceland and Rockall Bank. But the northward movement of the U-boats was not conducive to co-operation with I/KG.40, whose aircraft, being based at Bordeaux, could only reach the south-east corner of the area.'[12]

During the winter of 1940/41 the aircraft of I/KG.40 only managed to home the U-boats on to one convoy. This was OB288 which was set upon by a pack of five U-boats (U69, U73, U95, U96 and the Italian U-boat *Bianchi*) on the night of 23/24 February. They sank eight ships grossing 43,718 tons and damaged one ship of 9,718 tons. However, the problem for the Germans of successful interception on a large scale remained unsolved. The other major debilitating factor, lack of *Frontboote* in adequate numbers, which was in turn a contributory factor in the interception problem, and had bedevilled the *BdU*'s attempts at pack tactics, was about to be overcome by the rapid acceleration in the growth of the U-boat fleet. During the nine

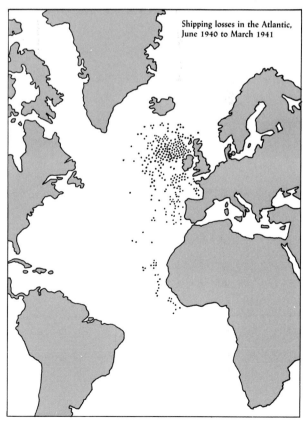

Shipping losses in the Atlantic, June 1940 to March 1941

Left: *U89* a 770-ton Type VIIC. This type formed the backbone of the U-boat fleet; 567 were commissioned from 1940 to 1944.

Left: The large 1,120-ton Type IXC Atlantic boat *U66*. She was sunk in a depth-charge attack by USN aircraft of the US escort carrier *Block Island* and the US destroyer *Buckley* off Cape Verde Islands, 6 May 1944.

months from April to December 1941 the number in commission would rise from 121 to 250. This rapid expansion facilitated Dönitz's intention to evolve the strategy of the U-boat campaign into strictly controlled pack operations against convoys – an evolution that would intensify the scale of the U-boat campaign into the full fury of the Battle of the Atlantic.

U-boat losses June 1940 to March 1941

Date	Boat	Cause and location
21 June	U122	Unknown: North Sea.
3 July	U26	Depth-charged by RN corvette *Gladiolus* and RAAF aircraft: SW of Bishops Rock.
3 Aug	U25	Mined: N of Terschelling.
20 Aug	U51	Torpedoed by RN submarine *Cachalot*: Bay of Biscay.
21 Aug	U102	Unknown: North Sea.
3 Sept	U57	Accident. Rammed by SS *Rona*: Brunsbüttel.
30 Oct	U32	Depth-charged by RN destroyers *Harvester* and *Highlander*: NW of Ireland.
2 Nov	U31	Depth-charged by RN destroyer *Antelope*: NW of Ireland.
21 Nov	U104	Depth-charged by RN corvette *Rhododendron*: S of Rockall.
? Nov	U560	Accident: collision off Memel.
7 March	U47	Depth-charged by RN corvettes *Arbutus* and *Camellia*: off Rockall.
8 March	U70	Depth-charged by RN destroyer *Wolverine*: S of Iceland.
17 March	U99	Torpedoed by RN destroyer *Walker*: NW of Hebrides.
17 March	U100	Rammed by RN destroyer *Vanoc*: NW of Hebrides.
23 March	U551	Depth-charged by RN trawler *Visenda*: S of Iceland.

U-boat strength during the Second Phase: June 1940 to March 1941

and success rate expressed as tonnage sunk per U-boat per day at sea

Month	Total no. U-boats	No. of *Frontboote*	Training and trials boats	Monthly average of daily number of boats at sea	Average tonnage sunk per U-boat per day at sea
1940					
June	51	27	24	18	694
July	53	30	23	11	592
Aug	55	27	28	13	715
Sept	61	27	34	13	739
Oct	68	30	38	12	976
Nov	74	24	50	11	550
Dec	83	27	56	10	826
1941					
Jan	94	22	72	8	540
Feb	103	21	82	12	730
March	109	27	82	13	586

Analysis of causes

Cumulative total in parentheses

Surface vessels	8	(21)
Shared by surface vessels and naval aircraft	–	(0)
Shared by surface vessels and shore-based aircraft	1	(2)
Naval aircraft	–	(1)
Shore-based aircraft	–	(1)
Shared by naval and shore-based aircraft	–	(1)
Torpedoed by submarine	1	(4)
Mines	1	(5)
Accidental causes	2	(3)
Unknown causes	2	(2)
Total	*15*	*(40)*

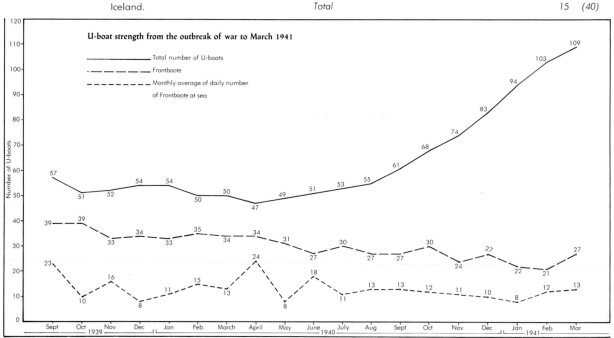

U-boat strength from the outbreak of war to March 1941

——— Total number of U-boats
·—·—·— *Frontboote*
- - - - - Monthly average of daily number of *Frontboote* at sea

The War in the Ether
The third phase, April to December 1941

BdU centralized control

During the twelve months 1 May 1940 to 1 May 1941, the total number of U-boats at Germany's disposal (excluding Italian boats) rose from 49 to 139 and subsequently very rapidly, despite war losses, to 184 by August, soaring to 250 by 1 December 1941. The latter figure was 94 in excess of the total number available in April 1917, when the U-boats achieved their greatest success, and 73 in excess of the highest number available in the entire course of the First World War (177 in September 1918). From April to December 1941, however, only an average of 33.69 per cent of the total were *Frontboote*, the remainder being either employed as school boats or undergoing training and trials. Moreover, because each *Frontboote* had to undergo periods in dock for refuelling and overhaul after each patrol, the average *monthly* number of *Frontboote* at sea daily throughout the nine months of the Third Phase was only 27.35. Yet it was with this small number that Dönitz embarked on his strategic policy of *BdU* control of pack operations against the convoy system.

The *raison d'être* of this decision was quite simply that Dönitz had no alternative. Strengthened British A/S sea and air defences had forced the U-boats westward into the open Atlantic, where convoys could be attacked either before the homeward A/S escorts joined the convoy or after the outward A/S escorts had left. But this gave the British the advantage of having a larger area of sea in which to carry out evasive routing of the convoys, while it consequently imposed the disadvantage on the Germans of minimizing the chances of interception. In an attempt to overcome this problem, groups of U-boats were deployed in broad patrol lines across the convoys' probable line of advance. But as broad dispositions would make it difficult for the most distant boats of the patrol line to close up with the other boats to make a pack attack on the convoy, when one or other of the boats made a sighting, it was imperative that immediate warning be given. This was best achieved by central control from *BdU* Command Headquarters at Lorient. Hessler explains the strategical and tactical methods hitherto employed once a U-boat had made contact with a convoy.

'The shadower's task [i.e., the boat that had first made contact] was to remain by the convoy, while the other boats set course to intercept the target, some of them from distances up to 300 or 400 miles. Whenever possible the shadower had to make hourly shadowing reports. Shadowing entailed constant opening and closing, submerging, surfacing and pursuing – a task calling for the highest skill, tenacity and nerve on the part of the commander. His task was vital to subsequent operations, perhaps even to the success

of a whole period, and for him the actual attack was a secondary consideration. If the convoy escort were strong, the *BdU* Command Headquarters had to forbid the commander to attack as long as only he was within range of the enemy ... Within a few hours the enemy would probably deduce the presence of a shadower from the nature, frequency and bearings of his radio messages, even if the boat had not already been sighted or located by radar. Every effort was made to shake off this unwanted observer, to force him to submerge, or to prevent his attacks. Therefore it might be better that the sighting U-boat, after making her first report, should refrain from running comments by radio, or severely curtail them.

After much discussion in the communications section and among the staff of the *BdU*, it was finally decided that shadowing reports must be continuous in order to concentrate the other boats. There was all the difference between the evaluation of the shadowing reports in the U-boats and in the plotting room of the *BdU*. The staff officer at Headquarters could often forecast the convoy's probable diversionary course, detect the shadower's mistakes in dead reckoning, and sometimes warn the boats of enemy counter-measures, as revealed by *B-Dienst*. If contact was lost and not likely to be regained with the existing dispositions, the boats were directed to carry out special search operations. At first these were simple, entailing only a systematic search for the lost convoy, or the formation of a patrol line ahead of the probable diversionary course of the enemy. The patrol line was also used, if there were danger of missing the convoy at night ... In the *BdU* Command Headquarters plotting room calculations were made on the basis of the estimated visibility, the positions, search courses, and speeds of the boats. In practice, changes in the weather and other conditions in the Atlantic often caused the boats to be badly out of position. In such cases long-wave homing signals – which contained the estimated true bearings and distance of the shadower from the centre of the convoy – allowed other boats to set an accurate course for interception. The request for homing signals came either from other boats – if they had not found the convoy by dead reckoning – or from *BdU* Command Headquarters. Although communications orders stipulated frequent changes in the wave-length of homing signals, it was obvious that the convoy escorts would also take bearings on the shadower. The risk had to be taken as these signals were the only means of checking the navigation of the boats.

In pre-war exercises in controlled U-boat operations every opportunity to attack by day or night had to be exploited. Submerged and surface attacks were regarded as equally valuable. The first year of the war saw a change in this respect, for experience showed that it was much better to attack on the surface at night, using a high speed to assume a good attacking position and then to evade pursuit. In cases where the same boats would be able to attack a convoy on two successive nights, the *BdU* forbade them to attack in daylight. The U-boats, steaming towards the target by day, no longer spent themselves in submerged day attacks followed by the inevitable pursuit; they maintained contact just within visual range and when darkness fell, formed up on all sides. The greater their number the more difficult it was for the convoy to shake them off.

When U-boats had less than 24 hours remaining to reach their night attack positions, attacks were in no way restricted. The radio message "Attack when darkness falls" indicated that the BdU had completed arrangements for the concentration of boats. After this, BdU Command Headquarters observed the development of the situation and intervened only if contact should be lost ... If the escort were close to the convoy the attack could be made from outside it, from, say 1,000–3,000 yards.

Usually it was necessary to find a gap in the escort line, through which the U-boat must penetrate. Many commanders purposely drove into the midst of the convoy, for once among the ships they were protected from the escorts and were often able to expend all their torpedoes. A strong escort, as usually found on the second night of a convoy operation, would often keep the boats far from the ships, compel them to submerge or chase them far ahead or astern. It was therefore vital to continue shadowing reports throughout the night. Should this be forgotten in the heat of battle or only incompletely accomplished, BdU Command Headquarters intervened by making a particular boat responsible for shadowing. Every night attack was made on the surface. German boats never employed the tactics of approaching the enemy half-submerged, with tanks already flooded. This method, not unknown in other navies, was considered ill-advised. At dawn the boats had to withdraw promptly from the immediate vicinity of the convoy. If they left it too late they were forced to submerge by the escorts and pursued and held off for a long time. Under such conditions it was difficult to maintain unbroken contact. For this reason BdU Command Headquarters were not perturbed if shadowing reports ceased for a few hours after daybreak.'[1]

The westward shift of the attack

From February to April 1941 the main operational area of the U-boats had shifted farther and farther westward beyond 20° West. Convoy surface and air escorts and patrols operating up to 20° West had become so strong (many convoys had up to eight and more escorts) that it was very difficult for the U-boats operating independently to penetrate the strong enemy screens. An even further shift to the west was brought about by the necessity, in the employment of wolf-pack tactics, of having a vast amount of sea room to allow the U-boats furthest from an intercepted convoy time in which to close on the prey. This had particular relevance to east-bound (homeward) convoys, which had to be intercepted at a sufficient distance from the coast of the UK to allow the boats to concentrate in daylight, without being forced to submerge (and consequently lose the advantage of their high surface speed) by air patrols. Consequently the U-boat patrol lines were drawn up in the area bounded by the meridians 25°–35° West to the south-east of Iceland, where the convoys were inadequately protected and the most distant U-boats would have time to concentrate for an attack.

The Italian U-boats were allocated to the area 47° 30′ North–57° 30′ North and 15°–25° West (i.e., to the south-west of the German boats), where they would not prejudice German operations, and if they were sighted might assist the German boats by causing traffic to move into the German zone of operations.

The order for the westward shift of the German boats was given on 8 May 1941. Of the five boats already operating to the

south of Iceland on that date, four were already pursuing Convoy OB318 in a westerly direction. This outward-bound convoy had been sighted by U110 on 7 May, and was attacked by four boats (U94, U110, U201 and U556) over four days and nights which resulted in the loss of seven merchant ships grossing 39,250 tons and damage to a further two of 10,955 tons. In the attack one U-boat (U110) was lost when the corvette Aubretia and two destroyers, Broadway and Bulldog, forced her to surface with well-aimed depth-charge attacks. U110 (Lemp) surfaced about three-quarters of a mile away from Bulldog which at once turned to ram, 'but on reflection her captain thought there might be a chance to capture the U-boat and countermanded his previous order ... About a cable's length from U110 the Bulldog stopped and sent a boarding-party over in a whaler. By this time the crew of U110 had abandoned ship. Several loads of confidential books and papers were ferried over to Bulldog and the greatest prize of all, an Enigma machine complete with a signal set up ready for transmission [of which see below]. After rescuing survivors [Lemp was not among them] U110 was taken in tow by Bulldog, but sank on 11 May.'[2]

After this operation the three surviving boats formed up with four others to form the Western Group which were disposed in a patrol line (each boat twenty miles apart) 350 miles south-east of Cape Farewell, Greenland. The group remained there, maintaining radio silence, for a week without any result. On 15 May they were ordered 240 miles to the south-west where they formed another patrol line with better results. On 19 May Convoy HX126 ran into the western flank of the patrol line. Although the convoy took evasive action to the north-west, a pack of five boats caught up with it on the second night of the chase and sank nine ships grossing 54,451 tons and damaged one ship of 13,037 tons. No further convoys were intercepted during May and only one convoy, HX133, was intercepted in June. Most of the sinkings (72.35 per cent) for the three months April–June had been accomplished by lone boats and not by deliberately positioned patrol lines of closely spaced boats across the probable convoy tracks. The most successful were the six U-boats operating independently off the Azores and West African coast, where the bulk of shipping still sailed as independents and those in convoy had no A/S escorts. During these three months only four wolf-pack attacks on convoys had materialized (in April Convoy SC26 had been attacked by six boats in 28° West before the A/S escort had joined – nine ships were sunk – but this was before Dönitz's BdU-controlled operations commenced):

The interception problem

The failure to intercept and bring about convoy battles by the patrol lines gave rise to the suspicion that it was not only the inherent factors such as the dispersion of the convoy routes over a vast area and too few Frontboote, but that radio transmissions by the boats (the major weak point in the control of operations by the BdU) had enabled the enemy to locate and avoid them by direction-finding (i.e., by taking cross-bearings on the U-boat

Right: *U48*, Type VIIB 750-ton Atlantic boat. She eventually became the most successful U-boat of the Second World War. She sank 53 ships of 318,111 tons.

Below: *U68* (Type IXC) undergoing trials in the Baltic, April 1941; she was sunk in April 1944 after being depth-charged by aircraft of the escort carrier *Guadalcanal* north of Madeira.

transmissions which would give an angle of intersection, or fix, and thus give away the approximate position of the boats). In an effort to minimize this possibility Dönitz issued a standing order designed to eliminate the less important radio messages:

'*In attack area*: Radio is to be used only for messages of tactical importance or on request from the command, or if the enemy is already aware of the boats' positions.

On passage: As above. Occasional transmissions of less important information may be made if it is certain that succeeding boats or those already in the area concerned will not be endangered.

Technical: Wavelengths are to be changed frequently; additional channels to be introduced; new radio procedure to make it difficult for the enemy to take bearings.'[3]

The eastward shift of the attack

When it became obvious that these measures had done nothing to solve the problem of interception it was deemed necessary to abandon the western zone of operations and shift the weight of the attack eastwards nearer the more heavily patrolled waters of the UK. 'For ten weeks the Eastern Atlantic had been unoccupied', Hessler explains, 'because of enemy patrols which restricted their freedom of movement ... [but] it now seemed necessary to accept these difficult conditions rather than to operate in less dangerous areas [to the west] where traffic could not be located.'[4] The return of the boats to the eastern Atlantic facilitated another attempt at direct co-operation with air reconnaissance. With more aircraft available the Condors of I/KG.40 were able to make two or three daily reconnaissance sorties, but only in two cases were the U-boats able to take action to intercept convoys and attack as a result of sighting reports from aircraft (this was against Convoys OG69 and S181). Moreover, the shift back into eastern Atlantic waters only made matters worse: from the beginning of July up to 12 September only four convoys were attacked by wolf-packs. And such was the strength of the defences that the average monthly sinkings fell from the 309,268 tons achieved in the previous three months to 99,113 tons during July and August. 'British A/S forces had increased to an astonishing degree,' laments the German authority.

'Not only had the number of escort vessels and aircraft risen, but their methods of keeping the U-boats at a distance had improved. Where a few months ago one U-boat had been adequate for shadowing, a group was now required. As far as the U-boat commanders and air observers could ascertain the convoys had both inner and outer screens. The latter increased the difficulties of making contact, for the boats were kept at a distance from which they could not discover the position of the convoy in relation to the escorts. Even if they did find this out and prepared to attack, they had first to haul ahead, by-pass the escorts or proceed under them, which entailed a considerable loss of time and often meant losing the forward attacking position for which they had striven. By day it was impossible to haul ahead inside the outer screen. At night these escort vessels usually closed in round the ships to increase the direct protection.'[5]

The Enigma factor

Although Britain's strength in A/S forces had increased considerably from the 180 vessels of all kinds when war broke out

to 695 by June 1941 (destroyers 248; corvettes 99; sloops 48 and 300 trawlers and A/S yachts) and the average number of escorts per convoy had not only risen from one during the summer of 1940 to five, but were also being used far more effectively since the introduction of the escort groups, this was only a part of the reason why the German attack had been largely thwarted during the summer months. The situation with regard to the problem of interception had profoundly altered in Britain's favour when the cryptanalysts of the GC and CS (Government Codes and Cipher School, of which GCHQ is the modern equivalent) at Bletchley Park broke and began to read the German Naval Enigma machine cipher settings, common to both the German surface fleet and to the U-boats, for home waters and the Atlantic. The first substantial break into these settings occurred in the latter part of March, but this only allowed the cryptanalysts to read the radio traffic for the previous month. The real break came on 9 May, when the capture of *U110* by the destroyer *Bulldog* yielded an Enigma machine and also the short-signal code-books which enabled GC and CS to read from then onwards the *Kurzsignale* (short signals in which the U-boats transmitted their sighting reports). By August complete mastery over the home waters and Atlantic Enigma settings had been achieved, allowing the cryptanalysts to read concurrently the U-boats' *Kurzsignale*.

This breakthrough on the cryptanalytic front proved decisive in that it led to a great improvement in the successful evasive routing of convoys away from the U-boat patrol line dispositions, resulting in so few interceptions as to thwart the u-boat commanders and the *BdU* in what they had expected to achieve. For despite the comparatively low average of monthly sinkings (191,559 tons for the whole year) by the U-boats, Britain's position was none the less precarious. The combined output of new shipping from the UK and all the Commonwealth yards was only 1,000,000 tons during 1941, whereas the losses from *all causes* during the year was 4,328,558 tons, of which the U-boats were responsible for 53.15 per cent. Britain needed to import a minimum of 36,000,000 tons of dry cargo and 720 tanker-cargoes of oil per annum, and the shipping losses in 1941 resulted in a deficit of 7,000,000 tons of supply-imports and 2,000,000 tons of food. Oil stocks, already nearing the danger point, shrunk by another 318,000 tons. Although the shortages were met by withdrawals from existing reserves of stock, it seriously depleted the margin above the irreducible minimum with which Britain would need to continue prosecuting the war. It is obvious, therefore, that the U-boat campaign, despite an average monthly sinking rate which was only 38 per cent of the 1917 average, still had decisive capabilities and could well have been decisive in 1941 had it not been for the breaking of the Enigma settings. 'That the Enigma breakthrough made a decisive contribution ... may be judged by the scope of the intelligence it provided,' the official historian of British Intelligence points out.

'From May onwards, with the British intercept stations receiving *every* signal transmitted by or to the U-boats, and with the U-boat

Right: The commissioning of *U118*, Type XB 1,760-ton minelaying U-boat, in December 1941. The white circle on the conning tower denotes that the boat is under training. She was sunk in a depth-charge attack by USN aircraft of the escort carrier *Bogue*, west of the Canary Islands on 12 June 1943.

Command employing the home waters settings of the Enigma, *every signal was being deciphered*. Nor was that all. The U-boat Command [having] decided that in the north Atlantic it must exercise a centralized co-ordination over their dispositions and attacks ... involved it in transmitting comprehensive situation reports and patrol instructions on the basis of which the Admiralty Operational Intelligence Centre (OIC) and GC and CS were able to make a detailed study of the capacities, the tactics and methods of attack of the U-boats and the OIC was able to produce, day after day, a virtually complete chart of their dispositions.'

Nor was the Enigma breakthrough the only method by which the German attack was blunted.

The development of British counter-measures
From 18 June the minimum speed limit for independently routed ships was raised from thirteen to fifteen knots, and a

Monthly breakdown of losses

Month	Independent sailings	Ships in convoy	Stragglers	Dispersals	Total
April	(24) 148,372	(12) 73,395	(3) 9,122	(2) 8,830	(41) 239,719
May	(40) 223,588	(16) 98,970	(4) 23,141	(3) 16,569	(63) 362,268
June	(40) 200,240	(19) 86,070	(4) 19,158	(3) 20,349	(66) 325,817
July	(14) 73,297	(10) 30,393	—	(2) 8,934	(26) 112,624
August	(9) 18,483	(18) 67,120	—	—	(27) 85,603
September	(14) 48,072	(39) 151,184	(4) 12,981	—	(57) 212,237
October	(11) 88,143	(17) 82,643	—	—	(28) 170,786
November	(6) 36,675	(7) 30,850	(2) 8,531	—	(15) 76,056
December	(17) 67,090	(6) 26,136	—	—	(23) 93,226

dramatic decline in losses of independents ensured. From an average of 34.66 per month for the three months April–June, the figure dropped to an average of 11.8 during the subsequent six months.

Convoys were also routed north, nearer to Iceland, where an advanced fuelling base came into operation at Hvalfiord which served to extend the limit of RN convoy escorts to 35° West. Moreover, the introduction of continuous A/S escort right across the width of the Atlantic became possible in June when a base for Canadian A/S escorts was opened at St. John's, Newfoundland (the Canadian escorts met the convoys at the limit of the RN escorts' range). The acquisition by way of Lend-Lease from the USA, and the construction of long-range aircraft together with the opening of an air base in Iceland, also extended the range of air cover to a maximum distance of 700 miles from the British Isles, 600 miles from the coast of Canada and some 400 miles to the south of Iceland. Although this still left a gap about 300-miles wide in mid-Atlantic where no air cover could be provided, the 'system of routing the convoys to the north so as to keep close to the air and surface escort bases in Iceland had the effect that in the long summer days of these latitudes the enemy had either to attack by day or not at all. Air cover prevented pursuit by day and so left the U-boats insufficient time to overhaul and attack a convoy by night.'[6]

New innovations in A/S technology also made the U-boats' task more difficult and dangerous. The fitting to A/S vessels of High Frequency Direction Finders (HF/DF, known as 'Huff Duff') made it possible to detect the approximate direction of the short-wave radio signals which the U-boats employed in making sighting reports and in massing for an attack on a convoy. The Germans believed it was impossible to D/F a short-wave radio signal and that anyway the *Kurzsignale* were of too short a duration to be homed on by direction-finders. Although the 'Huff Duff' gave errors in direction of up to 30 per cent, this was not critical because its real value was to rob the U-boats of the element of surprise by warning the escort commanders that an attack was imminent, and an idea of the number of U-boats that were massing. The first U-boat to be sunk as a direct result of an HF/DF bearing was *U587* (Borcherdt), which sent sighting reports of Convoy WS17 on 27 March 1942. Homing on the HF/DF bearings, four of the escort destroyers sank *U587* with a depth-charge attack. The U-boats also lost their immunity to air attack at night when aircraft were fitted with 'Leigh Lights' (named after the Commander who invented the idea). A 24in naval searchlight with a range of 5,000 yards was installed in a retractable ventral housing beneath the aircraft, fitted in a mounting which gave a 20° movement in the horizontal and vertical planes. The brightness of the light caused some pilots to be drawn down and unwittingly fly into the sea. This problem, and the dazzle from the beam, was overcome by lowering the beam so that only the tip of it was used to illuminate the target U-boat. But it was the breaking of the Enigma settings, above all else, with the resulting ability to intercept convoys, that had the decisive result.

Westwards again

Because sinkings had been slight in July and August after the shift to the east, the *BdU* once more decided to shift the areas of operations back to the west. 'Despite the unsatisfactory results of the first search across the Atlantic in May and June,' states Hessler, 'it was now considered that a westward thrust could be risked, particularly as the number of available boats had greatly increased.'[7] The total number of commissioned boats in September was 197 of which 73 were *Frontboote*. This time, in an attempt to overcome the interception problem, it was decided to sweep the whole of the north Atlantic between Britain and Newfoundland, and from Greenland south to the Azores, with groups of boats forming patrol lines which were to be kept moving rapidly over great areas. The Germans were of course unaware that the Enigma settings had been compromised and although the boats scoured practically the whole of the north Atlantic only five convoys (SC42, SC44, HG73, SC48, SC52) were sighted and attacked from mid-September until early in November: a total of 46 ships grossing 198,079 tons were sunk in these convoy battles.

Disappointed and baffled by the meagre results, the *BdU*, on 19 November, abandoned the strategy of broad patrol lines in favour of small groups. Dönitz gave his reasons for this in the War Diary:

'The (broad) patrol line ... brought no success and has been dissolved. Theoretically a narrow patrol line has more chance of intercepting enemy traffic than a wide formation of single boats. In practice, however, single boats have found convoys, whereas with one exception, no patrol line has located the enemy without the help of a previous sighting report from a detached boat. Why this should be is not clear. It cannot depend on chance, because chance does not always favour the one side, and this state of affairs will soon have existed for more than nine months. *It is possible that from some source or other the British obtain information on our concentrated formations, and take diversionary measures which occasionally lead them into the path of detached boats* [author's italics]. Their information might be gained:
(a) As a result of treachery ... (b) *By decrypting our radio messages: the Naval Staff continually checks up on this possibility, but regards it as out of the question.* (c) By co-ordinating radio traffic analysis and sighting reports: we cannot judge this as we do not know how much information the enemy gains from sighting reports and radio traffic, or how accurate is his D/F organization. *BdU* has this question constantly in mind ... (d) By radar: this may be helping the enemy to take avoiding action, but so far we have no confirmation.

All these possibilities are not enough to explain the failure of our concentrated formations, and it has therefore been decided to employ another method. The boats will be formed into several groups, not too far apart, so that if any boat sights a convoy, the others will be able to come up relatively quickly. I do not intend these groups to be stationary, but to move about constantly, to make it more difficult for the enemy to escape ...'[8]

Suspension of Atlantic operations

Before this new strategic card could be played, a crisis in the Mediterranean led to a suspension of operations in the Atlantic and the plans for the new operational dispositions were not realized. On 18 November 1941, the British Eighth Army began an advance in Cyrenaica, code-named Operation 'Crusader', before which Rommel's Africa Korps was in full retreat. To assist Rommel by attacking British supply traffic sailing from Gibraltar along the North African coast, eleven U-boats were immediately dispatched from the north Atlantic into the Mediterranean. These were followed by a second wave, so that by 15 December a total of twenty U-boats had passed through the Straits of Gibraltar, three (*U95*, *U208*, *U451*) being lost in the run through the heavily patrolled 'mousetrap'. By this date only five U-boats were left in the Atlantic, and these were concentrated off Gibraltar to attack any inward or outward convoys, so indirectly helping the situation in North Africa. Apart from scoring major successes by sinking the aircraft carrier *Ark Royal* (*U81* – Guggenberger – on 13 November) and the battleship *Barham* (*U331* – von Tiesenhausen – on 25 November) the Mediterranean boats sank only twelve merchant ships grossing 40,684 tons up to the end of December: a small return averaging 2,034 tons or 0.6 ships per boat.

The North Atlantic had also been denuded of boats to form, on Hitler's personal orders, a Northern Waters Group based on Norway to attack any British convoys attempting to ferry supplies to Russia (which Germany had invaded on 22 June). The results achieved by these six boats was even more dismal than the Mediterranean boats. From August to December the British ran nine PQ convoys to Russia and four QP return

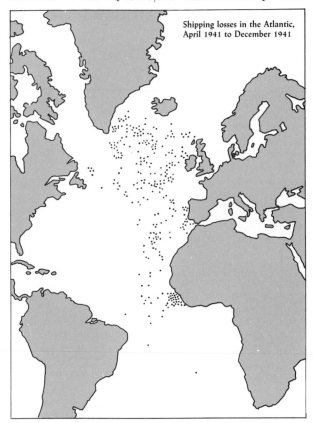

Shipping losses in the Atlantic, April 1941 to December 1941

convoys, with the loss of only one Russian merchant ship. Three Russian independents were also accounted for, bringing the total to four ships of 8,548 tons: an average per boat of a mere 1,424 tons. These excursions into the Mediterranean and to northern waters Dönitz rightly viewed as auxiliary tasks uselessly dividing the strength he needed in the tonnage war in the Atlantic, as he objected in the War Diary: 'The war will ultimately be decided by attacks on Britain's imports, which are the main objective.' When the Japanese attacked the American Fleet at Pearl Harbor on 7 December, prompting Hitler to declare war on the United States four days later, Dönitz saw a golden opportunity to renew the tonnage war in the Atlantic with a rich harvest of easy targets being offered in the American coastal area, where, he rightly predicted 'there can hardly be any question of an efficient patrol, at least patrol used to U-boats. Attempts must be made as quickly as possible to utilize these advantages . . . and to *beat the drum* along the American coast.'[9]

U-boat losses April to December 1941

Date	Boat	Cause and location
5 April	U76	Depth-charged by RN destroyers *Wolverine* and sloop *Scarborough*: S of Iceland.
28 April	U65	Depth-charged by RN corvette *Gladiolus*: S of Iceland.
9 May	U110	Depth-charged by RN destroyers *Broadway* and *Bulldog* and corvette *Aubretia*. Captured and foundered in tow: SW of Ireland.
2 June	U147	Depth-charged by RN destroyer *Wanderer* and corvette *Periwinkle*: NW of Ireland.
18 June	U138	Depth-charged by RN destroyers *Faulknor*, *Fearless*, *Forester*, *Foresight* and *Foxhound*: 100 miles W Cape Trafalgar.
27 June	U556	Depth-charged by RN corvettes *Celandine*, *Gladiolus* and *Nasturtium*: SW of Iceland.
29 June	U651	Depth-charged by RN destroyers *Malcolm* and *Scimitar* and minesweeper/sloop *Speedwell* and corvettes *Arabis* and *Violet*: S of Iceland.

Date	Boat	Cause and location
3 Aug	U401	Depth-charged by RN destroyers *St Albans* and *Wanderer* and corvette *Hydrangea*: SW of Ireland.
9 Aug	U144	Torpedoed by Russian submarine *Shch. 307*: Gulf of Finland.
25 Aug	U452	Depth-charged by RN trawler *Vascama* and RAF aircraft (209 Sqn): S of Iceland.
27 Aug	U570	Depth-charged by RAF aircraft (269 Sqn): 80 miles S of Iceland; captured and commissioned into RN as HMS *Graph*.
10 Sept	U501	Depth-charged by RCN corvettes *Chambly* and *Moosejaw*: S of Greenland.
11 Sept	U207	Depth-charged by RN destroyers *Leamington* and *Veteran*: Denmark Strait.
4 Oct	U111	Depth-charged by RN trawler *Lady Shirley*: WSW of Tenerife.
19 Oct	U204	Depth-charged by RN sloop *Rochester* and corvette *Mallow*: Straits of Gibraltar.
11 Nov	U580	Accident: collision off Memel.
15 Nov	U583	Accident: collision in Baltic.
16 Nov	U433	Depth-charged by RN corvette *Marigold*: S of Malaga.
28 Nov	U95	Torpedoed by R.Neth.N. submarine *0.21*: E of Gibraltar.
30 Nov	U206	Depth-charged by RAF aircraft (502 Sqn): W of St-Nazaire.
11 Dec	U208	Depth-charged by RN corvette *Bluebell*: W of Gibraltar.
15 Dec	U127	Depth-charged by RN destroyer *Nestor*: SW of Cape St. Vincent.
16 Dec	U557	Accident: collision with Italian torpedo-boat: SW of Crete.
17 Dec	U131	Depth-charged by RN destroyers *Stanley*, *Blakeney* and *Exmoor* and sloop *Stork*, corvette *Pentstemon*, and aircraft of escort carrier *Audacity* (802 Sqn): off Cape St. Vincent.
18 Dec	U434	Depth-charged by RN destroyers *Stanley* and *Blakeney*: SW of Cape St. Vincent.
19 Dec	U574	Rammed RN sloop *Stork* off Lisbon.
21 Dec	U451	Depth-charged by RN aircraft of escort carrier *Audacity* (812 Sqn): off Tangier.
21 Dec	U567	Depth-charged by RN sloop *Deptford* and corvette *Samphire*: N of Azores.
23 Dec	U79	Depth-charged by RN destroyers *Hasty* and *Hotspur*: off Bardia.
28 Dec	U75	Depth-charged by RN destroyer *Kipling*: off Mersa Matruh.

U-boat strength during the Third Phase: April to December 1941

and success rate expressed as tonnage sunk per U-boat per day at sea

Month 1941	Total no. U-boats	No. of *Frontboote*	Training and trials boats	Monthly average of daily number of boats at sea	Average tonnage sunk per U-boat per day at sea
April	121	28	93	19	420
May	139	33	106	24	486
June	150	38	112	32	339
July	169	53	116	27	134
Aug	184	64	120	36	76
Sept	197	73	124	36.5	193
Oct	219	75	144	36	153
Nov	238	81	157	38	66
Dec	250	88	162	25	120

Analysis of causes

Cumulative total in parentheses

Surface vessels	20	(41)
Shared by surface vessels and naval aircraft	1	(1)
Shared by surface vessels and shore-based aircraft	1	(3)
Naval aircraft	1	(2)
Shore-based aircraft	2	(3)
Shared by naval and shore-based aircraft	—	(0)
Torpedoed by submarine	2	(6)
Mines	—	(5)
Accidental causes	3	(6)
Unknown causes	—	(2)
Total	30	(69)

Paukenschlag
The fourth phase, January to July 1942

The campaign in American waters

The entry of the United States into the war made it imperative for the Germans to achieve a greater rate of sinking than ever before. Because much of the US merchant marine and shipbuilding potential would now be at the disposal of Great Britain, the *BdU* estimated that a monthly sinking rate of 800,000 tons (which was 200,000 tons in excess of Holtzendorff's 600,000-ton equation for victory in 1917) would be necessary if a mortal blow was to be dealt and victory made certain. During the last six months of 1941 the U-boats had only sunk ships at the rate of 125,088 tons per month, or a mere 15.63 per cent of the desired total. However, the *BdU*'s optimism that the 800,000 ton a month rate could be achieved was occasioned by the fact that he had started 1941 with a mere handful of 22 *Frontboote*, and that during the second half of 1941 the number of *Frontboote* actually engaged in operations in the Atlantic had averaged from fourteen to seventeen boats, whereas the number of *Frontboote* available at the beginning of 1942 was 91 and would rise gradually to 138 by July.

As single ship traffic could be expected along the entire eastern American seaboard, it was imperative that a tremendous and sudden blow be struck before the United States had time to introduce a convoy system and expand their A/S forces. Unfortunately only two 1,050-ton Type IXB (*U123* – Hardegen and *U109* – Bleichroot) and three 1,120-ton Type XC (*U130* – Kals, *U125* – Folkers and *U66* – Zapp) were immediately available out of the suitably large boats. 'Operation '*Paukenschlag*' [drum roll] was carried out by these five boats disposed between the St. Lawrence and Cape Hatteras ... As a simultaneous strike by all five promised the best results, they were instructed to move unobserved from the Newfoundland Bank to the US coast. Their progress westward was plotted at U-Boat Headquarters, and it was not until 12th January that they were ordered to launch the attack ... Despite the delayed start and the small number of attackers, results were excellent. Traffic of independent ships between New York and Cape Hatteras was so dense that it was impossible to seize all the opportunities.'[1]

Defences were practically non-existent apart from a few unpractised sea and air patrols, and at times each U-boat had up to ten ships in sight sailing with lights as in peacetime. Realizing how effective '*Paukenschlag*' was progressing, from the numerous intercepted distress calls from merchant ships off the US seaboard, the *BdU* at once decided to assemble every available large boat and dispatch them to the area. '*U103, U106* and *U107* arrived in the vicinity of Chesapeake Bay before the first boats had to return and thus the continued occupation of

the coast between New York and Cape Hatteras was temporarily assured.'[2]

Simultaneously with Operation '*Paukenschlag*' a group of seven medium-size 770-ton boats (one Type VIIB – *U87* – and six Type VIIC – *U582, U135, U552, U203, U86* and *U754*) named Group *Ziethen*, began operations off Newfoundland between the south coast of the island and latitude 43° North in contiguous attack areas. This disposition would have proved effective, as most of the group found targets in single vessels and small weakly escorted convoys near the coast. But the intense cold and the heavy ground swell on the Newfoundland Banks caused considerable problems. Freezing conditions, snow storms, fog and heavy seas caused torpedo failures and many misses, adversely affecting the results to the extent that each boat only succeeded in sinking two or three ships. However two Type VIIC boats (*U575* and *U96*) which followed in the wake of Group *Ziethen* in February, moved south on their own initiative to avoid the adverse conditions and began operating between New York and Cape Hatteras. The endurance of these medium-size boats was greater by three weeks than the U-boat Command had thought possible, and the *BdU* quickly capitalized on the knowledge by sending further groups of medium-size boats to probe the weak spot in the shipping defences off the US coast. 'One of the most surprising facts regarding the havoc wrought off the American coast ...,' writes Captain Roskill, ... 'is that there were never more than about twelve U-boats working in those waters at any one time – no greater strength than the enemy had sometimes mustered to make a "pack attack" on a single one of our convoys.'[3]

American coastal convoys instituted

Although New York was no further from the U-boat bases than Freetown, where the U-boats were regularly operating, the Americans had failed to make any contingency plans for a U-boat offensive off their eastern seaboard. And even when the attack developed, they failed to institute an interlocking convoy system to marry up with the North Atlantic convoys, and employed their sparse A/S forces uselessly in A/S hunting patrols, ignoring the British experience and seemingly forgetting President Wilson's deprecation of the method in the first war as 'hunting the hornets all over the farm'. It was only with prodding by the First Sea Lord (Admiral Pound) and Churchill, together with the catastrophic losses, that a coastal convoy system was started in the middle of May – a full four months after the slaughter of their independently routed shipping had commenced. But with the introduction of these convoys the U-boats

Right: *U71* crash-diving to survive this Sunderland attack in the Bay of Biscay 1942, only to be scuttled in Wilhelmshaven at the end of the war.

switched the weight of their attack to the Gulf of Mexico and the Caribbean, which the US convoy system initially did not embrace, and the great flow of independently routed US shipping continued to offer the U-boat virtually undefended targets. The extension of the operational area this far afield was made possible by the arrival in the Atlantic of the first of the Type XIV U-tankers (U459) which became known as *Milchkühe* (milch cows). Carrying 720 tons of diesel fuel, of which up to 600 tons (depending on the time spent at sea) was available for replenishing the operational boats in distant waters, they enabled up to twelve medium boats to carry out operations in the remotest parts of the Caribbean. When convoy was eventually introduced in these waters during July the results were immediate and losses dropped substantially from the peak they reached in May and June.

In conjunction with the losses in all theatres for the 7-month period January–July, the U-boats sank a total of 3,376,966 tons of shipping, or a monthly average of 482,423 tons, which was only 60 per cent of Dönitz's 800,000-ton equation for victory, and was only 78 per cent of the average

monthly sinkings achieved from February to August 1917. The score would undoubtedly have been greater if Hitler had not interfered with the dispositions. Fearful that the Allies would invade Norway in response to Stalin's demands for a second front to help relieve the pressure on his hard-pressed armies, the *Führer* decided, in February, that every available surface craft and twenty medium-size *Frontboote* should be sent to defend the Norwegian coast. As the provision of these twenty U-boats seriously prejudiced the results attainable in the US theatre, Dönitz, who was perturbed at this misdirection of forces, protested that '... The Allied problem is chiefly one of shipping and escort vessels. The more ships that are sunk, and the more protection the enemy is obliged to provide for his vital supplies from across the Atlantic, the less he will be able to spare for a landing [in Norway] which, without adequate supplies would be foredoomed to failure ...'[4]

However, the Naval Staff evidently saw no reason to oppose Hitler's obsession with Norway and vetoed Dönitz's argument pointing out that 'although there can be no doubt that every ton of enemy shipping sunk diminishes the enemy's potential for operations overseas, the Naval Staff considers that despite losses, the enemy still has sufficient ships for action against Norway'.[5] Thus the proposed, and as it turned out, unremunerative dispositions went ahead, depriving the *BdU* of twenty units that would have added substantially to the slaughter being wreaked off the US coast.

Monthly breakdown of losses

Month	Independent sailings	Ships in convoy	Stragglers	After dispersal	Total
January	(43) 224,475	(6) 34,146	(5) 26,410	(2) 16,193	(56) 301,224
February	(61) 359,382	(10) 62,959	(1) 6,914	–	(72) 429,255
March	(89) 485,176	(3) 17,226	(1) 5,112	–	(93) 507,514
April	(78) 399,345	(3) 18,816	–	–	(81) 418,161
May	(115) 534,143	(14) 82,692	–	–	(129) 616,835
June	(122) 569,916	(14) 67,010	–	–	(136) 636,926
July	(62) 263,180	(12) 61,883	(3) 20,998	(19) 120,990	(96) 467,051

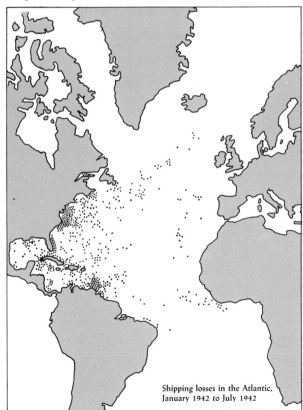

Shipping losses in the Atlantic, January 1942 to July 1942

While dealing with the dissipation of forces, it is interesting to note that the U-boats operating from the extreme north of Norway against the Arctic convoys to Russia, netted only 25 ships of 117,246 tons from January to July 1942, or an average of 3.57 ships a month (sixteen of the ships lost being from the ill-fated Convoy PQ17 which had scattered when it was erroneously believed that the convoy was under threat of attack by the battleship *Tirpitz*).

Allied shipbuilding capacity

As we have seen, despite their success during the first seven months of 1942, the average monthly sinkings by U-boat action was 40 per cent short of the *BdU*'s demand. To make matters worse it now came to light that German forecasts of British and American ship construction capabilities had been grossly underestimated. During June the German Naval Intelligence Division came up with revised estimates which suggested that during 1942 the combined output of British and US yards would be seven million tons (only fractionally above the actual figure of 6.99 million tons that was turned out), while in 1943 it was forecast that 10.8 million tons was possible (which was 4.31 million tons short of the actual figure). These startling figures

revealed that if any effective reduction were to be made in the aggregate tonnage of the Allies, the average rate of sinkings per month would have to be stepped up from the original 800,000-ton target to at least 900,000 tons a month (or 10.8 million tons per annum) if they were to be decisive (loss by other causes, i.e., Axis aircraft, surface craft and the U-boats of the Italian and Japanese Navies could push the total of losses over the rate of new construction).

The enormous output in Allied ship construction was made possible by what Morison, the official historian of US Naval Operations, has described as 'one of the mightiest of the many miracles of production by American industry'.[6] After designing a merchant ship that could be built quickly, inexpensively and in large numbers by modern assembly line and mass-production methods – the famous welded hull, 7,176 gross ton Liberty ship – eighteen new shipyards with 171 slipways were constructed to produce the ships. By April 1943 the goal of constructing 140 Liberty ships a month had been passed, and by 1944 the average time to build a Libery ship was only 42 days! During 1942–43, nearly 82 per cent of the total Allied aggregate of 21.38 million tons of new shipping was produced in the USA.

Dönitz, however, did not believe that 'the race between the enemy new building and U-boat sinkings is in no way hopeless'. He based this belief on the fact that US 'shipbuilding industries lie in the eastern states. Shipbuilding and ancillary industries depend mainly on oil fuel. The most important US oilfields lie

U-boat strength during the Fourth Phase: January to July 1942

and success rate expressed as tonnage sunk per U-boat per day at sea.

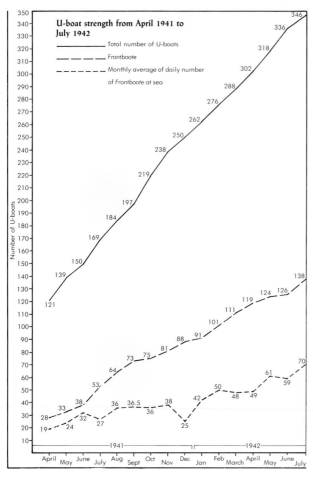

U-boat strength from April 1941 to July 1942

Month 1942	Total no. U-boats	No. of *Frontboote*	Training and trials boats	Monthly average of daily number of boats at sea	Average tonnage sunk per U-boat per day at sea
Jan	262	91	171	42	231
Feb	276	101	175	50	296
March	288	111	177	48	341
April	302	119	183	49	284
May	318	124	194	61	326
June	336	126	210	59	359
July	346	138	208	70	215

on the Gulf of Mexico. Consequently the greater part of US tanker tonnage is in the coastal traffic from the oil area to the industrial area. In the period (15.1–10.5, 1942) we sank 112 tankers of a total 927,000 tons. With every tanker sunk the American loses not only the ship for transporting oil, but he experiences immediate damage to his *new* construction . . .'[7] But the Naval Staff was less optimistic and believed that 'American industry could still have sufficient oil by the exercise of economy in other directions'.[8] Moreover, when the names of the sunken tankers were analysed, it transpired that a large proportion of them were destined for Great Britain, so that their loss affected British war industries rather than the US shipbuilding industry. Whatever the case, it was obvious that unless the U-boats could sink *at least* 900,000 tons of shipping a month, the race between enemy construction and what the U-boats could sink in excess of this figure would indeed be hopeless.

As the sinkings in US and Caribbean waters declined in the face of coastal convoys and the increasing ascendancy of US A/S forces, the *BdU* decided to withdraw the boats eastwards into the Atlantic and resume *Rudeltaktik* operations against the convoys, which it was hoped would give optimum results. A large increase in the number of available *Frontboote* would, it was confidently expected, overcome the interception problem. 'By June', Hessler explains, 'the German shipyards were able to make good the delays caused by earlier shortages of labour and the severe weather of the previous winter. The port of Kiel became a hive of activity, as a stream of new boats left on their first operation.'[9] The climax of the Battle of The Atlantic was about to begin.

U-boat losses January to July 1942

Date	Boat	Cause and location
9 Jan	U577	Depth-charged by RAF aircraft (230 Sqn): NW of Mersa Matruh.
12 Jan	U374	Torpedoed by RN submarine *Unbeaten*: E of Catania.
15 Jan	U93	Depth-charged by RN destroyer *Hesperus*: W of Cape St. Vincent.
2 Feb	U581	Depth-charged by RN destroyer *Westcott*: SW of Azores.
6 Feb	U82	Depth-charged by RN sloop *Rochester* and corvette *Tamarisk*: Azores area.
1 March	U656	Depth-charged by USN aircraft (VP.82): E of Newfoundland.
14 March	U133	Mined: off Salamis.
15 March	U503	Depth-charged by USN aircraft (VP.82): off Newfoundland.
24 March	U655	Rammed RN Minesweeper/sloop *Sharpshooter*: N of Hammerfest.
27 March	U587	Depth-charged by RN destroyers *Volunteer*, *Leamington*, *Aldenham* and *Grove*: SW of Ireland.
29 March	U585	Depth-charged by RN destroyer *Fury*: NE of Vardo.
4 April	U702	Unknown: North Sea.

Date	Boat	Cause and location
14 April	U85	Depth-charged by USN destroyer *Roper*: off Cape Hatteras.
14 April	U252	Depth-charged by RN sloop *Stork* and corvette *Vetch*: SW of Ireland.
1 May	U573	Interned Cartagena after depth-charge attack by RAF aircraft (233 Sqn): NW of Algiers. Commissioned into Spanish Navy as G.7.
2 May	U74	Depth-charged by RN destroyers *Wishart* and *Wrestler* and RAF aircraft (202 Sqn): SE of Valencia.
9 May	U352	Depth-charged by USCG cutter *Icarus*: off Raleigh Bay, North Carolina.
28 May	U568	Depth-charged by RN destroyers *Hero*, *Eridge* and *Hurworth*: off Tobruk.
2 June	U652	Torpedoed by *U.81* to scuttle her after depth-charge attack by RN (815 Sqn) and RAF (203 Sqn) aircraft: off Sollum.
13 June	U157	Depth-charged by USCG cutter *Thetis*: N of Havana.
30 June	U158	Depth-charged by USN aircraft (VP.74): W of Bermuda.
3 July	U215	Depth-charged by RN armed yacht *Le Tigre*: off Nantucket Island.
5 July	U502	Depth-charged by RAF aircraft (172 Sqn): W of La Rochelle.
7 July	U701	Depth-charged by USAAF aircraft (396 Sqn): off Cape Hatteras.
11 July	U136	Depth-charged by RN sloop *Pelican*, frigate *Spey* and French destroyer *Léopard*: NW of Canary Islands.
13 July	U153	Depth-charged by USN destroyer *Landsdowne*: off Colon.
15 July	U576	Depth-charged by USN aircraft (VS.9) and gunfire from auxiliary *Unicoi*: off Wilmington.
17 July	U751	Depth-charged by RAF aircraft (61 and 502 Sqns): NW of Cape Ortegal.
24 July	U90	Depth-charged by RCN destroyer *St. Croix*: North Atlantic.
31 July	U213	Depth-charged by RN sloops *Erne*, *Rochester* and *Sandwich*: W of Punta Delgada.
31 July	U588	Depth-charged by RCN destroyer *Skeena* and corvette *Wetaskiwin*: N. Atlantic.
31 July	U754	Depth-charged by RCAF aircraft (113 Sqn): S of Nova Scotia.

Analysis of causes

Cumulative total in parentheses

Surface vessels	17	(58)
Shared by surface vessels and naval aircraft	–	(1)
Shared by surface vessels and shore-based aircraft	1	(4)
Naval aircraft	3	(5)
Shore-based aircraft	5	(8)
Shared by naval and shore-based aircraft	2	(2)
Torpedoed by submarine	1	(7)
Mines	1	(6)
Accidental causes	–	(6)
Unknown causes	1	(3)
Interned	1	(1)
Total	32	*(101)*

Left: The Type VIID minelayer *U213* was sunk in a depth-charge attack by the sloops *Erne*, *Rochester* and *Sandwich*, west of Punta Delgada, 31 July 1942.

La Débâcle

The fifth phase, August 1942 to May 1943

Atlantic wolf-pack attacks

The *BdU*'s decision to revert to pack operations against the North Atlantic convoys was motivated and aided by two important factors. During February 1942, *B-Dienst* broke British Naval Cypher No. 3, which carried the bulk of Allied communications concerning the North Atlantic convoys. *B-Dienst* was able to read 80 per cent of the signals which figured in Naval Cypher No. 3, with only two short breaks, up until June 1943. Not only did this cryptanalytic success give the U-boat Command advance information of Allied convoy movements, but *B-Dienst* also frequently decrypted the daily signal in which the Admiralty issued its estimate of U-boat dispositions to the escort groups. The situation swung even further in the German's favour when, also during February, a fourth enciphering wheel was added to the naval Enigma machine, after the *BdU* had become suspicious of the security of the home waters cipher settings. This additional setting baffled the British GC and CS to the extent that they were unable to read the U-boat Enigma communications settings for the remainder of 1942.

Secondly, the total strength of the U-boat fleet rose in a steep curve from 250 boats in December 1941 to 358 by August 1942 and 420 by May of 1943: 120 in excess of the number that Dönitz had considered necessary for a successful blockade of the UK at the outbreak of war. However, only 52.67 per cent of the total, during the 10-month period, August 1942–May 1943, were *Frontboote*, of which a monthly average of 103.6 were at sea daily (all theatres), which was 56.6 more boats than the average number of *Frontboote* at sea during the climacteric month of April 1917.

The strategy to be employed against the North Atlantic convoys was set down in the *BdU* War Diary:

'Our counter-measures to the enemy's A/S developments being relatively backward, we have to use a large number of boats in order to disperse the surface escorts and to ensure continuity of contact with the convoy. In view of the wide areas involved, and the lack of depth in our U-boat patrol lines, it may take days to concentrate the boats for attack. Convoys should therefore be picked up early to allow the attack to be spaced over several days. Secondly, the attacks should whenever possible be launched in areas where the convoys have no air escorts. Thus ON and ONS convoys (i.e., UK–North America westward bound) must be picked up 300 to 500 miles west of the North Channel, and HX and SC convoys (i.e., Halifax/New York–UK and Sydney, Cape Breton–UK eastward bound) 300 to 500 miles to the north or south-west of Cape Race. These conditions govern the disposition of our boats. The best method of using fresh outward-bound boats is to assemble them in a formation against an ON convoy. They will pursue the convoy to the south-west, and on terminating the operation in the area of the

Newfoundland Bank, they should refuel east of Cape Race. They should then form a patrol line north-east of the Newfoundland Bank, the distance out depending on the state of fog, and attempt to pick up an SC or HX convoy. If, after a reasonable interval, the group should fail to pick up an ON or ONS convoy near the North Channel, then the boats should start a sweep to the south-west on the chance of picking up an HX or SC convoy.'[1]

The combination of a large number of *Frontboote* at sea, the *B-Dienst* decrypts and the strategy of trawling in broad formations over vast areas of the North Atlantic, did serve to solve, in large measure, the interception problem, but the result was disappointing. From the beginning of August until October 1942, 23 convoys were intercepted in the North Atlantic by U-boats in group formations: thirteen of these were by chance sightings and ten as a direct result of *B-Dienst* decrypts. Of the total number intercepted, contact was lost with eight convoys by the shadowing boats before a pack attack could develop, and in only three convoys (SC9, SC104 and SL125) were more than four ships sunk as a result of pack attacks. Of the fifteen convoys attacked by wolf-packs, 67 ships grossing 340,871 tons were sunk (68.36 per cent of the total convoy losses during the period), which was roughly 37 per cent greater than the total sunk by U-boats acting independently firing 'browning shots' at passing convoys (31 ships of 207,119 tons). However, the total losses achieved by the wolf-packs was only 22.18 per cent of the overall losses by U-boat action from August until the end of October. The sinking of independents in the Caribbean, off the coast of Brazil, north-west Africa and as far south as Capetown (a far-flung net of operations made possible by the U-tankers) yielded by far the richest harvest of 179 ships grossing 937,889 tons:

British counter-measures and German technical developments

Although bad weather – fogs and gales – had played a part in robbing the wolf-packs of better results, it was the development of Allied A/S measures that confounded them. The success of a wolf-pack attack on a convoy depended in the first instance on the U-boat that first made contact, and subsequently became the shadower, being able to transmit regular contact signals to enable the other boats of the group to close on the target. By virtue of a large number of escorts being fitted with HF/DF sets, they were able to take accurate bearings on the shadower and pin-point her position by obtaining cross-bearings, and in many instances drive her off and force her to remain submerged thus preventing her making the vital reports and bearing signals.

Right: A Type VIID in the U-boat pen in Brest.

Monthly breakdown of losses

Month	Independent sailings	Ships in convoy		Stragglers	After dispersal	Total
August	(65) 313,816	(45) 243,826	(6) 26,383	(1) 3,220	(117) 587,245
September	(60) 275,151	(28) 138,720	(8) 47,923	–	(96) 461,794
October	(54) 348,922	(25) 165,444	(10) 69,324	–	(89) 583,690

When an attack was able to develop, the escorts were now able more effectively to counter night surface attacks due to the development of a more efficient radar set. The primitive 286M radar set had the drawback of the aerial being fixed to the mast, which limited the arc of detection to 120° ahead of the ship. The improved 271M set, which began to be fitted in escort vessels during September 1941, had the advantage of full 360° cover due to the transmitter, receiver and aerial being all contained in a revolving scanner fitted above the bridge. This all-round scan, which was capable of detecting a surfaced U-boat up to four miles distant, and just eight feet of periscope at 1,300 yards, enabled the Escort Group Commander (and the captains of the individual escorts) to see at a glance both the position of the ships in the convoy as well as approaching U-boats. Together with the TBS (talk between ships) system the Escort Group Commander was now able to deal with night surface attacks with well co-ordinated tactical counter-attacks.

Depth-charge attacks had also become more accurate with the development of an ahead-throwing weapon known as 'Hedgehog'. Before this innovation, the main shortcoming of a depth-charge attack was that the pattern of charges could only be positioned as accurately as the firing ship's stern could be manoeuvred. Hedgehog fired a pattern of 24 mortar bombs which landed 300 yards ahead of the attacking ship in a circle about 130 feet in diameter, with the distance between the bombs being about twenty feet, which was about the extreme beam of a U-boat. The only drawback was that the mortar bombs were fitted with an impact fuze that would only detonate on a direct contact with a U-boat: a miss, therefore, however near, would do no harm whatsoever, whereas a depth-charge, set to explode at a given depth, could damage a U-boat with a near miss, or at least give the U-boat's crew a severe shaking. The first success with Hedgehog was the destruction of *U581* on 2 February 1942 by HMS *Westcott*.

By the autumn of 1942 Coastal Command had only one squadron of ten very long range (VLR) aircraft capable of reaching out 800 miles, from Iceland and Northern Ireland, into mid-Atlantic. As Dönitz's strategy was to locate the convoys before they reached the air gap in mid-Atlantic (i.e., beyond the reach of aircraft based on both sides of the Atlantic and in Iceland), then to concentrate against them while they were traversing it, and finally to withdraw when the convoys reached the area within air cover limits, aircraft only played a peripheral role during the convoy battles of the autumn and winter of

1942–43. However, since mid-1941 Coastal Command had been carrying out regular patrols of the U-boat transit area in the Bay of Biscay, and from the spring of 1942 these patrols were intensified. Aircraft of these patrols, equipped with Leigh Lights and ASVII radar sets, and armed with new Mk VIII aerial depth-charges (250lb), destroyed four U-boats (*U502*, *U751*, *U578*, *U165*) from July to September 1942 and severely damaged three others. Writes Hessler:

'Should this rate of casualties continue the consequence would be most serious, and it was decided to equip the boats with radar search receivers at the earliest possible moment. A suitable receiving instrument which had been produced for a different purpose by the French firm *Metox* happened to be available, and it required only slight modification and the addition of an auxiliary aerial. Production was hastened so that delivery could commence within six weeks. Meanwhile the only thing to do was to deny the enemy aircraft the chance of attacking, so all boats were ordered to remain submerged day and night when traversing the Bay of Biscay, surfacing only to recharge batteries.'[2]

This of course had the adverse effect of lengthening the time it took the boats to reach their operational areas and consequently reduced the limit of their endurance.

'The first delivery of the radar search receiver (*Metox*) was made early in August. This equipment was deliberately kept simple in order to hasten its production. It took the form of an ordinary receiver in the radio room, connected by a flexible cable to an aerial mounted on a wooden cross. Every time the boat broke surface, this contraption was rushed up to the fore end of the conning tower and mounted in a socket. It had to be turned through 90 degrees at frequent intervals in order to eliminate the dead sectors characteristic of this instrument. The equipment in this primitive form was not popular, for in heavy seas or when having to dive suddenly the wooden cross would suffer damage and the cable would get in the way when closing the conning tower hatch.'

Despite its primitive nature *Metox* proved effective in giving early warning of approaching aircraft (by detecting ASVII radar transmissions) and it is estimated that 95 per cent of U-boats in transit across the Bay of Biscay were able to dive before the approaching aircraft could get within range to launch an attack. To a large extent this rendered both day and night A/S patrols of Coastal Command over the Bay of Biscay ineffective, for both relied on the ASVII radar. *Metox* remained effective until February 1943, when the ASVII was replaced by ASVIII 10 centimetre radar, the transmissions of which *Metox* was unable to detect. Hessler explains:

'It was also essential to strengthen the U-boats' A.A. armament. But as the necessary structural alterations would require some months, the boats were meanwhile supplied with four 8mm machine-guns in improvised mountings on the conning tower rail, which could be taken below before diving. At best these had a certain morale value, for their low penetrating power afforded little protection to any boat incapable of diving.'[3]

Further developments had also been carried out with torpedoes as a result of continuing difficulties with these weapons. In the War Diary, Dönitz complained (24 June 1942) that,

'... compared with the First World War, we now have two main improvements – the bubble-free discharge and the trackless run, which, however, has reduced the speed of the torpedo to 30 knots. Yet the depth-keeping and detonation qualities of the torpedo have not even reached the level attained in 1918, although we have now had 2½ years of trials and strenuous efforts. The destructive effect of the warhead when used with an impact pistol is insufficient, as is shown by the many cases of ordinary freighters needing more than one torpedo to sink them.'[4]

An analysis of the results of torpedo hits with the impact pistol for the first six months of 1942 divulged that it had required 806 *hits* to sink 404 ships (figures from *BdU* records). 'Had we been able to use a magnetic pistol,' Hessler states, 'which requires only one torpedo to sink a ship, this would have virtually doubled the opportunities for destruction of shipping. The sinkings in the first half of 1942 would certainly have been much bigger.'[5] To overcome this unsatisfactory state of affairs a newly developed magnetic proximity fuze (Pi2) became operational at the beginning of November 1942, along with two newly developed torpedoes: the TIII electrically propelled and the G7a FAT (*Federapparat* or spring-loaded) torpedoes. The G7a FAT was designed especially for use against convoys, being designed to run a zigzag course after a predetermined length of straight run. If the torpedo missed its intended target, the period of zigzagging amidst the columns of ships in convoy, would have a far greater probability of hitting another ship than a conventional straight-running torpedo. G7a FAT was regarded as highly successful, for it raised the number of hits in convoy attacks to 75 per cent of shots fired. 'At first the U-boat crews were taken aback when the torpedo did not hit until perhaps [it had run] the third or fourth loop.'[6]

North African waters

On 8 November 1942 the *BdU* was informed of the Allied invasion of North Africa (Operation 'Torch') and the majority of boats operating in the North Atlantic were immediately ordered to hurry towards Gibraltar and the Atlantic coast of Morocco. Too late to interfere with the actual landings, the purpose was to attack the stream of shipborne supplies and reinforcements that would have to follow the invasion. By the middle of November a dozen U-boats had concentrated to the west of Gibraltar, while another group of seven penetrated the Straits into the Mediterranean. Although a great flow of traffic was passing in both directions through the waters to the west of Gibraltar the U-boats had scant success against them. This was due to the convoys being so very strongly protected by escort vessels and aircraft, that no loophole for attack could be found. They were forced to remain almost continuously submerged, even finding it difficult to surface long enough to recharge their batteries. During the remainder of November they sank six transports, the escort carrier *Avenger*, the depot ship *Hecla*, and damaged the destroyer *Marne*. But in return two U-boats (*U173* and *U98*) were lost and four so seriously damaged that they had to return to base.

Right: *U464*, Type XIV U-tanker supply boat (*Milchkühe*), was sunk in a depth-charge attack by USN aircraft, NW of Rockall on 20 August 1942.

justified, nor could I accept Naval High Command's opinion that the very sharp decline in sinkings in the Atlantic would be more than counter-balanced by the infinitely more valuable sinking of ships carrying supplies and reinforcements to the Mediterranean.'[7]

As events proved, sinkings by U-boats in the rest of the Atlantic – particularly among independents off Freetown, the coast of Brazil, Trinidad, Cape Town and in the South Atlantic – far from declining actually increased to the extent that November 1943 became the climactic month of the Second World War. Losses in all theatres reached the level of 126 ships grossing 802,160 tons: a loss rate second only to that achieved in April 1917 (860,334 tons). 'The fact that, in spite of the withdrawal of so many U-boats,' Dönitz maintained, 'our successes in the Atlantic in November were as great as they were – thanks to the concentration of enemy escort resources on the North African operations – raises the whole question whether this intervention by U-boats in the invasion was a sound move or not. Be that as it may, had they been allowed to remain in the "tonnage battle" area, their successes would have been far greater than that which they achieved off the coast of North Africa.'[8]

The reason for the fall in the level of results achieved during December (only 42 per cent of the November total) was due, in the main, to the number of U-boats operating in the remotest and most profitable areas of the Atlantic falling to twelve by mid-December. A lot of the boats, which had been supplied by U-tankers, had been in distant waters for three months or more, and had to return to the Biscay bases for long periods of overhaul and refit. For the whole of 1942 the average monthly rate of sinkings was 512,456 tons, which although only 56.93 per cent of the *BdU*'s requirement of 900,000 tons a month, had, none the less nearly proved decisive.

The results of the fifth phase
The official historian of the War at Sea explains:

'During the closing days of 1942 the Admiralty reviewed yet again the problems and prospects of the Atlantic battle. "Our shipping situation", reported a senior member of the Naval Staff, "has never been tighter"; and our surface and air escorts were still far too few. In spite of the success of the North African landings, grave anxiety was felt that future offensive plans might be delayed or even frustrated for lack of shipping. In particular fuel stocks had fallen to a very low figure. In mid-December there were only 300,000 tons of commercial bunker fuel in Britain, and consumption was running at about 130,000 tons a month ... As to the losses we had suffered during the year, it was beyond question that the enemy had done us great damage ... [and that] a further deficit of about a million tons of shipping had been added ... British imports fell below 34 million tons – one-third less than the 1939 figure ... To the British Admiralty it was plain that the Battle of the Convoy Routes was still to be decided, that the enemy had greater strength than ever before, *and that the crisis in the long-drawn struggle was near* [author's italics].'[9]

The crisis
During the middle of December GS and CS finally managed to break the U-boats' four-wheel Enigma settings, which had

Monthly breakdown of losses

Month	Independent sailings	Ships in convoy	Stragglers	After dispersal	Total
November	(87) 545,141	(35) 234,06	(3) 19,107	(1) 3,845	(126) 802,160
December	(38) 199,553	(17) 85,327	(8) 44,282	(1) 8,456	(64) 337,618

In the face of such an unfavourable exchange rate, Dönitz withdrew the boats farther to the west, into waters which were less strongly patrolled, to operate against the supply convoys bound for North Africa from the USA. On 6 December a transport and three merchant ships sailing independently were sunk to the west of the Azores, but the convoys were routed further south than the U-boat command believed and they reached Casablanca unscathed. When these U-boats were forced to return to the Biscay bases to refuel, the Naval High Command, on 23 December, cancelled their previous orders to maintain the attack on the North Africa traffic and U-boat operations against the Allied traffic supporting the invasion forces came to an end. Dönitz for his part had been opposed in principle to the continued employment of the U-boats off the Straits of Gibraltar.

'In this area the boats were being wasted and some of them would inevitably be lost without any real hope of achieving success, while at the same time there were other parts of the Atlantic which offered admirable opportunities for extensive sinkings. For there is no doubt that conditions in the rest of the Atlantic had, just as that moment, become particularly favourable for U-boat operations, because the enemy had been compelled to concentrate his available escort resources for the protection of the North Africa landings. I did not believe that a continuation of U-boat operations off Gibraltar was baffled all attempts since the previous February. This break-through was largely made possible by the recovery of the code-book which the U-boats used for their short weather reports, from *U559*, sunk sixty miles NE of Port Said on 30 October 1942. However, this advantage was temporarily nullified by *B-Dienst*'s continuing success against Naval Cypher No. 3. Not only was *B-Dienst* able to read the Admiralty's daily U-boat disposition signal, which allowed the Germans to forecast the areas through which the convoys would probably be routed, but they were also able to read the orders, resulting from the Enigma decrypts, diverting the convoys from the U-boat patrol lines, thus enabling them to redispose their forces to counter the attempted evasion. According to Hessler, nearly all the U-boat dispositions in the North Atlantic in the period January–May 1943 were based almost entirely on *B-Dienst*'s decrypts. More-over, the number of *Frontboote* reached its peak in this period (rising from 213 in January to 240 by May), allowing the *BdU* to dispose the U-boat patrol lines so widely, that evasive routing of the convoys around them would be difficult in the extreme. Despite these advantages the number of convoys intercepted and attacked during January and February was disappointing. Constant gales in the North Atlantic, which ate up the U-boats' fuel and consequently shortened the operational period, adversely affected the situation during January, although, according to Hessler, the *BdU* was of the opinion that:

'The failure to intercept was also due to the inexperience of the young U-boat Commanders and the unskilled interpretation of hydrophone noises. The case of *U201* which had pursued a school of whales for several hours, led to the embarkation in some boats of special ratings. These were to take gramophone records of the noises characteristic of schools of whales and dolphins. The noises were somewhat similar to propeller noises of a distant convoy or of a single steamship. The records were used in the training of U-boat officers and hydrophone operators.'[10]

It was not until 29 January that a convoy was actually intercepted by boats of a patrol line that led to a wolf-pack attack (*Haudegen* Group, south of Cape Race, trawling eastward towards Newfoundland). This was the westward-bound Convoy HX224, which was shadowed during a heavy westerly gale over a period of three days by *U456*, before a total of five boats could concentrate for attack. Only three ships from this convoy, grossing 24,823 tons were sunk, one of which was a straggler. In return a Flying Fortress sank *U265*. A survivor from a tanker sunk in the attack on HX224 informed the Commander of *U632* that a large convoy was following on the same route. A few hours later this convoy, SC118, passed through the centre of the *Pfeil* group patrol line. A total of twenty U-boats from the *Pfeil* and *Haudegen* Groups concentrated for the attack, and from 4 to 9 February eleven ships of 59,765 tons were sunk (three of them stragglers) and one ship of 9,272 tons was damaged. During the attack on SC118, which was heavily protected by sea and air, three U-boats were lost and four were damaged, two by air attack and two by surface escort depth-charge attack, which was a very unfavourable exchange rate for

Left: 20mm AA gunners of
U802 under training in the
Baltic, 1943.

the Germans. Equally unfavourable in terms of individual performance was the fact that of the twenty U-boats involved in the attack only three (or 15 per cent of the total force) successfully pressed home their attacks: six of the eight ships sunk (not including the stragglers) were accounted for by von Forstner in *U402* (who also accounted for the one damaged ship) while *U262* and *U614* sank one ship each. 'It was realized', Hessler states, 'that only the most experienced attackers could achieve results in face of the formidable defences of this convoy.'[11]

But experienced commanders were becoming a rarity. Since the outbreak of war up to the end of January 1943, 160 U-boats had been lost along with most of the Aces and best commanders. Also, the rapid rise in the number of new U-boats and the need to get as many as possible to sea as quickly as possible, led to a reduction in the training time for both new commanders and crews. It also led to a dilution of experienced crew members for training purposes and to stiffen the inexperienced crews manning the host of new boats. Moreover, not all the new officers being given command possessed the combination of guts and instinctive good judgement necessary to launch successful attacks against well-protected convoys. This goes a long way to explaining why only 15 per cent of the attacking force against SC118 achieved any success and why 75 per cent of the results achieved were accounted for by only one commander. The performance of the remaining commanders is seen as even more inadequate when the nature of the convoy escort is analysed. Although twelve warships were protecting the convoy at the height of the attack, double the strength of a normal escort group, about half the number was made up of American reinforcements from Iceland. 'But', explains Roskill, 'the reinforcements could not pull their full weight because they lacked training as part of an integrated group: we had long since learnt that training was more important than were numbers.'[12] A sentiment echoed by Admiral Horton at the time, 'it could not be too often stressed that the trained group was the basis of protection, not mere numbers'.[13] This criteria of quality rather than mere numbers was equally applicable in respect of the U-boats' potential. During the remainder of February five further convoys were intercepted on the North Atlantic routes, but only against one convoy, the westward-bound ON166, did a pack attack develop: thirteen boats concentrated for the attack from 21 to 25 February, of which seven boats sank seven ships grossing 45,312 tons and damaged a further four.

In the area to the west of Gibraltar, the boats disposed to attack convoys bearing supplies for the North African campaign intercepted four convoys during January and February. But only one attack on a convoy of tankers (TM1) was successful (seven tankers of 57,313 tons were sunk). Other attacks were spoiled by strong surface and air escorts, which forced the boats to remain submerged day and night preventing them from attaining attack positions. The *BdU* concluded: 'Running attacks on convoys near land, in areas heavily patrolled by aircraft, are no longer possible, because of the high performance of the

enemy's sea and airborne radar.' Despite the large number of *Frontboote* at sea, the total losses during January and February 1943 by U-boat action fell off noticeably from the 1942 monthly average: only 34.23 per cent of the losses being ships in convoy:

Month	Independent sailings	Ships in convoy	Stragglers	Total
January	(21) 146,514	(10) 67,479	(13) 93,203	(44) 307,196
February	(27) 113,569	(28) 175,170	(12) 73,342	(67) 362,081

The reasons why, in so many cases during February, a pack attack did not develop after a convoy was intercepted is explained by Hessler:

'The numerical increase of escort vessels and their universal equipment with radar had greatly increased our difficulties and dangers in attacking convoys ... Our boats experienced the greatest inconvenience from the outer screen, which was usually between 10 and 30 miles ahead of the main body. We found that the attempt to attain a forward position occupied far more time than formerly. Whenever an escort vessel or an aircraft appeared, the boats had to evade or dive, for depth-charge and air attacks invariably followed. When many U-boats were trying to attain the forward position, the escort vessels would not devote much time to any one U-boat, but after dropping one or two lines of depth-charges, would usually direct their attention to the next shadower, in order to force him under water. If a boat were forced to submerge for 30 minutes, it would lose four miles in relation to the convoy, and since in the normally bad weather of the Atlantic its surface speed would not exceed that of the convoy by more than three or four knots, two or three hours would be needed to regain bearing.'[14]

If in the meantime, as invariably happened, the convoy made an evasive change of course, and gales and heavy seas reduced visibility to a minimum, contact was lost. Despite these difficulties and continuing bad weather in the North Atlantic, during March the advantages of *B-Dienst* decrypts and the large number of *Frontboote* at sea finally paid dividends. From 7 to 11 March wolf-pack attacks developed against two convoys. SC121, despite evading two U-boat patrol lines as a result of Enigma decrypts, ran into a third group. Boats of all three groups then concentrated against the convoy and during 7–10 March nine boats sank twelve ships grossing 55,661 tons (five in convoy and seven which had straggled because of the heavy seas). On 9 March *B-Dienst* decrypted a message giving the position of HX228. The *BdU*, anticipating that the enemy would be aware of the group positions and would deviate the course of the convoy accordingly, countered by moving the U-boat dispositions 120 miles northward. This resulted in an attack on HX228 in which only four boats managed to press home attacks, resulting in the sinking of four ships of 24,175 tons and damage to a further three. Boats that had taken part in the attacks on SC121 and HX228, and still had sufficient fuel remaining, were formed into two groups *Stürmer* and *Dränger*. The boats in these groups had formed up by 15 March. According to Hessler:

'... it was intended that the latter should be used against convoy HX229, whose position and course on the 13th had been derived from *B-Dienst* decrypts. On the afternoon of the 14th we learnt from a further enemy signal that SC122, which included at least 49 ships in 14 columns, had received orders on the 13th to steer 067 degrees from the position 49°N, 46°W. Under these circumstances it was essential to use the *Raubgraf* group [which had been looking for Convoy ON170 north-east of Newfoundland] to close and shadow the SC122 convoy.'[15]

These dispositions led to the biggest and most successful convoy battle of the war.

The attack on convoys HX229 and SC122

'In heavy weather on the evening of the 15th one of the southern boats of the *Raubgraf* group sighted a destroyer steering northeast. Search measures yielded no results, but on the following morning a returning U-boat located a convoy not far to the southeast of the patrol line. This was presumed to be SC122. Further radio intelligence showed that HX229 was being deliberately diverted from its original line of advance of 089 degrees to a course which followed the east coast of Newfoundland. The original intention to use group *Dränger* against this convoy was therefore cancelled, and with all other groups [totalling 40 boats] it now hurried to the attack of the presumed SC122. Contact was made on the morning of the 16th, and by midday the first boats of the *Raubgraf* group had gone in to the attack. In the course of the day and the following night eight boats made contact with the convoy, and claimed sinking 14 ships and damaging six others.'[16]

This claim was wildly exaggerated. In this initial attack five boats sank only four ships and damaged four.

'On the night of the 16th a second convoy was reported 120 miles ahead of the first. This second convoy being identified as an SC [SC122], it was now realized that the one being attacked was an HX [HX229]. The speed of advance of SC122 was 1½ knots less than that of HX229. The two convoys were therefore closing, so that towards the end of the operation, when separated by only a few miles, they formed a common objective to all boats. Since the convoys were not steering the same course, this had the disadvantage of confusing the objective to the searching boats, which in some cases failed to find it.'[17]

The following description of the subsequent course of the operation is taken from the *BdU* War Diary.

'After our successes of the first night, the enemy on the 17th used air escorts, which allowed only five boats to make submerged attacks, resulting in the sinking of eight ships and damage to four more. Four of those sunk had been damaged in the previous night's attack. The ever-increasing air defence caused us to lose contact with both convoys on the night of the 17th, and the operation became increasingly difficult owing to the deterioration of the weather and visibility, with the result that only one boat was successful against the SC convoy. Improved visibility on the 18th allowed nine boats again to make contact, of which one carried out a bold and successful underwater attack in the middle of the convoy, in high seas, and sank two ships. On the night of the 18th and during the 19th eight further ships and one destroyer were sunk by five of our boats. Two of these attacked the main convoy and three attacked the easterly convoy. On the morning of the 20th, in increasing difficulties, due at night to near full moon and in daytime to stronger air defences, the operation had to be broken off . . .'[18]

The boats claimed to have sunk 32 ships aggregating 136,000 tons and damaged nine. The *BdU* commented that, 'This

Left: *U124*, Type IXB, was sunk in a depth-charge attack by the sloop *Black Swan* and the corvette *Stonecrop*, west of Opporto on 2 April 1943.

unprecedently successful convoy battle was all the more satisfactory in that only one U-boat [U384] was lost, while nearly half the participating boats had scored results.'[19] In fact, of the 44 U-boats that concentrated on SC122 and HX229, only sixteen (or 36.36 per cent) successfully pressed home their attacks, but they had sunk a total of 22 ships grossing 146,596 tons (nine of the ships sunk being stragglers after damage sustained by torpedoes during the attack on the convoys): no escort vessels were accounted for, and apart from the one U-boat sunk, three boats were also badly damaged. The success of this operation was attributable quite simply to the large number of boats that had concentrated, saturating the defence. But rather than mark the beginning of a more successful and perhaps decisive phase in U-boat strategy, the operation was destined to be one of the last successful wolf-pack attacks on a convoy.

The ascendancy of British counter-measures

The sum total of all the Allied A/S measures which had been developing slowly since 1915 had reached the stage of proving, in combination, to be a panacea to the U-boat menace. In addition to convoy, ASDIC, HF/DF, TBS, Leigh Lights, radar, depth-charges, ahead-throwing weapons, well-trained escort groups and the breaking of the U-boat Enigma, new developments introduced in the spring of 1943 finally proved decisive. The mid-Atlantic air gap was finally closed by the provision of an adequate number of Very Long Range aircraft and the innovation of merchant ships being converted to escort aircraft carriers. By May 1943, fifty VLR aircraft were operating from bases in Newfoundland, Iceland and Northern Ireland, while three escort carriers equipped with forty aircraft between them accompanied the convoys. 'Air cover for even only a few hours in mid-Atlantic was several times effective in breaking up attacking U-boat formations. Experience showed that surface escorts might become so disorganized by a concentrated attack and the resultant breaks in formation as to be ineffective for defence and U-boat killing, but given air escort they had time in which to rally while the U-boats were driven down and as a result became themselves disorganized.'[20]

In addition, the rise in the number of A/S vessels allowed the formation of five support groups which were used to reinforce the escorts of threatened convoys. The primary object of the groups was to hunt to destruction U-boats located in the vicinity of convoys. The vessels of the escort groups were necessarily limited to counter-attacks in the area of the convoy they were protecting. Independent of this limitation the support groups were able to dog U-boats over long distances and continue to press home attacks until a kill was made. The innovation of 10cm ASVIII radar, which the German *Metox* radar search receivers could not detect, also resulted in an intensification of aircraft patrols over the U-boat transit area in the Bay of Biscay, in an effort to prevent the U-boats reaching their operational areas. From 20 March to 13 April 1943, a total of 66 U-boats crossed the area and Coastal Command made two kills (U376 and U665), both by Leigh Light ASVIII equipped

Wellingtons of 172 squadron. In an attempt to counter the large number of night attacks by aircraft in the Bay of Biscay, Dönitz once again ordered (27 April) that the U-boats cross the Bay submerged at night, surfacing by day to charge their batteries when visibility would give more time to spot an approaching aircraft and submerge to avoid it. The resulting lack of night sightings of U-boats by the aircraft led to a concentration on day patrols. This resulted in 71 sightings, during the first week of May alone, and 43 attacks in which two U-boats (U465 and U663) were sunk and a further three damaged.

The new 10cm radar was also fitted to surface A/S vessels and '... Naval and air radar location coupled with the steadily increasing efficiency of the co-operation between surface and air forces not only made it very difficult for U-boats to approach convoys sufficiently closely to carry out an attack, but also provided the escorts with details of the positions of U-boats, thus allowing for successful tactical evasive routing.'[21] The ascendancy of these technical and tactical measures over the U-boats became apparent in the spring of 1943.

Only one further convoy (HX230) was intercepted in March. A hurricane prevented the boats concentrating for an attack, and intense air patrols, although unable to make accurate attacks because of the weather, were effective in preventing the boats attacking the numerous stragglers from the storm scattered convoy. Only one ship of 7,176 tons was sunk. During April four convoys were attacked (HX231, ON176, HX232 and HX234). Escort carrier-borne and land-based aircraft prevented the majority of the boats in the packs, which concentrated against three of these convoys, from attaining favourable attacking positions, and the total losses from all three convoys amounted to only eleven ships of 67,586 tons (five of these being stragglers). The attack on the fourth and last convoy in April (HX234), resulted in failure because of gale force winds, high seas and drifts of fog and snow, and commanders, for the most part inexperienced, who were unable to cope with these conditions. Of the nineteen boats that concentrated against HX234 only two managed to press home an attack: U306 sank two ships and U954 damaged one.

The surface escorts proved their mastery over wolf-pack attacks during the operation against Convoy OBS5 during the first week of May. A total of sixty U-boats from four groups concentrated against the convoy, which was protected by eighteen escort vessels. During a battle which extended over three nights, thirteen ships grossing 61,958 tons were sunk (four being stragglers) and one ship was damaged. But in return, during depth-charge and gunfire attacks by the escorts six U-boats were sunk and four were badly damaged: a further two (U439 and U659), running through the night in chase, collided and were lost. These losses resulted in the totally unacceptable exchange rate of 1.62 ships per U-boat lost. Of the sixty U-boats only nine (15 per cent) had managed to press home their attacks. Hessler says:

'In the past the *BdU* had believed that the normal surface escorts of a convoy could be effectively scattered if sufficient U-boats were concentrated. It had been constantly impressed on Commanding Officers that they should strive to deliver their attacks on the first or the second night, before air escorts appeared on the scene, for the latter would eventually force the boats to drop behind. Up to now it had seemed that the primary danger came from the enemy's air escorts and from bad weather. But in this last operation the surface escorts alone had sufficed to inflict grave losses on an exceptionally strong concentration of attackers. The U-boats were blind in the fog [which descended on the second night of the attack], whereas the escorts could attack them with radar-controlled gunfire. In short, unless the U-boats had some means of countering the radar menace, their position would be desperate.'[22]

The hopelessness of the situation was driven home to the BdU by the total failure of the pack attacks employed against four further convoys during May. The attack on HX237 was held off by strong escorts and carrier-borne aircraft: only three ships were sunk in return for the loss of three U-boats. No ships were accounted for in the attack by eleven boats on SC129, but once again the Germans lost three U-boats in addition to which many were seriously damaged in depth-charge attacks by surface escorts and carrier-borne aircraft. Attacks on SC130 and HX239 were defeated for the same reasons. No ships were sunk but in both attacks three U-boats were lost, including U954 in which Dönitz's son was serving. The monthly breakdown of the losses from U-boat action charts the sudden collapse of the offensive:

Month	Independent sailings	Ships in convoy	Stragglers	Total
March	(39) 213,836	(47) 279,010	(24) 140,885	(110) 633,731
April	(10) 57,244	(34) 193,982	(6) 35,911	(50) 287,137
May	(14) 74,756	(24) 122,945	(7) 39,481	(45) 237,182

The May total was the lowest since December 1941. To make matters worse a total of 41 U-boats were lost during that month; the first time since April 1940 that the monthly U-boat losses were greater than the number of new boats commissioned. Yet it is in judging the U-boat Commanders' individual performances, expressed as tonnage sunk per U-boat per day-at-sea, that the extent of the offensive's collapse is realized. In May 1943 this averaged 64 tons per boat, which was only 25.80 per cent of the May 1940 average (248 tons); 13.16 per cent of the May 1941 figure (486 tons); 19.63 per cent of the May 1942 average (326 tons); and a mere 6.55 per cent of that achieved in October 1940 (976 tons) – the most successful month of the war in these terms.

The feebleness of the individual performance in May 1943, was the result of interrelated factors: the youth and inexperience of many of the Commanders and the breakdown of morale due to life for the U-boat crews being made unbearably difficult and dangerous by the Allied A/S measures, especially the ubiquitous air patrols. Hessler sums up the German view of the situation:

'... failure in a whole series of convoy battles had shown beyond doubt that the offensive power of the U-boat was incapable of dealing with the defence. This situation was due firstly to outstanding developments in enemy radar, and secondly to effective co-operation between surface escorts, support groups, and carrier-borne aircraft. Moreover, we had numerous indications that the

Allies' huge construction programme for escort carriers, escort vessels, and aircraft had not yet reached its peak. On the other hand, there was no increase in the destructive power of the U-boat. Yet the crux of the U-boat campaign was the maintenance of the offensive against the Allied life-line in the North Atlantic. But now the staggering realization came upon us that we could no longer pursue this offensive in its existing form. Indeed, the latest experiences had shown that the striking power of the U-boat threatened to collapse in every theatre of war.'[23]

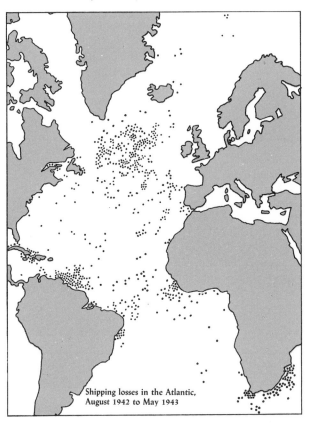

Shipping losses in the Atlantic, August 1942 to May 1943

U-boat strength during the Fifth Phase: August 1942 to May 1943

and success rate expressed as tonnage sunk per U-boat per day at sea.

Month	Total no. U-boats	No. of Frontboote	Training and trials boats	Monthly average of daily number of boats at sea	Average tonnage sunk per U-boat per day at sea
1942					
Aug	358	149	209	86	220
Sept	366	172	194	100	153
Oct	374	195	179	105	179
Nov	385	207	178	95	281
Dec	403	204	199	97	112
1943					
Jan	419	213	206	92	107
Feb	421	221	200	116	111
March	432	229	203	116	176
April	435	236	199	111	86
May	420	240	180	118	64

Dönitz concedes defeat

The disastrous losses of U-boats during May and the complete failure of *Rudeltaktic* against the convoys during the spring of 1943, obliged the *BdU* to concede defeat and on 24 May Dönitz ordered the withdrawal of the U-boats from the North Atlantic convoy routes. Dönitz wrote in the War Diary:

'The situation in the North Atlantic now forces a temporary shifting of operations to areas less endangered by aircraft ... the Caribbean Sea, the area off Trinidad, the area off the Brazilian and West African coasts ... With the boats at present in the North Atlantic, operations will be made against the traffic between the U.S.A. and Gibraltar – as far as these boats are able to do this with their fuel. The North Atlantic cannot, however, be entirely denuded of boats. It is necessary, by means of single boats, to leave the enemy in ignorance as long as possible regarding these alterations in tactics ...

It is intended to attempt attacks on convoys only under particularly favourable conditions, i.e., in the time of the new moon ... These decisions comprise a temporary deviation from the former principles for the conduct of U-boat warfare. This is necessary in order not to allow the U-boats to be beaten at a time when their weapons are inferior, by unnecessary losses while achieving very slight success. It is, however, clearly understood that the main operational area of U-boats is, as it always was, in the North Atlantic ... It is ... anticipated that after equipment with quadruples [the fitting of quadruple AA guns] from the autumn, the battle of the North Atlantic will be completely resumed once more. In the meantime ... the excessive losses and the lack of success in operations against the latest convoys now force us to take [these] decisive measures until the boats are equipped again with better defence and attack weapons.'[24]

In short, Dönitz regarded the May crisis as a temporary setback which was remediable.

U-boat losses August 1942 to May 1943

Date	Boat	Cause and location	Date	Boat	Cause and location
1 Aug	U166	Depth-charged by USCG aircraft (V.212): off New Orleans.	2 Oct	U512	Depth-charged by USAAF aircraft: N of Cayenne.
3 Aug	U335	Torpedoed by RN submarine *Saracen*: NE of Shetlands.	5 Oct	U582	Depth-charged by RAF aircraft (269 Sqn): SW of Iceland.
4 Aug	U372	Depth-charged by RN destroyers *Sikh*, *Zulu*, *Croome* and *Tetcott* and RAF aircraft (221 Sqn): off Jaffa.	8 Oct	U179	Depth-charged by RN destroyer *Active*: off Capetown.
6 Aug	U210	Depth-charged by RCN destroyer *Assiniboine*: North Atlantic.	9 Oct	U171	Mined: off Lorient.
			12 Oct	U597	Depth-charged by RAF aircraft (120 Sqn): SSW of Iceland.
8 Aug	U379	Depth-charged by RN corvette *Dianthus*: North Atlantic.	15 Oct	U619	Depth-charged by RN destroyer *Viscount*: North Atlantic.
10 Aug	U578	Depth-charged by RAF aircraft (311 Czech Sqn): N of Cape Ortegal.	15 Oct	U661	Depth-charged by RAF aircraft (120 Sqn): North Atlantic.
20 Aug	U464	Depth-charged by USN aircraft (UP.73): NW of Rockall.	16 Oct	U353	Depth-charged by RN destroyer *Fame*: North Atlantic.
22 Aug	U654	Depth-charged by USAAF aircraft (45 Sqn): off Colon.	20 Oct	U216	Depth-charged by RAF aircraft (224 Sqn): WSW of Ireland.
28 Aug	U94	Depth-charged by RCN corvette *Oakville* and USN aircraft (UP.92): S of Haiti.	22 Oct	U412	Depth-charged by RAF aircraft (179 Sqn): N of Faroes.
2 Sept	U222	Accident: collision off Danzig.	24 Oct	U599	Depth-charged by RAF aircraft (224 Sqn): N of Azores.
3 Sept	U162	Depth-charged by RN destroyers *Pathfinder*, *Quentin* and *Vimy*: NE of Trinidad.	27 Oct	U627	Depth-charged by RAF aircraft (206 Sqn): S of Iceland.
3 Sept	U705	Depth-charged by RAF aircraft (77 Sqn.): W of Scillies.	30 Oct	U520	Depth-charged by RCAF aircraft (10 Sqn): E of Newfoundland.
3 Sept	U756	Depth-charged by RAF aircraft: SW of Iceland.	30 Oct	U559	Depth-charged by RN destroyers *Hero*, *Packenham*, *Petard*, *Dulverton* and *Hurworth* and RAF aircraft (47 Sqn): 60 miles NE of Port Said.
14 Sept	U589	Depth-charged by RN aircraft of escort-carrier *Avenger* (825 Sqn) and RN destroyer *Onslow*: Bear Island area.	30 Oct	U658	Depth-charged by RCAF aircraft (145 Sqn): E of Newfoundland.
14 Sept	U88	Depth-charged by RN destroyer *Onslow*: Bear Island area.	5 Nov	U132	Depth-charged by RAF aircraft (120 Sqn): S of Cape Farewell.
15 Sept	U261	Depth-charged by RAF aircraft (58 Sqn): off Hebrides.	5 Nov	U408	Depth-charged by USN aircraft (VP.84): N of Iceland.
16 Sept	U457	Depth-charged by RN destroyer *Impulsive*: N of Murmansk.	12 Nov	U272	Accident: collision with German depot ship *Hela*: Baltic.
21 Sept	U446	Mined: Baltic.			
23 Sept	U253	Depth-charged by RAF aircraft (210 Sqn): S of Jan Mayen Island.	12 Nov	U660	Depth-charged by RN corvettes *Lotus* and *Stalwort*: NE of Oran.
27 Sept	U165	Depth-charged by RAF aircraft (825 Sqn): Bay of Biscay.			

Date	Boat	Cause and location	Date	Boat	Cause and location
13 Nov	U605	Depth-charged by RN corvettes *Lotus* and *Poppy*: off Algiers.	17 Feb	U201	Depth-charged by RN destroyer *Fame*: SE of Greenland.
14 Nov	U595	Depth-charged by RAF aircraft (500 Sqn) N of Oran.	17 Feb	U205	Depth-charged by RN destroyer *Paladin* and SAAF aircraft (15 Sqn): off Benghazi.
15 Nov	U411	Depth-charged by RN destroyer *Wrestler*: off Bone.	19 Feb	U268	Depth-charged by RAF aircraft (172 Sqn): W of St-Nazaire.
15 Nov	U259	Depth-charged by RAF aircraft (500 Sqn): NW of Algiers.	19 Feb	U562	Depth-charged by RN destroyers *Isis* and *Hursley* and RAF aircraft (38 Sqn): NE of Benghazi.
16 Nov	U173	Depth-charged by USN destroyers *Quick*, *Swanson* and *Woolsey*: off Casablanca.	21 Feb	U225	Depth-charged by USCG cutter *Spencer*: North Atlantic.
17 Nov	U331	Depth-charged by RN aircraft of fleet carrier *Formidable* (820 Sqn) and RAF aircraft (500 Sqn): NW of Algiers.	21 Feb	U623	Torpedoed by RAF aircraft (120 Sqn): North Atlantic.
19 Nov	U98	Depth-charged by RAF aircraft (608 Sqn): W of Gibraltar.	22 Feb	U606	Depth-charged by USCG cutter *Campbell* and Polish destroyer *Burza*: North Atlantic.
20 Nov	U184	Depth-charged by RNN corvette *Potentilla*: NE of Newfoundland.	23 Feb	U443	Depth-charged by RN destroyers *Bicester*, *Lamerton* and *Wheatland*: NW of Algiers.
21 Nov	U517	Depth-charged by RN aircraft of fleet carrier *Victorious* (817 Sqn): SW of Iceland.	23 Feb	U522	Depth-charged by RN cutter *Totland*: SW of Madeira.
8 Dec	U254	Damaged in collision with *U410* and depth-charged by RAF aircraft (120 Sqn): S of Cape Farewell.	24 Feb	U649	Accident: collision with *U232*: Baltic.
			4 March	U83	Depth-charged by RAF aircraft (500 Sqn): E of Cartagena.
10 Dec	U611	Depth-charged by USN aircraft (VP.84): S of Iceland.	4 March	U87	Depth-charged by RCN destroyer *St. Croix* and frigate *Shediac*: W of Opporto.
15 Dec	U626	Depth-charged by USCG cutter *Ingham*: North Atlantic.	7 March	U633	Depth-charged by RAF aircraft (220 Sqn): S of Iceland.
26 Dec	U357	Depth-charged by RN destroyers *Hesperus* and *Vanessa*: NW of Rockall.	8 March	U156	Depth-charged by USN aircraft (VP.53): E of Barbados.
27 Dec	U356	Depth-charged by RCN destroyer *St. Laurent*, frigate *St. John* and corvettes *Battleford*, *Chilliwack* and *Napanee*: N of Azores.	11 March	U432	Depth-charged by French corvette *Aconit*: North Atlantic.
			11 March	U444	Depth-charged by RN destroyer *Harvester* and French corvette *Aconit*: North Atlantic.
6 Jan	U164	Depth-charged by USN aircraft (VP.83): off Natal (Brazil).	12 March	U130	Depth-charged by USN destroyer *Champlin*: W of Azores.
13 Jan	U224	Depth-charged by RCN corvette *Ville de Quebec*: W of Algiers.	19 March	U5	Accident: collision: Baltic.
			20 March	U384	Depth-charged by RAF aircraft (201 Sqn): SW of Iceland.
13 Jan	U507	Depth-charged by USN aircraft (VP.83): off Parnahyba.	21 March	U163	Torpedoed by USN submarine *Herring*: Bay of Biscay.
15 Jan	U337	Depth-charged by RAF aircraft (206 Sqn): SW of Iceland.	22 March	U524	Depth-charged by USAAF aircraft (1 Sqn): S of Madeira.
21 Jan	U301	Torpedoed by RN submarine *Sahib*: W of Cape Bonifacio.	22 March	U665	Depth-charged by RAF aircraft (172 Sqn): W of St-Nazaire.
28 Jan	U553	Unknown: North Atlantic.	25 March	U469	Depth-charged by RAF aircraft (206 Sqn): S of Iceland.
3 Feb	U265	Depth-charged by RAF aircraft (220 Sqn): S of Iceland.	27 March	U169	Depth-charged by RAF aircraft (206 Sqn): N of Rockall.
4 Feb	U187	Depth-charged by RN destroyers *Beverley* and *Vimy*: 600 miles SE of Cape Farewell.	28 March	U77	Depth-charged by RAF aircraft (48 and 233 Sqns): E of Cartagena.
7 Feb	U609	Depth-charged by French corvette *Lobelia*: North Atlantic.	30 March	U416	Mined off Bornholm: salved and recommissioned.
7 Feb	U624	Depth-charged by RAF aircraft (220 Sqn): North Atlantic.	2 April	U124	Depth-charged by RN sloop *Swan* and corvette *Stonecrop*: W of Opporto.
10 Feb	U519	Depth-charged by USAAF aircraft (2 Sqn): NE of Azores.	5 April	U167	Depth-charged by RAF aircraft (233 Sqn): off Canary Islands.
12 Feb	U442	Depth-charged by RAF aircraft (48 Sqn): SW of Lisbon.	6 April	U632	Depth-charged by RAF aircraft (86 Sqn): S of Iceland.
14 Feb	U620	Depth-charged by RAF aircraft (202 Sqn): NW of Lisbon.	6 April	U635	Depth-charged by RN frigate *Tay*: SW of Iceland.
15 Feb	U529	Depth-charged by RAF aircraft (120 Sqn): SE of Cape Farewell.	7 April	U644	Torpedoed by RN submarine *Tuna*: SE of Jan Mayen Island.
17 Feb	U69	Depth-charged by RN destroyer *Viscount*: North Atlantic.			

Date	Boat	Cause and location
10 April	U376	Depth-charged by RAF aircraft (172 Sqn): W of St-Nazaire.
14 April	U526	Mined off Lorient.
17 April	U175	Gunfire of USCG cutter *Spencer*: SW of Cape Clear.
23 April	U189	Depth-charged by RAF aircraft (120 Sqn): SW of Iceland.
23 April	U191	Depth-charged by RN destroyer *Hesperus*: SW of Iceland.
23 April	U602	Depth-charged by RAF aircraft (560 Sqn): off Oran.
24 April	U710	Depth-charged by RAF aircraft (206 Sqn): S of Iceland.
25 April	U203	Depth-charged by RN aircraft of escort-carrier *Biter* (811 Sqn) and destroyer *Pathfinder*: 290 miles SE of Cape Farewell.
27 April	U174	Depth-charged by USN aircraft (VB.125): SE of Newfoundland.
30 April	U227	Depth-charged by RAF aircraft (455 Sqn): N of Faroes.
2 May	U332	Depth-charged by RAAF aircraft (461 Sqn): off Scilly Isles.
3 May	U439	Accident: collision with *U659*: W of Cape Finisterre.
3 May	U659	Accident: collision with *U439* W of Cape Finisterre.
4 May	U109	Depth-charged by RAF aircraft (86 Sqn): S of Ireland.
4 May	U630	Depth-charged by RCAF aircraft (5 Sqn): S of Cape Farewell.
5 May	U192	Depth-charged by RN corvette *Pink*: S of Greenland.
6 May	U125	Depth-charged by RN destroyer *Vidette*: SE of Newfoundland.
6 May	U438	Depth-charged by RN sloop *Pelican*: North Atlantic.
6 May	U531	Gunfire RN corvette *Snowflake* and rammed by destroyer *Oribi*: NE of Newfoundland.
6 May	U638	Depth-charged by RN corvette *Loosestrife*: off Newfoundland.
7 May	U447	Depth-charged by RAF aircraft (233 Sqn): W of Gibraltar.
7 May	U465	Depth-charged by RAAF aircraft (10 Sqn): NW of Cape Ortegal.
7 May	U663	Depth-charged by RAF (58 Sqn): W of Brest.
11 May	U528	Depth-charged by RN sloop *Fleetwood* and RAF aircraft (58 Sqn): SW of Ireland.
12 May	U186	Depth-charged by RN destroyer *Hesperus*: N of Azores.
13 May	U456	Depth-charged by RN destroyer *Pathfinder*, frigate *Lagan*, RCN corvette *Drumheller* and RAF aircraft (423 Sqn): North Atlantic.
14 May	U657	Depth-charged by USN aircraft (VP.84): SW of Iceland.
14 May	U266	Depth-charged by RAF aircraft (86 Sqn): SW of Ireland.
14 May	U89	Depth-charged by RN destroyer *Broadway*, frigate *Lagan* and aircraft of escort carrier *Biter* (811 Sqn): North Atlantic.

Date	Boat	Cause and location
15 May	U176	Depth-charged by Cuban sub-chaser CS13 and USN aircraft (VS.62): N of Havana.
15 May	U463	Depth-charged by RAF aircraft (58 Sqn): SW of Scillies.
15 May	U753	Unknown: North Atlantic.
16 May	U182	Depth-charged by USN destroyer *Mackenzie*: NE of Madeira.
17 May	U128	Depth-charged by USN destroyers *Jouett* and *Moffett* and aircraft (VP.74): 200 miles ENE of Bahia.
17 May	U640	Depth-charged by RN frigate *Swale*: SE of Cape Farewell.
17 May	U646	Depth-charged by RAF aircraft (269 Sqn): S of Iceland.
19 May	U954	Depth-charged by RAF aircraft (120 Sqn): SE of Cape Farewell.
19 May	U209	Depth-charged by RN frigates *Jed* and *Sennen*: North Atlantic.
19 May	U273	Depth-charged by RAF aircraft (269 Sqn): S of Iceland.
19 May	U381	Depth-charged by RN destroyer *Duncan* and corvette *Snowflake*: S of Cape Farewell.
20 May	U258	Depth-charged by RAF aircraft (120 Sqn): North Atlantic.
21 May	U303	Torpedoed by RN submarine *Sickle*: off Toulon.
22 May	U569	Depth-charged by USN aircraft of escort carrier *Bogue* (VC.9): North Atlantic.
23 May	U752	Rocket fire of RN aircraft from escort carrier *Archer* (819 Sqn): 750 miles W of Ireland.
25 May	U414	Depth-charged by RN corvette *Vetch*: NE of Oran.
25 May	U467	Depth-charged by USN aircraft (VP.84): SE of Iceland.
26 May	U436	Depth-charged by RN frigate *Test* and corvette *Hyderabad*: W of Cape Ortegal.
28 May	U304	Depth-charged by RAF aircraft (120 Sqn): S of Cape Farewell.
28 May	U755	Depth-charged by RAF aircraft (608 Sqn): N of Balearic Islands.
31 May	U440	Depth-charged by RAF aircraft (201 Sqn): W of Cape Ortegal.
31 May	U563	Depth-charged by RAF aircraft (58 and 228 Sqns) and RAAF aircraft (10 Sqn): SW of Brest

Analysis of causes
Cumulative total in parentheses

Surface vessels	47	(105)
Shared by surface vessels and naval aircraft	6	(7)
Shared by surface vessels and shore-based aircraft	5	(9)
Naval aircraft	12	(17)
Shore-based aircraft	62	(70)
Shared by naval and shore-based aircraft	1	(3)
Torpedoed by submarine	5	(12)
Mines	4	(10)
Accidental causes	6	(12)
Unknown causes	2	(5)
Interned	0	(1)
Total	*150*	*(251)*

Too Few, Too Late
The sixth phase, June to September 1943

From June to September 1943, while U-boat Command set about strengthening the U-boats' Flak armament, the main area of U-boat operations was to the south-west of the Azores, their attack being directed against the troop and supply convoys running between the United States and the Mediterranean. Boats were also deployed off South and West Africa, Brazil and in the Caribbean. It was assumed by the *BdU* that the United States–Mediterranean convoys would be beyond the range of air cover. He was sadly mistaken because the Americans employed five escort carriers with which to support the mid-Atlantic route and, during the Sixth Phase, aircraft from these carriers accounted for sixteen U-boats, while only six ships grossing 42,857 tons from the mid-Atlantic convoys fell victim to U-boat attack (seven ships of 43,598 tons were sunk in North Atlantic convoys during this period – all during September). During these four months sinkings of independents accounted for 85.26 per cent of the total losses:

Month	Independent sailings	Ships in convoy	Stragglers	Total	
June	(16) 71,870	(1) 4,220	–	(17)	76,090
July	(37) 199,140	(5) 38,637	–	(42)	237,777
August	(19) 84,208	–	(1) 8,235	(20)	92,443
September	(9) 55,254	(7) 43,598	–	(16)	98,852

The exchange rate of ships sunk per U-boat lost during this phase was a dismal 1.06 ships (or 5,675 tons) per boat.

The Bay of Biscay offensive
Of the 89 U-boats lost, 64 were accounted for by aircraft: twenty of these being sunk in the Biscay transit area.

'As U-boats continued to be surprised by aircraft and to be attacked before they could get to a safe depth the experiment was now made – it was first ordered on the 29th May – of U-boats making the passage across the Bay in company, in order to give mutual support in the event of attack, enable a better all-round aircraft watch to be kept, and to bring a more deadly volume of fire to bear on attacking aircraft. The procedure adopted was for outward groups of from two to five boats to proceed in company on the surface by day as far as 15°W. By night the orders were to proceed submerged and independently reforming at dawn if necessary. After reaching longitude 15°W they were to disperse. If surprised, groups were to remain surfaced and fire back. At all costs boats were to keep together. Similar orders were given to incoming groups which formed up at rendezvous west of 15°W. Boats approaching and leaving the Bay area between 15°W and 18°W, and in the approach area in the North Atlantic west and south of Ireland, were to proceed submerged day and night except when it was necessary to change batteries; this operation was to be carried out by day.

These orders merely prolonged the passage time of U-boats to the operational areas. But for boats actually in the operational areas the orders inflicted virtual paralysis since, in any weather in which surprise air attack was deemed possible, they were allowed to proceed only submerged by day and by night, and were allowed to relax this rule only if they could find a ship – or convoy – to attack … the German's tactics in the Bay had been successful in that night air patrols had made no attacks on, and had got no sightings of, U-boats. Day patrols, which in May had destroyed seven U-boats and damaged seven, although nearly doubled in June had destroyed only two and damaged seven so that casualties had been reduced from fourteen to nine. However, owing to the policy of refraining from convoy operations until the U-boats had been re-equipped and rearmed the number of U-boat passages had been fewer by 30 per cent. Therefore the proportion of casualties in the Bay had not, in fact, been appreciably reduced by the new tactics. Nevertheless, in view of the conflicting reports it received from U-boat commanders and of absence of precise information, the U-boat Command felt justified in continuing these group sailings.'[1]

But Coastal Command was quick to counter the group dispositions by the aircraft attacking in groups. The immediate response of the *BdU* to group air attacks was to abandon the tactic of fighting it out on the surface. The groups of U-boats were now to surface only to charge batteries and only by day, and were to remain surfaced if sighted by aircraft only if they were surprised. During the subsequent fortnight of this order being made (14 June) results were promising: of the twelve U-boats which entered the Biscay bases and the seventeen which sailed, none was sunk and only four were damaged. But during July, of the total of eighty U-boats which traversed the Bay, twelve were sunk and one was damaged by Coastal Command aircraft. As a result, on 2 August, the *BdU* ordered the immediate dispersal of all groups on passage, and from then on the boats were to proceed independently. It was, by now, obvious to the Germans that the Allies had found a way of rendering the *Metox* radar search receivers obsolete. The sailings of all boats was therefore cancelled until a new type of interception gear known as *Wanze* was installed. This instrument, the *Hagenuk-Wellenanzeiger* more commonly known as *Wanze*, covered a wider waveband, which it swept automatically, and, being fitted with an optical indicator, was capable of registering intermittent radiations and wavelengths which were undetectable by the *Metox* receiver.

'This new gear was to prove no more successful than the *Metox* in detecting the 10cm transmissions of the radar sets used by all Allied aircraft. Nevertheless the Germans had inadvertently stumbled upon the correct tactics for evading the air patrols. From the 3rd August, 1943, to the opening of the Second Front [June 1944] U-boats crossed the Bay with insignificant casualties. By scattering the boats over all the Bay of Biscay, by diverting a proportion around the Spanish coast where they were extremely difficult to locate with radar owing to the coastal background, the enemy made the physical problem of intercepting them so difficult that many got through entirely undetected. By returning to the policy of surfacing to charge batteries only by night, which had been abandoned at the end of April, the *BdU* restored to the U-boats their former virtual invulnerability to air attack in the Bay. Although almost all of the attacks made upon U-boats in the Bay between September 1943 and May 1944 were made at night only three U-boats were destroyed as a result of them, compared with seven by day attacks. Had the Germans not made the change of tactics that they did make at the end of April 1943, and had they adopted instead the tactics which they adopted in early August, there would have been no 'Bay Offensive' in the now generally accepted sense of the term. The 97 days of remunerative operations from 27th April 1943 to 2nd August 1943 would not have occurred. That they did occur was because, having defeated the U-boats in the Atlantic with convoy air and surface escorts the British were in a position to exploit to the fullest the tactical error which the Germans concurrently made in the Bay.'[2]

The correction of the tactical error had immediate and lasting results. Thereafter the kills made by Coastal Command in the Bay averaged, as before May 1943, only one a month. By June 1943 a total of 428 U-boats were in commission of which 214 were *Frontboote*.

Inadequate U-boat technical developments

Taking 1943 as a whole, the average monthly rate of new commissionings was 3.83 above the average monthly losses. But the fact was that all these boats, of all types, had been rendered obsolete by the combination of all Allied A/S measures. Hessler says:

'The restrictions imposed on the U-boats by the improved enemy A/S measures could only be effectively countered *by using high submerged speed*. Such a boat would not have to struggle on the surface against heavy odds to attain a good attacking position, but once having sighted, heard or located a convoy, *would be able to proceed underwater to a suitable position for attack*. [author's italics] The enemy

would find himself confronted by a new and surprising type of submarine, against which the existing A/S devices would be largely ineffective. As early as 1937 Dönitz had made contact with the engineer, Professor Walter. Thereafter Dönitz made vain efforts to interest the Naval Staff in the possibilities of the Ingolin-driven turbine as invented by Walter, which might be equally suitable for surface or submerged propulsion. Walter was eventually allowed to produce his first U-boat. This was a small experimental version of the real thing, and by the Spring of 1940 it was undergoing preliminary trials in the Bay of Danzig. V.80, as it was called, had a displacement of 80 tons, and actually attained *a submerged speed of over 23 knots*.

In January, 1940, the Naval Staff had authorized Walter to proceed with a prototype [the V.300] of an Atlantic U-boat. This experimental 550-ton boat was to resemble the existing standard Atlantic type, but with the Walter propulsion and a streamlined superstructure with Plexiglass covering, it was hoped to achieve a maximum submerged speed of 19 knots. Meanwhile, the trials of V.80 in 1940–41, and the latest experience with operational U-boats had convinced the *BdU* that an entirely new design of hull was needed. At the beginning of 1942 Dönitz sought the approval of the Naval Staff to scrap V.300 and start again, but this was not granted, and in February the Germania Yard was ordered to proceed with the original design. At this time designs were also being produced for a smaller [250 ton] U-boat, to embody the lessons of the V.80 experiments. In July, 1942, Dönitz's proposal to scrap V.300 was eventually accepted in the light of further research, and an entirely new design known as V.301 was started. Contracts for two smaller *Walter* boats, of 250 tons each, were given to Blohm & Voss, and to Germania, both yards being allowed considerable latitude in their design. These smaller boats were intended to procure data before embarking on mass production of the larger *Walter* boats.'[3]

Progress with this revolutionary type of propulsion involved numerous delays, and only seven *Walter* boats had been completed by the end of the war: all of them were still running trials. A further two were almost near completion when they suffered bomb damage during an air raid: they were scrapped on the stocks after the war. The dire necessity for boats of high submerged speed also led to designs being drawn up (by June 1943) for what became known as the *Electro* boats; so called because of the mass of electrical equipment they carried. Adopting the streamline form of the *Walter* boat, the traditional

Right: *U514*, 1,140-ton. Type IXC/40 Atlantic boat, running trials in the Baltic. She was sunk in a depth-charge attack by RAF aircraft of 224 squadron, NE of Cape Finisterre on 8 July 1943.

form of propulsion was used, but the number of batteries carried was doubled which provided a high enough underwater speed capable of outpacing the average speed of enemy convoys, thus permitting tactical submerged use against them in the face of strong opposition from air and sea. The projected submerged speed was 18 knots for 1½ hours, or 12 to 14 knots for ten hours, which represented an immense advance on the existing types of U-boat, whose full submerged speed did not exceed 6 knots for 45 minutes. The first *Electro* boat to be designed was the 1,600-ton Type XXI Atlantic boat. By virtue of the deep-diving capacity of this type, along with improved manoeuvrability and long endurance at high silent-running speed (60 hours at 5 knots as compared with the existing boats' 20 to 30 hours at 1.5 knots), the chances of eluding pursuit or withstanding a protracted counter-attack would be greater. Large fuel capacity extended the radius of action to the whole of the North and South Atlantic without reliance on U-tankers.

As the large size of the Type XXI rendered them unsuitable for operations in the North Sea and shallow-water areas, a small 232-ton coastal *Electro* boat, designated Type XXIII, was also designed. Although the *Electro* boats' designed speed was inferior by 7.82 knots to that of the *Walter* boats, precedence was given to the building of the *Electro* boats because the propulsion was of a more traditional type and they could, therefore, be built more quickly.

'Transition to the building of Types XXI and XXIII was ordered on 13th August 1943, with the stipulation that the change-over must in no way interrupt the continuity of U-boat production. At the same time the building of the Type VIIC/42, of which only a few of the 180 ordered had been laid down, was cancelled, while the building programme of the Types VII and IX was allowed to lapse. It was estimated that if U-boat losses continued on the same scale as in July and August 1943 (37 and 25 respectively), the current building programme would provide, up to the summer of 1944, sufficient reinforcements of old-type boats to enable us to maintain pressure on the enemy.'[4]

To expedite the construction of the *Electro* boats, assembly line production methods of prefabricated sections was introduced. The sections were produced by a large number of steel firms widely dispersed in the interior of Germany, which allowed additional labour forces to be made available for U-boat construction. The sections were then transported to the shipyards where they were welded together. By the war's end, 123 Type XXI had been completed of which 55 were commissioned; and 59 Type XXIII were completed with 35 commissioned. The introduction of a large number of these boats into service might well have won back the initiative for Germany, but it was a case of too few too late.

Right: *U106 being machine-gunned and depth-charged by Sunderlands of 461 and 228 Squadrons during August 1943.*

Below: *U2332, Type XXIII prefabricated coastal 'Electro' U-boat, running constructors' trials, Kiel. She was scuttled in May 1945, to avoid capture.*

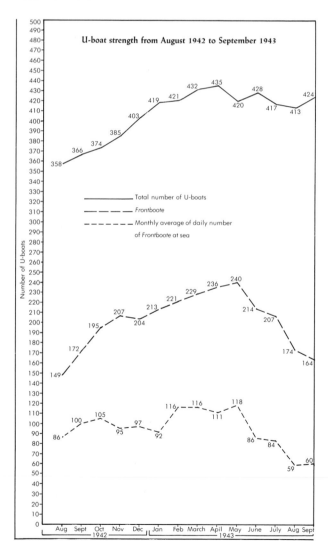

U-boat strength from August 1942 to September 1943

Total number of U-boats
Frontboote
Monthly average of daily number of Frontboote at sea

U-boat strength during the Sixth Phase: June to September 1943

and success rate expressed as tonnage sunk per U-boat per day at sea.

Month 1943	Total no. U-boats	No. of Frontboote	Training and trials boats	Monthly average of daily number of boats at sea	Average tonnage sunk per U-boat per day at sea
June	428	214	214	86	29
July	417	207	210	84	91
Aug	413	174	239	59	50
Sept	424	165	259	60	54

U-boat losses June to September 1943

Date	Boat	Cause and location
1 June	U202	Depth-charged by RN sloop *Starling*: 315 miles S of Cape Farewell.
1 June	U418	Depth-charged by RAF aircraft (236 Sqn): NW of Cape Ortegal.
2 June	U105	Depth-charged by French aircraft (141 Sqn): off Dakar.
2 June	U521	Depth-charged by USN sub-chaser *PC 565*: SE of Baltimore.
4 June	U308	Torpedoed by RN submatine *Truculent*: off Faroes.
4 June	U594	Depth-charged by RAF aircraft (48 Sqn): SW of Gibraltar.
5 June	U217	Depth-charged by USN aircraft of escort carrier *Bogue* (VC.9): North Atlantic.
11 June	U417	Depth-charged by RAF aircraft (206 Sqn): S of Iceland.
12 June	U118	Depth-charged by USN aircraft of escort carrier *Bogue* (VC.9): W of Canary Islands.
14 June	U334	Depth-charged by RN sloop *Pelican* and frigate *Jed*: SW of Ireland.
14 June	U564	Depth-charged by RAF aircraft (10 Sqn): NW of Cape Ortegal.
16 June	U97	Depth-charged by RAAF aircraft (459 Sqn.): S of Cyprus.
20 June	U388	Depth-charged by USN aircraft (VP.84): S of Cape Farewell.
24 June	U119	Depth-charged by RN sloop *Starling*: NW of Cape Ortegal.
24 June	U194	Depth-charged by RAF aircraft (120 Sqn): SW of Iceland.
24 June	U200	Depth-charged by USN aircraft (VP.84): SW of Iceland.
24 June	U449	Depth-charged by RN sloops *Kite*, *Wild Goose*, *Woodpecker*, and *Wren*: NW of Cape Ortegal.
3 July	U126	Depth-charged by RAF aircraft (172 Sqn): NW of Cape Ortegal.
3 July	U628	Depth-charged by RAF aircraft (224 Sqn): NW of Cape Ortegal.
5 July	U535	Depth-charged by RAF aircraft (53 Sqn): off Cape Finisterre.
7 July	U951	Depth-charged by USAAF aircraft (1st A/S Sqn): NW of Cape St. Vincent.
8 July	U232	Depth-charged by USAAF aircraft (2nd A/S Sqn): W of Opporto.
8 July	U514	Depth-charged by RAF aircraft (224 Sqn): NE of Cape Finisterre.
9 July	U435	Depth-charged by RAF aircraft (179 Sqn): W of Figueria.
9 July	U590	Depth-charged by USN aircraft (VP.94): off Amazon estuary.
12 July	U409	Depth-charged by RN destroyer *Inconstant*: N of Algiers.
12 July	U506	Depth-charged by USAAF aircraft (1st A/S Sqn): W of Vigo.
12 July	U561	Torpedoed by *MTB 81*: off Lipari.
13 July	U487	Depth-charged by USN aircraft of escort carrier *Core* (VC.13): North Atlantic.
13 July	U607	Depth-charged by RAF aircraft (228 Sqn): NW of Cape Ortegal.
14 July	U160	Depth-charged by USN aircraft of escort carrier *Santee* (VC.29): W of Azores.
15 July	U135	Depth-charged by RN sloop *Rochester* and corvettes *Balsam* and *Mignonette*: off Canary Islands.
15 July	U159	Depth-charged by USN aircraft (VP.32):S of Haiti.
15 July	U509	Depth-charged by USN aircraft of escort carrier *Santee* (VC.29): SE of Azores.
16 July	U67	Depth-charged by USN aircraft of escort carrier *Core* (VC.13): Saragossa Sea.
19 July	U513	Depth-charged by USN aircraft (VP.74): off Santos.

Date	Boat	Cause and location
20 July	U558	Depth-charged by USAAF aircraft (19 Sqn): NW of Cape Ortegal.
21 July	U662	Depth-charged by USN aircraft (VP.94): off Para.
23 July	U527	Depth-charged by USN aircraft of escort carrier *Bogue* (VC.9): S of Azores.
23 July	U598	Depth-charged by USN aircraft (VB.107): off Fernando Norohna.
23 July	U613	Depth-charged by USN destroyer *George E. Badger*: S of Azores.
24 July	U459	Depth-charged by RAF aircraft (172 Sqn): NW of Cape Ortegal.
24 July	U622	Bombed by USAAF aircraft: Trondheim.
16 July	U759	Depth-charged by USN aircraft (VP.32): SE of Jamaica.
28 July	U359	Depth-charged by USN aircraft (VP.32): S of San Domingo.
28 July	U404	Depth-charged by RAF (224 Sqn) and USAAF aircraft (4 Sqn): NW of Cape Ortegal.
29 July	U614	Depth-charged by RAF aircraft (172 Sqn): off Cape Finisterre.
30 July	U43	Depth-charged by USN aircraft of escort carrier *Santee* (VC.29): SW of Azores.
30 July	U375	Depth-charged by USN sub-chaser PC.624: NW of Malta.
30 July	U461	Depth-charged by RAF aircraft (461 Sqn): N of Cape Finisterre.
30 July	U462	Depth-charged by RAF aircraft (502 Sqn): NW of Cape Ortegal.
30 July	U504	Depth-charged by RN sloops *Kite*, *Wild Goose*, *Woodpecker* and *Wren*: NW of Cape Ortegal.
30 July	U591	Depth-charged by USN aircraft (VB.127): off Pernambuco.
31 July	U199	Depth-charged by USN aircraft (VP.74) and Brazilian aircraft: off Rio de Janeiro.
1 Aug	U383	Depth-charged by RAF aircraft (228 Sqn): W of Brest.
1 Aug	U454	Depth-charged by RAAF aircraft (10 Sqn): N of Cape Finisterre.
2 Aug	U106	Depth-charged by RAF and RAAF aircraft (228 and 461 Sqns): NW of Cape Ortegal.
2 Aug	U706	Depth-charged by USAAF aircraft (4 Sqn): off Cape Ortegal.
3 Aug	U572	Depth-charged by USN aircraft (VP.205): NE of Georgetown.
3 Aug	U647	Mined: Iceland/Faroes area.
4 Aug	U489	Depth-charged by RAF aircraft (423 Sqn): S of Iceland.
5 Aug	U34	Accident: collision with German depot ship *Lech*: off Memel.
7 Aug	U117	Depth-charged by USN aircraft of escort carrier *Card* (VC.1): W of Flores.
7 Aug	U615	Depth-charged by USN aircraft (VB.130, VP.204 and 205) and USAAF aircraft: S of Curaçao.
9 Aug	U664	Depth-charged by USN aircraft of escort carrier *Card* (VC.1): W of Azores.
11 Aug	U468	Depth-charged by RAF aircraft (200 Sqn): WSW of Bathurst.
11 Aug	U525	Depth-charged by USN aircraft of escort carrier *Card* (VC.1): NW of Azores.
11 Aug	U604	Scuttled E. of Pernambuco after depth-charge attack by USN destroyer *Moffett* and USN aircraft (VB.107 and 129).
17 Aug	U403	Depth-charged by RAF aircraft (200 and 697 French Sqns): off Dakar.
20 Aug	U197	Depth-charged by RAF aircraft (259 and 265 Sqns): S of Madagascar.
21 Aug	U670	Accident: collision in Baltic.
22 Aug	U458	Depth-charged by RN destroyer *Easton* and RHN *Pindos*: off Pantellaria.
24 Aug	U84	Depth-charged by USN aircraft of escort carrier *Core* (VC.13): Azores area.
24 Aug	U134	Depth-charged by RAF aircraft (179 Sqn): off Vigo.
24 Aug	U185	Depth-charged by USN aircraft of escort carrier *Core* (VC.13): North Atlantic.
25 Aug	U523	Depth-charged by RN destroyer *Wanderer* and corvette *Wallflower*: W of Vigo.
27 Aug	U847	Depth-charged by USN aircraft of escort carrier *Card* (VC.1): Saragossa Sea.
30 Aug	U634	Depth-charged by RN sloop *Stork* and corvette *Stonecrop*: NE of Azores.
30 Aug	U639	Torpedoed by Russian submarine *S101*: Kara Sea.
7 Sept	U669	Depth-charged by RCAF aircraft (407 Sqn): NW of Cape Ortegal.
8 Sept	U760	Interned Vigo after suffering damage.
8 Sept	U983	Accident: collision with *U988*: off Loba.
12 Sept	U617	Scuttled off Melilla after depth-charge attack by RN corvette *Hyacinth*, RAN minesweeper/sloop *Wollongong*, RN trawler *Haarlem* and RAF aircraft (179 Sqn).
19 Sept	U341	Depth-charged by RCAF aircraft (10 Sqn): SW of Iceland.
20 Sept	U338	Depth-charged by RAF aircraft (120 Sqn): SW of Iceland.
20 Sept	U346	Accident – marine casualty – off Hela, Baltic.
22 Sept	U229	Depth-charged by RN destroyer *Keppel*: North Atlantic.
27 Sept	U161	Depth-charged by USN aircraft (VP.74): NE of Bahia.
27 Sept	U221	Depth-charged by RAF aircraft (58 Sqn): SW of Ireland.

Analysis of causes

Cumulative total in parentheses

Surface vessels	16	(121)
Shared by surface vessels and naval aircraft	1	(8)
Shared by surface vessels and shore-based aircraft	0	(9)
Naval aircraft	27	(44)
Shore-based aircraft	36	(106)
Shared by naval and shore-based aircraft	1	(4)
Torpedoed by submarine	2	(14)
Mines	1	(11)
Accidental causes	4	(16)
Unknown causes	0	(5)
Interned	1	(2)
Total	89	(340)

Twilight and Defeat
The seventh and eighth phases, October 1943 to May 1944 and June 1944 to May 1945

Revised tactics and new weapons

It was on 13 September 1943 that Dönitz decided the time was ripe to resume the U-boat offensive against the North Atlantic convoys. 'All the essentials for a successful campaign are to hand', he signalled to the U-boats. By essentials he was referring to the improved anti-aircraft guns (the quick-firing 20mm twin) that had been fitted to the boats; the *Wanze* radar search receiver and the new T5 (*Zaunkönig*) acoustic torpedo, which had been specifically designed for use against the fast-moving surface escorts.

'Four months having elapsed since the last convoy battle, it was essential, for psychological reasons, that the next one should prove successful. Since success could only be expected if the crews were familiar with the new weapons and the commanders thoroughly conversant with the combined-attack tactics, officers and men underwent special training courses in July and August. The Commanding Officers were instructed at U-boat headquarters, where they were familiarized with the operational possibilities presented by the new weapons. The U-boats' objective was to remain the same, namely to attack enemy merchant ships, while the new weapons were only to be used to force a breach in the enemy air and surface escorts should the boats fail to approach the convoy unobserved. Opportunities for attack would be greatest if the enemy were taken by surprise, so it was essential that the boats should remain unobserved when taking up formation, when seeking to gain bearing on a convoy and also in the first stage of the attack. Lookouts and *Wanze* had therefore to be employed to the best effect, but, in case U-boat commanders should be over-influenced by *Wanze* warnings, it was necessary to remind them that this instrument was only intended as a safeguard against surprise attack and that they should not submerge unless the enemy was actually in sight.

In the second stage of the attack, namely before the arrival of the enemy support groups, there was still no need for the boats to expose themselves; only in the last and most difficult stage was this necessary, if, because of heavy opposition from air and sea, they were unable to reach an attacking position unobserved. In giving battle to the enemy air escorts, all boats in the vicinity of the convoy were, as far as possible, to engage simultaneously. In contrast to former practice, the boats had now to synchronize their tactics, but unfortunately they had no R/T equipment to facilitate this ... It was therefore laid down that the signal '*Remain surfaced to engage aircraft*' should be obeyed by all boats and that they should then refrain from submerging in the event of air attack. It was important that the boats should, as far as possible, assemble evenly round the convoy, preferably in groups of two, and larger groups were to be avoided ... should a large bunch of U-boats be located by several escort vessels, all would be forced temporarily to withdraw from the battle. On the other hand, the location of, say, six well-separated boats, or of several groups of two or three, would draw at least six escort vessels from the convoy and thereby attenuate the convoy escort ... Two boats in company are better able to protect

themselves against air attack, besides providing mutual support in engagements with destroyers ... The requisite concentration of U-boats ahead of the convoy was to be achieved during daylight, the boats using their T5 torpedoes against pursuing escort vessels, with the object of reducing their numbers, and engaging the enemy air escorts on the surface.

The actual attack was to take place at night, when the boats would thrust their way to the ships of the convoy with their T5 torpedoes. Every opportunity for firing torpedoes had instantly to be seized, both when attacking and when being pursued, and hence the few T5 torpedoes initially available were carried two forward and two aft. For attacks on merchant ships, four G7a FAT and four G7e torpedoes were carried. "The convoy battle", wrote Dönitz in the War Diary, "will demand more from officers and men in the way of alacrity, courage and tactical knowledge and ability than formerly. But the war situation and dire necessity will inspire everyone to do his utmost." [1]

Right: *U378*, Type VIIC, under air attack by USN aircraft of the escort carrier *Core*; North Atlantic, 20 October 1943. The U-boat was sunk in the attack.

The first wolf-pack attack on a convoy in the new offensive inspired confidence in the revised tactics and the new weapons. Twenty-two boats of Group *Leuthen* intercepted (on 20 September) and concentrated against the combined mass of shipping of Convoys ON202 and ONS18 which had joined company. Despite very strong air and surface escorts the U-boats sank three escorts and damaged one, together with the sinking of six merchant ships of 36,422 tons. Further results would undoubtedly have been obtained if not for thick fog off the Newfoundland Bank which caused the boats to break off the operation. In return three U-boats were sunk (two by aircraft) and three were badly damaged. For the *BdU*, the real criterion of success was the apparent efficacy of the T5 *Zaunkönig* torpedoes and the apparent deterrent effect of the new anti-aircraft armament: despite strong land-based and carrier-borne air escort the boats had been able to maintain contact and gain bearing on the convoy. However, the *BdU*'s evaluation of the T5 torpedo was based on the U-boats' grossly over-estimating the results obtained. From the U-boats' radio messages, the result of this four-day battle appeared to be twelve destroyers definitely and three probably sunk: this was an 80 per cent exaggeration. The reasons for the U-boats' exaggerated claims are explained by Hessler:

'As on dark nights and in bad visibility, U-boats and destroyers not infrequently encountered each other unexpectedly at ranges below 1,000 metres, the *Zaunkönig* had to be capable of being fired at very short range. The first of these torpedoes had, therefore, an arming range of 400 metres, which meant that the acoustic mechanism did not become operative until the torpedo had travelled 400 metres. It then reacted to the loudest noise-source detected, principally from the forward sector. At such short range the torpedo constituted a real danger to the firing boat, since it could not distinguish between the propeller noises of friend and foe. Thus, as a safeguard, it was laid down that, immediately after firing an above-water bow shot, the U-boat was to crash-dive to a maximum of 60 metres. After a stern shot, she was to proceed for several minutes at her slowest, quiet speed, an instruction all very well in theory but not always possible in practice, for the stern shot was most frequently used against pursuing destroyers and the U-boat had often to crash-dive immediately after firing. In either case, if her torpedo missed, the U-boat was likely to be depth-charged and a diving depth of 60 metres was insufficient; the U-boats accordingly sought a greater depth, between 160 and 180 metres.

An analysis of the first *Zaunkönig* operation revealed that most of the T5 torpedoes were fired at a range of about 3,000 metres at directly approaching targets, in which circumstances there was no necessity either for a short arming run or for the U-boat to place herself at a tactical disadvantage by having to dive. Accordingly, on 24th December Dönitz put forward a request for a torpedo with an arming run adjustable up to 800 metres, by which the U-boat would not be endangered and should have no need to dive. As a result of having to dive after firing *Zaunkönig* – an order that remained in force for the first few months of operation with this weapon – the result of a shot could only be assessed by ear and hydrophone. Propeller noises, asdic impulses, torpedo and depth-charge detonations, sinking noises and foxers (a device towed by A/S vessels designed to produce a noise louder than a ship's machinery and propellers) presented the naked ear with a peculiar, but often

impressive, cacophony of sounds. The difficulty of drawing the correct conclusions from these confused noises, in a skirmish with a destroyer and the vicinity of a convoy, can only be appreciated by one who has experienced it ... For a long time the belief persisted that the *Zaunkönig* had given the U-boats a strong advantage over the enemy destroyers, and it was not until 1944 that Dönitz began to regard the U-boats' claims with reserve. A very great discrepancy existed between the results he accredited to the U-boats and the actual results shown by British records.'[2]

After the comparatively successful attack on Convoys ON202/ ONS18, and despite the *BdU*'s confidence, the new offensive suddenly collapsed. During the remainder of September and the whole of October, the U-boats intercepted only one convoy and in their attempt to concentrate for an attack on ONS20 the *BdU*'s confidence in the U-boats' new anti-aircraft armament was also shattered. Boats of Group *Schlieffen* made contact with ONS20 on 15 October, but a strong air escort reinforced by Iceland-based A/S aircraft kept the boats almost continuously submerged and contact could only be maintained by the boats

Above: *U966 coming under attack from a Liberator of Coastal Command (311 Czech Squadron) which sank the U-boat north-west of Cape Ortegal, 10 November 1943.*

Above: *U793*, Type XVII Wa201 'Walter' experimental boat.

The abandonment of wolf-pack tactics

So unsuccessful did the switch to the eastern Atlantic prove to be (from November 1943 until March 1944 only 'eight ships were sunk in convoy) that by March the *BdU* decided to abandon wolf-pack tactics altogether.

Month	Independent sailings	Ships in convoy	Stragglers	Total
1943				
September	(8) 52,774	(8) 46,078	–	(16) 98,852
October	(15) 71,333	(4) 13,337	(1) 6,625	(20) 91,295
November	(9) 30,726	–	–	(9) 30,726
December	(8) 55,794	–	–	(8) 55,794
1944				
January	(6) 38,751	(5) 36,065	–	(11) 74,816
February	(11) 47,742	(3) 18,301	–	(14) 66,043
March	(16) 94,721	–	–	(16) 94,721
April	(5) 38,941	(3) 16,953	(1) 6,625	(9) 62,149
May	(4) 24,423	–	–	(4) 24,423

'The U-boats no longer hung together to prey upon convoys. They were now stationed singly in attack areas 20–40 miles broad and widely scattered between 48°N and 61°N. During the day they submerged to favourable depths for listening or, if it was necessary for W/T communications, to periscope depth. They surfaced only at dusk.'[4]

'For five months the U-boats had toiled relentlessly at the task of intercepting convoys on the North Atlantic routes, all reverses being borne in the belief that the new weapons and devices gradually coming into operational use, helped by air reconnaissance, would once again turn the convoy war in the U-boats' favour. Recent events had finally demonstrated that all the new weapons together could not give back to the old-type boats their striking power. While it was important that U-boat operations should continue, if only because of their value in tying down enemy forces which might otherwise be used elsewhere, in present circumstances the U-boat command was faced with the danger of there being insufficient boats left to sustain the war, and it became necessary to place greater value on conservation. Costly convoy attacks were therefore abandoned and, beginning in March 1944, U-boats were operated singly and concentrated upon tactics designed to contain the enemy's enormous resources until such time as a strong U-boat arm of new types was ready to resume the battle with, it was hoped, greater prospects of success.'[5]

It was too late. The Germans had played their last card in the strategic pack and lost. In 1917–18 they failed because they did not develop the *Rudeltaktik* – meeting the concentration in defence (the convoy system) with concentration in attack. In the Second World War they failed because they put all their bets on the *Rudeltaktik* concept and neglected, until too late, to counter Allied A/S technology with the necessary technological advances in the shape of the *Walter* and *Electro* boats. Only one of the Type XXI and six of the Type XXIII Electro boats were completed in time to carry out operational sorties (seven in all) before the war ended. In fact the only advance in technology completed in time to influence events was the *Schnorkel*: a ventilating apparatus which allowed the boat to remain submerged while recharging her batteries and which also expelled the exhaust gases.

remaining on the surface. The boats were, however, scattered over a large area and so were unable to provide mutual support as intended, but Dönitz nevertheless signalled *Remain surfaced. Shoot your way to the convoy with Flak.* The tactic of fighting it out on the surface was to be fully tested. The result was a heavy defeat for the Germans who lost six U-boats, against the loss of one ship of 6.625 tons from ONS20.

It ws the British cryptanalysts' success in breaking the four-wheel U-boat Enigma settings that proved decisive. This allowed the British to carry out evasive routing around the U-boat patrol lines with great success. Nor could this advantage be countered by the cryptanalysts of *B-Dienst*, who after June 1943, found themselves unable to read the British naval cyphers, apart from sporadic partial breakthroughs lasting for short periods. In fact for the remainder of the war *B-Dienst* failed to re-establish the standard of decryption that existed from 1942 up to May 1943. In an attempt to revitalize the offensive, the western Atlantic, where the patrol lines had operated throughout September and October, was abandoned. From the beginning of November the operational area was confined to the north-eastern Atlantic to facilitate a strategy which, it was hoped, would overcome the interception problem by reducing the size of the area in which to search for convoys, and bring the sphere of operations within range of German shore-based reconnaissance aircraft. This strategy proved equally unproductive.

'While the German reconnaissance aircraft, by long sweeps into the Atlantic, tried to locate the convoys, the U-boats were disposed in small groups along the convoy routes in positions in which it was hoped that, acting upon the aircraft reports, they would be able to intercept the convoys at night. Chief activity inevitably took place on the north-south convoy route between the United Kingdom and Gibraltar, this being the most favourable from the German point of view from which to operate air reconnaissance and U-boat attack. On the other hand, since October Allied aircraft equipped for both day and night operations had been based on the Azores where they were in a favourable position to give added protection to the convoys on this route. Also with the convoys were escort carriers equipped now with night as well as day fighter aircraft and which proved effective in preventing adequate enemy air reconnaissance.'[3]

U-boat losses October 1943 to May 1944

Date	Boat	Cause and location
4 Oct	U279	Depth-charged by RAF aircraft (120 Sqn): SW of Iceland.
4 Oct	U336	Depth-charged by USN aircraft (VB.128): SW of Iceland.
4 Oct	U422	Depth-charged by USN aircraft of escort carrier Card (VC.9): N of Azores.
4 Oct	U460	Depth-charged by USN aircraft of escort carrier Card (VC.9): N of Azores.
5 Oct	U389	Depth-charged by RAF aircraft (169 Sqn): SW of Iceland.
8 Oct	U419	Depth-charged by RAF aircraft (86 Sqn): North Atlantic.
8 Oct	U610	Depth-charged by RCAF aircraft (423 Sqn): North Atlantic.
8 Oct	U643	Depth-charged by RAF aircraft (86 and 120 Sqns): North Atlantic.
13 Oct	U402	Depth-charged by USN aircraft of escort carrier Card (VC.9): WSW of Iceland.
16 Oct	U470	Depth-charged by RAF aircraft (59 and 120 Sqns): SW of Iceland
16 Oct	U533	Depth-charged by RAF aircraft (244 Sqn): Gulf of Oman.
16 Oct	U844	Depth-charged by RAF aircraft (59 and 68 Sqns.): SW of Iceland.
16 Oct	U964	Depth-charged by RAF aircraft (86 Sqn): SW of Iceland.
17 Oct	U540	Depth-charged by RAF aircraft (59 and 120 Sqns): E of Cape Farewell.
17 Oct	U631	Depth-charged by RN corvette Sunflower: S of Cape Farewell.
17 Oct	U841	Depth-charged by RN frigate Byard: E of Cape Farewell.
20 Oct	U378	Depth-charged by USN aircraft escort carrier Core (VC.13): North Atlantic.
23 Oct	U274	Depth-charged by RN destroyers Duncan and Vidette and RAF aircraft (224 Sqn): SW of Iceland.
24 Oct	U566	Depth-charged by RAF aircraft (179 Sqn): off Opporto.
26 Oct	U420	Depth-charged by RCAF aircraft (10 Sqn): North Atlantic.
28 Oct	U220	Depth-charged by USN aircraft of escort carrier Block Island (VC.1): off Newfoundland.
29 Oct	U282	Depth-charged by RN destroyers Duncan and Vidette and corvette Sunflower: North Atlantic.
30 Oct	U431	Torpedoed by RN submarine Ultimatum: off Toulon.
31 Oct	U306	Depth-charged by RN destroyer Whitehall and corvette Geranium: NE of Azores.
31 Oct	U584	Depth-charged by USN aircraft of escort carrier Card (VC.9): North Atlantic.
31 Oct	U732	Depth-charged by RN destroyer Douglas and trawler Imperialist: off Tangier.
1 Nov	U340	Depth-charged by RN destroyers Active and Witherington and sloop Fleetwood and RAF aircraft (179 Sqn): off Tangier.
1 Nov	U405	Gunfire of USN destroyers Borie: North Atlantic.

U-boat strength during the Seventh Phase: October 1943 to May 1944

and success rate expressed as tonnage sunk per U-boat per day at sea.

Month	Total no. U-boats	No. of Frontboote	Training and trials boats	Monthly average of daily number of boats at sea	Average tonnage sunk per U-boat per day at sea
1943					
Oct	425	175	250	86	34
Nov	429	162	267	78	13
Dec	452	159	293	67	26
1944					
Jan	456	169	287	66	36
Feb	455	168	287	68	34
March	453	168	285	68	44
April	453	163	290	57	36
May	449	162	287	43	18

Date	Boat	Cause and location
5 Nov	U848	Depth-charged by USAAF and USN aircraft (VB.107): 290 miles SW of Ascension.
6 Nov	U226	Depth-charged by RN sloops Kite, Starling and Woodcock: off Newfoundland.
6 Nov	U842	Depth-charged by RN sloops Starling and Wild Goose: off Newfoundland.
9 Nov	U707	Depth-charged by RAF aircraft (220 Sqn): North Atlantic.
10 Nov	U966	Depth-charged by RAF (311 Czech Sqn) and USN aircraft (VB.103 and 110 Sqns): NW of Cape Ortegal.
12 Nov	U508	Depth-charged by USN aircraft (VB.103): N of Cape Ortegal.
16 Nov	U280	Depth-charged by RAF aircraft (86 Sqn): North Atlantic.
18 Nov	U718	Accident: collision in Baltic.
19 Nov	U211	Depth-charged by RAF aircraft (179 Sqn): off Azores.
20 Nov	U536	Depth-charged by RN frigate Nene and RCN corvettes Calgary and Snowberry: North Atlantic.
20 Nov	U768	Accident: collision in Baltic.

Above: The launch of U3001, Type XXI Atlantic 'Electro' U-boat, at A. G. Weser's yard at Bremen on 30 May 1944.

Date	Boat	Cause and location	Date	Boat	Cause and location
20 Nov	U769 U770	Bombed by Allied aircraft, while building: Wilhelmshaven.	6 Feb	U177	Depth-charged by USN aircraft (VB.107): NW of Ascension.
21 Nov	U538	Depth-charged by RN sloop *Crane* and frigate *Foley*: SW of Ireland.	8 Feb	U762	Depth-charged by RN sloops *Wild Goose* and *Woodpecker*: SW of Ireland.
23 Nov	U648	Depth-charged by RN frigates *Bazely*, *Blackwood* and *Drury*: N of Azores.	9 Feb	U238	Depth-charged by RN sloops *Kite*, *Magpie* and *Starling*: SW of Ireland.
25 Nov	U600	Depth-charged by RN frigates *Bazely* and *Blackwood*: N of Punta Delgada.	9 Feb	U734	Depth-charged by RN sloops *Starling* and *Wild Goose*: SW of Ireland.
25 Nov	U849	Depth-charged by USN aircraft (VB.107): W of Congo estuary.	10 Feb	U545	Depth-charged by RAF aircraft (612 Sqn): W of Hebrides.
28 Nov	U542	Depth-charged by RAF aircraft (179 Sqn): N of Madeira.	10 Feb	U666	Depth-charged by RN aircraft of escort carrier *Fencer* (842 Sqn): W of Iceland.
29 Nov	U86	Depth-charged by USN aircraft of escort carrier *Bogue* (VC.19): Azores area.	11 Feb	U283	Depth-charged by RCAF aircraft (407 Sqn): SW of Faroes.
13 Dec	U172	Depth-charged by USN aircraft of escort carrier *Bogue* (VC.19) and destroyers *Clemson*, *Dupont*, *George E. Badger* and *George W. Ingram*: 600 miles NNW of Cape Verde Islands.	11 Feb	U424	Depth-charged by RN sloops *Wild Goose* and *Woodpecker*: SW of Ireland.
			14 Feb	U738	Accident: collision off Gdynia.
			14 Feb	UIT23	Torpedoed by RN submarine *Tallyho*: Straits of Malacca.
13 Dec	U391	Depth-charged by RAF aircraft (53 Sqn): NW of Cape Ortegal.	18 Feb	U7	Accident, marine casualty: W of Pillau.
13 Dec	U593	Depth-charged by USN destroyer *Wainwright* and RN destroyer *Calpe*: NE of Djidjelli.	18 Feb	U406	Depth-charged by RN frigate *Spey*: North Atlantic.
16 Dec	U73	Depth-charged by USN destroyers *Trippe* and *Woolsey*: off Oran.	19 Feb	U264	Depth-charged by RN sloops *Starling* and *Woodpecker*: WSW of Ireland.
20 Dec	U850	Depth-charged by USN aircraft of escort carrier *Bogue* (VC.19): W of Madeira.	19 Feb	U386	Depth-charged by RN frigate *Spey*: WSW of Ireland.
21 Dec	U284	Scuttled following air attack: North Atlantic.	24 Feb	U257	Depth-charged by RCN frigate *Waskesiu*: North Atlantic.
23 Dec	U345	Bombed: Kiel.	24 Feb	U713	Depth-charged by RN destroyer *Keppel*: off Narvik.
24 Dec	U645	Depth-charged by USN destroyer *Schenck*: North Atlantic.	24 Feb	U761	Depth-charged by RN destroyers *Anthony* and *Wishart* and RAF (202 Sqn) and USN aircraft (VP.63 and VB.127): off Tangier.
? Jan	U377	Accident: torpedoed by U-Boat?	25 Feb	U91	Depth-charged by RN frigates *Affleck*, *Gore* and *Gould*: North Atlantic.
? Jan	U972	Accident: torpedoed by U-Boat?			
8 Jan	U426	Depth-charged by RAAF aircraft (10 Sqn): W of St-Nazaire.	25 Feb	U601	Depth-charged by RAF aircraft (210 Sqn): 250 miles NW of Lofoten Islands.
8 Jan	U757	Depth-charged by RN frigate *Bayntum* and RCN corvette *Camrose*: SW of Ireland.	? March	U28	Accident, marine casualty: off Neustadt, Baltic.
9 Jan	U81	Bombed by USAAF aircraft: Pola.	? March	U851	Unknown: North Atlantic.
9 Jan	UIT19	Bombed by USAAF aircraft: Pola.	1 March	U358	Depth-charged by RN frigates *Affleck*, *Garlies*, *Gore* and *Gould*: N of Azores.
13 Jan	U231	Depth-charged by RAF aircraft (172 Sqn): W of Cape Finisterre.	1 March	U603	Depth-charged by USN destroyer *Bronstein*: North Atlantic.
16 Jan	U544	Depth-charged by USN aircraft of escort carrier *Guadalcanal* (VC.13): NW of Azores.	1 March	U709	Depth-charged by USN destroyers *Bostwick*, *Bronstein* and *Thomas*: North Atlantic.
17 Jan	U305	Depth-charged by RN destroyer *Wanderer* and frigate *Glenarm*: WSW of Ireland.			
19 Jan	U641	Depth-charged by RN corvette *Violet*: SW of Ireland.	4 March	U472	Rocket fire from RN aircraft of escort carrier *Chaser* (816 Sqn) and depth-charged by RN destroyer *Onslaught*: SE of Bear Island.
20 Jan	U263	Mined: off La Pallice.			
28 Jan	U271	Depth-charged by USN aircraft (VB.103): W of Limerick.	5 March	U366	Rocket fire from RN aircraft of escort carrier *Chaser* (816 Sqn): NW of Hammerfest.
28 Jan	U571	Depth-charged by RAAF aircraft (461 Sqn): W of Galway.	6 March	U744	Depth-charged by RN destroyers *Icarus* and RCN *Chaudière* and *Gatineau* and RCN frigate *St. Catherines*; RCN corvettes *Chilliwack* and *Fennel* and RN *Kenilworth Castle*: North Atlantic.
30 Jan	U314	Depth-charged by RN destroyers *Meteor* and *Whitehall*: Barents Sea.			
30 Jan	U364	Depth-charged by RAF aircraft (172 Sqn): W of Bordeaux.	6 March	U973	Rocket fire from RN aircraft of escort carrier *Chaser* (816 Sqn): NW of Narvik.
31 Jan	U592	Depth-charged by RN sloops *Magpie*, *Starling* and *Wild Goose*: W of Ireland.	10 March	U343	Depth-charged by RN trawler *Mull*: SE of Sardinia.
4 Feb	U854	Mined: off Swinemünde.			

Date	Boat	Cause and location	Date	Boat	Cause and location
10 March	U450	Depth-charged by RN destroyers *Blankney*, *Blencathra*, *Brecon* and *Exmoor*: off Anzio.	16 April	U550	Depth-charged by USN destroyers *Gandy*, *Joyce* and *Peterson*: ESE of New York.
10 March	U625	Depth-charged and gunfire by RCAF aircraft (422 Sqn): W of Ireland.	17 April	U342	Depth-charged by RCAF aircraft (162 Sqn): SW of Iceland.
10 March	U845	Depth-charged by RN destroyer *Forester* and RCN *St. Laurent* and RCN frigates *Owen Sound* and *Swansea*: North Atlantic.	17 April	U986	Depth-charged by USN minesweeper *Swift* and sub-chaser *PC.619*: SW of Ireland.
11 March	U410	Bombed by USAAF aircraft: Toulon.	19 April	U974	Torpedoed by RNN submarine *Ula*: off Stavanger.
11 March	U380	Bombed by USAAF aircraft: Toulon.	20 April	UIT 4	Bombed by Allied aircraft: Monfalcone.
11 March	UIT22	Bombed by SAAF aircraft (226 and 279 Sqns): S of Cape of Good Hope.		UIT 5	
13 March	U575	Depth-charged by USN aircraft of escort carrier *Bouge* (VP.95); destroyer *Haverfield*; minesweeper/destroyer *Hobson*; RCN frigate *Prince Rupert* and RAF aircraft (172, 296 and 220 Sqns): N of Azores.	24 April	U311	Depth-charged by RCAF aircraft (423 Sqn): W of Ireland.
			26 April	U488	Depth-charged by USN destroyers *Barber*, *Frost*, *Huse* and *Snowden*: NW of Cape Verde Islands.
15 March	U653	Depth-charged by RN aircraft of escort carrier *Vindex* (825 Sqn.) and sloops *Starling* and *Wild Goose*: North Atlantic.	27 April	U803	Mined: Swinemünde.
			28 April	U193	Depth-charged by RAF aircraft (612 Sqn): W of St-Nazaire.
16 March	U392	Depth-charged by RN destroyer *Vanoc*, frigate *Affleck* and USN aircraft (VP.63): Straits of Gibraltar.	29 April	U421	Bombed by USAAF aircraft: Toulon.
			1 May	U277	Depth-charged by RN aircraft of escort carrier *Fencer* (842 Sqn): SW of Bear Island.
16 March	U801	Depth-charged by USN aircraft of escort carrier *Block Island* (VC.6); destroyers *Corry* and *Bronstein*: W of Cape Verde Islands.	2 May	U674	Depth-charged by RN aircraft of escort carrier *Fencer* (842 Sqn): NW of Narvik.
17 March	U1013	Collision: Baltic.	2 May	U959	Depth-charged by RN aircraft of escort carrier *Fencer* (842 Sqn): S of Jan Mayen Island.
19 March	U1059	Depth-charged by USN aircraft of escort carrier *Block Island* (VC.6): SW of Cape Verde Islands.			
25 March	U976	Depth-charged by RAF aircraft (248 Sqn): off Charente estuary.	3 May	U852	Depth-charged by RAF aircraft (8 and 621 Sqns): SE of Socotra.
29 March	U961	Depth-charged by RN sloop *Starling*: ESE of Faroes.	4 May	U371	Depth-charged by RN destroyer *Blankney*; French frigate *Sénégalais* and USN destroyers *Pride* and *Joseph E. Campbell*: W of Bougie.
30 March	U223	Depth-charged by RN destroyers *Laforey*, *Tumult*, *Blencathra* and *Hambledon*: NE of Palermo.	4 May	U846	Depth-charged by RCAF aircraft (407 Sqn): N of Cape Ortegal.
1 April	U355	Depth-charged by RN aircraft of escort carrier *Tracker* (846 Sqn) and destroyer *Beagle*: SW of Bear Island.	5 May	U473	Depth-charged by RN sloops *Starling*, *Wild Goose* and *Wren*: NW of Palma.
			5 May	U1234	Accident: collision off Gydnia: Baltic.
2 April	U360	Depth-charged by RN destroyer *Keppel*: NW of Hammerfest.	6 May	U66	Depth-charged by USN aircraft of escort carrier *Block Island* (VC.55) and destroyer *Buckley*: W of Cape Verde Islands.
3 April	U288	Depth-charged by RN aircraft of escort carriers *Activity* (819 Sqn) and *Tracker* (846 Sqn): SE of Bear Island.	6 May	U765	Depth-charged by RN aircraft of escort carrier *Vindex* (825 Sqn) and frigates *Aylmer*, *Bickerton* and *Bligh*: North Atlantic.
6 April	U302	Depth-charged by RN frigate *Swale*: off Azores.			
6 April	U455	Unknown: off Spezia.	14 May	U616	Depth-charged by USN destroyers *Ellyson*, *Emmons*, *Gleaves*, *Hambleton*, *Hilary P. Jones*, *Macomb*, *Nields* and *Rodman* and RAF aircraft (36 Sqn): NE of Oran.
7 April	U856	Depth-charged by USN destroyers *Champlin* and *Huse*: S of Sable Island.			
8 April	U2	Accident: collision west of Pillau, Baltic.	15 May	U731	Depth-charged by RN sloop *Kilmarnock*, trawler *Blackfly* and USN aircraft (VP.63): off Tangier.
8 April	U962	Depth-charged by RN sloops *Crane* and *Cygnet*: NW of Cape Finisterre.			
9 April	U515	Depth-charged by USN aircraft of escort carrier *Guadalcanal* (VC.58); destroyers *Pope*, *Chatelain*, *Flaherty* and *Pillsbury*: N of Madeira.	16 May	U240	Depth-charged by RAF aircraft (330 Norwegian Sqn): 200 miles W of Trondheim.
			18 May	U241	Depth-charged by RAF aircraft (210 Sqn): NE of Faroes.
10 April	U68	Depth-charged by USN aircraft of escort carrier *Guadalcanal* (VC.58): N of Madeira.	19 May	U960	Depth-charged by USN destroyers *Ludlow* and *Niblack* and RAF aircraft (36 and 500 Sqns): N of Oran.
11 April	U108	Bombed by Allied aircraft: Hamburg.			
14 April	U448	Depth-charged by RN sloop *Pelican* and RCN frigate *Swansea*: NW of Cape Finisterre.	19 May	U1015	Accident: collision: W of Pillau, Baltic.

Date	Boat	Cause and location
21 May	U453	Depth-charged by RN destroyers *Tenacious*, *Termagant* and *Liddesdale*: E of Cape Spartivento.
24 May	U476	Depth-charged by RAF aircraft (210 Sqn): NE of Trondheim.
24 May	U675	Depth-charged by RAF aircraft (4 OTU): W of Aalesund.
25 May	U990	Depth-charged by RAF aircraft (59 Sqn): NW of Trondheim.
27 May	U292	Depth-charged by RAF aircraft (59 Sqn): W of Aalesund.
29 May	U549	Depth-charged by USN destroyers *Ahrens* and *Eugene E. Elmore*: SW of Madeira.
31 May	U289	Depth-charged by RN destroyer *Milne*: Arctic.

Analysis of causes
Cumulative total in parentheses

Surface vessels	52	(173)
Shared by surface vessels and naval aircraft	10	(18)
Shared by surface vessels and shore-based aircraft	5	(14)
Naval aircraft	24	(68)
Shore-based aircraft	51	(157)
Shared by naval and shore-based aircraft	1	(5)
Torpedoed by submarine	3	(17)
Mines	3	(14)
Accidental causes	11	(27)
Unknown causes	2	(7)
Interned	0	(2)
Total	162	(502)

The final phase
The eighth and final phase commenced with all available U-boats in the Biscay ports either being ordered into the English Channel to attack the D-Day invasion fleet off the coast of Normandy and the subsequent cross-Channel troop and supply convoys, or disposed to form a reconnaissance line in the Bay of Biscay as a precaution against an Allied landing on that particular stretch of the French coast. By 6 June (D-Day), the Allied escort groups, consisting of 54 vessels, were in position along the main assault routes (to counter the U-boats). In addition Coastal Command put on intensive air patrols over the western entrance to the channel and in the Bay of Biscay. These measures were additional to close air and surface assault convoy escorts and were taken with the object of making the approaches to the channel area a difficult and exhausting operation for the U-boat. As soon as the landings were known to the enemy, the U-boats streamed out of the Biscay ports – Brest, St-Nazaire, Lorient, La Pallice. Some attempted to penetrate into the Channel, the others took up defensive positions off the ports. In the five days, 6–10 June, some forty U-boats were sighted and 24 attacked, eighteen at night. All of them fought back furiously. Six were destroyed by air patrols covering the convoys, and as many were damaged. The Germans were then forced to resort exclusively to the use of *Schnorkel*-fitted boats: this was effective and the number of contacts fell sharply, and there was only one more kill outright by aircraft in June. Surface vessels, however, with air co-operation, sank two more and three others

Right: *U505*, Type IXC, was captured by the USS destroyer *Nemo* NW of Dakar on 4 June 1944. She now survives as a naval relic at Chicago.

were destroyed, two by surface support groups and one by surface escort. Altogether in the Channel and Bay in the month of June eleven U-boats were sunk at the cost of only five ships.

With the breakout on land from the invasion area in the first week of August the Biscay ports were threatened and the U-boats, giving up their efforts in the Channel area, made for the Norwegian ports. This exodus enabled the Allied A/S forces to reap a rich harvest in the Bay in mid-August. Here surface patrols sank four, detected when submerged, and a fifth with air assistance; the surface patrols also assisted in destroying two other U-boats, sighted on the surface by aircraft. Aircraft destroyed, unaided, two on the surface and one submerged. Thus the total of U-boats destroyed in coastal waters in August came to fifteen; three in the Channel, twelve in the Bay, including two by mines. The three U-boats sunk in the Channel were destroyed in the convoy assault area, two by escorts and one by patrol. Of these, two were submerged and one was on the surface. The falling off in aircraft kills reflected the increasing use of *Schnorkel*. Having been driven from the Biscay bases and forced to operate from extemporized and temporary Norwegian bases which were vulnerable to air attack, U-boat strategy regressed to that of 1918, with a feeble campaign being directed against shipping in British coastal waters by boats operating as individual units. There was also some activity in Canadian and US eastern coastal waters. They achieved little:

Month	Independent sailings	Ships in convoy	Total
1944			
June	(6) 26,371	(6) 31,035	(12) 57,406
July	(12) 52,719	(2) 8,676	(14) 61,395
August	(11) 58,653	(6) 32,803	(17) 91,454
September	(2) 13,092	(6) 37,698	(8) 50,790
October	(4) 1,659	—	(4) 1,659
November	(1) 10,198	(4) 14,995	(5) 25,193
December	—	(11) 53,268	(11) 53,268
1945			
January	(2) 8,821	(12) 58,589	(14) 67,410
February	(5) 17,464	(13) 58,447	(18) 75,911
March	(3) 10,852	(12) 55,049	(15) 65,901
April	(6) 10,090	(6) 54,442	(12) 64,532
May	(4) 10,722	—	(4) 10,722

The average monthly loss rate for these twelve months was a mere 11.16 ships grossing 52,136 tons, despite the fact that monthly average of the daily number of *Frontboote* at sea was 48, which compares favourably with the average number at sea during the climactic month of April 1917. That the U-boats had finally been decisively defeated is beyond all doubt when the exchange rate of the number of ships sunk per U-boat lost during the last year of the war is considered: 0.42 ships (or 1,961 tons) per U-boat.

During the Second World War 830 U-boats took part in 3,000 operations in all theatres and sank 2,927 ships totalling 14,915,921 tons. During the First World War 320 U-boats took part in 3,274 operations and sank 5,282 merchant ships of all types grossing 12,284,757 tons – adding up to a grand total of

U-boat strength during the Eighth Phase: June 1944 to May 1945

and success rate expressed as tonnage sunk per U-boat per day at sea.

Month	Total no. U-boats	No. of *Frontboote*	Training and trials boats	Monthly average of daily number of boats at sea	Average tonnage sunk per U-boat per day at sea
1944					
June	435	178	257	47	40
July	423	177	246	34	58
Aug	406	158	248	51	57
Sept	401	146	255	68	24
Oct	403	131	272	45	1.17
Nov	418	130	288	41	20
Dec	428	135	293	51	33
1945					
Jan	453	139	314	39	55
Feb	453	156	297	47	57
March	445	165	280	56	37
April	389	166	223	54	39
May	349	no figures available		45	7.6

Above: *U2361*, Type XXIII 'Electro', fitting out at the Deutsche Werft, Hamburg, February 1945.

1,150 U-boats sinking 8,209 ships grossing 27,200,678 tons during 6,274 operations. During the two wars a total of 999 U-boats were lost, along with 33,087 officers and men who laid down their lives for their country. Apart from only two instances,* the U-boat arm fought bravely and fairly, preserving their discipline and morale, capitulating only after a battle of unparalleled heroism.

*After sinking the hospital ship *Llandovery Castle* on 27 June 1918, *Oberleutnant zur See* Helmut Patzig, commander of *U86*, fired on the survivors. In the Second World War a similar case occurred when *Kapitänleutnant* Eck, commander of *U852*, torpedoed the Greek steamer *Peleus* on 13 March 1944. These are the only stains on the honour of the U-boat arm.

Shipping losses in the Atlantic, June 1943 to May 1945

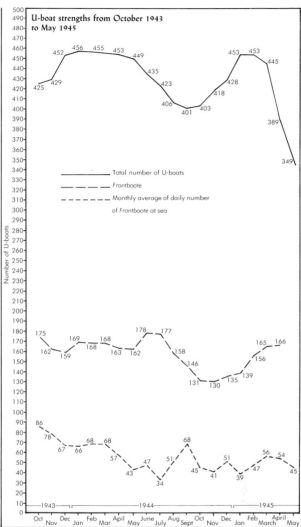

U-boat strengths from October 1943 to May 1945

Number of U-boats

Total number of U-boats

Frontboote

Monthly average of daily number of Frontboote at sea

425 429 452 456 455 453 449 435 423 406 401 403 418 428 453 453 445 389 349

175 162 159 169 168 168 163 162 178 177 158 146 131 130 135 139 156 165 166

86 78 67 66 68 68 57 43 47 34 51 68 45 41 51 39 47 56 54 45

1943   1944   1945

Oct Nov Dec Jan Feb Mar April May June July Aug Sept Oct Nov Dec Jan Feb March April May

Right: Three Type XXI U-boats scuttled in Hamburg harbour during May 1945; in the background is the wreck of the liner *New York* which used to run from Hamburg to America before the war.

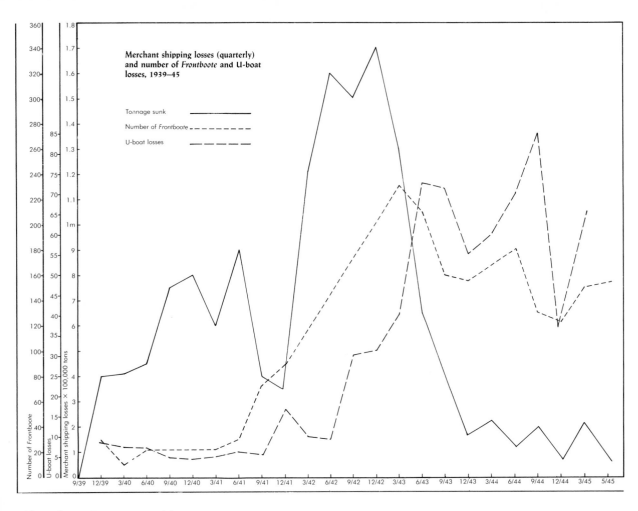

Merchant shipping losses (quarterly) and number of *Frontboote* and U-boat losses, 1939–45

Tonnage sunk ————
Number of *Frontboote* – – – – –
U-boat losses – – – – –

U-boat losses June 1944 to May 1945

Date	Boat	Cause and location
3 June	U477	Depth-charged by RAF aircraft (162 Sqn): NW of Christiansand.
4 June	U505	Captured after depth-charge attack by USN aircraft of escort carrier *Guadalcanal* (VC.8), and destroyers *Chatelain*, *Jenks* and *Pillsbury*: NW of Dakar. Naval relic at Chicago.
5 June	U987	Torpedoed by RN submarine *Satyr*: SE of Jan Mayen Island.
7 June	U955	Depth-charged by RAF aircraft (201 Sqn): N of Cape Ortegal: Salved 1971 – relic at Kiel.
7 June	U970	Depth-charged by RAF aircraft (228 Sqn): W of Bordeaux.
8 June	U373	Depth-charged by RAF aircraft (224 Sqn): off Brest.
8 June	U629	Depth-charged by RAF aircraft (224 Sqn): off Brest.
9 June	U740	Depth-charged by RAF aircraft (120 Sqn): W of Scillies.
9 June	U821	Depth-charged by RAF aircraft (206 and 248 Sqns): off Brest.
11 June	U980	Depth-charged by RCAF aircraft (162 Sqn): NW of Bergen.
12 June	U490	Depth-charged by USN aircraft of escort carrier *Croatan* (VC.25) and destroyers *Frost*, *Huse* and *Inch*: NW of Azores.
13 June	U715	Depth-charged by RCAF aircraft (162 Sqn): E of Faroes.
15 June	U860	Depth-charged by USN aircraft of escort carrier *Solomons* (VC.9): SSE of St. Helena.
17 June	U423	Depth-charged by RAF aircraft (333 Norwegian Sqn): NW of Christiansand.
18 June	U441	Depth-charged by RAF aircraft (304 Polish Sqn): 34 miles NE of Ushant.
18 June	U767	Depth-charged by RN destroyers *Fame*, *Havelock* and *Inconstant*: 10 miles NW of Pointe de Talbat.
24 June	U971	Depth-charged by RN destroyer *Eskimo* and RCN *Haida* and RAF aircraft (311 Czech Sqn): N of Ushant.

Date	Boat	Cause and location
24 June	U1225	Depth-charged by RCAF aircraft (162 Sqn): NW of Bergen.
25 June	U269	Depth-charged by RN frigate *Bickerton*.
25 June	U1191	Depth-charged by RN frigates *Affleck* and *Balfour*: 25 miles SE of Start Point.
26 June	U317	Depth-charged by RAF aircraft (86 Sqn): E of Shetlands.
26 June	U719	Depth-charged by RN destroyer *Bulldog*: off NW coast of Ireland.
27 June	U998	Paid-off at Bergen after depth-charge attack by RAF aircraft (333 Norwegian Sqn): E of Shetlands 16 June 1944.
29 June	U988	Depth-charged by RN frigates *Cooke, Duckworth, Domett* and *Essington* and RAF aircraft (224 Sqn): off Lorient.
30 June	U478	Depth-charged by RAF aircraft (86 Sqn) and RCAF (162 Sqn) aircraft: NW of Christiansand.

Date	Boat	Cause and location
2 July	U543	Depth-charged by USN aircraft of escort carrier *Wake Island* (VC.58): SW of Tenerife.
3 July	U154	Depth-charged by USN destroyers *Frost* and *Inch*: W of Madeira.
5 July	U233	Depth-charged by USN destroyers *Baker* and *Thomas*: SE of Halifax.
5 July	U390	Depth-charged by RN destroyer *Wanderer* and frigate *Tavy*: Seine Bay.
5 July	U586	Bombed by USAAF aircraft: Toulon.
5 July	U642	Bombed USAAF aircraft: Toulon.
6 July	U678	Depth-charged by RCN destroyers *Kootenay* and *Ottawa* and RN corvette *Statice*: 23 miles SSW of Brighton.
8 July	U243	Depth-charged by RAAF aircraft (10 Sqn): W of St-Nazaire.
11 July	U1222	Depth-charged by RAF aircraft (201 Sqn): W of La Rochelle.
14 July	U415	Mined: Baltic.
15 July	U319	Depth-charged by RAF aircraft (206 Sqn): WSW of The Naze.
17 July	U347	Depth-charged by RAF aircraft (210 Sqn): W of Lofoten Islands.
17 July	U361	Depth-charged by RAF aircraft (86 Sqn): W of Narvik.
18 July	U672	Depth-charged by RN frigate *Balfour*: 32 miles S of Portland Bill.
18 July	U742	Depth-charged by RAF aircraft (210 Sqn): W of Narvik.
21 July	U212	Depth-charged by RN frigates *Curzon* and *Ekins*: 47 miles SE of Brighton.
22 July	U1166	Accident, internal explosion: Kiel.
23 July	U239	Bombed by RAF aircraft: Kiel.
23 July	U1164	Bombed by RAF aircraft: Kiel.
26 July	U214	Depth-charged by RN frigate *Cooke*: 16 miles SSE of Start Point.
29 July	U872	Bombed by USAAF aircraft: Bremen.
29 July	U890 U891 U892	Bombed by Allied aircraft: Bremen: construction abandoned.
29 July	U2323	Mined: Baltic.
30 July	U250	Depth-charged by Russian sub-chasers *DS 910* and *MO 103* and aircraft: Koivisto Straits.
31 July	U333	Depth-charged by RN sloop *Starling* and frigate *Loch Killin*: W of Scillies.
? Aug	U996	Bombed by RAF aircraft: Hamburg: construction abandoned.
? Aug	U1196	Accident, internal explosion.
4 Aug	U671	Depth-charged by RN destroyer *Wensleydale* and frigate *Stayner*: 25 miles SE of Brighton.
6 Aug	U471	Bombed by USAAF aircraft: Toulon.
6 Aug	U736	Depth-charged by RN sloop *Starling* and frigate *Loch Killin*: SW of Belle Ile.
6 Aug	U952	Bombed by USAAF aircraft: Toulon.
6 Aug	U969	Bombed by USAAF aircraft: Toulon.
11 Aug	U385	Depth-charged by RN sloop *Starling* and RAAF aircraft (461 Sqn): W of La Rochelle.
11 Aug	U967	Scuttled: Toulon.

Growth of the U-boat arm, 1939–1945 (half yearly figures)

——— Total number of U-boats
- - - - *Frontboote*

Date	Boat	Cause and location
12 Aug	U198	Depth-charged by RIN sloop *Godarvari*; RCN frigate *Findhorn*; RN aircraft of *Begum* (832 Sqn) and *Shah* (851 Sqn): NW of Seychelles.
12 Aug	U981	Depth-charged by RAF aircraft (502 Sqn): Gironde estuary.
13 Aug	U270	Depth-charged by RAAF aircraft (461 Sqn): W of La Rochelle.
14 Aug	U618	Depth-charged by RN frigates *Duckworth* and *Essington* and RAF aircraft (53 Sqn): W of St-Nazaire.
15 Aug	U741	Depth-charged by RN corvette *Orchis*: 32 miles NW of Fécamp.
18 Aug	U107	Depth-charged by RAF aircraft (201 Sqn): W of La Rochelle.
18 Aug	U621	Depth-charged by RCN destroyers *Chaudière*, *Kootenay* and *Ottawa*: off La Rochelle.
19 Aug	U466	Scuttled: Toulon.
19 Aug	U608	Depth-charged by RN sloop *Wren* and RAF aircraft (53 Sqn): W of Ile d'Yeu.
20 Aug	U9	Bombed by Russian aircraft: Constanza.
20 Aug	U178	Scuttled: Bordeaux.
20 Aug	U188	Scuttled: Bordeaux.
20 Aug	U413	Depth-charged by RN destroyers *Forester*, *Vidette* and *Wensleydale*: S of Brighton.
20 Aug	U984	Depth-charged by RCN destroyers *Chaudière*, *Kootenay* and *Ottawa*: SW of Ushant.
20 Aug	U1229	Depth-charged by USN aircraft of escort carrier *Bogue* (VC.42): SE of Newfoundland.
21 Aug	U230	Scuttled: Toulon.
22 Aug	U180	Mined: off Gironde estuary.
24 Aug	U344	Depth-charged by RN destroyer *Keppel*; sloops *Mermaid* and *Peacock*; frigate *Loch Dunvegan* and RN aircraft of escort carrier *Vindex* (825 Sqn): NE of North Cape.
24 Aug	U445	Depth-charged by RN frigate *Louis*: W of St-Nazaire.
25 Aug	U354	Depth-charged by RN aircraft of escort carrier *Vindex* (825 Sqn): NE of Bear Island.
25 Aug	U667	Mined: off La Pallice.
25 Aug	U1000	Mined: Baltic.
25 Aug	UIT21	Scuttled: Bordeaux.
1 Sept	U247	Depth-charged by RCN frigates *St. John* and *Swansea*: S of Land's End.
2 Sept	U394	Depth-charged by RN destroyers *Keppel* and *Whitehall*; sloops *Mermaid* and *Peacock* and aircraft of escort carrier *Vindex* (825 Sqn): S of Jan Mayen Island.
4 Sept	UIT1	Bombed by RAF aircraft: Genoa.
5 Sept	U362	Depth-charged by Russian minesweeper *T116*: Kara Sea.
9 Sept	U484	Depth-charged by RCN frigate *Dunver*; corvette *Hespeler* and RCAF aircraft (423 Sqn): off Inner Hebrides.
9 Sept	U743	Depth-charged by RN frigate *Helmsdale* and corvette *Portchester Castle*: NW of Ireland.
10 Sept	U18	Scuttled: Constanza.
	U24	

Left: The interior of the bomb-proof U-boat pens at Trondheim on 19 May 1945 following Germany's surrender.

Bottom left: *U889*, Type IXC/40, surrendering to the Royal Navy at the end of the war. The large pipe running the length of the conning tower was a part of the *Schnorkel* apparatus.

Below: These two Type VII boats were part of a group of fifteen which surrendered to the Royal Navy on 19 May 1945.

Date	Boat	Cause and location
10 Sept	U19	Scuttled: Black Sea (off Turkish coast).
	U20	
	U23	
18 Sept	U925	Unknown: Faroes/Iceland area.
19 Sept	U407	Depth-charged by RN destroyers *Garland*, *Terpsichore* and *Troubridge*: S of Mylos.
19 Sept	U865	Depth-charged by RAF aircraft (206 Sqn): NE of Shetlands.
19 Sept	U867	Depth-charged by RAF aircraft (224 Sqn): NE of Shetlands.
23 Sept	U859	Torpedoed by RN submarine *Trenchant*: off Penang.
24 Sept	U565	Bombed by USAAF aircraft: Salamis.
24 Sept	U596	Bombed by USAAF aircraft: Salamis.
24 Sept	U855	Depth-charged by RAF aircraft (244 Sqn): off Bergen.
26 Sept	U871	Depth-charged by RAF aircraft (220 Sqn): NW of Azores.
29 Sept	U863	Depth-charged by USN aircraft (VB.107): Ascension area.
30 Sept	U703	Mined: off east coast of Iceland.
30 Sept	U921	Depth-charged by RN aircraft of escort carrier *Campania* (813 Sqn): SW of Bear Island.
30 Sept	U1062	Depth-charged by USN destroyer *Fessenden*: SW of Cape Verde Islands.
? Sept	U3509	Bombed by Allied aircraft Bremen: construction abandoned.
? Oct	U2331	Accident, marine casualty: off Hela, Baltic.
4 Oct	U92	Bombed by RAF aircraft: Bergen.
	U228	
	U437	
	U993	
5 Oct	U168	Torpedoed by R.Neth.N submarine *Zwaardvisch*: off Java.
15 Oct	U777	Bombed by RAF aircraft: Wilhelmshaven.
16 Oct	U673	Accident. Collision with German minesweeper: N of Stavanger.
16 Oct	U1006	Depth-charged by RCN frigate *Annan*: W of Shetlands.
20 Oct	U116	Depth-charged by USN aircraft (VP.74): Atlantic.
21 Oct	U957	Accident. Collision with German transport: off Lofoten Islands.
23 Oct	U985	Accident. German mine: off S Norway.
27 Oct	U1060	Depth-charged by RN aircraft of fleet carrier *Implacable* (1771 Sqn) and RAF aircraft (311 Czech and 502 Sqns): NW of Namsos.
28 Oct	U1226	Unknown: North Atlantic.
? Nov	U547	Mined: Baltic.
9 Nov	U537	Torpedoed by USN submarine *Flounder*: E of Surabaya (Java).
11 Nov	U771	Torpedoed by RN submarine *Venturer*: off Harstadt.
11 Nov	U1200	Depth-charged by RN corvettes *Kenilworth Castle*, *Launceston Castle*, *Pevensey Castle* and *Portchester Castle*: W of Scillies.
25 Nov	U322	Depth-charged by RN frigate *Ascension* and RAF aircraft (330 Norwegian Sqn): NW of Orkneys.

Date	Boat	Cause and location
28 Nov	U80	Accident. marine casualty: Baltic.
30 Nov	U196	Unknown: Sunda Strait.
6 Dec	U297	Depth-charged by RN frigates *Goodall* and *Loch Insh*: 31 miles NE of Cape Wrath.
9 Dec	U387	Depth-charged by RN corvette *Bamborough Castle*: off Murmansk.
12 Dec	U416	Accident. Collision: W of Pillau, Baltic.
12 Dec	U479	Mined: Gulf of Finland.
13 Dec	U365	Depth-charged by RN aircraft of escort carrier *Campania* (813 Sqn): E of Jan Mayen Island.
17 Dec	U400	Depth-charged by RN frigate *Nyasaland*: 38 miles off Cork.
18 Dec	U1209	Accident, marine casualty: wrecked Wolf Rock.
19 Dec	U737	Accident. Collision German minesweeper: West Fiord, Norway.
26 Dec	U2342	Mined: E of Swinemünde.
27 Dec	U877	Depth-charged by RCN corvette *St. Thomas*: NW of Azores.
28 Dec	U735	Bombed by RAF aircraft: off Horten, Norway.
30 Dec	U772	Depth-charged by RCAF aircraft (407 Sqn): 30 miles S of Portland Bill.
31 Dec	U906	Bombed by Allied aircraft: Hamburg.
	U908	
	U1011	
	U1012	
	U2532	
? Jan	U382	Accident, collision: Baltic.
? Jan	U650	Unknown: off NE coast of Scotland.
? Jan	U1020	Unknown: Moray Firth.
10 Jan	U679	Mined: Baltic.
16 Jan	U248	Depth-charged by USN destroyers *Hayter*, *Hubbard*, *Otter* and *Varian*: North Atlantic.
16 Jan	U482	Depth-charged by RN sloops *Amethyst*, *Hart*, *Peacock* and *Starling* and frigate *Loch Craggie*: North Channel.
17 Jan	U2523	Bombed by Allied aircraft: Hamburg.
21 Jan	U1199	Depth-charged by RN destroyer *Icarus* and corvette *Mignonette*: 16 miles off Land's End.
24 Jan	U763	Bombed by Russian aircraft: Königsberg.
26 Jan	U1172	Depth-charged by RN frigates *Aylmer*, *Bentinck*, *Calder* and *Manners*: 32 miles NE of Dublin.
27 Jan	U1051	Depth-charged by RN frigates *Bligh*, *Keats* and *Tyler*: 26 miles ENE of Wexford.
31 Jan	U3520	Mined: off Eckernforde.
? Feb	U923	Mined: Baltic.
3 Feb	U1279	Depth-charged by RN frigates *Bayntun*, *Braithwaite* and *Loch Eck*: NW of Shetlands.
4 Feb	U745	Unknown: Gulf of Finland.
4 Feb	U1014	Depth-charged by RN frigates *Loch Scavaig*, *Loch Shin*, *Nyasaland* and *Papua*: North Channel.
9 Feb	U864	Torpedoed by RN submarine *Venturer*: W of Bergen.
14 Feb	U989	Depth-charged by RN frigates *Bayntum*, *Braithwaite*, *Loch Dunvegan*, *Loch Eck*: E of Shetlands.
15 Feb	U1053	Accident while exercising: off Bergen.

Left: *U532* (Type IXC) entering Gladstone dock, Liverpool on 17 May 1945.

Bottom left: *U802* surrendering to the Royal Navy at Lisahally, Northern Ireland, on 14 May 1945. In all, 156 U-boats surrendered, while 221 scuttled themselves rather than fall into Allied hands.

Below: Type XXIII coastal 'Electro' boats tied up alongside *U541* (Type IXC) at Lisahally.

Above: *U541* (Type IXC) surrendering at the war's end to HMS *Lowestoft* off Gibraltar.

Date	Boat	Cause and location
16 Feb	U309	Depth-charged by RN frigate *St. John*: 55 miles NE of Cromarty.
17 Feb	U425	Depth-charged by RN sloop *Lark* and corvette *Alnwick Castle*: off Murmansk.
17 Feb	U1273	Mined: off Horten.
17 Feb	U1278	Depth-charged by RN frigates *Bayntum* and *Loch Eck*: NNW of Shetlands.
18 Feb	U2344	Accident: collision off Heiligenhaven.
19 Feb	U676	Mined: Gulf of Finland.
20 Feb	U1208	Depth-charged by RN sloop *Amethyst*: 46 miles ESE of Cork.
22 Feb	U300	Depth-charged by RN minesweeper/sloops *Pincher* and *Recruit* and armed yacht *Evadne*: SW of Cadiz.
24 Feb	U480	Depth-charged by RN frigates *Duckworth* and *Rowley*: SW of Land's End.
24 Feb	U927	Depth-charged by RAF aircraft (179 Sqn): SW of Lizard.
24 Feb	U3007	Bombed by USAAF aircraft: Bremen.
27 Feb	U327	Depth-charged by RN sloop *Wild Goose*; frigates *Labuan* and *Loch Fada* and USN aircraft (VPB.112): SW of Lizard.
27 Feb	U1018	Depth-charged by RN frigate *Loch Fada*: S of Lizard.
28 Feb	U869	Depth-charged by USN destroyer *Fowler* and French sub-chaser *L'Indiscret*: off Casablanca.
2 March	U3519	Mined: off Warnemünde.
7 March	U1302	Depth-charged by RN frigates *La Hulloise*, *Strathadam* and *Thetford Mines*: 25 miles NW of St. David's Head.

Date	Boat	Cause and location
10 March	U275	Mined: off Newhaven.
11 March	U681	Accident. Wrecked on Scillies: later bombed by USN aircraft (VPB.103).
11 March	U2515	Bombed by USAAF aircraft: Hamburg.
11 March	U2530	Bombed by USAAF aircraft: Hamburg.
12 March	U260	Mined: 50 miles SW of Kinsale.
12 March	U683	Depth-charged by RN sloop *Wild Goose* and frigate *Loch Ruthven*: SW of Land's End.
14 March	U714	Depth-charged by RN destroyer *Wivern* and SAN frigate *Natal*: 10 miles NE of Berwick.
15 March	U367	Mined: off Hela.
18 March	U866	Depth-charged by USN destroyers *Lowe*, *Menges*, *Mosley* and *Pride*: SE of Sable Island.
20 March	U1003	Rammed by RCN frigate *New Glasgow*: off Lough Foyle.
20 March	U905	Depth-charged by RAF aircraft (86 Sqn): 43 miles NW of Orkneys.
22 March	U296	Depth-charged by RAF aircraft (120 Sqn): North Channel.
26 March	U399	Depth-charged by RN frigate *Duckworth*: off Lizard.
27 March	U722	Depth-charged by RN frigates *Byron*, *Fitzroy* and *Redmill*: 23 miles SW of Dunvegan.
27 March	U965	Depth-charged by RN frigate *Conn*: 23 miles W of Cape Wrath.
29 March	U246	Depth-charged by RN frigate *Duckworth*: SE of Lizard.
29 March	U1106	Depth-charged by RAF aircraft (224 Sqn): NW of Shetlands.
30 March	U72	Bombed by USAAF aircraft: Bremen.
30 March	U96	Bombed by USAAF aircraft: Wilhelmshaven.
30 March	U329	Bombed by USAAF aircraft: Bremen.
30 March	U348	Bombed by USAAF aircraft: Hamburg.
30 March	U350	Bombed by USAAF aircraft: Hamburg.
30 March	U429	Bombed by USAAF aircraft: Wilhelmshaven.
30 March	U430 U870	Bombed by USAAF aircraft: Bremen.
30 March	U884 U886	Bombed by USAAF aircraft: Bremen. Construction abandoned.
30 March	U1021	Depth-charged by RN frigates *Conn* and *Rupert*.
30 March	U1167 U2340	Bombed by USAAF aircraft: Hamburg.
30 March	U3508	Bombed by USAAF aircraft: Wilhelmshaven.
31 March	U682	Bombed by RAF aircraft: Hamburg.
? April	U326	Unknown: off UK coast.
? April	U3036 U3042 U3043	Bombed by Allied aircraft: Bremen. Construction abandoned.
2 April	U321	Depth-charged by RAF aircraft (304 Polish Sqn): SW of Ireland.
3 April	U1221	Bombed by USAAF aircraft (7 Sqn): Kiel.
3 April	U1276	Depth-charged by RAF aircraft (224 Sqn): NE of Shetlands.
3 April	U2542	Bombed by USAAF aircraft: Kiel.

Date	Boat	Cause and location	Date	Boat	Cause and location
4 April	U237	Bombed by USAAF aircraft: Kiel.	21 April	U636	Depth-charged by RN frigates *Bazely*, *Bentinck* and *Drury*: 90 miles NE of Donegal.
	U749				
	U3003				
5 April	U1169	Mined: 20 miles SE of Carnsore Point.	22 April	U518	Depth-charged by USN destroyers *Carter* and *Neal A. Scott*: NW of Azores.
6 April	U1195	Depth-charged by RN destroyer *Watchman*: 12 miles SE of Sandown.	23 April	U183	Torpedoed by USN submarine *Besugo*: Java Sea.
7 April	U857	Depth-charged by USN destroyer *Gustafson*: W of Cape Cod.	23 April	U396	Depth-charged by RAF aircraft (86 Sqn): SW of Shetlands.
8 April	U677	Bombed by Allied aircraft: Hamburg.	24 April	U546	Depth-charged by USN destroyers *Chatelain*, *Flaherty*, *Harry E. Hubbard*, *Jansen*, *Keith*, *Neunzer*, *Pillsbury* and *Varian*: NW of Azores.
	U747				
	U982				
	U2509				
	U2514		24 April	UIT2	Scuttled: Genoa.
	U2516			UIT3	
	U2537				
8 April	U774	Depth-charged by RN frigates *Bentinck* and *Calder*: SW of Ireland.	25 April	U1107	Depth-charged by USN aircraft (VPB.103): SW of Ushant.
8 April	U1001	Depth-charged by RN frigates *Byron* and *Fitzroy*: 150 miles off Scillies.	28 April	U56	Bombed by RAF and USAAF aircraft: Kiel.
8 April	U2547	Bombed by Allied aircraft: Hamburg.	28 April	U1223	Bombed by Allied aircraft: off Weser estuary.
	U2549	Construction abandoned.	29 April	U286	Depth-charged by RN frigates *Anguilla*, *Cotton* and *Loch Shin*: off Murmansk.
	U2550				
	U2552		29 April	U307	Depth-charged by RN frigate *Loch Insh*: off Murmansk.
8 April	U3512	Bombed by RAF aircraft: Kiel.			
9 April	U804	Rocket fire from RAF aircraft (143, 235 and 248 Sqns): Little Belt.	29 April	U1017	Depth-charged by RAF aircraft (120 Sqn): NW of Ireland.
9 April	U843	Rocket fire from RAF aircraft (143, 235 and 248 Sqns): Kattegat.	30 April	U242	Depth-charged by RN destroyers *Havelock* and *Hesperus*: off UK coast.
9 April	U1065	Cannon fire from RAF aircraft (235 Sqn): Skagerrak.	30 April	U325	Depth-charged by RN destroyers *Havelock* and *Hesperus* and RAF aircraft (201 Sqn): N of Anglesey.
9 April	U1131	Bombed by RAF aircraft: Kiel.			
9 April	U1227	Bombed by RAF aircraft: Kiel.	30 April	U548	Depth-charged by USN destroyers *Bostwick*, *Coffman*, *Thomas* and frigate *Natchez*: E of Cape Hatteras.
10 April	U878	Depth-charged by RN destroyer *Vanquisher* and corvette *Tintagel Castle*: S of Ireland.			
12 April	U486	Torpedoed by RN submarine *Tapir*: W of Bergen.	30 April	U1055	Depth-charged by USN aircraft (VPB.63): SW of Ushant.
12 April	U1024	Depth-charged by USN frigate *Loch Glendhu*: sank in tow 23 miles NW of Holyhead.	? May	U398	Unknown: east coast of Scotland.
			? May	U785	Bombed by Allied aircraft: Kiel.
			2 May	U717	Scuttled at Flensburg after bombing by Allied aircraft.
14 April	U235	Accident: depth-charged in error by German torpedo-boat *T 17*: Kattegat.	2 May	U1007	Bombed by RAF aircraft and mined: off Wismar.
14 April	U1206	Accident: 30 miles NE of Aberdeen.			
15 April	U103	Bombed by Allied aircraft: Gdynia.	2 May	U2359	Bombed by RAF (143, 235, 248 and 303 Norwegian Sqns) and RCAF (404 Sqn) aircraft: Kattegat.
15 April	U285	Depth-charged by RN frigates *Grindal* and *Keats*: SW of Ireland.			
15 April	U1063	Depth-charged by RN frigate *Loch Killin*: W of Land's End.	3 May	U958	Scuttled: Kiel.
			3 May	U1210	Bombed by RAF aircraft: off Eckernforde.
15 April	U1235	Depth-charged by USN destroyers *Frost* and *Stanton*: North Atlantic.	3 May	U2524	Scuttled E of Samso after cannon and rocket fire from RAF aircraft (236 and 254 Sqns): SE of Aarhus.
16 April	U78	Gunfire from Russian shore batteries: off Pillau.			
			3 May	U2540	Scuttled off Flensburg after attack by RAF aircraft (2 TAF): Great Belt.
16 April	U880	Depth-charged by USN destroyers *Frost* and *Stanton*: North Atlantic.	3 May	U3028	Bombed by Allied aircraft: Great Belt.
16 April	U1274	Depth-charged by RN destroyer *Viceroy*: 6 miles E of Sunderland.	3 May	U3030	Depth-charged by RAF aircraft (2 TAF): Little Belt.
19 April	U251	Depth-charged by RAF aircraft: (143, 235, 248 and 333 Norwegian Sqns): S of Gothenburg.	3 May	U3032	Depth-charged by RAF aircraft (2 TAF): Little Belt.
			3 May	U3505	Bombed by USAAF aircraft: Kiel.
19 April	U879	Depth-charged by USN destroyers *Buckley* and *Reuben James*: 150 miles SSE of Halifax.	4 May	U236	Scuttled at Schleimündung after bomb damage by RAF aircraft (236 and 254 Sqns).

Right: Four Type XXI Atlantic 'Electro' boats *U3017*, *U2502*, *U3514* and *U2518* (nearest Quay) at Lisahally. Note the *Schnorkel* fitted to *U3017*.

Far right, top: *U1009* (Type VIIC/41) under the White Ensign after surrendering at Lisahally. Note the *Schnorkel* fitting running alongside the conning tower.

Right: *U2502*, *U3514* and *U3017* (all Type XXI) at Lisahally. Note the 30mm Flak guns in turrets.

Far right, bottom: *U826*, 770-ton Type VIIC Atlantic U-boat at Lisahally, under the White Ensign.

Right: *U293* (Type VIIC/41) under the White Ensign and under way for Lisahally.

Date	Boat	Cause and location
4 May	U393	Scuttled after depth-charge attack by RAF aircraft (236 and 254 Sqns): N of Fyn Islands.
4 May	U711	Depth-charged by RN aircraft of escort carriers Queen (853 Sqn), Searcher (882 Sqn) and Trumpeter (846 Sqn): off Harstad.
4 May	U746	Scuttled in Geltinger Bight after bombing by RAF aircraft.
4 May	U2338	Depth-charged by RAF aircraft (236 and 254 Sqns): Little Belt.
4 May	U2503	Cannon and rocket fire from RAF aircraft (236 and 254 Sqns): Little Belt.
4 May	U3525	Scuttled Kiel, after attack by Allied aircraft.
4 May	U4708	Bombed by Allied aircraft: Kiel.
4 May	U4709	Bombed by Allied aircraft: Kiel.
	U4711	Construction abandoned.
	U4712	
5 May	U534	Depth-charged by RAF aircraft (206 Sqn): Kattegat.
5 May	U579	Depth-charged by RAF aircraft: Little Belt.
5 May	U733	Scuttled at Flensburg after bombing by RAF aircraft.
5 May	U876	Scuttled Eckernforde after bombing by RAF aircraft.
	U904	
5 May	U2367	Accident. Collision with German U-boat while under attack: Great Belt.
5 May	U2521	Bombed by RAF aircraft (547 Sqn): SE of Aarhus.
5 May	U3523	Bombed by RAF aircraft (224 Sqn): off Aarhus.
6 May	U853	Depth-charged by USN destroyer Atherton and frigate Moberly: off Long Island.
6 May	U881	Depth-charged by USN destroyer Farquar: SE of Cape Race.
6 May	U1008	Depth-charged by RAF aircraft (86 Sqn): Kattegat.
6 May	U2534	Bombed by RAF aircraft (86 Sqn): Kattegat.
7 May	U320	Depth-charged by RAF aircraft (210 Sqn): W of Bergen.
8 May	U2365	Scuttled in Skagerrak after bombing by RAF aircraft (311 Czech Sqn).
8 May	U3503	Scuttled off Gothenburg after attack by RAF aircraft (86 Sqn): Kattegat.
9 May	U963	Accident. Wrecked off Lisbon.
9 May	U2538	Mined: off SW coast of Aero bi Marstal.

Analysis of causes

Cumulative total in parentheses

Surface vessels	79	(252)
Shared by surface vessels and naval aircraft	5	(23)
Shared by surface vessels and shore-based aircraft	8	(22)
Naval aircraft	11	(79)
Shore-based aircraft	146	(303)
Shared by naval and shore-based aircraft	1	(6)
Torpedoed by submarine	8	(25)
Mines	20	(34)
Accidental causes	18	(45)
Unknown causes	8	(15)
Interned	0	(2)
Scuttled	14	(14)
Shore batteries	1	(1)
Total	*319*	*(821)*

Flotilla dispositions from the fall of France, June 1940, until the end of the war, May 1945

Befehlshaber der Unterseeboote (BdU): Grossadmiral Karl Dönitz (Dönitz also became *Oberbefehlshaber der Marine (ObdM)* – supreme CinC, Navy, after the resignation of *Generaladmiral* Erich Raeder (30 Jan 1943) but retained the office of *BdU* although much of the day-to-day operations were commanded by *BdU* op, *Konteradmiral* Eberhard Godt.

I. U-Flotille
FdU, West
Base: Brest
Boats: Types VIIB, VIIC, VIID and XB
Commanding officers:
Jan 1940 to Oct 1940 Korvettenkapitän Hans Eckermann
Nov 1940 to Feb 1942 Korvettenkapitän Hans Cohausz
Feb 1942 to July 1942 Kapitänleutnant Heinz Buchholz
July 1942 to Sept 1944 Korvettenkapitän Werner Winter
Frontboote that served in the flotilla:
U7–U24, U56–U63, U79–U81, U83–U86, U116–U117, U137–U147, U149, U150, U201–U204, U208, U209, U225, U238, U243, U247, U263, U268, U271, U276, U292, U301, U304–U307, U311, U331, U336, U353, U354, U370–U372, U374, U379, U392, U394, U396, U401, U405, U413, U415, U418, U422, U424, U426, U435, U439– U441, U456, U471, U556–U559, U561–U566, U574, U582, U584, U597, U599, U603, U625, U628, U629, U632, U637, U643, U651, U653, U656, U665, U669, U722, U731, U732, U736, U740, U741, U743, U754, U767, U773, U821, U925, U956, U963, U987, U1007, U1199, UB, UD1.

II. U-Flotille
FdU, West
Base: Lorient
Boats: Mainly Type IX
Commanding Officers:
Jan 1940 to May 1940 Korvettenkapitän Werner Hartmann
June 1940 to Oct 1940 Korvettenkapitän Heinz Fischer
Oct 1940 to Jan 1943 Korvettenkapitän Viktor Schütze
Jan 1943 to May 1945 Kapitän zur See Ernst Kals
U25–U38, U41, U43, U44, U64–U68, U103–U111, U116, U117, U122–U131, U153–U154, U156–U157, U161–U162, U168, U173, U183–U184, U189–U191, U193, U501–U505, U507, U518–U522, U531, U532, U534, U536, U538, U545, U547–U548, U801–U802, U841–U843, U856, U868, U1223, U1225–U1228, UD3.

Below: *U1009,* Type VIIC/41 surrendering at Lisahally.

Above: *U802* (IXC/40), *U293*, *U1105* (both VIIC/41) and *U826* (VIIC) – nearest the camera – at Lisahally.

III. U-Flotille

FdU, West
Bases: La Pallice and La Rochelle
Boats: originally Type II, then Types VIIB and VIIC
Commanding Officers:
March 1941 to July 1941 Korvettenkapitän Hans Rösing
July 1941 to March 1942 Kapitänleutnant Herbert Schultze
March 1942 to June 1942 Kapitänleutnant Heinz von Reiche
June 1942 to Oct 1944 Korvettenkapitän Richard Zapp
U8, U10, U12, U14, U16, U18, U20, U22, U24, U82, U85, U132,
U134, U137–U138, U141, U143, U146–U147, U205–U206, U212,
U231, U241–U242, U245–U246, U257–U259, U262, U275, U280,
U289, U332–U334, U341, U343–U344, U352, U373, U375–U376,
U378, U384, U391, U398, U402, U423, U431–U433, U444, U451–
U452, U458, U466, U468–U469, U476, U478, U483–U484, U553,
U567–U573, U596, U600, U611, U613, U615, U619–U620, U625,
U630, U635, U645, U652, U657, U661, U671, U677, U701, U706,
U712, U719, U734, U752–U753, U760, U763, U952–U953, U957,
U960, U970–U971, U975, U992–U993, UB, UD1, UD3, UD4.

IV. and V. U-Flotillen

FdU, East
Used for the final fitting out of new boats before dispatch to the front flotillas.

VI. U-Flotille

FdU, West
Base: St-Nazaire
Boats: Types VIIB and VIIC
Commanding Officers:
Sept 1941 to Oct 1943 Korvettenkapitän Wilhelm Schulz
Oct 1943 to Aug 1944 Kapitänleutnant Carl Emmermann
U37–U44, U87, U136, U209–U210, U223, U226, U228–U229, U251–
U253, U260–U261, U264, U269–U270, U277, U290, U308, U312,
U319, U335, U337, U340, U356–U357, U376–U377, U380,
U385–U386, U404–U405, U411, U414, U417, U436–U437, U445,
U456–U457, U465, U477, U585–U592, U598, U608–U610, U614,
U616, U623, U626–U627, U640, U642, U648, U655, U658, U666,
U668, U672–U673, U675, U680, U703, U705, U742, U756–U758,
U766, U964, U967, U972, U981–U982, U986, U999.

VII. U-Flotille

FdU, West
Bases: Kiel and St-Nazaire (from June 1941 St-Nazaire only, later moved to Norway)
Boats: Mainly Type VII
Commanding Officers:
Jan 1940 to May 1940 Korvettenkapitän Hans Rösing
May 1940 to Feb 1940 Korvettenkapitän Herbert Sohler
Feb 1944 to March 1944 Korvettenkapitän Adolf Piening
U45–U55, U69, U70–U71, U73–U77, U88, U93–U102, U133, U135,
U207, U213, U221, U224, U227, U255, U265–U267, U274, U278,
U281, U285, U300, U303, U310, U338, U342, U358–U359, U364,
U381–382, U387, U390, U397, U403, U406, U410, U427, U434,
U436, U442, U448–U449, U453–U455, U479, U481, U551–U553,
U567, U575–U578, U581, U593, U594, U602, U607, U617–U618,
U624, U641, U647, U650, U662, U667, U678, U702, U704, U707–
U708, U710, U714, U751, U765, U962, U969, U974, U976, U980,
U985, U988, U994, U1004, U1191–U1192, UA.

VIII. U-Flotille

FdU, East
Used for training purposes
Bases: Eastern Baltic ports

IX. U-Flotille

FdU, West
Base: Brest
Boats: Types VIIC and VIID
Commanding Officers:
Nov 1941 to March 1942 Kapitänleutnant Jürgen Oesten
March 1942 to Aug 1944 Korvettenkapitän Heinrich Lehmann-Willenbrock
U89, U90–U92, U210–U211, U213–U218, U230, U232, U240, U244,
U247–U248, U254, U256, U273, U279, U282–U284, U293, U296,
U302, U309, U317, U347–U348, U365, U377, U383, U388–U389,
U403, U407–U409, U412, U421, U425, U438, U443, U447, U450,
U473, U480, U482, U591, U595, U604–U606, U621, U631, U633–
U634, U638, U659–U660, U663–U664, U709, U715, U739, U744,
U755, U759, U761–U762, U764, U771–U772, U951, U954–U955,
U966, U979, U984, U989, U997, U1165.

X. U-Flotille

FdU, West
Base: Lorient
Boats: Mainly Types IXC and XB
Commanding Officer Jan 1942 to Oct 1944 Korvettenkapitän Günter Kuhnke
U118, U155, U158–U160, U163–U167, U169–U172, U174–U179,
U181, U185–U188, U192–U194, U459–U464, U506, U508–U517,
U523–U530, U533, U535, U537, U539–U544, U546, U549–U550,
U804, U844–U846, U853, U855, U865–U866, U1221–U1222, U1229–
U1230, UD2, UD3, UD5.

XI. U-Flotille

FdU, Norway
Base: Bergen
Boats: Type VIIC
Commanding Officer May 1942 to Jan 1945 Fregattenkapitän Hans Cohausz
U88, U117, U209, U212, U218, U244, U246, U248, U251, U255,
U269, U275, U278, U285, U286, U290, U294–U297, U299–U300,
U302, U304, U309, U312–U315, U318, U321–U322, U324–U328,
U334, U339, U344, U347, U354–U355, U361, U363, U376–U378,
U394, U396, U399–U400, U403, U405, U408, U419–U420, U425–

U427, U435–U436, U456–U457, U467, U470, U472, U480, U482–
U483, U485–U486, U586, U589, U591–U592, U601, U606, U622,
U625, U629, U636, U639, U644, U646, U650, U654, U657, U663,
U674, U680–U683, U703, U711, U713, U716, U722, U735, U764,
U771–U775, U778, U825–U827, U867, U901, U905, U907, U926–
U927, U956–U957, U963, U965, U978–U979, U987, U990–U992,
U994, U1002–U1006, U1009–U1010, U1014, U1017–U1024, U1051,
U1053, U1055, U1058, U1063–U1064, U1104, U1107, U1109, U1163,
U1165, U1169, U1171–U1172, U1195, U1199, U1200, U1202–U1203,
U1206, U1208–U1209, U1231, U1272–U1273, U1276–U1279, U1302,
U2322, U2324–U2326, U2328–U2330, U2334–U2335, U2502–U2503,
U2506, U2511, U2513, U2518, U3008.

XII. U-Flotille

FdU, West
Base: Bordeaux
Boats: mainly Types IX, XB and XIV
Commanding Officer Oct 1942 to Aug 1944 Korvettenkapitän
Klaus Scholtz
U117–U119, U177–U182, U195–U200, U219–U220, U233, U459–
U463, U487–U490, U847–U852, U859–U863, U871, U1059–U1062,
UIT21–UIT25.

XIII. U-Flotille

FdU, Norway
Base: Trondheim
Boats: Type VIIC
Commanding Officer June 1943 to May 1945 Fregattenkapitän
Rolf Rüggeberg
U212, U251, U255, U277–U278, U286, U288–U289, U293–U295,
U299, U302, U307, U310, U312, U313, U315, U318, U354, U360
U362–U363, U365–U366, U387, U425, U427, U586, U601, U622,
U625, U636, U639, U668, U673, U703, U711, U713, U716, U737,
U739, U742, U771, U921, U956–U957, U959, U965, U968, U992,
U994–U995, U997, U1163.

XIV. U-Flotille

FdU, Norway
Base: Narvik
Boats: Type VIIC
Commanding Officer Dec 1944 to May 1945 Korvettenkapitän
Helmut Mohlmann
U294, U299, U318, U427, U995, U997.

XV., XVI. and XVII. U-Flotillen

Did not become operational.

XVIII. U-Flotille

Operational in the Baltic shortly before the end of the war.
U1161, U1162, UA, UD4.

XIX. U-Flotille

Training flotilla
Base: Pillau; transferred to Kiel at the end of the war.

XX. U-Flotille

Training flotilla
Base: Pillau (abandoned in Feb 1945).

XXI. and XXII. U-Flotillen

U-boat school flotillas.

XXIII., XXIV., XXV., XXVI., XXVII. U-Flotillen

Training flotillas.

XXVIII. U-Flotille

Did not become operational.

XXIX. U-Flotille

FdU, Mediterranean
Bases: La Spezia, Toulon, Pola, Marseilles, Salamis.
Commanding Officers:
Dec 1941 to May 1942 Korvettenkapitän Franz Becker
June 1942 to July 1943 Korvettenkapitän Fritz Freuenheim
Aug 1943 to Sept 1944 Korvettenkapitän Günther Jahn
U73–U75, U77, U81, U83, U97, U205, U223, U230, U301, U303,
U331, U343, U371–U372, U374–U375, U380, U407, U409–U410,
U414, U421, U431, U443, U450, U453, U455, U458, U466, U471,
U557, U559, U561–U562, U565, U568, U573, U577, U586, U593,
U596, U602, U605, U616–U617, U642, U652, U660, U755, U952,
U967, U969.

XXX. U-Flotille

Black Sea
Bases: Constanza and Feodosia
Commanding Officers:
Oct 1942 to May 1944 Kapitänleutnant Helmut Rosenbaum
June 1944 to Oct 1944 Kapitänleutnant Klaus Petersen
Oct 1944 – Kapitänleutnant Clemens Schöler
U9, U18, U19, U20, U23, U24.

XXXI. U-Flotille

FdU, East
Training flotilla
Bases: Hamburg, Wilhelmshaven and Wesermünde.

XXXII. U-Flotille

FdU, East
Training flotilla
Bases: Königsberg and Hamburg.

XXXIII. U-Flotille

FdU, West
Bases: Flensburg and ports in Asia
Commanding Officers:
Sept 1944 to Oct 1944 Korvettenkapitän Georg Schewe
Nov 1944 to May 1945 Korvettenkapitän Günther Kuhnke
U155, U168, U170, U181, U183, U190, U195–U196, U219, U234,
U245, U260, U262–U267, U281, U309, U382, U398, U510, U516,
U518, U530, U532, U534, U537, U539, U541, U546–U548, U714,
U758, U763, U802, U804–U806, U843, U853, U857–U858, U861–
U862, U864, U866, U868–U870, U873–U875, U877–U881, U889,
U953, U989, U1025, U1170, U1205, U1221, U1223, U1226–U1228,
U1230, U1232–1233, U1235, U1271, U1305, UIT24–UIT25.

Below: The large 1,600-ton
Type IXD/42 U-Cruisers *U874*,
U875 and *U883* moored at
Lisahally. During January 1946,
110 of the surrendered U-boats
were taken out to sea in groups
and sunk about 30 miles north of
Malin Head.

Conclusion

The question is often asked, would the outcome of the First World War have been different had the Germans begun with a much larger number of U-boats than they in fact possessed in August 1914? Such a question is historically meaningless since, as we have seen, the strategic value of the U-boat as a weapon was only realized empirically as a direct result of war experience. It is also asked, more pertinently, why orders were not placed for a much larger number of new boats than were actually contracted for in 1915, by which time the U-boats' potential was realized. But, once again, such a question is dependent on hindsight as no one in 1915 could foresee how long the war would last. A large building programme begun early in 1915 could not have produced adequate results until 1917, by which time, it was expected, the war would have come to an end. Anyway it is doubtful that German industrial capacity in the First World War could have coped with any greater demands than were in fact made upon it. Moreover, addressing the problem of an effective maritime blockade of Britain was not as dependent on the quantitive factor, as it was on the qualitative factor, in terms of correct strategic and tactical application of existing resources. There can be no doubt that had the tactical expedient of attacking convoys with U-boats concentrated in packs been adopted in the late summer of 1917, the U-boat offensive would have been the decisive factor in determining the outcome of the war in Germany's favour. Without ASDIC, radar or HF/DF equipment the convoy escorts in 1917, which were totally inadequate in numbers anyway, would have been impotent in the face of wolf-pack attacks carried out on the surface at night. The existing number of *Frontboote* would have been adequate. During the spring of 1917 the monthly average of the daily number at sea was only 41, yet these were able to account for a monthly average of 648,414 tons of shipping: a crippling score which could have been easily maintained, and more than probably improved upon, by pack tactics. But rather than develop their tactics the Germans clung blindly to the conviction that they could achieve victory with ever greater numbers of *Frontboote*. However, Dönitz's complaint (made in June 1945), with regard to the Second World War, that 'Germany was never prepared for a naval war against England', and that 'a realistic policy would have given Germany a thousand U-boats at the beginning' is pertinent despite the exaggerated number. That Germany only had 57 U-boats in commission when war broke out was a direct result of Hitler's faulty foreign policy. He was absolutely certain that Britain and France would shrink from a general war and would not honour their guarantees to Poland. When, contrary to Hitler's belief, the Western democracies tendered their War Ultimatums to the Reich, Admiral Raeder lamented that 'Today there began a war with Britain and France with which – to judge from all the Führer's utterances hitherto – we should not have had to reckon with before about 1944 (by which time Germany would have about 200 U-boats in accordance with the 'Z' plan of December, 1939).' If Germany had begun the war with 200 boats (let alone a thousand) it is highly probable that during the Second Phase (June 1940–March 1941) when the convoys were denuded of escorts (to counter the invasion threat) and A/S technology was not sufficiently advanced to counter surfaced, night time, pack attacks, the 'Happy Time' might very well have become the decisive period. As it turned out, by the time the numerical strength of the U-boat Fleet had reached the proportions that Dönitz had deemed necessary to effect a successful blockade of the British Isles (358 U-boats by August 1942), allied A/S measures were sufficiently developed to defeat surfaced, night-time, pack attacks, and had rendered existing types of U-boats, with their relatively low underwater speed, as good as obsolete. Once again, in the last analysis, the qualitative factor, this time in terms of the lack of U-boats with high underwater speed and endurance (*Walter* and *Electro* boats) proved to be the decisive factor, rather than the quantitive on which the Germans staked so much.

In comparing the First and Second World Wars, the exchange rate taken over the whole of the two periods distinctly favours the performance of the U-boat commanders in the First World War. During the 51 months of the First War the exchange rate was 29.67 merchant ships or 69,015 tons per U-boat lost. During the 69 months of the second war this fell to a mere 3.84 ships or 18,167 tons. The reason for this disparity in performance is quite simply the ascendancy of Allied A/S measures in the second war, which accounted for 72.59 per cent of the total number of U-boats commissioned in that period, in comparison to 51.44 per cent of the total commissioned in the first war The most important single factor in bringing about this disparity was air power, which only played a marginal role in the first war (accounting for the destruction of one U-boat) but became a major factor in the second war, being solely responsible for the destruction of 388 U-boats (47.25 per cent of the total losses) apart from assisting surface vessels in the destruction of a further 45. But it must not be thought that air power alone was the panacea to the U-boat menace. The panacea was *Convoy with both air and surface escorts*. This was the surest method of not only *protecting merchant ships* but also *bringing to action and defeating the U-boats*. The final proof is in the eating of the pudding:

between September 1943 and May 1945, out of the tens of thousands of ships escorted, U-boats sank only 100 ships in convoy world-wide, but lost in return 150 U-boats to air and sea convoy escorts. The efficacy of convoy as the correct *defensive* and *offensive* antidote to a submarine offensive against merchant shipping is one of the main lessons of this book. It is a hard learnt lesson of history which is in danger of being forgotten, for as Admiral J. R. Hill has pointed out in his recent book *Anti-Submarine Warfare* (Ian Allen Ltd, 1984) . . . 'Many people, naval officers included, doubt the continuing efficacy of convoys as a means of ensuring the safe and timely arrival of merchant shipping and the defeat of submarines attempting to inhibit it.' What they advocate in the place of convoy is a reversion to the strategically discredited 'Protected Lane' concept guarded by patrol and hunting groups : a strategy that almost brought Britain to her knees before the institution of the convoy system in 1917.

Above: Kapitänleutnant Lothar von Arnauld de la Perière, supreme U-boat Ace of the two world wars, who sank 194 merchant ships totalling 453,716 tons.

Above: Kapitänleutnant Walther Forstmann, Germany's second Ace of the two wars. He sank 146 ships of 384,304 tons.

Above: Kapitänleutnant Max Valentiner, Germany's third Ace of the first war. He sank 141 merchant ships grossing 299,326 tons.

The top five U-boat 'aces' of the First World War

Figures are in gross tons; numbers of ships are in parentheses.

Rank	Name	U-boats commanded	Merchant ships		Warships	
Kapitänleutnant	Lothar von Arnauld de la Perière	U35, U×&	(194)	453,716	(2)	2,500
Kapitänleutnant	Walther Forstmann	U12, U39	(146)	384,304	(1)	820
Kapitänleutnant	Max Valentiner	U38, U3, U38, U157	(141)	299,326	(1)	627
Kapitänleutnant	Otto Steinbrinck	U6, UB10, UB18, UC65, UB57	(202)	231,614	(2)	11,810
Kapitänleutnant	Hans Rose	U53	(79)	213,987	(1)	1,265

The top ten U-boat 'aces' of the Second World War

Figures are in gross tons; numbers of ships are in parentheses.

Rank	Name	U-boats commanded	Total ships	
Korvettenkapitän	Otto Kretschmer	U23, U99	(44)	266,629
Korvettenkapitän	Wolfgang Lüth	U13, U9, U138, U43, U181	(43)	225,713
Korvettenkapitän	Erich Topp	U57, U552	(34)	193,684
Korvettenkapitän	Karl-Friedrich Merten	U68	(29)	180,744
Korvettenkapitän	Victor von Schütze	U25, U103	(34)	171,164
Kapitänleutnant	Herbert Viktor Schütze	U48	(26)	171,122
Kapitänleutnant	Georg Lassen	U160	(28)	167,601
Korvettenkapitän	Heinrich Lehmann-Willenbrock	U5, U96, U256	(22)	166,596
Korvettenkapitän	Günther Prien	U47	(28)	164,953
Kapitänleutnant	Heinrich Liebe	U38	(30)	162,333

Above: Germany's supreme U-boat Ace of the Second World War, Korvettenkapitän Otto Kretschmer, who, while in command of *U23* and *U99*, sank 44 ships of 266,629 tons.

Above: Korvettenkapitän Eric Topp (centre, wearing the white cap), third-ranking Ace, in the conning tower of *U552*, who sank 34 ships grossing 193,684 tons with *U57* and *U552*.

Above: Korvettenkapitän Günther Prien who, apart from earning fame for his sinking of the battleship *Royal Oak* in Scapa Flow, was also rated ninth of the Second World War Aces. He sank 28 ships grossing 164,953 tons while in command of *U47* and was lost when corvettes *Arbutus* and *Camellia* depth-charged her off Rockall in March 1941.

Above: Kapitänleutnant Joachim Schepke, eleventh Ace, who led *U3*, *U19* and *U100* to sink 39 ships totalling 159,130 tons. He was lost when *U100* was depth-charged and rammed by destroyers *Vanoc* and *Walker*, north-west of the Hebrides in March 1941.

Above: Kapitänleutnant Robert Gysae, Germany's fifteenth Ace, who sank 25 ships grossing 144,901 tons while commanding *U98* and *U177*.

Above: Kapitänleutnant Engelbert Endrass, nineteenth of the U-boat Aces. He commanded *U46* and *U567* which sank 22 ships of 128,879 tons while under his charge; he died when *U567* was depth-charged by the sloop *Deptford* and corvette *Samphire* north of the Azores, December 1941.

Appendices

Merchant vessels (British, Allied and neutral) sunk by U-boats and minefields laid by U-boats with a breakdown of the successes obtained by the various flotilla groups 1914–18

Figures are in gross tons; numbers of ships are in parentheses.

Month	High Seas Fleet	Flanders	Mediterranean*	Constantinople	Baltic	U-Cruisers	Total
1914							
Aug							
Sept							
Oct	(1) 866						(1) 866
Nov	(2) 2,084						(2) 2,084
Dec							
Totals	(3) 2,950						(3) 2,950
1915							
Jan	(7) 17,577						(7) 17,577
Feb	(9) 22,785						(9) 22,785
March	(29) 89,517						(29) 89,517
April	(29) 30,926	(3) 9,713			(1) 849		(33) 41,488
May	(52) 107,515			(1) 19,380			(53) 126,895
June	(100) 101,211	(14) 14,080					(114) 115,291
July	(61) 85,732	(24) 6,998		(1) 5,275			(86) 98,005
Aug	(69) 155,637	(31) 7,709	(3) 4,067	(2) 11,154	(2) 4,205		(107) 182,772

Above: Some of the 176 surrendered U-boats moored at Harwich.

Month	High Seas Fleet	Flanders	Mediterrane[an]
Sept	(30) 75,881	(8) 793	(19) 53,
Oct	(19)	19,866 (18)	63,
Nov	(16)	14,091 (44)	152,
Dec	(4) 14,001	(16) 17,045 (18)	76,
Totals	(390) 700,782	(131) 90,295 (102)	350,
1916			
Jan	(16)	17,172 (9)	32,
Feb	(28)	47,711 (16)	47,
March	(21) 66,287	(40) 68,424 (7)	20,
April	(37) 93,524	(26) 37,775 (20)	56,
May	(17) 25,891	(9) 21,398 (37)	72,
June	(3) 2,259	(14) 18,389 (43)	67,
July	(52) 9,713	(7) 10,958 (33)	86,
Aug	(26) 19,621	(22) 7,929 (77)	129,
Sept	(43) 36,613	(83) 86,808 (44)	105,
Oct	(67) 127,719	(66) 84,487 (44)	125,
Nov	(32) 71,480	(101) 87,608 (40)	166,
Dec	(52) 55,638	(100) 115,492 (45)	136,
Totals	(350) 508,745	(512) 604,151 (415)	1,045,
1917			
Jan	(89) 165,494	(82) 84,356 (24)	78,
Feb	*280,602	134,140	105,
March	316,852	185,728	61,
April	447,913	156,472	254,
May	244,984	195,098	170,
June	356,054	143,054	164,
July	309,095	128,912	90,
Aug	249,991	129,788	79,
Sept	124,620	116,942	111,
Oct	177,482	115,699	144,
Nov	84,737	99,579	104,
Dec	133,159	117,621	148,
Totals	2,895,983	1,607,389	1,514,

* No numbers of ships sunk are found in German records

Month	High Seas Fleet	Flanders	Mediterrane[an]
1918			
Jan	(51) 114,094	(47) 57,280 (48)	103,
Feb	(53) 147,174	(33) 65,461 (32)	83,
March	(53) 111,650	(57) 99,395 (60)	110,
April	(42) 93,556	(39) 90,606 (37)	75,
May	(62) 113,211	(23) 39,277 (43)	112,
June	(34) 96,260	(31) 58,931 (23)	58,
July	(33) 119,471	(39) 53,612 (29)	76,
Aug	(41) 115,248	(28) 48,658 (18)	65,
Sept	(40) 82,063	(21) 35,725 (21)	35,
Oct	(26) 52,095	(9) 9,815 (11)	28,
Nov		(3)	10,
Totals	(435) 1,044,822	(327) 558,760 (325)	761,

'Pola.

Constantinople	Baltic	U-Cruisers	Total	
6,011			(58)	136,048
2,350			(39)	86,064
350 (1)	200		(63)	167,523
			(38)	107,739
44,520 (4)	5,254		(636)	1,191,704
			(25)	49,610
			(44)	95,090
5,350			(69)	160,536
			(83)	187,307
			(63)	119,381
5,420			(63)	93,193
3,453 (1)	172		(95)	110,728
2,666 (7)	3,561		(133)	163,145
731 (1)	1,679		(172)	231,573
3,041 (6)	964		(185)	341,363
116 (6)	1,355		(180)	326,689
			(197)	307,847
20,777 (21)	7,731		(1,309)	2,186,462
			(195)	328,391
				520,412
				564,497
251	787			860,334
	5,608			616,316
14,500	5,276	13,542		696,725
	413	26,760		555,514
40		13,004		472,372
799				353,602
2,175	1,426	25,157		466,542
1,201		12,603		302,599
		7,655		411,766
18,966	13,510	98,721		6,149,070
*				
12,408		(8) 8,110	(160)	295,630
161		(15) 38,449	(138)	335,202
2,891		(19) 44,354	(190)	368,746
4,221		(11) 35,820	(134)	300,069
97		(10) 31,280	(139)	296,558
		(22) 55,066	(110)	268,505
		(12) 31,108	(113)	280,820
3,904		(48) 76,993	(154)	310,180
1,833		(8) 16,495	(91)	171,972
7,315		(8) 19,005	(73)	116,237
			(3)	10,233
32,830		(161) 356,680	(1,305)	2,754,152

Merchant vessels (British, Allied and neutral) sunk by U-boats and Italian submarine action, 1939–45

I have compiled the monthly statistics according to theatre (which include losses from mines laid by U-boats) from Dr Jürgen Rohwer's *Axis Submarine Successes 1939–1945*. The information in this work, the result of three decades of meticulous research, provide the most accurate statistics available. For comparison and completeness I have also tabulated the British official figures of losses by submarine (which also include losses due to Japanese submarines) and total losses by all forms of enemy action (U-boats, aircraft, mines, warship and merchant raiders, E-boats, unknown and marine casualty). The latter have been compiled from the official history of *The War at Sea, 1939–1945* by Captain S. W. Roskill. (British figures of losses by submarine do not include ships sunk by mines laid by U-boats.) Figures are in gross tons; numbers of ships are in parentheses.

Month	Atlantic & North Sea	Arctic	Mediterranean	Baltic	Indian Ocean	Total	British Official Figures Submarines	British Official Figures Total All Causes
1939								
Sept	(48)					(48)	(41)	(53)
	178,621					178,621	153,879	194,845
Oct	(33)					(33)	(27)	(46)
	156,156					156,156	134,807	196,355
Nov	(27)					(27)	(21)	(50)
	72,721					72,721	51,589	174,269
Dec	(39)					(39)	(25)	(72)
	101,823					101,823	80,881	189,768
Totals	(147)					(147)	(114)	(221)
	509,321					509,321	421,156	755,237
1940								
Jan	(53)					(53)	(40)	(73)
	163,029					163,029	111,263	214,506
Feb	(50)					(50)	(45)	(63)
	182,369					182,369	169,566	226,920
March	(26)					(26)	(23)	(45)
	69,826					69,826	62,781	107,009
April	(6)					(6)	(7)	(58)
	30,927					30,927	32,467	158,218
May	(14)					(14)	(13)	(101)
	61,635					61,635	55,580	288,461
June	(63)		(2)		(1)	(66)	(58)	(140)
	356,937		9,917		8,215	375,069	284,113	585,496
July	(39)		(2)			(41)	(38)	(105)
	197,878		4,097			201,975	195,825	386,913
Aug	(55)		(1)			(56)	(56)	(92)
	287,136		1,044			288,180	267,618	397,229
Sept	(59)				(1)	(60)	(59)	(100)
	284,577				4,008	288,585	295,335	448,621
Oct	(66)					(66)	(63)	(103)
	363,267					363,267	352,407	442,985
Nov	(36)					(36)	(32)	(97)
	181,695					181,695	146,613	385,715
Dec	(46)					(46)	(37)	(82)
	256,310					256,310	212,590	349,568
Totals	(513)		(5)		(2)	(520)	(471)	(1,059)
	2,435,586		15,058		12,223	2,462,867	2,186,158	3,991,641

							British Official Figures	
Month	Atlantic & North Sea	Arctic	Mediterranean	Baltic	Indian Ocean	Total	Submarines	Total All Causes
1941								
Jan	(23) 129,711					(23) 129,711	(21) 126,782	(76) 320,240
Feb	(47) 254,118					(47) 254,118	(39) 196,783	(102) 403,393
March	(41) 236,549					(41) 236,549	(41) 243,020	(139) 529,706
April	(41) 239,719					(41) 239,719	(43) 249,375	(195) 687,901
May	(63) 362,268					(63) 362,268	(58) 325,492	(139) 511,042
June	(65) 322,012		(1) 3,805			(66) 325,817	(61) 310,143	(109) 432,025
July	(24) 105,320			(2) 7,304		(26) 112,624	(22) 94,209	(43) 120,975
Aug	(24) 80,542	(3) 5,061				(27) 85,603	(23) 80,310	(41) 130,699
Sept	(54) 208,713		(3) 3,524			(57) 212,237	(53) 202,820	(84) 285,942
Oct	(25) 165,333	(1) 3,487	(2) 1,966			(28) 170,786	(32) 156,554	(51) 218,289
Nov	(13) 63,699		(1) 6,600		(1) 5,757	(15) 76,056	(13) 62,196	(35) 104,640
Dec	(11) 56,957	(1) 2,185	(11) 34,084			(23) 93,226	(26) 124,070	(285) 583,706
Totals	(431) 2,224,941	(5) 10,733	(18) 49,979	(2) 7,304	(1) 5,757	(457) 2,298,714	(432) 2,171,754	(1,299) 4,328,558
1942								
Jan	(54) 295,776	(1) 5,135	(1) 313			(56) 301,224	(62) 327,357	(106) 419,907
Feb	(72) 429,255					(72) 429,255	(85) 476,451	(154) 679,632
March	(88) 491,818	(2) 11,507	(3) 4,189			(93) 507,514	(95) 537,980	(273) 834,164
April	(67) 389,635	(4) 19,066	(10) 9,460			(81) 418,161	(74) 431,664	(132) 674,457
May	(124) 588,521	(2) 12,344	(3) 15,970			(129) 616,835	(125) 607,247	(151) 705,050
June	(127) 626,158		(9) 10,768			(136) 636,926	(144) 700,235	(173) 834,196
July	(74) 358,461	(16) 102,296	(6) 6,294			(96) 467,051	(96) 476,065	(128) 618,113
Aug	(105) 540,765	(4) 6,295	(8) 40,185			(117) 587,245	(108) 544,410	(123) 661,133
Sept	(85) 420,470	(7) 40,511	(4) 813			(96) 461,794	(98) 485,413	(114) 567,327
Oct	(65) 427,292	(1) 163			(23) 156,235	(89) 583,690	(94) 619,417	(101) 637,833
Nov	(83) 524,917	(6) 36,541	(10) 95,407		(27) 145,295	(126) 802,160	(119) 729,160	(134) 807,754
Dec	(56) 292,632		(4) 27,617		(4) 17,369	(64) 337,618	(60) 330,816	(73) 348,902
Date not known								(2) 2,229
Totals	(1,000) 5,385,700	(43) 233,858	(58) 211,016		(54) 318,899	(1,155) 6,149,473	(1,160) 6,266,215	(1,664) 7,790,697

Month	Atlantic & North Sea	Arctic	Mediterranean	Bal
1943				
Jan	(33) 282,855	(2) 4,310	(9) 20,031	
Feb	(52) 301,719	(1) 7,460	(9) 21,206	
March	(85) 509,829	(3) 18,245	(12) 46,823	
April	(38) 223,067		(5) 13,934	
May	(37) 195,188		(1) 5,979	
June	(6) 28,917		(6) 23,720	
July	(23) 126,855	(2) 857	(6) 25,949	
Aug	(4) 21,749	(2) 3,472	(7) 20,821	
Sept	(9) 54,068	(2) 9,649	(2) 14,352	
Oct	(10) 44,935	(2) 4,757	(5) 28,543	
Nov	(6) 23,245		(3) 7,481	
Dec	(7) 47,785		(1) 8,009	
Totals	(310) 1,860,212	(14) 48,750	(66) 236,848	
1944				
Jan	(2) 14,535	(3) 21,530		
Feb	(2) 7,048		(6) 21,651	
March	(7) 34,500	(1) 7,062	(3) 29,231	
April	(5) 35,310	(1) 7,176	(2) 14,386	
May	(3) 17,276		(1) 7,147	
June	(9) 41,761			
July	(10) 38,395			
Aug	(7) 35,259	(2) 5,885		
Sept	(4) 23,303	(2) 14,395		
Oct				(- 1
Nov	(4) 14,995			
Dec	(8) 51,338	(3) 1,930		
Totals	(61) 313,720	(12) 57,978	(12) 72,415	(

Indian Ocean	Total	British Official Figures	
		Submarines	Total All Causes
	(44)	(37)	(50)
	307,196	203,128	261,359
(5)	(67)	(63)	(73)
31,696	362,081	359,328	403,062
(10)	(110)	(108)	(120)
58,834	633,731	627,377	693,389
(7)	(50)	(56)	(64)
50,136	287,137	327,943	344,680
(7)	(45)	(50)	(58)
36,015	237,182	264,852	299,428
(5)	(17)	(20)	(28)
23,453	76,090	95,753	123,825
(15)	(46)	(46)	(61)
84,116	237,777	252,145	365,398
(7)	(20)	(16)	(25)
46,401	92,443	86,579	119,801
(3)	(16)	(20)	(29)
20,783	98,852	118,841	156,419
(3)	(20)	(20)	(29)
13,060	91,295	97,407	139,861
	(9)	(14)	(29)
	30,726	66,585	144,391
	(8)	(13)	(31)
	55,794	86,967	168,524
(62)	(452)	(463)	(597)
364,494	2,510,304	2,586,905	3,220,137
(6)	(11)	(13)	(26)
38,751	74,816	92,278	130,635
(6)	(14)	(18)	(23)
37,344	66,043	92,923	116,855
(5)	(16)	(23)	(25)
23,928	94,721	142,944	157,960
(1)	(9)	(9)	(13)
5,277	62,149	62,149	82,372
	(4)	(4)	(5)
	24,423	24,424	27,297
(3)	(12)	(11)	(26)
15,645	57,406	57,875	104,084
(4)	(14)	(12)	(17)
23,000	61,395	63,351	78,756
(8)	(17)	(18)	(23)
50,310	91,454	98,729	118,304
(2)	(8)	(7)	(8)
13,092	50,790	43,368	44,805
	(4)	(1)	(4)
	1,659	7,176	11,668
(1)	(5)	(7)	(9)
10,198	25,193	29,592	37,980
	(11)	(9)	(26)
	53,268	58,518	134,913
(36)	(125)	(132)	(205)
217,545	663,308	773,327	1,045,629

Month	Atlantic & North Sea	Arctic	Mediterranean	Baltic	Indian Ocean	Total	British Official Figures	
							Submarines	Total All Causes
1945								
Jan	(13)			(1)		(14)	(11)	(18)
	66,770			640		67,410	56,988	82,897
Feb	(13)	(3)			(2)	(18)	(15)	(26)
	39,094	22,505			14,312	75,911	65,233	95,316
March	(13)	(2)				(15)	(13)	(27)
	51,515	14,386				65,901	65,077	111,204
April	(11)	(1)				(12)	(13)	(22)
	62,929	1,603				64,532	72,957	104,512
May	(4)					(4)	(3)	(4)
	10,722					10,722	10,022	17,198
Totals	(54)	(6)	(1)	(2)		(63)	(55)	(97)
	231,030	38,494	640	14,312		284,476	270,277	411,127

In addition the following losses were accounted for by German U-boats in the Pacific and Black Sea:

Pacific	Dec 1944	(1)	7,180
Black Sea	Nov 1941	(1)	1,975
	Feb 1943	(1)	4,648
	March 1943	(1)	8,228
	June 1943	(1)	1,783
	July 1943	(2)	11,794
	June 1944	(1)	1,850

} (7) 30,278 } (8) 37,458

Total } (8) 37,458

In July 1945 the British trawler *Kned* (352 tons) was sunk by a mine which had been laid by *U218* (Becker) off Lizard Head. This loss has not been added to the statistics of losses.

Summary of mercantile losses by year, 1939–45

The German figures include the addition of losses in the Pacific and the Black Sea, which are not included in the monthly tabulations. Figures are in gross tons; numbers of ships are in parentheses.

	1. German figures: losses by U-boats		2. British figures: losses by submarines		3. Variation between British & German figures (Cols 1&2)		4. British figures of total losses by all causes		5. Percentage of total losses (Col. 4) represented by losses from U-boats (Col. 1)
1939	(147)	509,321	(114)	421,156	(−33)	−88,165	(221)	755,237	67.43%
1940	(520)	2,462,867	(471)	2,186,158	(−49)	−276,709	(1,059)	3,991,641	61.70%
1941	(458)	2,300,689	(432)	2,171,754	(−26)	−128,935	(1,299)	4,328,558	53.15%
1942	(1,155)	6,149,473	(1,160)	6,266,215	(+5)	+116,742	(1,664)	7,790,697	78.93%
1943	(457)	2,536,757	(463)	2,586,905	(+6)	+50,148	(597)	3,220,137	78.77%
1944	(127)	672,338	(132)	773,327	(+5)	+100,989	(205)	1,045,629	64.29%
1945	(63)	284,476	(55)	270,277	(−8)	−14,199	(97)	411,127	69.19%
Totals	(2,927)	14,915,921	(2,827)	14,675,792	(−100)	−240,129	(5,142)	21,543,026	69.23%

The British figures of losses by submarines do not include ships sunk by mines laid by U-boats, and this accounts in part for the *minus* discrepancy in comparison with the German figures for the years 1939–41. For instance if the number of ships lost by mines for 1939 which are included in the German figures (71,031 tons) are added to the British total, the discrepancy in the 1939 statistics is reduced to a mere 17,134 tons. The *plus* discrepancy for the years 1942–44 is accountable by the fact that the British figures include ships sunk by Japanese submarines in the Indian and Pacific Oceans, which are not included in my tabulation of Rohwer's German figures.

Comparison between German and British Official statistics of the British, Allied and neutral merchant vessels sunk by U-boat action, 1914–18

The German official figures can be found in Volume 5 of Konteradmiral Arno Spindler's *Der Krieg zur See, 1914–1918: Der Handelskrieg mit U-Booten*. The British figures are derived from the Admiralty paper *Statistical Review of the War Against Merchant Shipping*, compiled by the Director of Statistics, dated 23 December 1918. The German official figures, the result of more than thirty years of research, are without doubt the more accurate of the two, including as they do *all* vessels sunk by U-boat action (including mining), whereas the British compilation only includes vessels of over 500 gross tons and excludes fishing vessels. Figures are in gross tons; numbers of ships are in parentheses.

	German Figures	British Figures	Variation
1914			
Aug			
Sept			
Oct	(1) 866	(1) 866	
Nov	(2) 2,084	(2) 2,084	
Dec			
Total	(3) 2,950	(3) 2,950	
1915			
Jan	(7) 17,577	(7) 17,126	
Feb	(9) 22,785	(9) 22,784	
March	(29) 89,517	(26) 72,441	
April	(33) 41,488	(23) 38,614	
May	(53) 126,895	(35) 106,293	
June	(114) 115,291	(58) 118,091	
July	(86) 98,005	(55) 105,145	
Aug	(107) 182,772	(74) 181,691	
Sept	(58) 136,048	(56) 151,271	
Oct	(39) 86,064	(30) 88,145	
Nov	(63) 167,523	(55) 153,277	
Dec	(38) 107,739	(40) 121,951	
Total	(636) 1,191,704	(468) 1,176,829	(−168) (−14,876)
1916			
Jan	(25) 49,610	(19) 64,451	
Feb	(44) 95,090	(40) 107,857	
March	(69) 160,536	(55) 169,863	
April	(83) 187,307	(81) 191,872	
May	(63) 119,381	(58) 122,592	
June	(63) 93,193	(64) 111,719	
July	(95) 110,728	(51) 110,084	
Aug	(133) 163,145	(121) 158,405	
Sept	(172) 231,573	(126) 224,876	
Oct	(185) 341,363	(185) 351,764	

Mercantile tonnage sunk by individual U-boats, 1914–18

Source pp. 372–93 of *Der Handelskrieg mit U-Booten*, volume 5, by Konteradmiral Arno Spindler. Figures are in gross tons. Note that only 3 ships of 2,950 tons were accounted for in 1914: *U17* Feldkirchner, (1) 866; and *U21* Hersing, (2) 2,084. These have been added to the grand totals of the U-boats concerned.

Boat	Commanders	1915	1916	1917	1918	Total
U6	Steinbrinck	(13) 4,654				(13) 4,654
	Lepsius					
U8	Stoss	(5) 15,049				(5) 15,049
U9	Weddigen	(13) 8,636				(13) 8,636
	Spiess					
U10	Stuhr	(7) 1,625				(7) 1,625
U12	Forstmann	(1) 3,738				(1) 3,738
	Kratzsch					
U16	Hansen	(10) 11,476				(10) 11,476
	Hillebrand					
U17	Feldkirchner	(11) 15,769				(12) 16,635
	Walther					
U19	Kolbe	(25) 9,464	(7) 20,959	(14) 34,393		(46) 64,816
	Weisbach					
	Spiess					
U20	Schwieger	(25) 111,170	(11) 32,510			(36) 144,300
U21	Hersing	(4) 9,219	(10) 16,253	(20) 51,156		(36) 78,712
U22	Hoppe	(7) 15,678	(9) 8,669	(7) 17,892	(20) 4,448	(43) 46,687
	Scherb					
	Hashagen, E.					
	Hasagen, H.H.					
U23	Weisbach	(7) 8,822				(7) 8,822
	Schulthess					
U24	Schneider	(25) 74,044	(2) 384	(6) 31,304		(33) 105,732
	Remy					
U25	Wünsche	(21) 14,126				(21) 14,126
U26	von Berckheim	(2) 2,849				(2) 2,849
U27	Wegener	(9) 29,402				(9) 29,402
U28	von-Forstner	(18) 43,760	(5) 14,299	(16) 35,723		(39) 93,782
	Schmidt, G.					

Boat	Commanders	1915	1916
U29	Platsch	(4) 12,934	
	Weddigen		
U30	von Rosenberg	(9) 22,005	(2) 2,9…
	Grünert		
U32	von Spiegel	(1) 2,247	(16) 44,2…
	Hartwig		
	Albrecht, K.		
U33	Gansser	(40) 121,246	(1) 5,3…
	Siehs		
	von Doemming		
U34	Rücker	(19) 56,530	(54) 102,9…
	Klasing		
	Canaris		
U35	Kophamel	(35) 89,192	(122) 266,6…
	von Arnauld		
	von Voigt, E.		
	von Heimburg		
U36	Graeff	(14) 12,688	
U37	Wilcke	(2) 2,811	
U38	Valentiner, M.	(68) 150,912	(53) 113,9…
	Wickel		
U39	Forstmann	(44) 102,476	(64) 169,7…
	Metzger		
U41	Hansen	(28) 58,949	
U43	Jürst		(13) 28,5…
	Bender		
	Kirchner		
U44	Wagenführ		(8) 26,6…
U45	Sittenfeld		(4) 6,7…
U46	Hillebrand		(17) 33,8…
	Saalwächter		
	Hillebrand		
	Meyer, W.		
U47	Metzger		(7) 14,5…
	Gercke		
	Gerth		

	German Figures	British Figures	Variation
Nov	(180) 326,689	(151) 326,003	
Dec	(197) 307,847	(174) 291,636	
Total	(1,309) 2,186,462	(1,125) 2,108,530	(−184) (−77,932)

1917

	German Figures	British Figures
Jan	(195) 328,391	(162) 331,466
Feb	520,412	(224) 497,095
March	564,497	(267) 553,189
April	860,334	(372) 867,834
May	616,316	(285) 589,603
June	696,725	(286) 674,458
July	555,514	(224) 545,021
Aug	472,372	(186) 509,142
Sept	353,602	(158) 338,242
Oct	466,542	(159) 448,923
Nov	302,599	(126) 289,095

	German Figures	British Figures	Variation
Dec	411,766	(160) 382,060	
Total	(2,609) 6,149,070	6,026,128	(−122,942)

1918

	German Figures	British Figures	Variation
Jan	(160) 295,630	(123) 302,088	
Feb	(138) 335,202	(115) 318,174	
March	(190) 368,746	(169) 244,814	
April	(134) 300,069	(112) 273,355	
May	(139) 296,558	(112) 294,019	
June	(110) 268,505	(101) 252,637	
July	(113) 280,820	(95) 259,901	
Aug	(154) 310,180	(104) 278,876	
Sept	(91) 171,972	(79) 186,600	
Oct	(73) 116,237	(52) 112,427	
Nov	(3) 10,233	(15) 26,857	
Total	(1,305)	(1,077)	(−228)

	German Figures	British Figures	Variation
	2,754,152	2,649,748	(−104,404)
1914	(3) 2,950	(3) 2,950	
1915	(636) 1,191,704	(468) 1,176,829	
1916	(1,309) 2,186,462	(1,125) 2,108,530	
1917	6,149,070	(2,609) 6,026,128	
1918	(1,305) 2,754,152	(1,077) 2,649,748	
Total	12,284,757	(5,282) 11,964,185	(−320,572)

When the 614 fishing vessels of 62,139 tons sunk by U-boats are added to the total of the British figures, the discrepancy between the British and German totals is reduced to a mere 258,433 tons.

1917	1918	Total
		(4) 12,934
(15) 22,465		(26) 47,383
(18) 53,573	(2) 5,652	(37) 105,740
(26) 46,427	(17) 56,575	(84) 229,598
(35) 58,789	(13) 44,649	(121) 262,886
(62) 170,672	(5) 13,234	(224) 539,741
	(14) 12,688	
	(2) 2,811	
(13) 24,107	(3) 10,992	(137) 299,985
(42) 121,447	(4) 10,788	(154) 404,478
	(28) 58,949	
(28) 79,314	(3) 8,746	(44) 116,590
(13) 42,649		(21) 72,332
(20) 38,832		(24) 45,622
(25) 75,197	(13) 41,390	(55) 150,399
(7) 9,496		(14) 24,075

Boat	Commanders	1915	1916	1917	1918	Total
	Schultze, E.					
	Bünte					
U48	Rutz		(4) 10,622	(30) 92,930		(34) 103,552
	Hashagen					
	Edeling					
U49	Hartmann		(17) 35,288	(21) 51,145		(38) 86,433
U50	Berger		(9) 25,308	(17) 67,456		(26) 92,764
U52	Walther		(4) 5,766	(24) 65,459	(2) 650	(30) 71,875
	Spiess					
	Krapohl					
U53	Rose		(6) 23,264	(60) 156,161	(24) 36,344	(90) 215,769
	von Schrader, O.					
U54	von Bothmer			(21) 62,182	(8) 28,745	(29) 90,927
	Heeseler					
	von Ruckteschell					
U55	Werner		(3) 9,605	(33) 51,082	(29) 84,326	(65) 145,013
U56	Lorenz		(4) 5,374			(4) 5,374
U57	von Georg		(23) 15,167	(32) 76,513	(3) 23,512	(58) 115,192
	Sperling					
	Gühler					
U58	Wippern		(3) 1,576	(18) 29,325		(21) 30,901
	Hermann					
	Scherb					
	Amberger					
U59	von Firks		(2) 422	(11) 18,341		(13) 18,763
U60	Schuster			(38) 80,357	(16) 33,801	(54) 114,158
	Grünert					
	Jasper					
U61	Dieckmann			(29) 68,135	(7) 22,635	(36) 90,770
U62	Hashagen, E.			(39) 95,903	(8) 33,163	(47) 129,066
	Wiebalcke					
U63	Schultze, O.		(18) 47,302	(40) 96,552	(16) 67,011	(74) 210,865
	Metzger					
	Schultze, O.					
	Hartwig					

Boat	Commanders	1915		1916		1917		1918		Total	
U64	Morath			(4)	9,635	(35)	94,109	(6)	28,422	(45)	132,166
U65	von Fischel			(1)	9,223	(40)	58,851	(11)	26,585	(52)	94,659
U66	von Bothmer Muhle			(12)	24,862	(12)	44,154			(24)	69,016
U67	von Rosenberg Nieland von Rabenau			(3)	8,988	(14)	30,705	(2)	9,276	(19)	48,969
U69	Wilhelms			(14)	38,288	(16)	66,183			(30)	104,471
U70	Wünsche			(15)	30,280	(37)	104,951	(2)	13,458	(54)	148,689
U71	Schmidt, H. Gude Schmidt, H. Scheuerling			(8)	6,585	(8)	4,948	(1)	120	(17)	11,653
U72	Kraft Feldkirchner Schultze, E. Böhm			(8)	19,765	(10)	18,806			(18)	38,571
U73	Siehs Rohne von Voigt, E. Bünte Saupe			(10)	76,157	(5)	4,534	(1)	3,030	(16)	83,721
U74	Weisbach			(1)	2,802					(1)	2,802
U75	Beitzen Schmolling			(5)	5,035	(4)	8,583			(9)	13,618
U76	Bender			(1)	1,146					(1)	1,146
U78	Dröscher Vollbrecht			(4)	8,297	(12)	18,381			(16)	26,678
U79	Jess Rohrbeck Thouret Meusel Thouret			(5)	9,560	(16)	24,171			(21)	33,731
U80	von Glasenapp Amberger Scherb Koopmann			(3)	5,563	(16)	39,349	(7)	5,036	(26)	49,948
U81	Weisbach			(2)	2,578	(29)	86,427			(31)	89,005
U82	Middendorf Adam Middendorf			(5)	1,957	(21)	66,507	(9)	40,166	(35)	108,630
U83	Hoppe			(1)	123	(4)	6,163			(5)	6,286
U84	Roehr					(25)	76,989	(2)	55,957	(27)	82,946
U85	Petz					(5)	23,127			(5)	23,127
U86	Crüsemann Götze Patzig					(13)	46,535	(20)	79,045	(33)	125,580
U87	von Speth- Schülzburg					(21)	59,170			(21)	59,170
U88	Schwieger					(13)	39,583			(13)	39,583
U89	Mildenberger					(4)	8,496	(2)	6,885	(6)	15,381
U90	Remy Petz Remy Schultze, H.					(10)	10,354	(25)	94,155	(35)	104,509
U91	von Glasenapp					(1)	2,274	(39)	93,976	(40)	96,250
U92	Bieler Ehrlich							(8)	19,790	(8)	19,790
U93	von Spiegel Ziegner Gerlach					(27)	72,756	(3)	6,068	(30)	78,824

Boat	Commanders	1915		1916	
U94	Saalwächter Schwab				
U95	Prinz				
U96	Petz				
U97	Schmidt, H. Wünsche von Mohl Götting				
U98	Andler				
U100	von Loë-Degenhart Götting				
U101	Koopmann Georg				
U102	Killmann Beitzen				
U103	Rücker				
U104	Bernis				
U105	Strackerjan				
U107	Starke Sievert				
U108	Nitzsche				
U110	von Schubert				
U111	Beyersdorff				
U113	Recke				
U117	Dröscher				
U118	Stohwasser				
U122	Korte				
U139	von Arnauld				
U140	Kophamel				
U151	Kophamel von Nostitz				
U152	Kolbe Franz				
U153	Pastuscznyck				
U154	Gercke				
U155	Meusel Eckelmann Studt				
U156	Gansser				
U157	Valentiner, M. Rabe V. Pappenheim Valentiner, M.				
UB2	Fürbringer, W. Neumann Vieber von Keyserlingk	(10)	706	(1)	6
UB4	Gross	(3)	10,883		
UB5	Smiths von Montigny	(5)	996		
UB6	Hacker Voigt, E. Neumann, K. von Heydebreck Steckelberg	(7)	3,922	(9)	3,0
UB7	Werner Lütjohann	(1)	6,011		
UB8	von Voight	(1)	19,380		
UB10	Steinbrinck Saltzwedel Buch Amberger	(27)	13,379	(2)	2,8

1917		1918		Total	
(15)	39,876	(5)	17,769	(20)	57,645
(12)	30,338	(2)	7,592	(14)	37,930
(21)	70,614	(11)	30,918	(32)	101,532
(2)	421	(2)	4,985	(4)	5,406
		(3)	9,120	(3)	9,120
(5)	13,901	(7)	42,307	(12)	56,208
(4)	7,886	(24)	52,821	(28)	60,707
(2)	7,605	(3)	5,640	(5)	13,245
(3)	7,001	(5)	15,248	(8)	22,249
(4)	8,145	(8)	28,567	(12)	36,712
(8)	29,553	(12)	26,131	(20)	55,884
		(6)	24,576	(6)	24,576
		(2)	8,445	(2)	8,445
(2)	5,105	(6)	27,036	(8)	32,141
		(3)	3,011	(3)	3,011
		(4)	6,734	(4)	6,734
		(24)	46,898	(24)	46,898
		(2)	10,439	(2)	10,439
		(1)	278	(1)	278
		(6)	7,208	(6)	7,208
		(7)	30,888	(7)	30,888
(12)	29,048	(39)	109,236	(51)	138,284
		(20)	37,726	(20)	37,726
		(4)	12,780	(4)	12,780
		(4)	8,158	(4)	8,158
(19)	53,306	(47)	134,795	(66)	188,101
(4)	7,353	(52)	56,442	(56)	63,795
(1)	302	(13)	10,463	(14)	10,765
				(11)	1,378
				(3)	10,883
				(5)	996
				(16)	7,007
				(1)	6,011
				(1)	19,380
(?)	6,379			(36)	22,583

Boat	Commanders	1915		1916		1917		1918		Total	
	von Rohrscheidt										
	Pilzecker										
	von Schmettow										
	von Rohrscheidt										
	Reimarus										
	Gregor										
	Lorenz										
	Stephan										
	von Montigny										
	Stephan										
	Emsmann										
	Stüben										
UB12	Nieland	(9)	424	(6)	5,313	(6)	4,405			(21)	10,142
	Kiel										
	Gerth										
	Niemer										
	Steindorff										
	Wigankow										
	Braun										
	Frhr. von Lyncker										
	Schöller										
UB13	Becker, S.	(4)	2,170	(6)	1,593					(10)	3,763
	Neumann, K.										
	Metz										
UB14	von Heimburg	(3)	13,467			(1)	155			(4)	13,622
	von Dewitz										
	von Heimburg										
	Schwarz, K.										
	Ulrich, E.										
UB16	Valentiner, H.	(11)	9,504	(11)	8,275	(1)	107	(2)	939	(25)	18,825
	Hundius										
	Müller-Schwarz										
	Niemer										
	Thielmann										
	Rhein										
	Bachmann, G.										
	Krameyer										
	von d. Lühe										
UB17	Wenninger	(6)	545	(6)	1,689	(1)	40			(13)	2,274
	Metz										
	Fürbringer, W.										
	Moecke										
	Suadicani										
	Degetau										
	Meier, U.										
	Niemeyer										
	Wigankow										
	Ries										
UB18	Steinbrinck			(88)	89,342	(38)	39,213			(126)	128,555
	Lafrenz										
	Meier, U.										
	Niemeyer, G.										
UB19	Becker, W. G.			(11)	11,558					(11)	11,558
	Noodt										
UB20	Viebeg			(4)	1,531	(9)	8,383			(13)	9,914
	Glimpf										
UB21	Hashagen, E.			(7)	2,491	(18)	23,841	(9)	13,593	(34)	39,925
	Walther, F.										
	Scheffler										
	Mahn										
UB22	Putzier Wacker			(7)	4,570	(20)	12,076			(27)	16,646

Boat	Commanders	1915	1916	1917	1918	Total
UB23	von Voight		(41) 21,482	(10) 12,840		(51) 34,322
	Ziemer					
	Lefholz					
	von Schmettow					
	Niemer					
UB27	Dieckmann		(10) 6,438	(2) 10,228		(12) 16,666
	Lübe					
	von Stein					
UB29	Pustkuchen		(29) 39,378			(29) 39,378
	Platsch					
UB30	Schapler		(6) 964	(4) 4,269	(12) 31,044	(22) 36,277
	von Montigny					
	Rhein					
	Stier					
UB31	Bieber			(22) 66,221	(7) 18,129	(29) 84,350
	Braun					
UB32	Sahl			(22) 42,889		(22) 42,889
	Ruprecht					
	Vieberg					
	Ditfurth					
UB33	Gregor, F.				(15) 14,152	(15) 14,152
UB34	Schultz, T.		(9) 5,494	(10) 20,412	(15) 22,822	(34) 48,728
	Schaashausen					
	von Ruckteschell					
	Förste					
	Weitzhaupt					
UB35	Gebeschus		(8) 5,826	(31) 28,192	(5) 13,198	(39) 47,216
	von Schrader					
	Gebeschus					
	Stöter					
UB36	Albrecht, K.		(3) 1,152	(8) 5,100		(11) 6,252
	von Keyserlingk					
UB37	Valentiner, H.		(26) 14,744	(4) 5,756		(30) 20,500
	Günther					
UB38	Wassner		(21) 16,799	(21) 26,973	(7) 10,219	(49) 53,991
	von Montigny					
	von Fischer					
	Bachmann					
UB39	Fürbringer, W.		(60) 66,599	(33) 23,211		(93) 89,810
	Küstner					
UB40	Neumann, K.		(12) 15,355	(56) 89,654	(35) 28,349	(103) 133,358
	Howaldt					
	Dobberstein					
UB41	von Sichartshofen			(8) 8,387		(8) 8,387
	Krause, G.					
	Ploen					
UB42	Wernicke		(2) 881	(7) 10,470	(2) 6,206	(11) 17,557
	Schwarz, K.					
	von Rohrscheidt					
	Schwarz, K.					
	von Montigny, G.					
UB43	Niebuhr		(13) 63,239	(9) 35,963		(22) 99,202
	von Mellenthin					
	Obermüller					
UB44	Wäger		(1) 3,409			(1) 3,409
UB45	Palis		(3) 11,666			(3) 11,666
UB46	Bauer, C.		(4) 8,099			(4) 8,099
UB47	Steinbauer, W.		(12) 42,949	(8) 32,885		(20) 75,834
	Wendlandt					
UB48	Steinbauer, W.			(16) 51,922	(20) 57,351	(36) 109,273
	Hinüber					

Boat	Commanders	1915	1916
UB49	von Mellenthin		
	Ehrensberger		
UB50	Becker, F.		
	Kukat		
UB51	Krafft		
	Gercke		
UB52	Launburg		
UB53	Sprenger		
UB54	von Werner		
	Hecht		
UB55	Wenninger		
UB56	Valentiner, H.		
UB57	Steinbrinck, O.		
	Lohs, F.		
UB58	Fürbringer, W.		
	Löwe		
UB59	Wassner		
UB61	Schultz, T.		
UB62	Putzier		
	Sperling		
	Putzier		
UB63	Gebeschus, R.		
UB64	von Schrader, O.		
	Gude, W.		
UB65	Schelle		
UB66	Wernicke		
	Petri		
UB67	Schulz, G.		
	von Doemming		
UB68	von Heimburg		
	Dönitz		
UB70	Remy, F.		
UB72	Creutzfeld		
	Träger		
UB73	Adam		
	Neureuther		
UB74	Neureuther		
	Steindorff		
UB75	Walther		
UB77	Meyer, W.		
	Maurer		
UB78	Stosberg		
UB80	Viebeg		
UB81	Saltzwedel		
UB82	Becker, G. W.		
UB83	Krause		
	Buntebart		
UB86	Trenk		
UB87	Petri		
	Hibsch		
UB88	Ries		
	von Rabenau, R.		
UB90	von Mayer, G.		
UB91	Hartwig		
UB92	Krapohl		
	Lautenschläger		
	Müller, F. P.		
UB94	Hamann		
UB95	Maass, O.		
UB103	Hundius		
UB104	Berlin		Bieber

1917	1918		Total	
41,546	(30)	56,154	(44)	97,700
36,139	(22)	73,053	(41)	109,192
26,661	(15)	26,867	(20)	53,528
	(14)	42,637	(14)	42,637
3,119	(18)	48,065	(20)	51,184
6,638	(10)	3,244	(16)	9,882
5,192	(13)	19,986	(20)	25,178
5,407			(4)	5,407
43,651	(36)	109,499	(53)	153,150
7,983	(2)	208	(8)	8,191
2,309	(6)	8,669	(7)	10,978
12,920			(2)	12,920
12,187	(3)	10,065	(8)	22,252
4,481	(4)	13,660	(6)	18,141
1,712	(29)	38,488	(30)	40,200
4,275	(6)	18,186	(9)	22,461
	(1)	200	(1)	200
	(1)	13,936	(1)	13,936
	(7)	16,993	(7)	16,993
	(6)	23,736	(6)	23,736
	(6)	12,578	(6)	12,578
	(10)	22,259	(10)	22,259
	(10)	19,530	(10)	19,530
9,529			(5)	9,529
	(2)	15,448	(2)	15,448
	(3)	1,511	(3)	1,511
9,942	(16)	31,329	(19)	41,271
3,218			(1)	3,218
	(1)	1,920	(1)	1,920
	(2)	1,770	(2)	1,770
	(7)	13,351	(7)	13,351
	(7)	34,380	(7)	34,380
	(13)	32,333	(13)	32,333
	(1)	1,420	(1)	1,420
	(5)	16,468	(5)	16,468
	(7)	16,459	(7)	16,459
	(2)	3,261	(2)	3,261
	(2)	5,282	(2)	5,282
	(15)	28,746	(15)	28,746
	(7)	14,442	(7)	14,442

Boat	Commanders	1915		1916		1917		1918		Total	
UB105	Marschall							(25)	69,641	(25)	69,641
	Petersen										
UB107	Howaldt							(12)	28,740	(12)	28,740
	von Prittwitz										
	u. Gaffron										
UB108	von Beulwitz							(2)	2,655	(2)	2,655
	Amberger										
UB109	Ramien							(5)	13,610	(5)	13,610
UB110	Fürbringer							(4)	7,686	(4)	7,686
UB111	von Werner							(8)	1,571	(8)	1,571
UB112	Reiche, F.							(9)	9,238	(9)	9,238
	Rhein										
UB113	von Reiche, C.							(2)	1,836	(2)	1,836
	Pilzecker										
UB115	Thomsen							(1)	336	(1)	336
UB117	Wassner							(6)	11,586	(6)	11,586
UB118	Krautz							(5)	23,967	(5)	23,967
UB119	Kolbe							(1)	2,100	(1)	2,100
UB120	Plum							(2)	7,219	(2)	7,219
UB122	Träger							(1)	3,150	(1)	3,150
	Schmitt, R.										
UB123	Ramm							(5)	4,490	(5)	4,490
UB125	Schubert							(6)	10,967	(6)	10,967
	Vater										
UB126	von Fischer, W.							(2)	3,078	(2)	3,078
UB128	Canaris							(1)	7,418	(1)	7,418
UB129	Neumann							(1)	9,217	(1)	9,217
UC1	von Werner	(11)	10,028	(25)	40,339	(2)	8,721			(38)	59,088
	Ramien										
	Küstner										
	Thielmann										
	Steckelberg										
	Thielmann										
	Warzecha										
	Mildenstern										
UC3	Weisbach	(15)	17,669	(4)	10,597					(19)	28,266
	Wassner										
	Keysern										
UC4	Vesper			(9)	11,432	(14)	12,844	(5)	2,859	(28)	27,135
	Moecke										
	Hamm										
	Bieber										
	Pilzecker										
	Howaldt										
	Reimarus										
	Steckelberg										
	Reimarus										
	Hecht										
	Schmitz, W.										
	Schmitt, E.										
UC5	Pustkuchen	(19)	21,915	(10)	14,373					(29)	36,288
	Mohrbutter										
UC6	von Schmettow	(20)	16,197	(32)	45,692	(2)	2,175			(54)	64,064
	Ehrentraut										
	Günther										
	von Zerboni di										
	Sposetti										
	Löwe										
	Reichenbach										
UC7	Wäger	(13)	20,819	(16)	24,451					(29)	45,270
	Haag										

Boat	Commanders	1915		1916		1917		1918		Total	
UC10	Nitzsche	(1)	2,229	(14)	27,849					(15)	30,078
	Saltzwedel										
	Nitzsche										
	Albrecht, W.										
UC11	Schmidt, W.	(3)	3,457	(10)	15,811	(11)	13,677	(5)	5,611	(29)	38,556
	Saltzwedel										
	Schmitz										
	von Ditfurth										
	Niemeyer										
	von Ditfurth										
	Dobberstein										
	Schwartz										
	Lange										
	Utke										
UC12	Palis			(5)	3,039					(5)	3,039
	Fröhner										
UC13	Kirchner	(3)	387							(3)	387
UC14	Bauer, C.	(1)	2,952	(7)	4,918	(6)	1,097			(14)	8,967
	Becker, F.										
	Klatt										
	Pilzecker										
	Lorenz										
	Feddersen										
UC15	von Dewitz			(1)	3,905					(1)	3,905
	Heller										
UC16	von Werner			(21)	20,277	(21)	22,799			(42)	43,076
	Reimarus										
UC17	Wenninger			(25)	14,128	(58)	105,659	(11)	24,083	(94)	143,870
	von Rohrscheidt										
	Fürbringer, W.										
	Pilzecker, U.										
	Stephan										
	Pilzecker, U.										
	Frhr. von Lynder										
UC18	Kiel			(19)	18,094	(15)	15,522			(34)	33,616
UC19	Nitzsche			(1)	275	(2)	3,080			(3)	3,355
UC20	Becker, F.			(2)	1,353	(16)	8,797	(6)	19,964	(24)	30,114
	von Lühe										
	Kümpel										
	Kukat										
	Rohne										
UC21	Saltzwedel			(22)	22,599	(73)	106,903			(95)	129,502
	von Zerboni di										
	Sposetti										
UC22	Heimburg			(6)	18,420	(9)	5,966	(9)	28,317	(24)	52,703
	Wiesenbach										
	Bünte										
	Weichhold										
UC23	Kirchner			(2)	14,598	(33)	8,167	(31)	17,409	(66)	40,174
	von Bothmer										
	Lübbe										
UC24	Willich					(4)	9,816			(4)	9,816
UC25	Feldkirchner					(10)	2,792	(7)	24,941	(17)	27,733
	Lippold										
	Frhr von Wangenheim										
	Dönitz										
UC26	von Schmettow			(22)	38,348	(13)	17,884			(35)	56,232
UC27	Vesper					(43)	31,078	(10)	36,912	(53)	67,990
	Schulz, G.										
	Canaris										
	List										

Boat	Commanders	1915		1916	
	Gercke				
	Ciliar				
UC29	Rosenow				
UC30	Stenzler			(1)	62
UC31	von Schrader			(1)	20
	Siewert				
	Bartholdy				
	Stüben				
UC32	Breyer			(2)	2,19
UC33	Schelle				
	Arnold				
UC34	Sprenger			(2)	46
	Obermüller				
	Schlüter				
	Wiedemann				
UC35	von Voigt				
	Korsch				
UC36	Buch				
UC37	Launburg				
	List				
	Kümpel				
UC38	Klatt				
	Wendlant				
UC39	Tornow				
	von d. Lühe				
	Ehrentraut				
UC40	Deuerlich				
	Menzel				
	Wischhausen				
UC41	Bernis				
	Förste, H.				
UC42	Tornow				
	Müller, A.				
UC43	Sebelin				
UC44	Tebbenjohanns				
UC45	Aust				
	Soergel				
	Ackermann				
UC46	Moecke			(5)	4,27
UC47	Hundius				
	Wigankow				
UC48	Ramien				
	Lorenz				
UC49	Petri				
	Arnold				
	Petri				
	Kükenthal				
UC50	Seuffer				
UC51	Schröder, W.				
	Galster, H.				
UC52	Sahl				
	von Doemming				
	Sahs				
	Dönitz, F.				
UC53	Albrecht, K.				
	Gerth				
UC54	Prinze zu Reutz				
	Heinrich XXXVII				
	Loyke				
	Berninghaus				
UC55	Schultz, T. von Lilienstern				

'17		1918		Total	
(7)	20,765			(17)	20,765
)	5,239			(9)	5,867
3)	38,091	(3)	15,336	(37)	53,627
)	4,649			(6)	6,847
5)	20,557			(35)	20,557
1)	40,306	(6)	24,780	(19)	65,546
4)	56,482	(8)	9,087	(42)	65,569
8)	28,348			(18)	28,348
1)	56,543	(35)	21,615	(66)	78,158
6)	52,525			(36)	52,525
)	5,249			(3)	5,249
8)	21,617	(14)	25,317	(32)	46,934
8)	18,233			(18)	18,233
3)	9,635			(13)	9,635
3)	24,727			(13)	24,727
7)	24,271			(27)	24,271
2)	16,809			(12)	16,809
6)	6,387			(10)	10,660
2)	65,884			(52)	65,884
4)	67,776			(34)	67,776
3)	34,859	(10)	28,336	(23)	63,195
6)	42,212	(3)	3,610	(29)	45,822
9)	34,394			(29)	34,394
5)	101	(15)	27,570	(20)	27,671
8)	25,584	(25)	38,438	(53)	64,022
)	3,453	(16)	65,906	(19)	69,359
)	12,988			(9)	12,988

Boat	Commanders	1915	1916	1917		1918		Total	
UC56	Kiesewetter					(2)	9,824	(2)	9,824
UC57	Wissmann			(1)	88			(1)	88
UC58	Vesper			(14)	3,927	(6)	16,808	(20)	20,755
	Schwartz, K.								
UC59	Lefholz					(8)	8,331	(8)	8,331
	Strasser, W.								
UC60	von Fischer			(1)	1,426			(1)	1,426
UC61	Gerth, G.			(11)	13,819			(11)	13,819
UC62	Schmitz, M.			(12)	20,035			(12)	20,035
UC63	Heydebreck			(36)	36,404			(36)	36,404
UC64	Müller-Schwarz			(15)	15,555	(12)	9,483	(27)	25,038
	Hecht, E.								
	Schwartz, F.								
UC65	Steinbrinck, O.			(103)	112,859			(103)	112,859
	Viebeg								
	Lafrenz								
UC66	Pustkuchen, H.			(33)	47,152			(33)	47,152
UC67	Neumann, K.			(29)	60,667	(24)	37,651	(53)	98,315
	Niemöller								
UC69	Wassner			(50)	88,138			(50)	88,138
	Thielmann								
UC70	Fürbringer, W.			(24)	12,347	(9)	14,576	(33)	26,923
	Dobberstein								
	Warzecha								
	Dobberstein								
UC71	Valentiner, H.			(49)	83,272	(20)	60,653	(69)	143,925
	Thielmann								
	Saltzwedel								
	Steindorff, E.								
	Schmidt, E.								
	Lange, W.								
UC72	Voigt, E.			(37)	64,323			(37)	64,323
UC73	Schapler			(6)	11,701	(12)	14,719	(18)	26,420
	Wiedemann								
	Gercke, O.								
	Hagen								
UC74	Marschall			(27)	71,807	(10)	25,092	(37)	96,899
	von d. Lühe, H.								
	Schüle								
	von d. Lühe, H.								
UC75	Paech			(39)	50,114	(17)	38,959	(56)	89,073
	Lohs, F.								
	Schmitz, W.								
UC76	Barten			(14)	6,006			(14)	6,006
	Ziegner								
	Palmgren								
UC77	von Rabenau			(28)	37,574	(4)	11,488	(32)	49,062
	Ries								
UC78	Kukat					(2)	13,000	(2)	13,000
UC79	Hacker			(7)	15,880	(3)	6,467	(10)	22,347
	Löwe, W.								
	Krameyer								

Above: *U123* of the UEII class of ocean minelayers. After the war, surrendered U-boats were put on display for the British public, as this picture shows.

U-boats ordered, 1905–18

U1 to *U4* were known as the *Karp* type, so called because they were improved and slightly enlarged versions of the three *Karp*-class U-boats that had been designed and built in Germany by Krupps for the Russian Navy. *U5* to *U18* were known as the *Desiderata* type, because they were designed to conform to certain desiderata (specifications) with regard to speed, endurance and armament formulated by the *Reich-Marine-Amt* (Navy Office). The *Mittel-U* (medium size) refers to the diesel-engined, ocean-going boats, variants of which were the UE ocean-going minelayers and the large UA cruisers. Displacements shown are for surface trim.

Date ordered	Type	Boats
Pre-war		
Feb 1905 to Aug 1907	4 × 238/421-ton *Karp* type	*U1–U4*
April 1908 to May 1910	14 × 505/564-ton *Desiderata* type	*U5–U18*
Nov 1910 to June 1914[1]	27 × 650/725-ton *Mittel-U*	*U19–U45*

Date ordered	Type	Boats
1914		
Aug	1 × 270-ton coastal boat (This boat was being built for Norway and was requisitioned)	*UA*
	5 × 725-ton *Mittel-U*	*U46–U50*
	6 × 715-ton *Mittel-U*	*U51–U56*
Oct	6 × 787-ton *Mittel-U*	*U57–U62*
	5 × 791-ton *Mittel-U* (These boats were being built for Austria and were requisitioned)	*U66–U70*
Nov	17 × 127-ton UBI coastal boats	*UB1–UB17*
	15 × 168-ton UCI minelayers	*UC1–UC15*

Date ordered	Type	Boats
1915		
Jan	4 × 755-ton UEI ocean minelayers	U71–U74
March	6 × 755-ton UEI ocean minelayers	U75–U80
April	12 × 265-ton UBII coastal boats	UB18–UB29
May	3 × 810-ton Mittel-U	U63–U65
June	6 × 808-ton Mittel-U	U81–U86
	6 × 757-ton Mittel-U	U87–U92
July	18 × 274-ton UBII coastal boats	UB30–UB47
Aug	18 × 400-ton UCII minelayers	UC16–UC33
Sept	12 × 838/750-ton Mittel-U	U93–U104
Nov	15 × 420-ton UCII minelayers	UC34–UC48
1916		
Jan	31 × 420-ton UCII minelayers	UC49–UC79
May[2]	10 × 800-ton Mittel-U	U105–U114
	12 × 1,200-ton Mittel-U	U127–U138
	10 × 1,160-ton UEII ocean minelayers	U117–U126
	24 × 516-ton UBIII coastal boats	UB48–UB71
Aug	3 × 1,930-ton UA cruisers	U139–U141

Date ordered	Type	Boats
Sept[3]	2 × 880-ton Mittel-U	U115–U116
	16 × 516-ton UBIII coastal boats	UB72–UB87
Nov[4]	9 × 2,160-ton UA cruisers	U142–U150
1917		
Feb[5]	6 × 800-ton Mittel-U	U158–U163
	45 × 510/519-ton UBIII coastal boats	UB88–UB132
	7 × 1,500-ton UA cruisers	U151–U157
June	9 × 800-ton Mittel-U[6]	U164–U172
	10 × 2,000-ton UA cruisers[7]	U173–U182
	37 × 533-ton UBIII coastal boats[8]	UB133–UB169
	39 × 491-ton UCIII minelayers[9]	UC80–UC118
June–Dec[10]	18 × 1,200-ton UA cruisers	U183–U200
Dec[10]	12 × 820-ton Mittel-U	U201–U212
	36 × 540-ton UBIII coastal boats	UB170–UB205
	34 × 510-ton UCIII minelayers	UC119–UC152
	20 × 360-ton UF coastal boats	UF1–UF20
1918		
Jan[10]	28 × 360-ton UF coastal boats	UF21–UF48
	16 × 1,380-ton Mittel-U	U213–U228
	48 × 900-ton Mittel-U	U229–U276
	44 × 523-ton UBIII coastal boats	UB206–UB249
	40 × 510-ton UCIII minelayers	UC153–UC192
	44 × 360-ton UF coastal boats	UF49–UF92

Total number of U-boats ordered

Karp	4
Desiderata	14
UA coastal	1
Mittel-U	191
UE minelayers	20
UA cruisers	47
UB coastal	249
UC minelayers	192
UF coastal	92
Total	810

Number completed before the war

Karp	4
Desiderata	14
Mittel-U	10
Total	28

Number completed during the war

UA coastal	1
Mittel-U	83
UE minelayers	20
UA cruisers	11
UB coastal	136
UC minelayers	95
Total	346

Number completed after the armistice

Mittel-U	2
UBIIII coastal	7
UCIII minelayers	9
Total	18

Total number of boats completed: 392
U42 (built in Italy) not delivered: 1

Boats building in November 1918 and scrapped on the stocks:

Mittel-U	28	
UA cruisers	30	149
UBIII coastal	57	
UCIII minelayers	34	

Boats projected but never laid down

Mittel-U	67
UA cruisers	6
UBIII coastal	49
UCIII minelayers	54
UF coastal	92
Total	268

Summary of U-boats completed from August 1914 until November 1918

	1914	1915	1916	1917	1918	Totals
Mittel-U	10	12	25	25	11	83
UE minelayers	–	3	7	–	10	20
UA cruisers	–	–	–	7	4	11
UA coastal	1	–	–	–	–	1
UBI coastal	–	17	–	–	–	17
UBII coastal	–	5	25	–	–	30
UBIII coastal	–	–	–	42	47	89
UCI minelayers	–	15	–	–	–	15
UCII minelayers	–	–	51	13	–	64
UCIII minelayers	–	–	–	–	16	16
Totals	11	52	108	87	88	346

Notes

1. There was no U42. The number was allotted to a boat ordered from Italy, which was retained and commissioned into the Italian Navy as the Balilla.

2. Only 2 of the 12 Mittel-U ordered were completed: U135 in June 1918 and U136 in Aug 1918. The remainder of the group U127–U134, and U137, U138 were between 80 to 85 per cent complete when the war ended, and were all scrapped on the stocks from 1919 to 1920.

3. Both U115 and U116 were about 90 per cent complete when the war ended and were scrapped on the stocks.

4. Only U142 was completed (Nov 1918) of this group of 9; the remainder, U143–U150 were 55 to 80 per cent complete when the war ended and were scrapped on the stocks from 1919 to 1920.

5. Four of this group of 6 Mittel-U were completed from May to August 1918. U158 and U159 were 95 per cent complete when the war ended and they were scrapped on the stocks in 1919.

6. Of this group of 9 Mittel-U only 4 were completed: U164 in October 1918 and U165 in November 1918, U166 and U167 after the armistice. The other 5, U168–U172 were 75 per cent complete when the war ended and were scrapped on the stocks in 1919.

7. None of these UA cruisers (U173–U182) were completed. All scrapped on the stocks in 1919.

8. A total of 11 from this group of 37 UBIII coastal boats were completed: 4 (UB142, UB143 and UB149) during the last months of the war; and 7 after the armistice (UB133, UB136, UB144, UB145, UB150, UB154, UB155). The remaining 26 were all scrapped on the stocks in 1919.

9. Of this group of 39 UCIII minelayers, 16 were completed during the latter months of 1918 (UC90–UC105 inclusive); 9 were completed after the armistice (UC106–UC114), while the remaining 14 (UC80–UC89 and UC115–UC118) were uncompleted when the war ended and were all scrapped on the stocks.

10. None of these 340 boats was completed. Of the 18 UA cruisers, only 12 (U183–U194) were actually laid down, the other 6 (U195–U200) were cancelled. Of the 76 Mittel-U, only 9 (U201–U209) were laid down, the remaining 67 (U210–U276) were all cancelled. Of the 80 UBIII coastal boats only 31 were actually laid down (UB170–UB175; UB178–UB184; UB188–UB205); the remaining 49 (UB176–UB177; UB185–UB187; UB206–UB249) were all cancelled. Of the 74 UCIII minelayers, only 20 were laid down (UC119–UC138), the other 54 (UC139–UC192) were cancelled. None of the 92 UF coastal boats (UF1–UF92) were laid down.

U-boats commissioned, 1939–45

Type	Description	Boats	Commissioned	Total
IA	Pre-war Atlantic U-boat	U25–U26	1936	2
IIA	250–300-ton coastal U-boat	U1–U6	1935	6
IIB	250–300-ton coastal U-boat	U7–U24	1935	
		U120–U121	1940	20
IIC	250–300-ton coastal U-boat	U56–U63	1938–40	
		U137	1940	9
IID	250–300-ton coastal U-boat	U138–U152	1940–41	15
VIIA	625-ton Atlantic U-boat	U27–U36	1936–37	10
VIIB	750-ton Atlantic U-boat	U45–U55	1938–39	
		U73–U76	1940	
		U83–U87	1941–42	
		U99–U102	1940	24
VIIC	770-ton Atlantic U-boat	U69–U72	1940–41	
		U77–U82	1941	
		U88–U98	1941–42	
		U132–U136	1941	
		U201–U212	1941–42	
		U221–U232	1942	
		U235–U291	1942–43	
		U301–U316	1942–43	
		U331–U394	1941–44	
		U396–U458	1941–44	
		U465–U473	1942–44	
		U475–U486	1942–44	
		U551–U683	1940–44	
		U701–U722	1941–43	
		U731–U768	1942–44	
		U771–U779	1943–44	
		U821–U822	1943–45	
		U825–U826	1944	
		U901	1944	
		U903–U907	1943–44	
		U921–U928	1943–44	
		U951–U994	1942–43	
		U1051–U1058	1944	
		U1131–U1132	1944	
		U1161–U1162	1943	
		U1191–U1210	1943–44	567
VIIC/41	770-ton Atlantic U-boat	U292–U300	1943	
		U317–U329	1943–44	
		U827–U828	1944	
		U929–U930	1944–45	
		U995	1943	
		U997–U1010	1943–44	
		U1013–U1025	1943–44	
		U1063–U1065	1944	
		U1103–U1110	1944	
		U1163–U1172	1943–44	
		U1271–U1279	1944–45	
		U1301–U1308	1944–45	92
VIIC/42	1,080-ton Atlantic U-boat	U1101–U1102	1943	2
VIID	960-ton minelaying U-boat	U213–U218	1941–42	6
VIIF	Torpedo transport U-boat	U1059–U1062	1943	4
IXA	1,030-ton Atlantic U-boat	U37–U44	1938–39	8
IXB	1,050-ton Atlantic U-boat	U64–U65	1939–40	
		U103–U111	1940	
		U122–U124	1940	14
IXC	1,120-ton Atlantic U-boat	U66–U68	1941	
		U125–U131	1941	
		U153–U160	1941	
		U161–U166	1941–43	

Type	Description	Boats	Commissioned	Total
		U171–U176	1941	30
IXC/40	1,140-ton Atlantic U-boat	U167–U170	1941–43	
		U183–U194	1942	
		U501–U550	1941–43	
		U801–U806	1943–45	
		U841–U846	1943	
		U853–U858	1943	
		U865–U870	1943	
		U877–U881	1944	
		U889	1944	
		U1221–U1235	1943–45	111
IXD/41	1,600-ton U-cruiser	U180	1942	
		U195	1942	2
IXD/42	1,600-ton U-cruiser	U177–U179	1942	
		U181–U182	1942	
		U196–U200	1942	
		U847–U852	1943	
		U859–U864	1943	
		U871–U876	1943–44	
		U883	1944	29
XB	1,760-ton minelaying U-boat	U116–U119	1941–42	
		U219–U220	1942–43	
		U233–U234	1943	8
XIV	1,690-ton supply U-boat	U459–U464	1941–42	
		U487–U490	1942–43	10

Prefabricated U-boats

To speed production these boats were constructed from prefabricated sections which were welded together. The pressure hull was formed by two flattened cylinders placed one over the other. The sections (eight for Type XXI and four for Type XXIII) were produced by a large number of steel firms widely dispersed in the interior of Germany so that additional labour forces could be available for U-boat construction. The sections were assembled at the shipyards of Blohm & Voss, Hamburg; A. G. Weser, Bremen and Schichau, Danzig.

Built by end of war	Commissioned by end of 1944
Type XXI Atlantic U-boat	
U2501–U2546, U2548–U2552,	U2501–U2519, U2521–U2522, U2524,
U3001–U3041, U3044, U3501–U3530	U2529, U2534, U2540, U3001–U3010,
Total 123	U3013, U3017, U3030, U3032, U3035,
	U3041, U3501–U3508, U3510–U3512,
	U3514–U3515, U3523
	Total 55
Type XXIII Coastal U-boat	
U2321–U2371, U4701–U4707, U4710	U2321–U2332, U2334–U2346, U2348,
Total 59	U2350–U2351, U2353–U2354, U2356,
	U2359, U2361, U2363, U4706
	Total 35

The German record of U-boats commissioned in 1945 is incomplete, but the number is estimated to be approximately 65.

'Walter'-type U-boats

New technology developed by Professor Walter made possible a high underwater speed provided by a fuel containing its own oxygen, the combustion of which did not exhaust the oxygen in the boat which the crew needed to breath. A number of 'Walter'-type U-boats were built but were still undergoing trials at the end of the war. They comprised:

Type XVII B	300-ton coastal boat	U1405–U1407	Built 1944–45
Type Wa 201	250-ton experimental boat	U792–U793	Built 1943–44
Type Wk 202	250-ton experimental boat	U794–U795	Built 1943–44
Total 7			

Summary of U-boats commissioned and built, 1939–45

Type	Built	Commissioned	Type	Built	Commissioned
IA	2	2	IXD/41	2	2
IIA	6	6	IXD/42	29	29
IIB	20	20	XB	8	8
IIC	9	9	XIV	10	10
IID	15	15	XXI	123	55[1]
VIIA	10	10	XXIII	59	35[1]
VIIB	24	24	'Walter' type	7	7
VIIC	567	567	Estimated number of U-boats commissioned in 1945		65
VIIC/41	92	92	Total	1,158	1,131
VIIC/42	2	2			
VIID	6	6	[1]To end 1944.		
VIIF	4	4			
IXA	8	8			
IXB	14	14			
IXC	30	30			
IXC/40	111	111			

Foreign submarines requisitioned or captured and commissioned into German service.

German Number	Original Name	Nationality	German Number	Original Name	Nationality
UA	Batiray[1]	Turkish	UIT17	CM1	
UB	Seal	British	UIT21	Giuseppe Finzi	
UC1	B5	Norwegian	UIT22	Alpino Bagnolini	
UC2	B6		UIT23	Reginaldo Giuliani	Italian
UD1	08		UIT24	Comandante Cappellini	
UD2	012		UIT25	Luigi Torelli	
UD3	025	Dutch	Total 18		
UD4	026				
UD5	027				
UF1	L'Africaine				
UF2	La Favorite	French	[1]Building in Germany and requisitioned		
UF3	L'Astrée				

Monthly analysis of U-boat gains, losses and total strength, 1914–18

Total strength includes training boats and boats undergoing trials and lengthy repairs.

Month	Boats commissioned	Boats lost, ceded and interned	Gains	Losses	Total strength
Number of boats commissioned before the war					28
1914					
Aug	UA, U29, U30	U13, U15	3	2	29
Sept	U31, U32, U33		3	–	32
Oct	U34		1	–	33
Nov	U35, U36	U18	2	1	34
Dec	U37, U38	U11, U5	2	2	34
1915					
Jan	U39, UB1	U31, U7; UB1 ceded to Austria	2	3	33
Feb	U40, U41, UB2, UB9		4	–	37
March	UB3, UB4, UB5, UB10, UB11, UB12, UB14	U8, U12, U29	7	3	41
April	U43, UB6, UB8, UB13, UB15, UC11	U37	6	1	46
May	U44, UB7, UB16, UB17, UC1, UC2, UC12, UC13	UB3	8	1	53
June	UC3, UC4, UC5, UC6, UC14, UC15	U14, U40; UB15 ceded to Austria	6	3	56
July	U66, UC7, UC8, UC9, UC10	U23, U36, UC2	5	3	58
Aug	U67, U68	U26, U27, UB4	2	3	57
Sept	U69, U70	U6, U41	2	2	57
Oct	U45, U73	UC9	2	1	58
Nov	U74, UB24	UC13; UC8 interned in Holland	2	2	58
Dec	U46, U71, UB18, UB19, UB25, UB26		6	–	64

Month	Boats commissioned	Boats lost, ceded and interned	Gains	Losses	Total strength
1916					
Jan	U72, UB28, UB29		3	–	67
Feb	U47, U51, UB20, UB21, UB27		5	–	72
March	U52, U63, U75, U77, UB22, UB23, UB30, UB31, UB42	U68, UC12	9	2	79
April	U48, U53, U64, U78, UB32, UB33, UB39, UB43	UB26, UB13, UC5	8	3	84
May	U49, U54, U65, U76, U79, UB36, UB37, UB44, UB45	U74, UC3, UC10; UB8 ceded to Bulgaria	9	4	89
June	U55, U56, U80, UB34, UB35, UB46, UC16, UC25		8	–	97
July	U50, U57, UB38, UB47, UC17, UC22, UC23, UC26, UC27	U77, U51, UC7	9	3	103
Aug	U58, U81, UB40, UB41, UC18, UC19, UC24, UC28, UC29, UC30	UB44, UC10	10	2	111
Sept	U59, U82, U83, UC20, UC21, UC31, UC32, UC33, UC34, UC46	UB7	10	1	120
Oct	U60, U84, U85, UC35, UC37, UC38, UC39, UC40, UC41,		12	–	132

Month	Boats commissioned	Boats lost, ceded and interned	Gains	Losses	Total strength
Nov	UC42, UC43, UC47 UC36, UC44, UC45, UC48, UC55, UC65, UC66, UC70, UC71, UC74, UC75, UC76, UC77	U20, U56, UB19, UB45, UC15	13	5	140
Dec	U61, U62, U86, UC49, UC50, UC56, UC61, UC67, UC68, UC69, UC72, UC73	UB29, UB46, UC19	12	3	149
1917					
Jan	UC51, UC57, UC62, UC63, UC78, UC79	U76, UB37	6	2	153
Feb	U87, U93, U155, UC64	U83, UC18, UC32, UC39, UC46	4	5	152
March	U94, U99, UC52, UC58	U85, UC43, UC68; UB6 interned in Holland	4	4	152
April	U88, U95, U96, U100, UC53	UC30	5	1	156
May	U97, U98, U101, UC54, UC59	U59, U81, UB36, UB39, UC24, UC26, UC36	5	7	154
June	U89, U102, UB48, UB49, UB54, UB60, UB61, UC60	UC29, UC66	8	2	160
July	U103, U105, U106, U151, UB50, UB51, UB55, UB56, UB57, UB62, UB63	U99, U69, UB20, UB27, UC1, UC61; UB43 and UB47 ceded to Austria; UB23 interned in Spain	11	9	162
Aug	U90, U104, U107, U156, UB52, UB53, UB58, UB59, UB64, UB65, UB66, UB67	U44, U50, UC41, UC44, UC72	12	5	169
Sept	U91, U110, U157, UB72, UB75, UB76, UB80, UB81	U28, U45, U49, U66, U88, UB32, UC6, UC21, UC33, UC42, UC55	8	11	166
Oct	U92, U152, UB68, UB69, UB70, UB73, UB74, UB77, UB78, UB79, UB82, UB83, UB84	U106, UB41, UC14, UC16, UC62	13	5	174
Nov	U109, U153, UB71, UB85, UB86	U48, U58, UB61, UC51, UC57, UC63, UC65, UC47	5	8	171
Dec	U108, U111, U154, UB87, UB103, U109	U75, U87, UB18, UB56, UB75, UB81, UC38, UC69	6	8	169
1918					
Jan	UB88, UB105, UB118	U84, U93, U95, U109, UB22, UB35, UB63, UB66, UB69, UC50	3	10	162
Feb	U113, UB89, UB106, UB107, UB119, UB121	U89, UB38	6	2	166

Month	Boats commissioned	Boats lost, ceded and interned	Gains	Losses	Total strength
March	U117, U140, UB90, UB104, UB108, UB110, UB120, UB122, UB126	U61, U110, UB17, UB54, UB58, UC79; UC48 interned in Spain	9	7	168
April	UB91, UB92, UB111, UB112, UB113, UB123, UB124, UB127, UB128	U104, UB33, UB55, UB71, UB82, UB85	9	6	171
May	U118, U122, U139, U160, UB93, UB114, UB115, UB116, UB117, UB125, UB129	U32, U103, U154, UB16, UB31, UB52, UB70, UB72, UB74, UB78, UB119, UC35, UC75, UC78; U39 and UC56 interned in Spain	11	16	166
June	U112, U114, U119, U135, U141, U161, UB94, UB95, UB130	U64, UC11, UC64	9	3	172
July	U123, U124, U162, UB96, UB97, UB131, UB132, UC90, UC91	UB65, UB107, UB108, UB110, UB124, UC77	9	6	175
Aug	U120, U136, U163, UB142, UB98, UC92, UC93, UC94	UB12, UB30, UB53, UB57, UB109, UC40, UC70	8	7	176
Sept	U121, U125, U99, UB100, UB148, UC95, UC96, UC97, UC98, UC99	U92, U102, U156, UB83, UB103, UB104, UB113, UB115, UB127	10	9	177
Oct	U126, U164, UB101, UB102, UB143, UB149, UC100, UC101, UC102, UC103, UC104, UC105	U78, UB68, UB90, UB116, UB123; UB10, UB40, UC59, UC4 scuttled on evacuation of Flanders; U47, U65, UB48, UC25, UC53, UC54, U73, UC34, UB129, U72 scuttled on evacuation of Adriatic bases	12	19	170
Nov	U142, U165	U34	2	1	171

		Gains	Losses
Total number of boats commissoned		346	—
Total number of boats lost by internment			6
	ceded to Austria		4
	ceded to Bulgaria		1
	war losses		178
	scuttled on evacuation of Flanders and Adriatic bases		14
	Total losses		203

Boats completed after the armistice: U166, U167, UB133, UB136, UB144, UB145, UB150, UB154, UB155, UC106, UC107, UC108, UC109, UC110, UC111, UC112, UC113, UC114   18

	Gains
Total number of boats completed	364

Monthly analysis of U-boat gains, losses and total strength, 1939–45

Total strength includes training boats and boats undergoing trials and lengthy repairs.

Month	Boats commissioned	Boats lost	Gains	Losses	Total strength
Number of boats commissioned before the war					57
1939					
Sept	UA	U39, U27	1	2	56
Oct		U12, U40, U42, U45, U16	–	5	51
Nov	U44, U55	U35	2	1	52
Dec	U50, U62, U64	U36	3	1	54
1940					
Jan	U63	U55	1	1	54
Feb	U65	U15, U41, U33, U53, U63	1	5	50
March	U101, U122	U31, U44	2	2	50
April	U99, U102, U120	U54, U64, U49, U1, U22, U50	3	6	47
May	U100, U121, U123	U13	3	1	49
June	U124, U137, U138	U122	3	1	51
July	U93, U103, U139	U26	3	1	53
Aug	U94, U95, U104, U140, U141	U25, U51, U102	5	3	55
Sept	U73, U96, U97, U105, U106, U142, U143	U57	7	1	61
Oct	U74, U98, U107, U108, U144, U145, U146, UC2	U32	8	1	68
Nov	U69, U70, U110, U149, U150, U551, UB, UC1, UD1	U31, U104, U560	9	3	74
Dec	U71, U75, U76, U109, U111, U147, U148, U552, U553		9	–	83
1941					
Jan	U66, U67, U72, U77, U151, U152, U201, U554, U555, U751, UD4		11	–	94
Feb	U68, U78, U83, U203, U556, U557, U558, U559, U651		9	–	103
March	U79, U125, U126, U202, U204, U331, U371, U560, U561, U562, U563	U47, U70, U99, U100, U551	11	5	109
April	U80, U81, U84, U127, U372, U401, U431, U432, U501, U564, U565, U566, U567, U652	U76, U65	14	2	121
May	U82, U128, U129, U132, U205, U206, U373, U402, U433, U451, U452, U502, U568, U569, U570, U571, U572, U653, U752	U110	19	1	139

Above: *U873* (Type IXD/42 U-cruiser) and *U234* (Type XB minelayer) in a US navy yard after surrender. Note the upright *Schnorkel* on the side of the conning tower of *U234*.

Month	Boats commissioned	Boats lost	Gains	Losses	Total strength
June	U85, U130, U207, U332, U351, U374, U403, U434, U453, U573, U574, U575, U576, U753, UD3	U147, U138, U556, U651	15	4	150
July	U86, U116, U131, U133, U134, U153, U161, U208, U375, U454, U503, U504, U577, U578, U579, U580, U581, U654, U701		19	–	169
Aug	U87, U135, U136, U154, U155, U213, U333, U352, U376, U404, U435, U455, U505, U582, U583, U584, U585, U655, U754	U401, U144, U452, U570	19	4	184
Sept	U156, U157, U158, U162, U251, U405, U436, U456, U506, U586, U587, U588, U589, U656, U702	U501, U207	15	2	197
Oct	U88, U117, U159, U160, U163, U171, U209, U252, U253, U334, U355, U377, U378, U406, U437, U507, U508, U590, U591, U592, U593, U594, U657, U703	U111, U204	24	2	219
Nov	U89, U164, U172, U173, U174, U214, U215, U254, U255, U379, U408, U438, U457, U459, U509, U510, U595, U596, U597, U598, U658, U704, U775, UD5	U580, U583, U433, U95, U206	24	5	238

Month	Boats commissioned	Boats lost	Gains	Losses	Total strength
Dec	U90, U118, U175, U176, U216, U256, U335, U356, U380, U407, U439, U458, U460, U511, U512, U599, U600, U601, U602, U659, U705, U756	U208, U127, U557, U131, U434, U574, U451, U567, U79, U75	22	10	250
1942 Jan	U91, U217, U218, U257, U409, U440, U461, U513, U514, U603, U604, U605, U606, U607, U660	U577, U374, U93	15	3	262
Feb	U165, U178, U210, U258, U259, U336, U381, U410, U441, U515, U608, U609, U610, U611, U661, U757	U581, U82	16	2	276
March	U92, U166, U177, U179, U211, U260, U261, U353, U411, U442, U462, U516, U517, U612, U613, U614, U615, U706	U656, U133, U503, U655, U587, U585	18	6	288
April	U119, U183, U212, U262, U354, U382, U412, U443, U463, U464, U518, U616, U617, U618, U619, U620, U662	U702, U85, U252	17	3	302
May	U180, U181, U184, U221, U222, U263, U264, U301, U337, U444, U445, U465, U519, U520, U621, U622, U623, U624, U663, U758	U573, U74, U352, U568	20	4	318
June	U182, U185, U223, U224, U265, U266, U302, U338, U357, U383, U413, U446, U466, U521, U522, U523, U625, U626, U627, U628, U664	U652, U157, U158	21	3	336
July	U167, U186, U187, U225, U267, U268, U303, U384, U414, U447, U467, U524, U525, U629, U630, U631, U632, U633, U665, U707, U708	U215, U502, U701, U136, U153, U576, U751, U90, U213, U588, U754	21	11	346
Aug	U188, U189, U226, U227, U269, U304, U339, U358, U385, U415, U448, U449, U468, U526, U634, U635, U636, U637, U666, U709, U759	U166, U335, U372, U210, U379, U578, U464, U654, U94	21	9	358
Sept	U168, U190, U195, U196, U228, U270, U271, U305, U417, U450, U527, U528, U529, U638, U639, U640, U641, U710, U711	U222, U162, U705, U756, U589, U88, U261, U457, U446, U253, U165	19	11	366
Oct	U191, U197, U229, U230, U272, U273, U306, U340, U359, U386, U418, U469, U530, U531, U642, U643, U644, U645, U646, U667, U731, U732, U760	U512, U582, U179, U171, U597, U619, U661, U353, U216, U412, U599, U627, U520, U559, U658	23	15	374
Nov	U169, U192, U198, U199, U231, U232, U274, U275, U307, U341, U360, U387, U416, U419, U532, U533, U647, U648, U649, U650, U668, U712, U733, UF2	U132, U408, U272, U660, U605, U595, U411, U259, U173, U331, U98, U184, U517	24	13	385
Dec	U193, U200, U219, U235, U276, U277, U308, U316, U388, U420, U487, U534, U535, U669, U713, U734, U735, U761, U951, U952, U953, U954, U955	U254, U611, U626, U357, U356	23	5	403
1943 Jan	U170, U194, U236, U237, U278, U309, U342, U421, U470, U536, U537, U670, U736, U737, U762, U847, U956, U957, U958, U959, U960, UD2	U164, U224, U507, U337, U301, U553	22	6	419
Feb	U238, U279, U280, U281, U310, U343, U362, U389, U422, U488, U538, U539, U714, U738, U841, U848, U961, U962, U963, U964, U965	U265, U187, U609, U624, U519, U442, U620, U529, U69, U201, U205, U268, U562, U225, U623, U606, U443, U522, U649	21	19	421
March	U220, U239, U282, U283, U311, U344, U363, U390, U423, U489, U490, U540, U541, U671, U715, U739, U740, U763, U801, U842, U843, U849, U966, U967, U968, U969, U970	U83, U87, U633, U156, U432, U444, U130, U5, U384, U163, U524, U665, U469, U169, U77, U416	27	16	432
April	U240, U284, U312, U391, U424, U425, U542, U543, U672,	U124, U167, U632, U635, U644, U376, U526, U175, U189,	18	15	435

Month	Boats commissioned	Boats lost	Gains	Losses	Total strength
May	U716, U741, U844, U850, U971, U972, U973, U974, U975, U285, U313, U345, U364, U392, U426, U471, U472, U544, U545, U673, U717, U742, U743, U764, U845, U846, U851, U921, U976, U977, U978, U979, U980, U1059, U1060	U191, U602, U710, U203, U174, U227, U332, U439, U659, U109, U630, U192, U125, U438, U531, U638, U447, U465, U663, U528, U186, U456, U657, U266, U89, U176, U463, U753, U182, U128, U640, U646, U954, U209, U273, U381, U258, U303, U569, U752, U414, U467, U436, U304, U755, U440, U563	26	41	420
June	U286, U288, U314, U346, U365, U427, U428, U473, U546, U547, U548, U674, U718, U744, U745, U765, U802, U852, U853, U981, U982, U983, U984, U985, U1062	U202, U418, U105, U521, U308, U594, U217, U417, U118, U334, U564, U97, U388, U119, U194, U200, U449	25	17	428
July	U241, U289, U290, U315, U347, U366, U393, U429, U475, U476, U549, U550, U675, U719, U746, U747, U748, U766, U854, U859, U986, U987, U988, U989, U990, U991	U126, U628, U535, U951, U232, U514, U435, U590, U409, U506, U561, U487, U607, U160, U135, U159, U509, U67, U513, U558, U662, U527, U598, U613, U459, U622, U759, U359, U404, U614, U43, U375, U461, U462, U504, U519, U199	26	37	417
Aug	U242, U291, U292, U316, U348, U367, U394, U430, U477, U676, U749, U750, U855, U856, U860, U922, U992, U993, U1061, U1161, U1221	U383, U454, U106, U706, U572, U647, U489, U34, U117, U615, U664, U468, U525, U604, U403, U197, U670, U458, U84, U134, U185, U523, U847, U634, U639	21	25	413
Sept	U233, U287, U293, U349, U478, U677, U720, U767, U803, U857, U858, U861, U903, U904, U994, U995, U997, U1162, U1191, U1192, U1222	U669, U760, U983, U617, U341, U338, U346, U229, U161, U221	21	10	424
Oct	U243, U244, U247, U294, U295, U317, U350, U369, U396, U479, U480, U678, U768, U821, U862,	U279, U336, U422, U460, U389, U419, U610, U643, U402, U470, U533, U844, U964, U540, U631,	27	26	425
Nov	U865, U923, U994, U999, U1163, U1164, U1193, U1194, U1223, U1224, UIT21, UIT22, U248, U249, U296, U297, U318, U370, U397, U481, U679, U721, U771, U792, U794, U863, U866, U924, U1000, U1001, U1002, U1101, U1165, U1195, U1196, U1225, U1226	U841, U378, U274, U566, U420, U220, U282, U431, U306, U584, U732, U340, U405, U848, U226, U842, U707, U966, U508, U280, U718, U211, U536, U768, U769, U770, U538, U648, U600, U849, U542, U86	25	21	429
Dec	U245, U250, U298, U299, U300, U319, U320, U398, U482, U483, U680, U722, U772, U804, U864, U867, U868, U925, U1003, U1004, U1005, U1166, U1167, U1197, U1198, U1199, U1227, U1228, UIT23, UIT24, UIT25	U172, U391, U593, U73, U850, U284, U345, U645	31	8	452
1944					
Jan	U246, U321, U368, U399, U484, U773, U869, U871, U1006, U1007, U1052, U1103, U1168, U1200, U1201, U1202, U1229, U1230, U1271, U1272	U377, U972, U426, U757, U81, UIT19, U231, U544, U305, U641, U263, U271, U571, U314, U364, U592	20	16	456
Feb	U322, U485, U681, U774, U805, U870, U872, U926, U1008, U1009, U1010, U1053, U1102, U1169, U1203, U1204, U1231, U1273, U1301	U854, U177, U762, U238, U734, U545, U666, U283, U424, U738, UIT23, U7, U406, U264, U386, U257, U713, U761, U91, U601	19	20	455
March	U234, U323, U400, U486, U775, U873, U877, U905, U1013, U1014, U1015, U1051, U1054, U1104, U1170, U1171, U1205, U1206, U1207, U1232, U1274, U1275	U28, U851, U358, U603, U709, U472, U366, U744, U973, U343, U450, U625, U845, U410, U380, UIT22, U575, U653, U392, U801, U1013, U1059, U976, U961, U223	23	25	453
April	U324, U682, U776, U793, U795, U806, U874, U875, U878, U879, U901, U1016,	U355, U360, U288, U302, U455, U856, U2, U962, U515, U68, U108, U448,	23	23	453

Month	Boats commissioned	Boats lost	Gains	Losses	strength	Month	Boats commissioned	Boats lost	Gains	Losses	strength
	U1017, U1018, U1055, U1056, U1172, U1208, U1209, U1210, U1236, U1276, U1303	U550, U342, U986, U974, UIT4, UIT5, U311, U488, U803, U193, U421				Nov	U1108, U1307, U2332, U2339, U2342, U2343, U2344, U2345, U2346, U2505, U2518, U2519, U2520, U2521, U2522, U3009, U3010, U3013, U3508, U3510, U3511, U3512	U547, U537, U771, U1200, U322, U80, U196	22	7	418
May	U325, U683, U777, U825, U826, U827, U876, U880, U881, U907, U1019, U1020, U1021, U1057, U1131, U1235, U1277, U1278, U1302	U277, U674, U959, U852, U371, U846, U473, U1234, U66, U765, U616, U731, U240, U241, U960, U1015, U453, U476, U675, U990, U292, U549, U289	19	23	449						
June	U326, U828, U927, U1022, U1023, U1024, U1058, U1105, U1132, U2321, U2501	U477, U505, U987, U955, U970, U373, U629, U740, U821, U980, U490, U715, U860, U423, U441, U767, U971, U1225, U269, U1191, U317, U719, U998, U988, U478	11	25	435	Dec	U930, U1306, U1405, U2333, U2347, U2348, U2349, U2350, U2351, U2523, U2525, U2526, U2527, U2528, U2530, U3011, U3012, U3014, U3015, U3019, U3020, U3513, U3514, U3515, U3516, U3517, U3518	U297, U387, U416, U479, U365, U400, U1209, U737, U2342, U877, U735, U772, U906, U908, U1011, U1012, U2532	27	17	428
July	U327, U778, U822, U906, U928, U1063, U1064, U1106, U1279, U2322, U2323, U2324, U2502, U3001, U3501	U543, U154, U233, U390, U586, U642, U678, U243, U1222, U415, U319, U347, U361, U672, U742, U212, U1166, U239, U1164, U214, U872, U890, U891, U892, U2323, U250, U333	15	27	423						
Aug	U779, U889, U1107, U1109, U2325, U2326, U2327, U2328, U2503, U2504, U2506, U3002, U3003, U3004, U3502	U996, U1196, U671, U471, U736, U952, U969, U385, U967, U198, U981, U270, U618, U741, U107, U621, U466, U608, U9, U178, U188, U413, U984, U1229, U230, U180, U344, U445, U354, U667, U1000, UIT21	15	32	406	**1945**					
						Jan	U1308, U2352, U2353, U2354, U2355, U2356, U2357, U2358, U2359, U2360, U2524, U2531, U2533, U2534, U2535, U3016, U3017, U3018, U3021, U3022, U3023, U3024, U3025, U3026, U3027, U3028, U3509, U3519, U3520, U3521, U3522, U3523, U3524, U3525, U4701, U4702, U4703	U382, U650, U1020, U679, U248, U482, U2523, U1199, U763, U1172, U1051, U3520	37	12	453
Sept	U328, U929, U1065, U110, U1304, U1305, U2329, U2330, U2331, U2334, U2335, U2336, U2507, U2508, U2509, U2510, U2511, U3005, U3505, U3504	U394, U247, UIT1, U362, U484, U743, U18, U24, U19, U20, U23, U925, U407, U865, U867, U859, U565, U596, U855, U871, U863, U703, U921, U1062, U3509	20	25	401						
						Feb	U1406, U1407, U2361, U2362, U2363, U2364, U2529, U2536, U2538, U2539, U2540, U2546, U3029, U3030, U3031, U3032, U3033, U3034, U4705, U4706, U4707	U923, U1279, U745, U1014, U864, U989, U1053, U309, U425, U1273, U1278, U2344, U676, U1208, U300, U480, U927, U3007, U327, U1018, U869	21	21	453
Oct	U2337, U2338, U2340, U2341, U2512, U2513, U2514, U2515, U2516, U2517, U3006, U3007, U3008, U3505, U3506, U3507	U2331, U92, U228, U437, U993, U168, U777, U673, U1006, U116, U957, U985, U1060, U1226	16	14	403						
						March	U883, U2365, U2366, U2367, U2537, U2541,	U3519, U1302, U275, U681, U2515, U2530, U260, U683,	26	34	445

Month	Boats commissioned	Boats lost	Gains	Losses	strength
	U2542, U2543, U2544, U2545, U2548, U3035, U3037, U3038, U3039, U3040, U3041, U3044, U3526, U3527, U3528, U3529, U3530, U4704, U4709, U4711	U714, U367, U866, U1003, U905, U296, U399, U722, U965, U246, U1106, U72, U96, U329, U348, U350, U429, U430, U870, U884, U886, U1021, U1167, U2340, U3508, U682			
April	U1025, U2368, U2369, U2370, U2371, U2551, U2552, U4712	U326, U3036, U3042, U3043, U321, U1221, U1276, U2542, U237, U749, U3003, U1169, U1195, U857, U677, U747, U982, U2509, U2514, U2516, U2537, U774, U1001, U2547, U2549, U2550, U2552, U3512, U804, U843, U1065, U1131, U1227, U878, U486, U1024, U235, U1206, U103, U285, U1063, U1235, U78, U880, U1274, U251, U879, U636, U518, U183,	8	64	389

Month	Boats commissioned	Boats lost	Gains	Losses	strength
		U396, U546, UIT2, UIT3, U1107, U242, U56, U1223, U286, U307, U1017, U325, U548, U1055			
May	U4710	U398, U785, U717, U1007, U2539, U958, U1210, U2524, U2540, U3028, U3030, U3032, U3505, U236, U393, U711, U746, U2338, U2503, U3525, U4708, U4709, U4711, U4712, U534, U579, U733, U876, U904, U2367, U2521, U3523, U853, U881, U1008, U2534, U320, U2365, U3503, U963, U2538	1	41	349
Total Commissioned	1,113*				
Total Losses		821			

*The difference in the total commissoned between this figure of 1,113 and the 1,149 (1,131 German plus 18 foreign U-boats) shown on page 132 are accountable to the discrepancy in the total between the German base records (on which this table is based) and the *BdU* war records. There is no way of verifying which is correct.

U-boat specifications, 1906–18

Sources: Spindler's *Der Handelskrieg mit U-booten* and Gröner's *Die Deutschen Kriegsschiffe*

Class	Builder[1]	Laid down – Commissioned	Displace-ment (tons)[2]	Length (feet	Beam (feet)	Speed (knots)[2]	Endurance (n.miles/ knots)[2]	Fuel (tons)[3]	Diving time (seconds)[4]	Torpedoes	Mines	Guns
U1	Germania	04–06	238 283	139.08	12.30	10.8 8.7	1,400/8 50/5	20	100	3 × 17.7in	–	Nil
U2	Kw. Dzg	06–08	341 430	149.02	18.04	13.2 9.0	1,600/13 50/5	44	86	6 × 17.7in	–	Nil
U3–U4	Kw. Dzg	07–09	421 510	168.249	18.373	11.8 9.4	3,000/9 55/4.5	46	80	6 × 17.7in	–	1 × 2in
U5–U8	Germania	08–11	505 636	188.263	18.373	13.4 10.2	3,300/9 80/5	53	65	8 × 17.7in	–	1 × 2in
U9–U12	Kw. Dzg	08–11	493 611	188.263	18.686	14.2 8.1	3,250/9 80/5	50	90	6 × 17.7in	–	1 × 2in
U13–U15	Kw. Dzg	09–12	516 644	189.90	19.686	14.8 10.7	3,500/9 90/5	64	78	6 × 17.7in	–	1 × 2in
U16	Germania	09–11	489 627	189.64	19.686	15.5 10.7	1,500/15 90/5	64	78	6 × 17.7in	–	1 × 2in
U17–U18	Kw. Dzg	10–12	564 691	204.57	19.686	14.9 9.5	1,300/13 75/5	71	70	6 × 17.7in	–	1 × 2in

Class	Builder[1]	Laid down – Commissioned	Displacement (tons)[2]	Length (feet)	Beam (feet)	Speed (knots)[2]	Endurance (n.miles/ knots)[2]	Fuel (tons)[3]	Diving time (seconds)[4]	Torpedoes	Mines	Guns
U19–U22	Kw. Dzg	10–13	650 / 837	210.476	20.01	15.4 / 9.3	9,700/8 / 80/5	U19, 20, 22: 52 + 47 U21: 54 + 22 U23–U24: 56 + 54	75	9 × 19.7in	–	1 × 3.4in (or 4.1in)
U23–U26	Germania	11–14	669 / 864	212.28	20.735	16.7 / 10.3	9,910/8 / 85/5	U23–U24: 56 + 54 U25–U26: 55 + 30	85	9 × 19.7in	–	1 or 2 × 3.4in
U27–U30	Kw. Dzg	12–14	675 / 867	212.28	20.735	16.7 / 9.8	8,420/8 / 85/5	U27–U28: 57 + 30 U29–U30: 57 + 44	45	10 × 19.7in	–	2 × 3.4in or 1 × 4.1in
U31–U41	Germania	12–15	685 / 878	212.28	20.735	16.4 / 9.7	8,790/8 / 80/5	56 + 55	50	6 × 19.7in	–	1 or 2 × 3.4in or 1 × 4.1in
U43–U50	Kw. Dzg	14–16	725 / 940	213.265	20.342	15.2 / 9.7	11,140/8 / 51/5	U43–U45: 57 + 75 U46–U50: 56 + 74	55	6 × 19.7in	–	1 or 2 × 3.4in or 1 × 4.1in
U51–U56	Germania	14–16	715 / 902	213.921	21.129	17.1 / 9.1	9,400/8 / 55/5	57 + 46	55	8 × 19.7in	–	1 × 4.1in 1 × 3.4in
U57–U59	Weser, Br	14–16	786 / 954	219.827	20.735	14.7 / 8.4	7,730/8 / 55/5	78 + 41	30	7 × 19.7in	–	1 × 4.1in or 1 × 3.4in
U60–U62	Weser, Br	14–16	768 / 956	219.827	20.735	16.5 / 8.4	11,400/8 / 49/5	76 + 52	30	7 × 19.7in	–	1 × 4.1in or 1 × 3.4in
U63–U65	Germania	15–16	810 / 927	224.289	20.67	16.5 / 9.0	9,170/8 / 60/5	78 + 30	30	8 × 19.7in	–	1 × 4.1in

Originally building for Austria but requisitioned

Class	Builder[1]	Laid down – Commissioned	Displacement (tons)[2]	Length (feet)	Beam (feet)	Speed (knots)[2]	Endurance (n.miles/ knots)[2]	Fuel (tons)[3]	Diving time (seconds)[4]	Torpedoes	Mines	Guns
U66–U70	Germania	13–15	791 / 933	228.029	20.67	16.8 / 10.3	7,880/7 / 115/5	47 + 40	30	12 × 17.7in	–	1 × 3.4in or 1 × 4.1in

UE I Class Ocean Minelayers (nicknamed 'The Children of Sorrow')

Class	Builder[1]	Laid down – Commissioned	Displacement (tons)[2]	Length (feet)	Beam (feet)	Speed (knots)[2]	Endurance (n.miles/ knots)[2]	Fuel (tons)[3]	Diving time (seconds)[4]	Torpedoes	Mines	Guns
U71–U72	Vulkan, Hbg	15–16	755 / 832	186.36	19.357	10.6 / 7.9	7,880/7 / 83/4	80 + 10	40	4 × 19.7in	34	1 × 3.4in or 1 × 4.1in
U73–U74	Kw. Dzg	1915	745 / 829	186.36	19.357	9.6 / 7.9	5,480/7 / 83/4	69 + 13	40	4 × 19.7in	34	1 × 3.4in or 1 × 4.1in
U75–U80	Vulkan, Hbg	15–16	755 / 832	186.36	19.357	9.9 / 7.8	7,880/7 / 83/4	80 + 10	40	4 × 19.7in	34–38	1 × 3.4in or 1 × 4.1in

Mittel-U

Class	Builder[1]	Laid down – Commissioned	Displacement (tons)[2]	Length (feet)	Beam (feet)	Speed (knots)[2]	Endurance (n.miles/ knots)[2]	Fuel (tons)[3]	Diving time (seconds)[4]	Torpedoes	Mines	Guns
U81–U86	Germania	15–16	808 / 946	229.866	20.67	16.8 / 9.1	11,220/8 / 56/5	81 + 38	45	10 × 19.7in	–	1 × 3.4in or 1 × 4.1in
U87–U92	Kw. Dzg	15–17	757 / 998	215.889	20.342	15.6 / 8.6	11,380/8 / 56/5	54 + 79	45	12 × 19.7in	–	1 or 2 × 4.1in
U93–U95	Germania	16–17	838 / 1,000	234.755	20.67	16.8 / 8.6	9,020/8 / 52/5	47 + 60	45	16 × 19.7in	–	1 × 3.4in or 1 × 4.1in
U96–U98	Germania	16–17	837 / 998	234.755	20.67	16.9 / 8.6	8,290/8 / 47/5	47 + 68	45	16 × 19.7in	–	1 × 3.4in or 1 × 4.1in
U99–U104	Weser, Br	16–17	750 / 952	221.795	20.735	16.5 / 8.8	10,100/8 / 45/5	46 + 68	45	7 × 19.7in	–	1 × 4.1in
U105–U110	Germania	16–17	798 / 1,000	234.755	20.67	16.4 / 8.4	9,280/8 / 50/5	47 + 60	45	12 × 19.7in	–	1 × 3.4in or 1 × 4.1in

Class	Builder[1]	Laid down – Commissioned	Displacement (tons)[2]	Length (feet	Beam (feet)	Speed (knots)[2]	Endurance (n.miles/ knots)[2]	Fuel (tons)[3]	Diving time (seconds)[4]	Torpedoes	Mines	Guns
U111–U114	Germania	17–18	798 / 996	234.755	20.67	16.4 / 8.4	8,300/8 50/5	47 + 57	45	12 × 19.7in	–	1 × 3.4in or 1 × 4.1in
U115–U116	Schichau, Dzg – none completed	1916	882 / 1,233	237.216	21.326	16.0 / 9.0	11,470/8 60/4.5	68 + 65	30	12 × 19.7in	–	1 × 3.4in or 1 × 4.1in

UE II Class Ocean Minelayers (known as the 'Omnibus' type)

Class	Builder	Laid down – Commissioned	Displacement	Length	Beam	Speed	Endurance	Fuel	Diving time	Torpedoes	Mines	Guns
U117–U121	Vulkan, Hbg	16–18	1,164 / 1,512	267.467	24.345	14.7 / 7.0	13,900/8 35/4.5	95 + 96	30	12 × 19.7in	42 + 30*	1 or 2 × 5.9in
U122–U126	B & V, Hbg	16–18	1,163 / 1,468	269.042	24.345	14.7 / 7.2	11,470/8 35/4.5	95 + 96	30	12 × 19.7in	42 + 30*	1 or 2 × 5.9in

Mittel-U

Class	Builder	Laid down – Commissioned	Displacement	Length	Beam	Speed	Endurance	Fuel	Diving time	Torpedoes	Mines	Guns
U127–U130	Germania – none completed	1916	1,221 / 1,649	269.20	24.738	17.6 / 8.1	10,000/8 50/4.5	53 + 138	30	14 × 19.7in	–	1 or 2 × 5.9in
U131–U134	Weser, Br – none completed	1916	1,160 / 1,527	270.682	24.738	17.6 / 8.1	10,000/8 50/4.5	53 + 138	30	14 × 19.7in	–	1 or 2 × 5.9in
U135–U138	Kw. Dzg	16–18	1,175 / 1,534	273.963	24.738	17.6 / 8.1	10,000/8 50/4.5	53 + 138	30	14 × 19.7in	–	1 × 5.9in

UA Cruisers

Class	Builder	Laid down – Commissioned	Displacement	Length	Beam	Speed	Endurance	Fuel	Diving time	Torpedoes	Mines	Guns
U139–U141	Germania	16–18	1,930 / 2,483	301.852	29.922	15.3 / 7.6	12,630/8 53/4.5	103 + 283	30	19 × 19.7in	–	2 × 5.9in
U142–U144	Germania	17–18	2,158 / 2,785	319.897	29.725	15.8 / 7.6	17,750/8 53/4.5	120 + 330	30	24 × 19.7in	–	2 × 5.9in

Only *U142* was completed (November 1918); the remainder were scrapped on the stocks after the war.

Class	Builder	Laid down – Commissioned	Displacement	Length	Beam	Speed	Endurance	Fuel	Diving time	Torpedoes	Mines	Guns
U145–U147	Vulkan, Hbg – none completed	1917	2,173 / 2,789	319.897	29.725	17.5 / 8.5	20,000/6 70/4.5	120 + 330	30	24 × 19.7in	–	2 × 5.9in
U148–U150	Weser, Br – none completed	1917	2,153 / 2,766	319.897	29.725	17.5 / 8.5	20,000/6 70/4.5	120 + 330	30	24 × 19.7in	–	2 × 5.9in

*in deck containers

UA Cruisers (ex-Mercantile Cruisers)

Class	Builder	Laid down – Commissioned	Displacement	Length	Beam	Speed	Endurance	Fuel	Diving time	Torpedoes	Mines	Guns
U151–U157	Various yards	16–17	1,512 / 1,875	213.265	29.20	12.4 / 5.2	25,000/5.5 65/3	148 + 137	50	18 × 19.7in	–	2 × 5.9in or 2 × 4.1in
U158–U159	Kw. Dzg –none completed	1917	811 / 1,034	233.443	20.342	16.0 / 9.0	12,370/8 55/5	58 + 87	35	12 × 19.7in	–	2 × 5.9in or 2 × 4.1in
U160–U172	Br. Vulkan	17–19	821 / 1,002	234.755	20.67	16.2 / 8.2	8,500/8 50/5	47 + 60	45	12 × 19.7in	–	1 or 2 × 5.9in

U160–U167 were completed; the remainder were all scrapped before completion.

Class	Builder	Laid down – Commissioned	Displacement	Length	Beam	Speed	Endurance	Fuel	Diving time	Torpedoes	Mines	Guns
U173–U200	B & V, Hbg – none completed	1918	2,158 / 2,785	319.897	29.725	17.5 / 8.5	20,700/6 70/4.5	120 + 330	30	24 × 19.7in	–	2 × 5.9in
U201–U212	Br. Vulkan, Vegesack – none completed	1918	820 / 1,000	234.755	20.67	16.0 / 9.0	6,500/8 60/4.5	47 + 60	45	12 × 19.7in	–	1 × 4.1in
U213–U218	Kw. Dzg – all cancelled	1918	1,335 / 1,830	289.056	25.919	18.0 / 9.0	12,000/8 90/4.5	53 × 138	30	16 × 19.7in	–	1 × 5.9in
U219–U224	Weser, Br	1918	1,400 / 1,900	287.415	25.919	18.0 / 9.0	12,000/8 90/4.5	53 × 138	30	16 × 19.7in	–	1 × 5.9in
U225–U228	B & V, Hbg – all cancelled											
U229–U246	Germania		900 / 1,210	242.794	21.982	16.5 / 9.0	11,400/8 50/5	71 + 67	45	12 × 19.7in	–	1 × 4.1in
U262	Br. Vulkan – all cancelled	1918										
U263–U276	Schichau, Dzg – all cancelled	1919	882 / 1,233	237.216	21.326	16.5 / 9.0	11,400/8 50/5	68 + 65	30	12 × 19.7in	–	1 × 4.1in

Class	Builder[1]	Laid down – Commissioned	Displacement (tons)[2]	Length (feet)	Beam (feet)	Speed (knots)[2]	Endurance (n.miles/ knots)[2]	Fuel (tons)[3]	Diving time (seconds)[4]	Torpedoes	Mines	Guns
Originally being built for Norway but requisitioned												
UA	Germania	13–14	270 / 342	153.222	15.683	14.2 / 7.3	900/10 76/3.3	13	67	5 × 17.7in	–	1 × 2in
UB I Class												
UB1–UB8	Germania	14–15	127 / 142	92.196	10.335	6.47 / 5.51	1,650/5 45/4	3.5	20	2 × 17.7in		1 × MG
UB9–UB17	Weser, Br	14–15	127 / 141	91.474	10.335	7.45 / 6.24	1,500/5 45/4	3	22	2 × 17.7in		1 × MG
UB II Class												
UB18–UB19	B & V, Hbg	1915	263 / 292	118.542	14.305	9.15 / 5.81	6,650/5 45/4	22 + 6	32	4 × 19.7in		1 × 2in or 1 × 3.4in
UB20–UB23	B & V, Hbg	15–16	263 / 292	118.542	14.305	9.15 / 5.81	6,450/5 45/4	22 + 6	32	4 × 19.7in		1 × 2in or 1 × 3.4in
UB24–UB29	Weser, Br	15–16	265 / 291	118.542	14.305	8.90 / 5.72	UB24, UB25 UB27–UB28 8,150/5 UB26, UB29 7,200/5	22 + 6	22	4 × 19.7in		1 × 2in
UB30–UB41	B & V, Hbg	15–16	274 / 303	121.068	14.337	9.06 / 5.71	UB30–UB35 8,150/5 UB36–UB41 7,030/5	21 + 7	30	4 × 19.7in	–	1 × 2in or 1 × 3.4in
UB42–UB47	Weser, Br	15–16	UB42 279 remainder 272 / 305	121.068	14.337	8.82 / 6.22	6,940/5 45/4	22 + 5	32	4 × 19.7in	–	1 × 2in or 1 × 3.4in
UB III Class												
UB48–UB53	B & V, Hbg	16–17	516 / 651	181.439	19.029	13.6 / 8.0	9,040/6 55/4	35 + 40	30	10 × 19.7in	–	1 × 3.4in or 1 × 4.1in
UB54–UB59	Weser, Br	16–17	516 / 646	183.243	19.029	13.4 / 7.8	9,020/9 55/4	36 + 39	30	10 × 19.7in	–	1 × 3.4in or 1 × 4.1in
UB60–UB65	Vulkan, Hbg	16–17	508 / 639	182.161	18.898	13.3 / 8.0	8,420/6 55/4	32 + 36	30	10 × 19.7in	–	1 × 3.4in or 1 × 4.1in
UB66–UB71	Germania	16–17	513 / 647	183.178	19.029	13.2 / 7.6	9,090/6 55/4	35 + 40	30	10 × 19.7in	–	1 × 3.4in or 1 × 4.1in
UB72–UB74	Vulkan, Hbg	16–17	508 / 639	182.161	18.898	13.4 / 7.5	8,420/6 55/4	32 + 36	30	10 × 19.7in	–	1 × 3.4in or 1 × 4.1in
UB75–UB79	B & V, Hbg	16–17	516 / 648	181.439	19.029	13.6 / 7.8	8,680/6 55/4	34 + 39	30	10 × 19.7in	–	1 × 3.4in or 1 × 4.1in
UB80–UB87	Weser, Br	16–17	516 / 647	183.243	19.029	13.4 / 7.5	8,180/6 50/4	34 + 34	30	10 × 19.7in	–	1 × 3.4in or 1 × 4.1in
UB88–UB102	Vulkan, Hbg	17–18	510 / 640	182.161	18.898	13.0 / 7.4	7,120/6 55/4	35 + 36	30	10 × 19.7in	–	1 × 3.4in or 1 × 4.1in

Class	Builder[1]	Laid down – Commissioned	Displacement (tons)[2]	Length (feet)	Beam (feet)	Speed (knots)[2]	Endurance (n.miles/knots)[2]	Fuel (tons)[3]	Diving time (seconds)[4]	Torpedoes	Mines	Guns
UB103–UB117	B & V, Hbg	17–18	519 / 649	181.439	19.029	13.3 / 7.5	7,420/6 / 55/4	35 + 36	30	10 × 19.7in	–	1 × 3.4in or 1 × 4.1in
UB118–UB132	Weser, Br	17–18	512 / 643	183.243	19.029	13.9 / 7.6	7,280/6 / 55/4	35 + 36	30	10 × 19.7in	–	1 × 3.4in or 1 × 4.1in
UB133–UB141	Germania	17–18	533 / 656	183.178	19.029	12.5 / 7.5	9,090/6 / 50/4	35 + 36	30	10 × 19.7in	–	1 × 4in
UB142–UB148	Weser, BR	17–18	523 / 653	183.243	19.029	12.5 / 7.5	7,280/6 / 50/4	35 + 36	30	10 × 19.7in	–	1 × 4.1ir
UB149–UB153		17–19										
UB154–UB166	Vulkan, Hbg	17–18	539 / 656	182.161	19.029	12.5 / 7.5	7,120/6 / 50/4	35 + 36	30	10 × 19.7in	–	1 × 4.1ir
UB167–UB169 – none completed		1918										
UB170–UB177	Germania – cancelled	1918	533 / 656	186.426	19.029	12.5 / 7.5	9,090/6 / 50/4	35 + 36	30	10 × 19.7in	–	1 × 4.1ir
UB178–UB187	Weser, Br	1918	555 / 684	186.36	19.029	13.6 / 8.0	7,280/6 / 50/4	35 + 36	30	10 × 19.7in	–	1 × 4.1ir
UB206–UB219 – cancelled												
UB188–UB205	Vulkan, HBG	1918	539 / 656	189.641	19.029	12.5 / 7.5	7,120/6 / 50/4	35 + 36	30	10 × 19.7in	–	1 × 4.1ir
UB220–UB249 – cancelled												

UC I Class

Class	Builder[1]	Laid down – Commissioned	Displacement (tons)[2]	Length (feet)	Beam (feet)	Speed (knots)[2]	Endurance (n.miles/knots)[2]	Fuel (tons)[3]	Diving time (seconds)[4]	Torpedoes	Mines	Guns
UC1–UC10	Vulkan, Hbg	14–15	168 / 183	111.521	10.335	6.20 / 5.22	780/5 / 50/4	3	23	–	12	1 × MG
UC11–UC15	Weser, Br	14–15	168 / 182	111.521	10.335	6.49 / 5.67	910/5 / 50/4	3	23	–	12	1 × MG

UC II Class

Class	Builder[1]	Laid down – Commissioned	Displacement (tons)[2]	Length (feet)	Beam (feet)	Speed (knots)[2]	Endurance (n.miles/knots)[2]	Fuel (tons)[3]	Diving time (seconds)[4]	Torpedoes	Mines	Guns
UC16–UC24	B & V, Hbg	15–16	417 / 493	161.917	17.126	11.6 / 7.0	9,430/7 / 55/4	14 + 15	35	7 × 19.7in	18	1 × 3.4in
UC25–UC33	Vulkan, Hbg	15–16	400 / 480	162.245	17.126	11.6 / 6.6	UC25–UC27 9,260/7 UC28–UC30 9,410/7 UC31–UC33 10,040/7 53/4	41 + 14	48	7 × 19.7in	18	1 × 3.4in
UC34–UC39	B & V, Hbg	15–16	427 / 509	165.198	17.126	11.9 / 6.8	10,180/7 / 54/4	40 + 15	35	7 × 19.7in	18	1 × 3.4in
UC40–UC45	Vulkan, Hbg	15–16	400 / 480	162.245	17.126	11.7 / 6.7	9,410/7 / 60/4	41 + 14	48	7 × 19.7in	18	1 × 3.4in
UC46–UC48	Weser, Br	15–16	420 / 502	170.119		11.7	7,280/7 / 54/4	14 + 14.5	30	7 × 19.7in	18	1 × 3.4in
UC49–UC51	Germania	16–17	434 / 511	172.875	17.126	11.8 / 7.2	8,820/7 9,450/7 56/4	41 + 15	30	7 × 19.7in	18	1 × 3.4in
UC52–UC54												
UC55–UC58	Kw. Dzg	16–17	415 / 498	165.756	17.126	11.6 / 7.3	8,660/7 9,450/7 52/4	41 + 15	30	7 × 19.7in	18	1 × 3.4in
UC59–UC60												
UC61–UC64	Weser, Br	16–17	422 / 504	170.119	17.126	11.9 / 7.2	8,000/7 / 59/4	43	30	7 × 19.7in	18	1 × 3.4in
UC65–UC73	B & V, Hbg	1916	427 / 508	165.198	17.126	12.0 / 7.4	10,420/7 / 52/4	41 + 15	35	7 × 19.7in	18	1 × 3.4in
UC74–UC76	Vulkan, Hbg	16–17	410 / 493	165.526	17.126	11.8 / 7.3	10,420/7 8,660/7 52/4	41 + 14	30	7 × 19.7in	18	1 × 3.4in
UC77–UC79												
UC80–UC86	Kw. Dzg – none completed	1917	474 / 560	184.064	18.176	11.5 / 6.6	8,200/7 / 40/4.5	41 + 15	15	7 × 19.7in	18	1 × 4.1in

Class	Builder[1]	Laid down – Commissioned	Displace-ment (tons)[2]	Length (feet)	Beam (feet)	Speed (knots)[2]	Endurance (n.miles/ knots)[2]	Fuel (tons)[3]	Diving time (seconds)[4]	Torpedoes	Mines	Guns
UC87–UC89	Weser, Br	1917 – none completed	480 566	184.064	18.176	11.5 6.6	8,200/7 40/4.5	55 + 11	15	7 × 19.7in	18	1 × 4.1in
UC III Class												
UC90–UC118	B & V, Hbg	17–18	491 571	185.409	18.176	11.5 6.6	9,850/7 40/4.5	55 + 11	15	7 × 19.7in	18	1 × 4.1in
UC119– UC138 UC153– UC192	B & V, Hbg	1918 – none completed	511 582	187.345	18.176	11.5 6.6	9,850/7 40/4.5	55 + 11	30	7 × 19.7in	18	1 × 4.1in
UC139– UC152	Kw. Dzg	1918 – cancelled	474 564	186.524	19.029	11.5 6.6	8,200/7 40/4.5	55 + 11	30	7 × 19.7in	18	1 × 4.1in
Single-hulled coastal boats												
UF1–UF92	Schichau, Elbg Tecklenborg Atlas-W, Br Neptun Seebeck	1918 – all cancelled	364 381	146.332	14.567	11.0 7.0	3,500/7 64/4	?	15	7 × 19.7in	–	1 × 3.4in

Diving depths

U1–U4 = 98 feet; U5–U116, U201–U212, all UB and UC types = 165 feet; U117–U200, U213–U228 and UF1–UF92 = 250 feet.

Notes
1. B & V, Hbg. = Blohm & Voss, Hamburg; Br, Vulkan = Bremer-Vulkan, Vegesack; Germania = Krupp's Germania Yard, Kiel; Kw. Dzg = Kaiserliche werft (Imperial Dockyard), Danzig; Schichau = Schichau, Danzig; Vulkan, Hbg. = Vulkan, Hamburg; Weser, Br. = A. G. Weser, Bremen.
2. Surfaced/submerged. **3.** Interior bunkers + saddle tanks. **4.** Boat under way.

U-boat specifications, 1935–45

Source: Admiralty MS: PRO Adm 186/8020

Type	Description	Displace-ment (tons)[1]	Length (feet)	Beam (feet)	Speed (knots)[1]	Endurance (n.miles knots)[1]	Fuel (tons)	Diving depth (feet)	Diving time (seconds)[2]	Torpedoes[3] and mines[4]	Guns	Crew
IA	Pre-war Atlantic U-boat	862 983	238.88	20.49	18.6 8.3	8,100/10 78/4	96	330	30	14 torpedoes (normal) or 4 torpedoes + 16 TMA mines or	1 × 4.1in (150 rounds) 1 × 20mm Flak single (2,000 rounds)	43
										28 TMA mines or 42 TMB mines — 4 torpedoes + 10 TMA and 9 TMB mines or — 4 torpedoes + 24 TMB mines or		
IIA	Coastal U-boat	253.8 303.1	134.97	13.467	13 6.9	2,000/8 35/4	12	330	–30	5 torpedoes (normal) 6 torpedoes (maximum) or 1 torpedo + 8 TMA mines or	1 × 20mm Flak twin (850 rounds)	25
										12 TMA mines or 18 TMB mines — 1 torpedo + 4 TMA and 6 TMB mines or — 1 torpedo + 10 TMB mines or		

Type	Description	Displacement (tons)[1]	Length (feet)	Beam (feet)	Speed (knots)[1]	Endurance (n.miles knots)[1]	Fuel (tons)	Diving depth (feet)	Diving time (seconds)[2]	Torpedoes[3] and mines[4]	Guns	Crew
IIB	Coastal U-boat	278.9 / 328.5	140	13.467	13 / 7	3,900/8 43/4	21	330	−30	As Type IIA	1 × 20mm Flak twin (1,000 rounds) or 1 × 20mm Flak twin and 1 × 20mm Flak single: 1,800 rounds (Black Sea boats)	25
IIC	Coastal U-boat	291 / 341	144.87	13.467	12 / 7	4,200/8 42/4	23	330	−25	As Type IIA	1 × 20mm Flak twin (1,200 rounds)	25
IID	Coastal U-boat	314 / 364	145.1	16.129	12.7 / 7.4	5,650/8 56/4	38	330	−25	As Type IIA	1 × 20mm Flak twin (1,200 rounds)	25
VIIA	Atlantic U-boat	626 / 745	212.88	19.302	17 / 8	6,800/10 90/4	67	309	30	11 torpedoes maximum or 3 torpedoes + 12 TMA mines or	1 × 3.5in (250 rounds) 1 × 37mm Flak (1,195 rounds) 2 × 20mm Flak twin (4,380 rounds)	44
VIIB	Atlantic U-boat	753 / 857	219.45	20.47	17.9 / 8	9,400/10 90/4	108	309	30	14 torpedoes maximum or 4 torpedoes + 16 TMA mines or	As Type VII	44
VIIC	Atlantic U-boat	769 / 871	221.43	20.47	17.7 / 7.6	9,700/10 80/4	113	309	30	As type VIIB	As type VII	44
VIIC/41	Atlantic U-boat	This type was the same in all respects as Type VIIC with the exception of a stronger pressure hull for deeper diving depth, which was 394 feet.										
VIIC/42	Atlantic U-boat	This type was virtually an expanded Type VIIC, redesigned to meet the new tactical requirements brought about by the increase in convoy speeds, greater dispersal of convoy routes, and improved A/S methods. The diving depth was increased, and new diesels were installed which, at a speed of 10 knots, provided nearly double the range of the Type VIIC.										
		1,084.5 / 1,098.92	225.49	20.34	18.6 / 7.6	12,600/10 80/4	159	394	30	As Type VIIC except for 2 reserve torpedoes		
VIID	Minelaying U-boat	965 / 1,080	252.3	20.9	16.7 / 7.3	13,000/10 69/4	169	330	30	12 torpedoes normal or 4 torpedoes + 16 TMA and 15 SMA mines or	1 × 3.5in (250 rounds) 1 × 37mm Flak (1,995 rounds) 2 × 20mm Flak twin (4,380 rounds)	44
VIIF	Torpedo supply U-boat	1,084 / 1,181	256.18	23.95	17.6 / 7.9	13,950/10 75/4	199	330	30	14 torpedoes normal and maximum	As Type VIID	46
IXA	Atlantic U-boat	1,032 / 1,153	252.45	21.48	18.2 / 7.7	11,350/10 82/4	154	330	35	19 torpedoes normal 22 torpedoes maximum or	1 × 4.1in (180 rounds) 1 × 37mm Flak (2,625 rounds) 2 × 20mm Flak twin (8,500 rounds)	48

VIIA torpedo/mine options box:
22 TMA mines or 33 TMB mines — 3 torpedoes + 8 TMA and 6 TMB mines or — 3 torpedoes + 18 TMB mines or

VIIB torpedo/mine options box:
26 TMA mines or 39 TMB mines — 4 torpedoes + 10 TMA and 9 TMB mines or — 3 torpedoes + 24 TMB mines or

VIID torpedo/mine options box:
39 TMA + 15 SMA mines — 26 TMA + 15 SMA mines or — 14 torpedoes + 15 SMA mines or — 4 torpedoes + 10 TMA, 9 TMB and 15 SMA mines or — 3 torpedoes + 24 TMB and 15 SMA mines or

VIIF: Based on Type VIIC with additional storage space for 21 torpedoes as cargo to replenish operational boats at sea.

IXA torpedo/mine options box:
44 TMA mines or 66 TMB mines or — 8 torpedoes + 14 TMA and 12 TMB mines or — 8 torpedoes + 33 TMB mines or — 8 torpedoes + 22 TMA mines or

Type	Description	Displacement (tons)[1]	Length (feet)	Beam (feet)	Speed (knots)[1]	Endurance (n.miles knots)[1]	Fuel (tons)	Diving depth (feet)	Diving time (seconds)[2]	Torpedoes[3] and mines[4]	Guns	Crew
IXB	Atlantic U-boat	1,051 / 1,178	252.45	22.308	18.2 / 7.3	12,400/10 64/4	165	330	35	As Type IX	As Type IX	48
IXC	Atlantic U-boat	1,120 / 1,232	237.18	22.308	18.3 / 7.3	16,300/10 63/4	208	330	35	As Type IX	As Type IX	48
IXC/40	Atlantic U-boat	1,144 / 1,257	237.18	22.688	18.3 / 7.3	16,800/10 63/4	214	330	35	As Type IX	As Type IX	48
IXD/41	U-cruiser	1,610 / 1,799	289.01	24.75	16.5 / 6.9	13,000/10 115/4	203	330	35	24 torpedoes maximum	1 × 4.1in (200 rounds) 1 × 37mm Flak (2,575 rounds) 2 × 20mm Flak twins (8,100 rounds)	57
IXD/42	U-cruiser	1,616 / 1,804	289.01	24.75	19.2 / 6.9	32,300/10 57/4	442	330	35	21 torpedoes normal or 8 torpedoes + 26 TMA mines or 8 torpedoes + 39 TMB mines	1 × 4.1in (200 rounds) 1 × 37mm Flak (2,575 rounds) 2 × 20mm Flak twins (8,100 rounds)	57
XB	Minelaying U-boat	1,763 / 2,177	296.34	30.36	17 / 16.4	21,000/10 93/4	368	376	−40	15 torpedoes + 66 SMA mines	1 × 4.1in (200 rounds) 1 × 37mm Flak (2,500 rounds) 2 × 20mm Flak twins (8,000 rounds)	52
XIV	(Milchkühe) U-tanker supply boat	1,688 / 1,932	221.43	30.85	14.9 / 6.2	12,300/10 55/4	203	396	?	Nil	1 × 37mm Flak (2,500 rounds) 2 × 20mm Flak twins (8,000 rounds)	53

Supply capacity: diesel oil 720 tons, lubricating oil 34 tons, fresh water 10.5 tons, distilled water 3 tons. Each U-tanker's supply of fuel oil could replenish 12 VIIC boats with four weeks' supply or five IXC boats with eight weeks' supply.

Type	Description	Displacement (tons)[1]	Length (feet)	Beam (feet)	Speed (knots)[1]	Endurance (n.miles knots)[1]	Fuel (tons)	Diving depth (feet)	Diving time (seconds)[2]	Torpedoes[3] and mines[4]	Guns	Crew
XXI	Prefabricated Electro Atlantic U-boat	1,621 / 1,819	237	21.78	15.6 / 17.18	15,500/10 365/5	250	376	18	20 torpedoes maximum	2 × 30mm Flak in twin mounting (3,800 rounds)	57
XXIII	Prefabricated Electro Coastal U-boat	232 / 256	114.44	9.9	9.75 / 9.7	4,300/6 175/4	18	330	−10	2 torpedoes maximum	Nil	14
XVIIB	'Walter'-type coastal	312 / 337	136.161	10.827	8.5 / 21.5	3,000/8 150/2	20 + 55 H₂O₂*	500	?	4 × 16.4in	Nil	19

*Hydrogen Peroxide (Aurol) fuel for 'Walter' turbine

Type	Description	Displacement (tons)[1]	Length (feet)	Beam (feet)	Speed (knots)[1]	Endurance (n.miles knots)[1]	Fuel (tons)	Diving depth (feet)	Diving time (seconds)[2]	Torpedoes[3] and mines[4]	Guns	Crew
Wa 201	'Walter'-type experimental	277 / 294	127.959	10.827	9 / 25.0	? / 117/20	18 + 43 H₂O₂	?	?	4 × 16.4in	Nil	12
Wk 202	'Walter'-type experimental	236 / 259	113.522	11.155	9 / 24.0	1,840/9 / ?	14 + 40 H₂O₂	?	?	4 × 16.4in	Nil	12

Notes

1. Surfaced/submerged. 2. Boat under way. 3. Torpedoes 21in unless otherwise specified. 4. TMA Mines (475lb explosive charge) = *Torpedo-Ankertaumine* (torpedo anchor mine). 5. TMB (1,280lb charge) and TMC (2,205lb charge) Mines = *Torpedo-Grundminen* (torpedo sea-bed mine); these were torpedo-shaped mines (about half the size of a normal torpedo) constructed for ejection through a U-boat's torpedo tubes. 6. SMA Mines = *Sonder-Mine A* (Shaft Mine Type A); this was a special type of anchor-mine with a 773lb explosive charge developed for Types XB and VIID Minelaying U-boats. 7. The TMA, TMB and TMC mines had remote detonation mechanisms, mostly magnetic and some acoustic. 8. The SMA Mines had magnetic remote detonators.

Problems of leadership in a submarine, by Kapitänleutnant Wolfgang Luth

The following is a lecture on the problems of leadership in a submarine, given at a convention of naval officers at Weimar on 17 December 1943. Luth was one of the outstanding German submarine comanders. He was born in 1913, and joined the German Navy in 1933. In August 1943 he received the swords and diamonds to the Oak Leaves award, worn with the Knight's Cross of the Iron Cross; he was the seventh man to receive this decoration, and the first member of the Navy. At that time it was *claimed* that he had sunk forty-six ships totalling 254,000 GRT. In addition he was credited with sinking one enemy submarine, damaging two more ships and a destroyer, and executing a successful mining operation. One of his cruises is said to have been the longest submarine cruise of the war. Luth was given the nickname 'der grosse Jäger' ('the great hunter').

Grand Admiral, Gentlemen:

It is my job as submarine commander to sink ships. To do this I need a cooperative crew so that everything clicks. If the men are really to cooperate, they not only have to know their jobs well – all the little details of their daily routine – but they also have to like their work.

I wish to describe to you here a number of episodes which are to show you along what lines I have directed life aboard, and how we live. I have spent a long time on enemy missions, the entire four years. What I am going to tell here is based only on my experiences; these are my own ideas. I shall try to skip basic principles, to avoid platitudes, and to relate only episodes which can serve as examples of how it can be done. Each trip was different, and each time I was surrounded by different officers and men. There is no formula which applies to all cases. I have learned new things during each of my sixteen missions, so that I had gathered considerable experience by the time I started on my last mission, which lasted more than seven and one half months.

I am now going to describe to you briefly conditions aboard a submarine, because they are so entirely different from those aboard other naval vessels.

Life aboard is monotonous for long periods. For many long weeks one must be able to bear failures, and when depth-charges are added life becomes a war of nerves – which, however, affects principally the leaders. We feel something like a flier in the air who is attacked, let us say, by three fighters. This man, however, must be able to hear clearly every shot which is intended for him, even if it misses, yes, even if it misses him by several thousand metres. Therefore he feels not only the shots that hit home, but every single shot that is fired. All these blasts have a

tormenting intensity. Then the lights go out and he sits in the dark, and when it is dark all men become more and more afraid. Unlike the plane the submarine cannot fly away, but has to remain motionless without being able to defend herself or shoot back. All that requires stouthearted men.

To this must be added that life aboard a submarine is unnatural and unhealthy compared to life on a sailing vessel, just as unhealthy as city life compared to life in the country.

There is no constant change between day and night, for the lights have to burn all the time inside the boat. There are no Sundays and no weekdays, and there is no regular change of seasons. Therefore life is monotonous and without rhythm, and the captain must attempt to compensate for these disadvantages as far as possible. Added to this is the continuous change of climate, which affects even the healthiest man after a certain length of time. The boat passes from the trade wind zones to the tropics, from humid regions to clear weather zones, and touches one climatic zone after the other, particularly en route to and from her zone of operations. There is no regular time for sleeping, since most of the fighting is done at night. Continuous responsibility rests with the captain for the physical and mental health of his men.

The necessary restrictions on both smoking and drinking by the men on board are also factors which must not be ignored, for both affect the men's stomachs and nerves, particularly if they indulge in them at night on an empty stomach. I have seen young fellows of twenty-three become unfit for submarine duty within two years. Of course, one must not get drunk too often when ashore; that is a peacetime luxury. During my enemy missions I have never drunk that very popular watch coffee, which tastes so horrible because it is much too strong; I have never smoked more than one to two cigars daily, and I have only seldom got drunk ashore.

The morale of the crew depends on the following factors:

(1) The discipline aboard.

(2) Success. If a commander is successful his crew will love him more, even if he is a numbskull, than one who is unsuccessful. However, for a commander who is not successful it is particularly important to have a crew with high morale.

(3) A well-organized daily routine aboard.

(4) The example and the correct attitude of the officers.

(5) Real spiritual leadership for the men, together with a genuine concern for their personal welfare.

It is the duty of the captain to see to it that a high esprit de corps prevails on his ship and that the opinions of incompetent men count little. He should act aboard perhaps like a gardener who roots out the weeds and tends the good plants. That is not too difficult, for we deal mostly with eager young men. The men are from twenty to twenty-two years old; the petty officers are twenty-three to twenty-five years old. It is also to our advantage that most of the men are skilled craftsmen who have served apprenticeships, and that there are hardly any intellectual misfits among them who got only part way through secondary schools because they were thrown out or were too stupid to continue. Such men can have a very adverse effect on the crew. However, if they are closely watched their talents can also be used to good advantage.

My crew included men from all regions of Germany. Twenty per-cent of them came from the Rhineland and the rest came from all other parts of Germany, even from Austria and the Sudetenland; in my daily dealings I have had good and bad experiences with all of them. Most petty officers were married and the rest were honestly engaged. I consider that an advantage. Though I know that a woman can break a man's fighting spirit, I also know that she can give him strength, and I have often observed that married men returned from their leave particularly well rested for a new mission. Married petty officers must be told what is required of the wife of a fighting man. I was glad to meet them and to be able to tell them that we expected them to be brave. I believe that afterwards several of them felt better able to bear their burden, and I asked my wife to write to them now and then and keep in touch with them.

Much has been written about the award of medals, and this subject will continue to be a controversial one. This only shows the importance of the problem. The fact must not be ignored that there are some men who, when decorated with the Iron Cross First Class, suddenly develop diseases which cannot be spotted by an X-ray machine and which are generally known by the catch-words of heart and stomach ailments and rhuematism. If every submarine man would submit to a conventional physical check-up, only few would be found fit for duty. It is necessary to appeal to a man's iron willpower to maintain his health and to overcome minor difficulties. If two men are up for the Iron Cross First Class and only one can receive it, I prefer to give it to the man who stays on board rather than to the one who is lucky enough to be advanced to petty officer or chief petty officer and therefore has to leave the ship.

On a long mission, for practical reasons, I cannot apply the penal provisions of the disciplinary punishment regulations, because I cannot imprison anybody and liberty restrictions or withholding of pay are also impractical. If I punish a man with two weeks in the brig I have to say to him: 'In a few months we shall be home again, and then you will have to sweat it out.' In the meantime we experience success and danger together in which the man proves his worth. We return home feeling triumphant at having accomplished something. Am I to lock the man up then for an offence committed months ago? I consider this unwise. Nevertheless, I do hold disciplinary hearings while

at sea. In the case of a grave offence all officers are present. I want everybody to be neatly and uniformly dressed. If, for instance, a man was impertinent to a superior or committed some other infraction, an offence for which he might get three days, I deprive him for three days of his bunk. In that case he has to sleep on deck without a mattress or a blanket, and, since this is uncomfortable, it is more effective than three days arrest. On long missions the younger men often break a lot of dishes. Admonitions, as you know, are of little avail, especially since mess duty is often difficult during rough weather. Now I have china muster every week, and if too much is missing the mess attendent has to eat out of a can for three days. To deprive a man of his smoking privilege is also hard punishment. To forbid a skat fan to play for three days also works miracles. On one trip our rations were short, yet one man obtained in an uncomradely manner additional rations in such quantities that I had to make an example of him. I punished him by giving him the silent treatment for two weeks, as used to be customary among cadets, and actually nobody talked to him and he slept on a hard bunk all that time. Afterwards the case was closed; nothing more was said about it, and comradeship was fully restored.

Once I had a chronic grumbler aboard who also liked to be disobedient towards superiors who could not handle him. He crabbed about everything, similar to some types in civilian life. Once when we had no success for weeks and his grumbling threatened the morale of the crew I called muster. I dived to forty metres, got everything settled, left three good men in the control and electro motor compartments, assembled the crew in the compartment and addressed the man in a loud voice: 'Either you return with me as my friend, or when you return I shall send you to a penal company at the Eastern Front. For the time being you will pull two weeks' extra duty according to an exact schedule.' I gave him this in writing and had him sign it. Then I had it printed in the ship's paper which hangs on the bulletin boards, one across from the radio room and one at the head in the aft compartment where it can be read with the necessary leisure. The man performed his extra duty in the tropics to my full satisfaction, he sorted out bad potatoes, cleaned the bilges, shifted the supplies, and relieved his comrades of the kind of work that is necessary but is very unpleasant to perform. He continued to do his work so well that he now wears the Iron Cross, and I have recommended him to my successor as combat helmsman.

I do not let the mess petty officer distribute fruit, chocolate, and similar things in a routine manner but I keep them under my thumb. Fruit as a reward for a job well done or withheld as punishment for greediness is a good means for education on a long trip.

These are all things which can be done very well on board. They are more effective when sensibly applied than the penalties provided by the disciplinary punishment regulations. It is important that the crew be notified of the punishment in a proper manner, either through the ship's paper or the bulletin board, or at muster. Any chicanery must be prevented, and the man must never notice that his captain is irritated.

Generally I had the tendency to punish as little as possible. This cannot be done by putting your hands in your lap and letting everything take its course, but by taking particularly good care of one's men, by truly leading and educating them, and by issuing clear orders to make obedience easier.

One day after I had received the Oak Leaves at sea my aft lookout spotted a destroyer too late. There was nothing for us to do but dive and wait. Our success was jeopardized and we were exposed to unnecessary danger. Nevertheless I did not punish the man. We had so much stuff thrown at us that we could not surface for fifteen hours. The looks he got from his comrades when the depth-charges started to explode were punishment enough. The fact that I did not punish the man paid off well; he is now an excellent man.

I have also had men with prison records aboard, and got along with them well. Naturally they must not be thieves who stole from their fellow crew members or similar inferior types. At one time a destroyer was attacking us with depth-charges, when suddenly at great depth a valve of the bilge waterline burst. Water rushed into the boat. The electric switchboard at the central control station caught fire, and the lights went out. Fortunately I had a man with a prison record aboard who wanted to redeem himself. He jumped into the fire and extinguished it. He received the Iron Cross First Class and is now a petty officer. It was a bargain for both of us, for him as well as for me. In almost every case the purpose of punishment is to educate the man, not to destroy him. The chance to redeem himself is often a strong incentive for such a man.

It is obvious that a precise routine must be adhered to on board. It is a matter of honour that the watch is relieved on time. I also stress the observance of military courtesy aboard. This naturally applies more in port than at sea, where it must suffice to call 'Attention' when the captain enters a compartment for the first time during the day, and to have the senior enlisted man report what is going on, just as the watch officer on the bridge has to report. While lying in port muster must be stood at least once a day. I feel that a dignified colour ceremony is particularly important. From time to time a locker muster must be held at sea, too, and one must constantly check to see that all gear is properly stowed. Besides this, it must be added that the captain must be accessible at all times aboard, so that important matters are not postponed our of misplaced respect for his person or fear of his bad mood.

The lookout is particularly important on a submarine. His qualifications depend even more on his character than on his good eyes. During all my cruises we spotted far more than 100 planes, but we were bombed only three times. Several times the lookout spotted planes even at night and twice he even heard them in time. Despite this I permit the men to talk and smoke while on watch. I know that young crews must be forbidden to do so while in training at home, where not a word may be spoken during watch. The lookout must first get a 'solid foundation'. But if you've been at sea for months, you can't let the men stand watch for four hours without speaking a single word. When I know that they are alert, I permit them to sneak up on each other back to back and exchange a few words with their eyes on their binoculars. Whether smoking is permitted at night is decided by the watch officer on the basis of visibility. I should like to remark here that I forbid the younger men to smoke on an empty stomach before breakfast from 0400 and 0800.

During one cruise one of my men was killed and several others wounded. As replacement I picked a volunteer ordinary seaman who had served on German ships since he was fourteen. He came aboard with a straw hat on his head and said: 'Day, Captain this is where I am supposed to get on'. He had no idea of military discipline. I assigned him my best petty officer to teach him military discipline and the basic facts. After two weeks we swore him in. For this occasion we submerged, decorated the bow compartment with flags, and turned this administration of the oath into a real ceremony. The man had previously learned the oath by heart. In my address I told him about the duties of a German soldier. The crew attended uniformly dessed in brown tropical shirts. Everyone got a decent haircut for the occasion. Appropriate songs for the ceremony had been prearranged, so that the singing really clicked. We also made the young seaman a present of the 'Duties of a Man-of-War's Man' which one of the men had carefully written down. One has to think of such trifles if ceremonies of this kind are being improvised, and military ceremonies are necessary from time to time to stimulate the enthusiasm of the men. He became an excellent man, who was awarded the Iron Cross and the submarine insignia, and he is staying on board without having to go through, the usual basic training. When he went on leave I sent a fellow crew member along for his protection so that he could tell him: 'You must salute this man, he is a superior; watch your step, this man belongs to the railroad patrol; but that admiral over there in that beautiful uniform is a railroad man who won't bother you'.

Normally no alcohol is allowed aboard. However, the men are very grateful if they can take a swig from a bottle now and then on a special occasion, as when a steamer has been sunk, if it's somebody's birthday, or if somebody got soaked while working on the upper deck.

The closer the petty officers co-operate with their officers, the better will be the discipline aboard. Therefore I support the petty officers on board whenever I can. I tell them not only all the things that are forbidden and the things they cannot do to establish discipline, but rather how many possibilities there are and what means they have at their disposal to gain the respect of the men. Most of them are so young that they need that advice. Sometimes when we are submerged I call them together, instruct them in disciplinary problems, and induce them to tell me all their troubles. After you have had a heart to heart talk with them you reproach yourself for not having talked with them before to help solve their problems. I also feel it is a mistake to treat a seasoned seaman like a boot. 'A soldier must be self-confident', is an old axiom. The seaman must, if possible, shoulder more responsibility than his younger comrades.

Success is easy to take; it raises morale. My efforts on board; however, are directed in keeping up the crew's morale when things are not going well too. The good soldier can show his true mettle only when the odds are against him. On enemy missions things never go as well, or for that matter as badly, as you expect them to. You just have to have the guts to stick it out. If you have success you have to let your crew share in it. It is a matter of temperament how a commander makes his crew feel their part in the fight. It is difficult for the submarine man; he cannot actively participate in the fight or just go out and perform heroic deeds. However, if somebody makes a single slip the shot carefully prepared long in advance misses the target.

At one time I ran smack into a convoy in the middle of the night. I barely dodged a destroyer and sneaked close by a steamer into the middle of the convoy. Visibility was limited, and I had not yet a clear view of the situation. I slowed down because I told myself that 'he who thinks slowly, must go slowly, or he might come to grief'. After I had manoeuvred into the centre of the convoy, I informed my Chief Officer of our position and he relayed it to the crew over the loud speaker. Since the men know what the game was I did not have to drive them on. Before the boat turned for the attack I called down: 'The run starts!' This not only gives the crew a heightened feeling of confidence, but also prepares them for the climax of the attack. For instance, when the torpedo is on its way I add: 'It will take at least forty seconds before it hits.' When the entire boat counts together, the victory bottle is uncorked in anticipation, and the victory march is prepared for playing over the loudspeaker, the seconds pass. And if after two minutes there is still no explosion, the waiting is ended with the expression 'Schiet'. If depth-charges are dropped after a hit, there usually is also an opportunity to tell the men a few more interesting details about the attack. If one manages to keep on the surface, a few deserving crew members are allowed to come up on the bridge for a moment to watch the sinking steamer. By day, while at periscope depth, there are always situations in which one can let some of the men look through the periscope. In the heat of battle such things are not often possible. For that very reason one should take advantage of good opportunities.

One day, after I had received my diamonds, I spotted a large steamer which had the same speed as the submarine. After a long chase I was able to sink her, so to speak in gratitude for the award. During such a long chase I gladly let the men take a look at the plotting chart and have them search through the ship register to try to identify the type and size of the steamer, so that the hunting fever gradually spreads through the entire boat. I permit a few men to come on the bridge to pick up the steamer through binoculars. The entire crew must be able to participate in such experiences.

Before entering port, I dive once more in the Bay of Biscay and hold muster, I tell the men what they can tell at home and what is forbidden. Since every German thinks that only secrets are interesting, I show them that many other things which are not secret can also be interesting. At one time I posted a sample letter on the bulletin board: 'Dear Erika, I have returned safely. We were very successful and sank several steamers. Once we even caught a shark and I won first prize in the chess tournament . . . ' I add a lot of other things, and they can pick out whatever suits them best.

The ordinary daily routine must be perfectly organized. The ship must become a home to the sailor. Naturally there must not be too much regimentation. Because rest periods are particularly necessary on a submarine, it is one of the submarine man's main principles that his off-duty hours and his sleep are inviolable. The rhythm of a normal life must be preserved as much as possible. Since the change from day to night cannot ordinarily be felt on a submarine it must be brought about by artificial means. During supper the dim lights are switched on, and we have an evening concert on records from half an hour before the watch changes (2000) until half an hour afterwards. Sunday is always a special occasion and begins with a recorded program, initiated regularly by the song 'Yes, this is my Sunday fun, to stay in bed at least till ten.' The evening concert always ends with a fine record, the 'Abendlied' sung by the Regensburg Domspatzen. I tell my men; 'If you do put on a clean shirt every once in a while, don't do it on Tuesday or Friday; do it on Sunday, so at least some of you will run around in Sunday clothes.' Every man brings along enough illustrated magazines so that it is possible to distribute six new ones every Sunday. We arrange it so that the last papers are given out when we reach port. Of course we also arrange the bill of fare accordingly, and the menu will contain items which indicate that it is a holiday.

Of course on a long mission it is necessary to have general ship cleaning. It is interesting that I was almost the only man aboard who really knew how to clean a ship, how to chip paint, and how to swab decks and benches. Hardly a member of the crew had ever been on a battleship, where you really learn these things. This general ship cleaning is done on Saturdays, accompanied by lively record music to make it more pleasant. The arrangement of the menu is difficult, for the men start to crab about the food all too easily. I therefore let the various compartments draw up the menu. Of course the longer we are out on a mission the closer I have to control the fare, so that all the best things will not be eaten up at the beginning. I also insist that the men have decent table manners, especially in the petty officers' quarters. I do not insist on these things because I am an aesthete, but because I believe that the authority of the petty officers suffers if they do not take care of themselves under all circumstances. I have seen petty officers who sat down at the table with dirty hands and unbottoned clothes, or who snapped at a mess attendant because the plate was not absolutely clean while at the same time a man was sitting next to them who dirtied his plate with his greasy hands. Such a difference of standards makes the mess crew feel insecure and leads to constant friction, and this can easily be avoided. One must see to it that the men crab about the food rarely and only in justified cases.

Bread is also baked aboard. Because our baking oven is out of order this was a difficult affair. We remedied the situation by arranging a baking contest. Four men who were professional bakers had to compete with each other, and we gave each new loaf of bread so much publicity over the radio and in the ship's paper that it could not have been done better at the Reichstag elections. This way we finally did get decent bread after all. But there are also other minor details which you must remember. If you have neither indelible ink nor name tags, and therefore the laundry which is hung up to dry in the electric motor compartment is not marked, it gets lost occasionally and unnecessary annoyance is caused. Experience has shown that it takes about two weeks for it to turn up again. The ship's store must also be watched; it must be run on the basis that every man gets an equal share, the captain not more than the youngest seaman. If exceptions are made in certain articles the men must be told about it very frankly. In all these the watch officer must really be the men's best comrade and the link between captain and crew. However, he can only inform the captain of any dissatisfaction if the men tell him about it; thus he must have their full confidence.

We did not hold sick call on board. I feel that this is not necessary for fifty healthy men. But I have always trained my men to see the doctor or the captain even about trifles. Not because they feel sorry for themselves or want to shirk their duty but, on the contrary, in order always to be fit for duty. It is every submarine man's duty to stay healthy for duty. It is better to have a boil treated immediately than to wait until it has become big for fear of being called a sissy. A healthy way of life is necessary on board. I not only order every man to wear his woollen waistband, but I also repeat the order every evening at dusk over the radio. I do not permit drinking ice water in the tropics. I have forbidden young hands to smoke on an empty stomach, and I see to it that the mid watch coffee is not made quite as strong as is usual in submarines.

On one mission we had a case of diphtheria. Fortunately we did not notice it until the man was already completely paralyzed and the danger of contagion had passed. Otherwise we would have been so worried that we would all have gargled until our throats were sore. After many weeks the paralyzed man is fit for duty once more, and during the last two months he did full duty although he had been lying in the aft compartment all this time and had scarcely seen daylight. Upon arrival in port he was declared unfit for submarine duty for some time. I was angry about that; there are physical defects in spite of which one can be a good submarine man. There are doubtless many submarine men who have been declared unfit for duty in keeping with the regulations, when nobody wanted to take the responsibility of sending them against the enemy again, though it would have been possible. But when so many soldiers are risking their lives, others should have to risk their health in this tough war. I have also had cases of gonorrhea and even syphilis on board which, however, could be cured by the doctor. Three days before shoving off I stop all shore leave without previous notice, so that the men will not make a last quick visit to a whorehouse.

I never had to contend with sexual problems on board, not even during the missions which lasted seven and one half months. To be sure, I have not permitted the men to hang pictures of nude girls on the bulkheads and over their bunks. If you are hungry you shouldn't paint bread on the wall. It is also advisable to leaf through the books aboard every once in a while. Time and again you turn up one which can be thrown overboard because it appeals only to man's lower instincts. When we arrive in port I like to see to it that the men buy as much as possible for their families, so that they spend their money in a sensible way. At the base the men should be left alone at times so that they can relax and do as they like. Many escape to the whorehouse simply because it is 'pleasanter and more interesting' there and they feel themselves unobserved.

The spirit of the crew depends mainly on an exemplary officers' corps. Up to now I have had seventeen officers on my ship, of whom only four had trouble getting adjusted; there were seven midshipmen, among them one failure. All the others were exceptionally good, and helped to shape life aboard so that 'every day was Sunday'.

Life in the officers' mess must be above reproach, for the crew looks up to their officers, whose esprit de corps transmits itself to them. I also address all my men as 'seamen'. After all they are all seafaring men; it doesn't matter whether a man works on the engines now or tended the sails in past decades – they are all doing it for their ship. Even such a minor detail can help to create the proper community spirit aboard.

You have to take pains with young officers. It is obvious that they are not all alike and are apt to get out of line at times. Nevertheless you can't let them hang the picture of the Fuehrer on the left side of the bulkhead in the officers' mess and on the right side one of a girl from a box of candy which they bought in Paris. That shows bad taste. The same is true if they like American and British jazz. Whether they like it or not has nothing to do was the matter. In a tough war everyone must have learned to hate his enemy without reservation. It is also obvious that obscenities and dirty jokes are not to be told on a crowded ship and on such a long journey. This is not only for moral reasons, but also because it is hard to stop such things once they have started, because it is hard to draw the line afterwards, and above all because the men are quick to pick up unsuitable habits.

Once I had a watch officer who always slept undressed in his bunk; as if that were not enough, he never came on battle station at night without dressing first. He never even forgot to put on his oilskin pants and hat. His well-being was so important to him before he came on battle station. He never drank coffee because he was a hypochondriac and belived he had something wrong with his stomach; he drank a cup of milk instead. Since we had no cows on board, and therefore not much milk, I forbade this. Then he poured some hot water into the milk and said that this was a substitute for coffee. Then he didn't eat this or that, and literally demanded an extra sausage for himself. Before something like that comes to the captain's attention the crew has of course spotted it long ago, and the officers' mess is brought into ridicule.

On the bridge I often talk to the watch officers. I ask them what we would do under today's weather conditions to dodge a suddenly approaching destroyer. When would we have to dive today if a plane approached, when we would remain surfaced? Under what conditions do we attack and from what side, etc.? With the aid of the chart I discuss the situation with them and let them offer suggestions. They must be positive suggestions dictated by an aggressive spirit, however, for I am scared enough myself and in that I don't need help from anybody else.

Naturally, the officers must be left alone in their mess often enough, to give them time to grumble about the captain. To be sure, the meals are taken together, however, in a decent looking uniform and on a white or at least tolerably white bed sheet for a tablecloth. Also the daily 'Doppelkopf' (card game), or whatever makes for pleasant conviviality, must not be forgotten. It is also pleasant to see a book make the rounds which one can discuss afterwards.

My experiences with midshipmen are good, In the beginning they are sometimes still very young and understand of course practically nothing about life on a submarine. At first I had to think about where to put them. There was no room in the officers' quarters, and neither did I want to put them into the petty officers' quarters, so I put them into the bow compartment. I did this first because it is the only way to learn from the bottom up how life is conducted on board, and second because it has been my experience that they will know more than the men within a fairly short time. Naturally they are invited to the officers' mess now and then to eat and play cards or for conversation. But otherwise I intentionally assign them more duties than other crew members. During their off-duty hours they have to calculate reckonings, make trim calculations, or receive instructions so that the men can only say: 'To be a midshipmen is not really as wonderful as it looks in the movies. They really have to work if they want to get somewhere'. The result of this treatment was that the midshipmen knew something, were efficient, and I liked to have them on my missions.

It is common knowledge that when depth-charges start to explode everybody looks at the officers. I had an officer who had such a dry sense of humour and was so calm that he fell sound asleep during a depth-charge attack. He only woke up when the instruments started to fall on his head. Since this was his off-duty period, he actually went right back to sleep and only mumbled something about 'turbulent times'. When we surfaced and found ourselves in a minefield, I asked him whether he thought we should keep more starboard or port. He gave me an honest answer. 'It doesn't matter; if we wake up tomorrow we have steered right.' That was not impertinence; it fit his soldierly temperament.

The Officer of the Watch sits at the hydrophone and hears the destroyer long before the crew knows anything about it. I forbid him to report the destroyer and her movements to me out loud. Each message is brought to me by a runner, who is a calm man and reports it to me in a low voice. The word destroyer is never mentioned, instead the term 'small vessel' is used so that some men do not become unnecessarily excited. The free watch must be induced to go to bed and sleep. One must see to it that they actually breathe through the potash cartridges; naturally this includes also the officers off duty, particularly because it is uncomfortable. After everything has been prepared, it is a good time for the captain to go to bed. That makes the crew happy, and the men begin to think that things are only half as bad as they seem. And I go through the ship and tell them all the things we are going to do to get the enemy; this is very important and must be done whenever possible.

The 1st watch officer should be the liaison man between the crew and the captain. This is not always easy for a young officer, especially with petty officers of the same age. I help him with advice. Only very few young officers can afford to address their men by their first name. That is by no means always necessary to gain their confidence. Since the chief engineer does not stand watch, he must make special efforts to hold frequent bull sessions with his men in order to establish a closer relationship.

The officers must be inventive in order to keep up the men's enthusiasm, particularly on such long trips. I do not arrange everything that should be done during off-duty hours myself, but call the officers and men together and tell them: 'See to it that we get something organized again. Perhaps we could do this or that, this way or that way.'; and I add some suggestions but remain in the background and let the men do the rest.

Chess and skat tournaments are easy to arrange. The score of each round is announced over the loud-speaker or through the ship's paper. The first couple of times everybody is enthusiastic, but later that becomes boring, too, and you have to think up something new again. There are the celebrations and holidays which can be arranged in a nice manner. At Christmas time candles on fir wreaths made of twisted towels and green coloured toilet paper were lit in every room. Christmas baking lasted for two weeks, and everybody was permitted to nibble at a little just like at home. On Christmas Eve a home made Santa Claus, who wears only a bed sheet in the tropics, stands in the festively decorated bow compartment and presents every man with some candy and a book with a dedication. All this, of course, is accompanied with appropriate verses and phrases. We sang Christmas carols and the captain gave a Christmas speech. After the celebration we ate supper on the gaily decorated tables. The officers' mess was dissolved and the officers ate with the men.

There is nothing new to write about the ceremony when crossing the Equator. It is prepared long in advance and can be arranged quite well despite the increased danger from air attack, though only in a limited way. The educational value of this ceremony, if it is rough enough, should not be underestimated. I am of the opinion that young men should experience once in this life how much a healthy body can endure; the captain's duty is to see that the rough play does not degenerate into sadism.

On a man's birthday the 'Birthday Serenade' by 'our' Paul Linke sounds over the loud-speaker. The captain and the officers appear in the central control room with a can of fruit, a cake, and a bottle of cognac, and everybody gets a sip to celebrate the day. The 'Birthday Serenade' is played until the ceremony is over. We say many other things on board with the accompaniment of music:
'We'll do it all right, we'll do it all right, we'll get the thing done yet' ('Wir schaffen es schon, wir schaffen es schon, wir werden das Ding schon dreh'n'), which we play for the chief engineer while he is regulating the trim. When we are about to surface we signal the watch to get ready with the march 'Today we shove off into the blue sea' ('Heut stechen wir ins blaue Meer').

If we sight whales, or even a dead whale floating around with an enormous oil trail, or life boats, or if there is a thunderstorm, or when a St. Elmo's light or an aurora borealis can be seen, the crew is called topside one by one, if possible, to let them share the experience.

All these things are trifles, of course; one can forget about them or do them in an altogether different way. However, there can be no doubt that on the whole they do affect the life and the spirit aboard.

The men must know what they are fighting for and must be eager to risk their lives for it. It is necessary to get rid of a certain passive philosophy in some of the men. On Sunday I sometimes dive and hold muster under water to tell them something about the Reich, and the centuries-old struggle for it, and about the greatest men of our history. On the Führer's birthday I tell them something about his life and about my visit to Führer Headquarters. I talk to the petty officers separately about women and other subjects which can be more easily discussed with them than with the entire crew. I have the officers hold lectures on the subjects they are interested in. The chief engineer, for instance, talks about coal as a raw material; an officer of the watch about the Atlantic, its climate and fauna, about the Gulf Stream, flying fishes, and the trade winds — all things which belong to the general education of a seaman. According to orders, we only avoid talking about religion. We speak about Germany, the Führer and his National Socialist movement.

Such lectures are very effective to fill out spare time. If one has introduced the men to something in their own language they will often talk about it for days, for the submarine man spends a large part of his spare time on his bunk shooting the breeze with his shipmates.

The men are also encouraged to read good books, and they have voluntarily read books by Beumelburg, Jelusich, and other historical writers. This or that problem 'casually' brought up in the bow compartment, and the ensuing discussion, can also arouse the interest for good books. Of course, to influence them that way the officers have to sit down with their men for lengthy conversations. An officer's entrance should not suddenly interrupt the men's conversation; on the contrary, they should be glad to be able to talk to an older comrade about things that are not yet clear to them.

During long missions we also had classes for the men. I set up loose curricula to which the officers and petty officers can adhere. Of course, it is impossible to make exact plans on an enemy mission. Every watch officer holds classes for the men of his own watch, on subjects which every seamen should but unfortunately doesn't know: about wind and waves, flags and insignia, plotting and chart reading, etc. As is customary, we also have a ship's paper. In the first section it brings short excerpts from the political news. I feel that this part is so important that I have always written it myself. The second part is for local news and contains humourous descriptions of the events of the last few days. Especially appreciated were the 'Special Submarine News' which in combination with the radio news service kept us so well informed about the political situation that after seven and a half months we knew perhaps more about it than the people at home, who are distracted from a larger perspective by the multitude of small things in every-day life.

Before the start of a mission it is important to see to it that enough books come on board. The library should consist of an intelligent mixture of good and lighter books, for a sailor likes to read when he lies on his bunk. And since books can influence a man very strongly, the reading material becomes the captain's responsibility. Another detail must be mentioned in this connection. It is practical to construct, with means available on board, little reading lamps for all cots in the crew quarters so that the men can really read fairly comfortably. After all, one cannot expect them to spend their spare time, too, in the more or less bumpy forecastle, where the lights are none too good for reading; this is sometimes not possible in any case, since torpedoes are often stored there. Furthermore, the men have stood on their feet long enough during the watch, and they want to lie down comfortably.

No matter how many records there are on board, during a long mission they soon become boring. Therefore I permit only one hour of music every day. Each compartment, and every man on his birthday, gets a chance to arrange a programme, so that every taste is satisfied. For this purpose I divide the records into several groups: Good but difficult music which is hard to understand and cannot be played on board, good and serious, but understandable music, like the Egmont Overture, Rienzi, the Prelude by Liszt, and so forth. One of these must be played every day at the beginning of the concert. A large part of the programme consists of good music that is easy to understand, taken mostly from German operettas. The rest of the programme is filled with pleasant easily understood music: I always see to it that not too many sentimental songs are played, since they often do not fit into a system which is to make the men tough. Our men have a much greater appreciation of German culture than is generally realized. If, for instance, we wanted to play Mozart's 'Kleine Nachtmusik', the first officer of the watch told the men in a few words over the loud-speaker something about the piece, and the men really did listen to it with a little more appreciation. Naturally, it is impossible as well as unnecessary to persuade the men to like only serious music, but now and then it must be possible to lift them above their everyday life.

In areas where the danger of air attack was not so serious, the off-duty watch sang at night in the bow compartment. They sang mostly seamen's songs which before the war had also been sung on the sailing training ships of the Navy. I stressed that, for if we seamen don't sing typical seamen's songs who else in the Navy or at home would do so? After all, we do not need too many marching songs since the Navy does not march very much.

I have talked about skat and chess tournaments. We also arranged other competitions, singing for instance. Everyone had to sing a song through the microphone, and the entire crew gave their verdict.

The first prize for a seaman was to start the diesel engine, or for a machinist to come to the bridge and direct the ship instead of the captain. We also arranged a real strength exhibition like the Olympic Games, complete with radio reporting and close-packed spectators. A heavy weight was attached to the end of a rope hanging from a stick fifty centimetres long. This weight had to be lifted by turning the stick until the rope was completely wound around it. Whoever could raise and lower the weight most often was the winner. I tell you these things in such detail only to show that there is an infinite variety of possibilities on board to arrange an hour of fun now and then for the crew. We also held a lying contest, and everybody had to tell the story over the loud-speaker that he would tell at home at his father's beer table, at least as exaggerated as Muenchhausen. We got some really wonderful tall stories, some of them fit to print.

To make the men remember the ship doctor's instructions on hygiene we arranged a poetry competition. Everyone had to compose a four to eight line verse which expressed in a humorous way what the doctor had said. We also held a drawing contest. The entries had to be drawings of funny incidents on board. Those who could not draw very well could explain their funny figures with a few words. A good idea and a sharp wit counted more than the ability to draw. All entries, of course, were put into the 'show window'. Furthermore, books of general educational value are also popular on board. Pamphlets with vocational instruction, and particularly maps and reference books are studied. As the time passes the most incredible questions arise. Somebody asks whether cows give more milk if a radio is played often in their vicinity; whether it is true that the holes in cheese are made with compressed air; or someone

maintains that you cannot hear the thunder during a thunderstorm at sea. Some believe that horse meat tastes bad because horses have no kidneys and sweat everything through the ribs. In such cases reference books have to be consulted to settle the argument. It goes without saying that we have maps on the wall which show our fronts. They hang near the bulletin board where the ship's paper is displayed, and next to the duty roster which we use as show window to exhibit particularly interesting pictures, types of warships, special announcements, or newspapers.

Handicraft is also popular and the men are quite skillful, but it is not as simple on board a submarine as the book says it is. I have almost never succeeded in getting the necessary materials on board. The proper wood for carving is especially scarce. The men in the engine room have the advantage in that respect, for some of the waste materials from the shipyard are quite useful.

I have mentioned here a number of general examples. They are meant merely to serve as suggestions, and can either be followed or changed according to temperament. One thing is clear, though: the captain must be concerned about his men and take care of them. It is not enough to issue orders and to punish a man now and then for noncompliance. Discipline and spartan training in the little routines of everyday duty are most important to the captain if he wants to be successful. But this is already well known, and therefore I will not go into further details. Beyond this, however, it must be demanded that the crew live for the ship, and gladly follow the captain. And now I wish to show on the basis of a few failures which I have experienced that there are situations which cannot be mastered simply by orders and obedience. In such cases the captain is dependent on the fact that he and the crew have their hearts set on the same thing.

We have been at sea for a hundred days and everything has clicked. Suddenly we had to crash dive, but we would not submerge. I looked at the manometer, but it was hardly moving. I thought: 'Well, it is always that way; when you are in a hurry it seems to take ages', then the vents in the diesel engine compartment would not open. What had happened after everything had gone smoothly a hundred times? While surfacing a 2nd class petty officer had checked the vent with a valve pin, but had forgotten to pull it out again. During the crash dive the air vent stayed shut. The man who stood by on that post only looked at his indicator panel, and when he heard the click was satisfied and reported 'Air vent open'. I ordered the air vent opened by hand, but that takes too long, and I surfaced to clear the situation. But just as I opened the conning tower hatch the air vent opened and the ship submerged again. I, the captain, had nearly fouled things up. We kept going down and were unable to blow out the negative buoyancy quick diving tank. That valve was always hard to turn, and we needed a wrench which was always fastened to a rope so that it would be ready at the right time. But on that day of all days it was missing! We sank rapidly. Then we started to blow the tanks. After a few minutes we noticed that the pumps were not sucking properly. The men in the trim corner had not paid close attention. When, after cruising underwater for some time, we wanted to pump the diesel bilges, that pump also failed to work properly – it had gradually accumulated all the pants buttons and rags which the crew of the bow compartment had dropped into the bilges. You just can't relax in making sure that all duties at sea are performed properly.

After a particularly long period in the shipyard far more than a third of my crew were new men, especially among the ratings. The first steamer which I spotted during that mission was a particularly fat morsel, proceeding at high speed. After a long chase we manoeuvered into attack position at night and I said to the 1st watch officer of the watch, who was on his first cruise: 'Now aim the the first shot at the foremast and the second shot calmly at the aftermast'. This watch officer wanted to make a particularly good job of it and said 'Tube 1 fire!' so calmly and quietly that the fire control man could not hear it in the conning tower. It did not seem loud enough to me, either, and I told him to order the second shot louder. He did so then, but the fire control man had forgotten to remove the safety pin before firing, and the second shot did not go off either. He was new on board and so was the torpedo mate, therefore the communication through the speaking tube did not function the way it had been practised before. Immediately I ordered a switch over to the remaining two tubes and fired them at the steamer. However, the distance had become very short. The tin fish were out, but now the steamer had seen us and was turning toward us. We were about to be rammed and the shots had missed! I wanted to turn hard to port and ordered: 'Hard left, starboard engine full speed ahead! Port engine full speed astern!' but our new helmsman turned the rudder at first to starboard and I had to correct him, so that the boat took a while to start turning. The machinist mate, an old experienced hand, started the port diesel engine at full speed astern and thought that the new mate was confused because the starboard diesel engine was now running full speed ahead. He jumped to the starboard diesel engine and switched it into reverse also. Now I stood there with both engines running full speed astern and the rudder in the wrong position. However we got clear and continued to chase the steamer, but she turned on the steam and ran the decisive mile faster than we could. When you finally realize that you have lost her and that the whole thing has been fouled up you feel like crying. But you must never weaken.

One day there was a terrible noise in the middle of the night. We thought of aerial bombs or some similar catastrophe. Instead, the wall of the compensating tank had burst and the air had escaped with a great roar. At the time the negative buoyancy quick diving tank was damaged and put out of order. The pressure gauge had been checked but had not indicated any critical pressure. This had not been done. On another occasion there was dense cloud obscuring the sun. When the sun finally broke through the low hanging clouds it was in the southeast at noon instead of the south. The compass seemed absolutely correct, and the chief engineer reported after some time to the captain that the compass was correct and the sun must be in the wrong position. After several exact reckonings we found that we had steered 30 degrees off our course for three days and had come uncomfortably close to minefields. But it is always the captain's fault. I had not bothered to see to it that the gyrocompass was compared with land bearings during our departure.

During one mission I had a very likeable chief quartermaster, who, however, had the constant habit of jumping the gun. When we passed through one of our own minefields I told him that tomorrow morning at 0300 he should begin zigzagging, because then it would begin to get light and we would have to count on enemy submarines; and I added that tomorrow at 0500 we would change our course from 300 degrees to 290 degrees. At 0500 in the morning I came on the bridge and saw that he had already changed the course without me. What had happened? At 0300 he had started to zigzag and changed course from 300 degrees to 290 degrees, and after he had proceeded on this course for some time he confused port with starboard and made the next tack to 240 degrees; we had been zagging for two hours in the mine area, because for two hours we had deviated 30 degrees from our course. It's an uncomfortable feeling, and it's annoying to be blown sky high because of such stupidity. I couldn't help saying: 'If we hit a mine now and blow up, even in heaven I'll kick you in the butt'. We turned at once and went back on the same course. What good is it for the captain to think while he is being blown up that it is somebody else's fault after all? No, he should check everything himself before it is too late. Enough bad experiences have been made already.

All such failures must and can be avoided for the most part. In the final analysis if something goes wrong it is always the captain's and the officers' fault. They must know that there are situations in which there can't be someone standing behind every crew member to give orders, in which orders may come too late, and in which it is decisive that the men are attached heart and soul to 'their boat'. I am convinced that many a boat was lost through such trifles, and that many were unsuccessful because of such incalculable and unexpected mishaps.

It is the duty of every captain to have faith in his men; he must want to have faith in them, even if they have disappointed him at one time or another. For beyond this we know for a fact that our young men are thirsting for action with unqualified devotion. This is an important advantage over the Anglo-Americans. If our men are led into action united in the National Socialist spirit with revolutionary ardour, then they will always follow gladly on new assignments and to new attacks. We must only show them respect and we must like them.

Bibliography

Unpublished

First World War

PRO Adm 186/395 *German views on Unrestricted Submarine Warfare (1917)*

PRO Adm 186/429 *The German Admiralty's Views on Unrestricted Submarine Warfare (1919)*

PRO Adm 137/3886 *Translation of Extracts from German Submarine Orders, Instructions and Regulations (1914–18)*

PRO Adm 186/629 *Mining Operations of German Submarines Around The British Isles 1915–18*

Naval Staff Historical Monographs:

The Dover Command (vol. 1)

Admiralty Statistical Review of The War Against Shipping (December 1918)

The History of British Minefields (2 vols., 1920)

Notes on The Convoy System of Naval Warfare: Part II. First World War (1960)

Convoy: The Core of Maritime Strategy (1956)

Naval Staff Technical History Monographs:

Aircraft v. Submarines, 1918

The Anti-Submarine Division of The Naval Staff. December 1916–November 1918

Anti-Submarine Development and Experiments Prior to December 1916

Second World War

PRO Adm 239/388 *History of German U-boat Policy, 1939–45*

PRO Adm 223/88 *Admiralty Use of Special Intelligence (Ultra) In Naval Operations 1939–45*

PRO Adm 239/246 *Anti-Submarine Warfare, vol. I: Development of the U-boat Campaign*

PRO Adm 219/14 *Statistical Analysis of Anti-Submarine Warfare In The Atlantic (1941)*

PRO Adm 234/466 *German Torpedo Development, 1939–45*

Naval Staff Historical Monographs:

Defeat of The Enemy Attack on Shipping, 1939–1945. Vol. IA – Text. Vol. IB – Tables and Plans

PRO Adm 186/802 *The U-Boat War in the Atlantic. vol. I.*

PRO Adm 234/67 *The U-Boat War in the Atlantic. vol. II.*

PRO Adm 234/68 *The U-Boat War in the Atlantic. vol. III.*

(This 3-volume monograph was written by Fregatten-kapitän Günther Hessler assisted by Alfred Hoschatt, who were both staff officers in the U-boat Command.)

Official Works – Published

Der Krieg zur See, 1914–1918 (German Official History):

Der Krieg in der Nordsee, vols. I to V by Fregatten-kapitän Otto Groos; vols. VI and VII by Admiral Walther Gladish (Berlin, Mittler, 1920–65)

Der Handelskrieg mit U-Booten, (5 vols.) *Konteradmiral* Arno Spindler (Berlin, Mittler, 1932–66)

Kriegstagebuch des Oberkommandos der Wehrmact, 1940–45, 4 vols. in 7 parts (Frankfurt, Bernard & Graefe, 1965)

History of The Great War (British Official History):

Naval Operations, (5 vols.), vols. I to III by Sir Julian Corbett; vols. IV and V by Sir Henry Newbolt, (Longmans, 1920–31);

Seaborne Trade, (3 vols.), C. E. Fayle (Murray, 1920–24)

The Merchant Navy, (3 vols.), Sir Archibald Hurd (Murray 1921–29)

The War In The Air, (6 vols.), vol. I by Sir Walter Raleigh; vols. II to VI by H. A. Jones, (Oxford, Clarendon Press, 1922–37)

History of The Blockade of Germany And The Countries Associated With Her In The Great War, 1914–1918, A. C. Bell. (Printed in 1931, this remained on the restricted list until it was finally published by HMSO in 1961.)

History of The Second World War (British Official History):

The War At Sea, (3 vols. in 4 parts), Captain S. W. Roskill, R.N. (HMSO, 1954–60)

Shipping And The Demands of War, I. C. Behrens, (HMSO, 1955)

British Intelligence In The Second World War, F. H. Hinsley (3 vols. in 4 parts HMSO, 1979–88)

History of Unites States Naval Operations, 15 vols., Samuel E. Morison, (Little, Brown & Co., Boston) vol. I *The Battle of The Atlantic 1939 – May 1943* vol. X *The Atlantic Battle Won, May 1943 – May 1945*

Published Works

Bacon, Admiral Sir Reginald. *The Dover Patrol 1915–1917.* Hutchinson, 1919 – *From 1900 Onwards*, 2 vols. Hutchinson, 1919

Bauer, Admiral Hermann. *Als Führer der U-boote im Weltkriege, 1914–18*, Leipzig, Koehler & Ameland, 1943

Bayly, Admiral Sir Lewis. *Pull Together! The Memoirs of Admiral Sir Lewis Bayly*, Harrap, 1939

Beesly, P. *Room 40 British Naval Intelligence 1914–18*, Hamish Hamilton, 1982

Birnbaum, Karl E. *Peace Moves and U-boat Warfare: a Study of Imperial Germany's Policy towards the United States 1916–17*, Stockholm, Almqvist & Wiskell, 1958

Brennecke, Jochen. *The Hunters and the Hunted*, Burke, 1958

Bucheim, Lothar-Günther. *U-Boat War*, Collins, 1978

Chatterton, E. Keble. *Fighting the U-boats*, Hurst & Blackett, 1940

— *Beating the U-boats*, Hurst & Blackett, 1943

Churchill, Sir W. S. *The Second World War*, 6 vols., Cassell, 1952

Compton-Hall, R. *The Underwater War 1939–1945*, Blandford Press, 1982

Cowie, Captain J. S. *Mines, Minelayers and Minelaying*, Oxford, 1949

Craig, Gordon A. *Germany 1866–1945*, Oxford, 1978

Des Vereines Deutscher Ingenieure. *Der Unterseeboot der Germaniawerft*, Berlin, 1923

Dönitz, Admiral Karl. *Memoirs: Ten Years and Twenty Days*, Weidenfeld & Nicolson, 1959

Falkenhayn, General Erich von. *General Headquarters 1914–1916*, Hutchinson, 1919

Ferro, Marc. *The Great War, 1914–18*, Ark paperbacks, 1987

Gayer, Lieutenant-Commander Albert. *Die Deutschen U-Boote in ihrer Kriegführung, 1914–18*, Berlin, Mittler, 1930

Gibson, R. H. and Prendergast, M. *The German Submarine War, 1914–1918*, Constable, 1931

Grant, R. M. *U-Boats Destroyed*, Putman, 1964

— *U-Boat Intelligence, 1914–1918*, Putnam, 1969

Gretton, Vice-Admiral Sir Peter. *Convoy Escort Commander*, Cassell, 1964

Gröner, Erich. *Die Deutschen Kriegsschiffe, 1815–1936*, Berlin, Lehmanns, 1937

Halpern, P. G. *The Keyes Papers*, vols. I and II, Navy Records Society, 1972–80

Herzog, Bodo. 60 *Jahre Deutsche U-boote, 1906–1966*, Lehmanns, Munich, 1968

Hezlet, Vice-Admiral Sir Arthur. *The Submarine and Sea Power*, Peter Davis, 1967

Jameson, Rear-Admiral Sir William. *The Most Formidable Thing*, Hart-Davies, 1965

Jellicoe, Admiral of the Fleet Earl. *The Crisis of the Naval War*, Cassell, 1920

— *The Submarine Peril*, Cassell, 1934

Keyes, Admiral Sir Roger. *The Naval Memoirs of Admiral of the Fleet Sir Roger Keyes*, 2 vols., Butterworth, 1934–5

Le Fleming, H. M. *Warships of World War I*, Ian Allan, 1962

Lenton, H. T. *German Warships of the Second World War*, Macdonald & Janes, 1975

Luedendorff, Erich. *My War Memories, 1914–1918*, 2 vols., Hutchinson, 1919

Macintyre, Captain Donald. *The Battle of The Atlantic*, Batsford, 1971

— *U-Boat killer*, Weidenfeld & Nicolson, 1956

Marder, Arthur J. *From the Dreadnought to Scapa Flow*, 5 vols., Oxford, 1961–70

Michelsen, Vizeadmiral Andreas. *Der U-boots Krieg, 1914–1918*, Leipzig, Koehler, 1925

Padfield, P. *Dönitz The Last Fuhrer*, Gollancz, 1984

Patterson, A. Temple (ed.) *The Jellicoe Papers*, 2 vols., Navy Records Society, 1966–68

Porten, E. P. Van der. *The German Navy in World War Two*, Arthur Barker, 1970

Raeder, Dr Erich. *Struggle For The Sea*, Kimber, 1959

Robertson, T. *The Golden Horseshoe*, Evans Bros., 1955

Rohwer, Jurgen. *Axis Submarine Successes, 1939–1945*, Patrick Stephens, 1983

— *The Critical Convoy Battles of March 1943*, Ian Allan, 1977)

Rössler, Eberhard. *The U-boat*, Arms & Armour Press and Naval Institute Press, 1981

Scheer, Admiral Reihard. *Germany's High Sea Fleet in The World War*, Cassell, 1920

Schofield, Vice-Admiral B. B. *British Sea Power in the Twentieth Century*, Batsford, 1967

Mallmann Showell, Jak P. *U-boats Under The Swastika*, Ian Allan, 1987

Simpson, Colin. *Lusitania*, Longman, 1972

Sims, Rear-Admiral William S. *The Victory at Sea*, Murray, 1920

Taylor, A. J. P. *English History, 1914–1945*, Oxford, 1965

Terraine, John. *A Time For Courage: The R.A.F. in The European War, 1939–1945*, Macmillan, 1985

Thomas, Lowell. *Raiders of The Deep*, Heinemann, 1932

Tirpitz, Grand-Admiral Alfred von. *My Memoirs*, 2 vols., Hurst & Blackett, 1919

Watts, Anthony. *The U-boat Hunters*, Macdonald & Jane's, 1976

Source Notes

Chapter 1
1. *Der Krieg in der Nordsee 1914–1918*, Band 1, Appendix 2 (hereafter cited as *Nordsee*).
2. Ibid, pp. 74–5.
3. Ibid, pp. 96–7.
4. Gibson and Prendergast, *The German Submarine War*, pp. 14–15 (hereafter cited as Gibson and Prendergast).
5. Scheer *Germany's High Seas Fleet in the World War*, p. 63. (hereafter cited as Scheer).

Chapter 2
1. Spindler, *Der Handelskrieg mit U-booten 1914–1918*: all the important German official memoranda advocating U-boat warfare against shipping can be found in the appendices of Band 1, pp. 177–269 (hereafter cited as Spindler).
2. Scheer, p. 216.
3. Ibid, pp. 222–3.
4. Spindler, Band 1, p. 87.

5. The diplomatic exchanges between Washington and Berlin can be found in A. C. Bell. *The History of The Blockade of Germany* (hereafter cited as Bell) and Karl Birnbaum's *Peace Moves and U-boat Warfare* (hereafter cited as Birnbaum).
6. Spindler, Band 1, pp. 129–30.

Chapter 3
1. Bell, p. 156.
2. Spindler, Band 1, pp. 153–4.
3. Bell, p. 157.
4. Churchill's remarks in the House of Commons, 15 February 1915, quoted in Bell, p. 421, footnote.
5. Admiral R. Bacon. *From 1900 Onwards*, p. 255.
6. The German official figures are in Spindler, Band 5, pp. 362–71.
7. The official British figures are in the Admiralty paper *Statistical Review of The War Against Shipping* (December 1918).

8. Spindler, Band 2, pp. 58–9.
9. Grant. *U-boats Destroyed*, p. 23.
10. Spindler, Band 2, pp. 59–60.
11. PRO Adm 186/629 *Mining Operations of German Submarines Around The British Isles, 1915–1918*.
12. Simpson C. *Lusitania*, p. 149.
13. American reactions to the sinking of the *Lusitania* can be found in Bell and Birnbaum.
14. Quoted in Bell, p. 423.
15. Churchill, *The World Crisis*, vol. 2, p. 292.
16. Fayle. *History of The Great War: Seaborne Trade*, vol. 1, (hereafter cited as Fayle).
17. Grant. *U-boats Destroyed*, p. 26.

Chapter 4
1. Fayle, vol. 2.
2. Spindler, Band 3, pp. 72–4.
3. Gibson and Prendergast, p. 92.
4. Spindler, Band 3, pp. 119–20.
5. Bell, p. 592.
6. Ibid, p. 594.

7. Scheer, p. 242.

Chapter 5
1. Quoted in Marder *From The Dreadnought to Scapa Flow*, vol. 3, pp. 253–4 (hereafter cited as Marder).
2. A full account of the decision-making in the autumn of 1916 can be found in Newbolt, H. *History of The Great War: Naval Operations*, vol. 4. (cited as *Naval Operations*).
3. Ibid.

Chapter 6
1. *Naval Operations*, vol. 4.
2. PRO Adm 186/613 *The Dover Command*, p. 131.
3. Ibid.
4. Ibid.
5. *Naval Operations*, vol. 4.
6. Jellicoe, *The Submarine Peril*.
7. Ibid.
8. Marder, vol. 4, p. 69.
9. Jellicoe to Beatty, 4 February 1917: quoted in Marder, vol. 4, p. 87.

10. *Naval Operations*, vol. 4, p. 343.
11. Jellicoe, *The Submarine Peril*, p. 7.
12. Admiralty MS. *The Atlantic Convoy System, 1917–1918*.
13. Marder, vol. 4, p. 73.
14. Quoted in Marder, vol. 4, p. 77.
15. Marder, vol. 4, p. 84.
16. Ibid, pp. 81–2.
17. Ibid.
18. Jones, H. A. *The War In The Air*, vol. 3.

Chapter 7
1. The decision-making that went into the unleashing of the unrestricted campaign can be found in *Naval Operations*, vol. 4.
2. Ibid.
3. Scheer, pp. 248–52.
4. Ibid, pp. 248–52.
5. Bell, p. 601.
6. Ibid, pp. 571–2.
7. PRO Adm 186/3886. *German Submarine Orders, Instructions and Regulations*.

8. Ibid.
9. Ibid.
10. Spindler, Band 4, pp. 2–3.
11. Fayle, vol. 3, pp. 92–3.

Chapter 8
1. Admiral Sims. *Victory at Sea*, pp. 6–7.
2. Fayle, vol. 3, p. 76.
3. Ibid, p. 76.
4. *Naval Operations*, vol. 5.
5. Quoted in Admiralty MS. *Notes on The Convoy System of Naval Warfare*, Part 2.
6. Ibid.
7. Vice-Admiral Hazlet. *The Submarine and Sea Power* (hereafter cited as Hazlet), pp. 94–5.
8. Spindler, Band 4, pp. 507–8.
9. Naval Operations, vol. 5, p. 55.
10. Marder, vol. 4, p. 185.
11. Hezlet, op. cit.
12. Rössler. *The U-boat*, p. 78.

Chapter 9
1. *Naval Operations, vol. 5.*
2. Admiralty MS. *Convoy: The Core of Maritime Strategy*, p. 9.
3. Rössler. *The U-boat*, p. 79.
4. Vizeadmiral Hermann Bauer, *Als Führer der U-boote im Weltkriege*, pp. 457–8.

Chapter 10
1. *Nordsee*, Band 7, p. 265.
2. Quoted in Marder, vol. 5, p. 74.

3. Admiral Sims, *Victory At Sea*, p. 250.
4. Vizeadmiral Andreas Michelsen, *Der U-bootskrieg 1914–1918*, p. 85.
5. Quoted in Marder, vol. 5, p. 74.
6. Admiralty MS. *Notes On The Convoy System of Naval Warfare*, Part 2.
7. Ibid.
8. Marder, vol. 5, p. 87.
9. Hezlet, pp. 94–5.
10. *Notes On The Convoy System Of Naval Warfare*, Part 2.
11. Marder, vol. 5, p. 79.
12. Quoted in Marder, vol. 5, pp. 94–5.
13. *Naval Operations*, vol. 5, p. 280.
14. Luedendorff. *My War Memories 1914–1918*, vol. 2.
15. Marder, vol. 5, p. 299.
16. Fayle, vol. 3, pp. 400–1.
17. Scheer, p. 349.
18. Marder, vol. 5, pp. 173–4.
19. Nordsee, Band 7, p. 341.
20. Gibson and Prendergast, p. 330.
21. Grant. *U-boats Destroyed*, p. 146.

Chapter 11
1. The naval terms of the armistice can be found in parliamentary paper, *Command 9212 (1918)*.
2. Gibson and Prendergast, p. 331.
3. Ibid, p. 331.
4. *Command 9212.*
5. PRO Adm 186/802, pp. 105–6.
6. Winston Churchill. *The Second World War*, vol. 1, p. 126. (hereafter

cited as Churchill).
7. Quoted in Padfield. *Dönitz, The Last Führer*, pp. 205–6.
8. Admiralty MS. *Convoy: The Core of Maritime Strategy*, p. 12. (hereafter cited as Barley Waters MS).
9. Joachim C. Fest *Hitler*, p. 915.

Chapter 12
1. Quoted in Padfield, p. 232.
2. PRO Adm 186/802, p. 10.
3. Ibid, p. 12.
4. Ibid, p. 16.
5. Ibid, p. 16.
6. Barley Waters MS, p. 14.
7. Roskill. *The War At Sea*, vol. 1, p. 60.
8. Ibid, pp. 103–4.
9. *The Defeat of The Enemy Attack on Shipping*, vol. 1A, p. 150.
10. Ibid, p. 49.
11. Barley Waters MS, p. 11.
12. *The Defeat of The Enemy Attack on Shipping*, vol. 1A, p. 55.
13. PRO Adm 186/802, p. 26.
14. Ibid, p. 26.
15. Ibid, p. 26.
16. Churchill, vol. 1, p. 392.

Chapter 13
1. PRO Adm 186/802, p. 27.
2. *The Defeat of The Enemy Attack on Shipping*, vol. 1A, p. 58.
3. PRO Adm 186/802, p. 48.
4. Ibid, p. 49.
5. Ibid, p. 50.
6. Ibid, p. 50.

7. Ibid, p. 52.
8. Ibid, pp. 51–2.
9. Ibid, p. 57.
10. Ibid, p. 58.
11. Ibid, p. 61.
12. Ibid, p. 67.

Chapter 14
1. PRO Adm 186/802, pp. 66–7.
2. Watts. *The U-boat Hunters*, pp. 43–4.
3. PRO Adm 186/802, p. 78.
4. Ibid, p. 79.
5. *The Defeat of The Enemy Attack on Shipping*, vol. 1A, p. 73.
6. Ibid, p. 71.
7. PRO Adm 186/802, p. 82.
8. Ibid, pp. 85–6.
9. Quoted in Padfield, p. 266.

Chapter 15
1. PRO Adm 234/67, p. 4.
2. Ibid, p. 4.
3. Roskill, vol. II, p. 96.
4. PRO Adm 234/67, p. 9.
5. Ibid.
6. Morison. *History of U.S. Naval Operations*, vol. I, p. 292.
7. Quoted in Padfield, p. 271.
8. PRO Adm 234/67, p. 17.
9. Ibid, p. 29.

Chapter 16
1. PRO Adm 234/67, pp. 51–3.
2. Ibid, p. 26.
3. Ibid.
4. Ibid.

5. Ibid, p. 48.
6. Ibid, p. 85.
7. Dönitz. *Memoirs*, p. 283.
8. Ibid, p. 296.
9. Roskill, vol. II, pp. 217–8.
10. PRO Adm 234/67, p. 75.
11. Ibid.
12. Roskill, vol. II, pp. 356–7.
13. Ibid, p. 357.
14. PRO Adm 234/67, p. 90.
15. Ibid, p. 94.
16. Ibid.
17. Ibid, p. 94.
18. Ibid, p. 95.
19. Ibid.
20. *The Defeat of the Enemy Attack on Shipping*, p. 90.
21. Ibid, p. 92.
22. PRO Adm 234/67, p. 106.
23. Ibid, pp. 111–12.
24. *The Defeat of the Enemy Attack on Shipping*, p. 97.

Chapter 17
1. *Defeat of the Enemy Attack on Shipping*, pp. 111–12.
2. Ibid, p. 113.
3. PRO Adm 234/67, p. 44.
4. PRO Adm 234/68, p. 7.

Chapter 18
1. PRO Adm 234/68, p. 24.
2. Ibid, pp. 26–7.
3. *The Defeat of the Enemy Attack on Shipping*, p. 107.
4. Ibid, pp. 120–21.
5. PRO Adm 234/68, p. 51.

Acknowledgements

I owe warm thanks to my publisher, Roderick Dymott, for his support and encouragement, also to Guss Britton of the submarine museum at H.M.S. Dolphin, Karl Wahnig who served in *U802*, Robert McMillan, Jak Mallmann Showell and the staffs of the WZ-Bilddienst, Wilhelmshaven, and the Imperial War Museum, for providing, and help in tracing, photographs. Thanks also to my brother David for all his help and to my sister, Tina Rothin, for her magnificent job in typing the manuscript. Finally, but not least, it is with warm affection that I thank my wife Val, who for the last fifteen months has patiently endured a house littered throughout with piles of books, manuscripts and plans which work on this book required. Without her support, this book could not have been written. The following publishers have kindly given permission to quote from the copyright material indicated: E. S. Mittler & Sohn, from the Official German History *Der Krieg zur See*: Captain Otto Groos and Admiral Walther Gladisch's *Der Krieg in der Nordsee*, and Konteradmiral Arno Spindler's *Der Handelskrieg mit U-Booten*: Cassell & Co. Ltd., from Admiral of the Fleet Earl Jellicoe's *The Submarine Peril*, Admiral Reinhard Scheer's *Germany's High Seas Fleet in the World War*, and Sir Winston Churchill's *The Second World War*: John Murray (Publishers) Ltd., from C. Ernest Fayle's *History of the Great War Seaborne Trade*, and Rear-Admiral W. S. Sims' *The Victory at Sea*: Constable and Co. Ltd., from R. H. Gibson and Maurice Prendergast's *The German Submarine War, 1914–1918*: Hutchinson Publishing Group Ltd., from Admiral Sir Reginald Bacon's *From 1900 Onwards*, and Erich Luedendorff's *My War Memoirs 1914–1918*: Oxford University Press., from Arthur J. Marder's *From The Dreadnought To Scapa Flow*: Putnam & Co. Ltd., From Grant's *U-Boats Destroyed*: The Longman Group Ltd., from Colin Simpson's *Lusitania*: Arms & Armour Press Ltd., from Eberhard Rössler's *The U-Boat*: Gollancz (Victor) Ltd., from Peter Padfield's *Dönitz: The Last Führer*: Macdonald & James., from Anthony Watt's *The U-Boat Hunters*: and Weidenfeld & Nicholson, from Karl Dönitz's *Memoirs: Ten Years and Twenty Days*. Quotes from official publications and unpublished Crown Copyright material is published by permission of the Controller of Her Majesty's Stationery Office.

Index

Photograph Acknowledgements
Photographs are reproduced by courtesy of the following persons and institutions, to whom the author extends his gratitude.
WZ Bilddienst, Wilhelmshaven pages 8, 10, 13, 14, 19, 20, 23, 24, 26, 42, 44, 45, 47, 52, 64, 69, 73, 78, 80, 81, 83, 84, 86, 90, 92, 93, 95, 99, 101, 106, 108, 111, 114, 123, 131, 132, 137, 146, 147, 165.
Imperial War Museum, London pages 2, 12, 29, 38, 47, 48, 57, 65, 69, 72, 79, 85, 86, 88, 104, 123, 126, 133, 137, 138, 139.
Gus Britton pages 7, 8, 19, 20, 22, 31, 32, 34, 37, 41, 48, 51, 55, 58, 63, 65, 66, 71, 76, 142, 148, 160.
Karl Wahnig pages 113, 138, 140, 143, 144.
R. McMillan pages 99, 147.